THE CRISIS OF LIBERAL INTERNATIONALISM

THE CRISIS OF LIBERAL INTERNATIONALISM

Japan and the World Order

Edited by

YOICHI FUNABASHI

G. JOHN IKENBERRY

BROOKINGS INSTITUTION PRESS
Washington, D.C.

Copyright © 2020
THE BROOKINGS INSTITUTION
1775 Massachusetts Avenue, N.W.
Washington, D.C. 20036
www.brookings.edu

All rights reserved. No part of this publication may be reproduced or transmitted in any form or by any means without permission in writing from the Brookings Institution Press.

The Brookings Institution is a private nonprofit organization devoted to research, education, and publication on important issues of domestic and foreign policy. Its principal purpose is to bring the highest quality independent research and analysis to bear on current and emerging policy problems. Interpretations or conclusions in Brookings publications should be understood to be solely those of the authors.

Library of Congress Cataloging-in-Publication Data
Names: Funabashi, Yōichi, 1944– editor. | Ikenberry, G. John, editor.
Title: The crisis of liberal internationalism : Japan and the world order / edited by Yoichi Funabashi, G. John Ikenberry.
Description: Washington, D.C. : Brookings Institution Press, [2020] | Includes bibliographical references and index.
Identifiers: LCCN 2019048172 (print) | LCCN 2019048173 (ebook) | ISBN 9780815737674 (paperback : alk. paper) | ISBN 9780815737681 (epub)
Subjects: LCSH: Liberalism. | Internationalism. | International organization. | Japan—Foreign relations—1945– | Japan—Politics and government—1945–
Classification: LCC JZ1745 .C75 2020 (print) | LCC JZ1745 (ebook) | DDC 327.52—dc23
LC record available at https://lccn.loc.gov/2019048172
LC ebook record available at https://lccn.loc.gov/2019048173

9 8 7 6 5 4 3 2 1

Typeset in Adobe Garamond Pro

Composition by Elliott Beard

Contents

Preface vii
YOICHI FUNABASHI

Introduction Japan and the Liberal International Order 1
YOICHI FUNABASHI | G. JOHN IKENBERRY

PART I
FOREIGN POLICY

1 Proactive Stabilizer: Japan's Role in 39
the Asia-Pacific Security Order
ADAM P. LIFF

2 Follower No More?: Japan's Leadership 79
Role as a Champion of the Liberal Trading Order
MIREYA SOLÍS

3 Reformist Status Quo Power: 107
Japan's Approach toward International Organizations
PHILLIP Y. LIPSCY

4 Universality to Plurality?: Values in Japanese Foreign Policy 133
MAIKO ICHIHARA

5   Atoms for Alliance Challenges: 167
    Japan in the Liberal International Nuclear Order
    NOBUMASA AKIYAMA

PART II
STATECRAFT

6   Japan's Homogenous Welfare State: 203
    Development and Future Challenges
    AKIHISA SHIOZAKI

7   Winds, Fevers, and Floating Voters: Populism in Japan   237
    KEN VICTOR LEONARD HIJINO

8   Japan's Incomplete Liberalism: 271
    Japan and the Historical Justice Regime
    THOMAS BERGER

9   The Perils and Virtues of Constitutional Flexibility: 303
    Japan's Constitution and the Liberal International Order
    KENNETH MORI McELWAIN

10 The Silent Public in a Liberal State: 325
    Challenges for Japan's Journalism in the Age of the Internet
    KAORI HAYASHI

11 Japan and the Liberal International Order: 359
    A Survey Experiment
    ADAM P. LIFF | KENNETH MORI McELWAIN

    Contributors   377

    Index   383

Preface

YOICHI FUNABASHI

The Brexit referendum and the election of Trump in 2016 served as a wake-up call. It reminded us of the fragility of the American-led liberal international order upon which Japan's prosperity and peace have been heavily reliant in the postwar era. In such a political environment, Japan must become a key player and stakeholder in upholding and shaping the liberal international order. How can Japan do this today and into the future? What are the challenges it faces both at home and abroad? What potential does Japan have to play this role and what are its limitations? These are the questions that have been at the core of our project.

Since I became a journalist fifty years ago, I have reported on many era-defining crises: the 1971 Nixon shock, the 1973 oil crisis, the 1980s U.S.-Japan trade wars, the 1990–91 Gulf War, escalation of the North Korean nuclear program, the 1997 Asian financial crisis, the 2008 Lehman shock, the Senkaku/Diaoyu island disputes, and the 2011 Fukushima nuclear disaster.

Yet I sense the unraveling of the liberal international order is perhaps more concerning for Japan than any previous crisis, for this order has been at the very heart of Japan's postwar success and prosperity. In Western democracies, and most notably the United States under Donald Trump, leaders have decidedly turned away from supporting an open and multilateral order, while populist and divisive domestic politics as exemplified by Brexit are weakening its foundations at home.

Although Japan has retained its commitment to multilateralism, questions remain as to whether this is sustainable given the geopolitical tensions Japan must navigate. Beyond the United States abdicating its role as leader of the liberal order, the clearest source of such tensions comes from an illiberal and authoritarian China, which increasingly threatens the rules-based order. At the same time, Russia is reasserting itself as a significant player in global politics, North Korea continues to escalate its nuclear program, and relations with South Korea remain soured by historical issues.

At home, the Abe administration has helped restore some degree of stability, especially in foreign policy, with Abe's long-term premiership ending the "revolving door" of prime ministers. Meanwhile, Japan, with its welfare state and tight immigration policies, has managed to stave off virulent strains of populism thus far. In this context, it is unsurprising that the world is turning to Japan to shoulder greater responsibility in shaping the liberal international order. Japan has begun taking on this mantle as the primary driver of the Comprehensive Progressive Trans-Pacific Partnership (CPTPP) negotiations after the U.S. withdrawal, and through signing an Economic Partnership Agreement with the EU. However, questions remain over the sustainability of Japan's role as a leader, for it is still riddled with many challenges—ageing population, deflationary pressures, and rising public debt—that persist from the Lost Decades. It is vital, therefore, that Japan strengthens its domestic foundations to ensure it can continue to play a proactive role in shaping the liberal international order.

In discussions I had with Professor John Ikenberry, it became clear we both believed that in this political environment there needed to be discussion on how Japan can do more to uphold the liberal international order while also managing the challenges it faces from within. This book is the product of these discussions, and our attempt to encourage thoughtful debate on Japan's role in the world by bringing together insights from leading Japan thinkers. I am fortunate enough to have known John since the 1990s, but it was his brilliant chapter on Japan's global role in the post–Cold War era for *Examining Japan's Lost Decades* (Routledge, 2016) that opened my eyes to the possibility of us working together on this book.

I thank John for offering invaluable guidance to the contributors and for sharing with us his wisdom as a leading academic on the theory of liberalism in international relations.

From the first core meeting, Adam Liff, Kenneth Mori McElwain, and Akihisa Shiozaki were heavily involved, and they played a crucial role in the early stages of the development of this book. They were later joined by Ken Hijino, Nobumasa Akiyama, Phillip Lipscy, Mireya Solís, Maiko Ichihara, Thomas Berger, and Kaori Hayashi as the contributors and coauthors of the book.

By the end of 2017, we started receiving drafts of the chapter contributions, and in May 2018, all contributors participated in a three-day conference in Tokyo for critical discussions and constructive dialogue on each of the chapters. I thank Kenneth Mori McElwain for negotiating with the University of Tokyo, who was generous enough to offer its facilities for the conference.

Throughout the project, the authors have shown true dedication to producing content of the highest quality possible, with Adam Liff and Kenneth Mori McElwain supplementing the written analysis of the book with an original survey into public attitudes toward Japan taking a leadership role at both the regional and global level. The authors have also drawn on over forty interviews of policymakers, diplomats, and academics organized by the Asia Pacific Initiative to provide fresh perspectives into policymaking in the Abe administration.

As they were writing their chapters, I asked the contributors to keep in mind that while the book is aimed at an international audience, it should also offer a critical review of the Abe administration from a nonpartisan perspective and make policy recommendations. I hope that the book finds this balance and offers fresh insights for everyday readers and scholars alike—anyone interested in developing a deeper understanding of what Japan stands for and how it can evolve in the twenty-first century.

When the Rebuild Japan Initiative Foundation was founded in September 2011, our emphasis was largely on matters of domestic governance related to the Fukushima nuclear disaster and its subsequent fallout. Since then, and especially after July 2017, when we restructured to become the Asia Pacific Initiative, our focus has become more international, with a greater emphasis on understanding Japan's place in the world. In particular, this book builds on our previous publication, *Reinventing Japan: New Directions in Global Leadership* (Praeger, 2018), where we looked at possibilities for Japanese leadership in soft power. In developing this book, we have drawn upon our past publications and experience, where we have covered different aspects of the liberal international order. These include *Quiet Deterrence: Building Japan's New National Security Strategy* (Rebuild Japan Initiative Foundation, 2014), *The Democratic Party of Japan in Power: Challenges and Failures* (Routledge, 2017), *Japan's Population Implosion: The 50 Million Shock* (Palgrave Macmillan, 2018), and *The Article II Mandate: Forging a Stronger Economic Alliance between the United States and Japan* (Center for Strategic and International Studies, Rowman & Littlefield, 2018), which was jointly produced with the Center for Strategic and International Studies. At the Asia Pacific Initiative, we hope that this book will also serve as a platform from which to further explore how Japan can work together with like-minded democracies and especially the EU, in light of the recently signed EU-Japan economic partnership agreement.

Once again, I thank all of the contributors and authors for their dedication throughout each stage of the development of the book. From the Asia Pacific Initiative, I must thank Harry Dempsey, the staff director for the project from its inception to the latter stages, for his Herculean efforts, and Shunta Takino and Patrick Madaj, who have seamlessly filled his role since Harry's departure. Yukari Utsumi, Takako Yatabe, Mika Takao, Fumino Sato, Yoshinori Ohnoki, and Ryu Tabata have actively assisted with logistics and coordination of the project.

The research team at the Asia Pacific Initiative has also played an important role in bringing the book to publication: Moe Suzuki, Saki Kuzushima, Merisa Mitsufuji (Keio University), Andrea Fischetti (University of Tokyo), Ryosuke Tanaka (London School of Economics), Lauren Altria (Waseda University), Takato Nakamura (University of Tokyo), Yiming Ma (The George Washington University), and Yuka Koshino (Georgetown University).

Since the earliest of stages, the National Endowment for Democracy has been a pillar of support for the book. I thank, in particular, Carl Gershman, Lynn Lee, Wilson Lee, and Andrea Forward for their contributions. Without them, the fruitful discussions among authors, editors, and academics, which were essential in the development of this book, would not have been possible. The support of the National Endowment for Democracy has extended far beyond financial and logistical matters, and it was thanks to them that we were able to hear the thoughts of Francis Fukuyama on the arguments made in the book during his visit to Japan in June 2018. I also thank Satoru Mori and Toshihiro Nakayama for offering their thoughts during the discussion session with Francis Fukuyama.

Last but not least, I thank Bill Finan, Kristen Harrison, Marjorie Pannell, and the entire staff at Brookings Institution Press for bringing this book to publication. It is an honor to have this book published by such an esteemed and prestigious organization that values the evidence-based research independent think tanks such as ours seek to promote.

THE CRISIS OF LIBERAL INTERNATIONALISM

Introduction

JAPAN AND THE LIBERAL INTERNATIONAL ORDER

YOICHI FUNABASHI | G. JOHN IKENBERRY

National Interest: The Fragile Blossom and Asian Anchor of Stability

Rising powers often tell themselves that their development was due to domestic causes, such as a hardworking population or a wise leader. However, it must not be forgotten that the most important thing to a country's development is its external environment and the order it finds itself embedded in. For the past seventy years, Japan has been the most significant beneficiary of the U.S.-led liberal international order. Since the 1970s, China has joined the ranks as one of the largest beneficiaries of the order, lifting hundreds of millions of Chinese citizens out of poverty. Without the security provided by the U.S. alliance system, the General Agreement on Tariffs and Trade based upon the principle of free trade, and the values-based system centered on democracy and human rights, security and peace in East Asia would not have been possible. It is an order that has allowed for Japan and China to prosper economically—and in Japan's case, to become a democratic and civilian power.[1]

The liberal international order that supported Japan's development is a set of rules, norms, and institutions that govern relations between states in an open manner, backed by hard power guaranteed by the United States. It has three pillars: the security order, the economic order, and the human rights order. The security order includes the UN- and U.S.-led alliances that seek to foster cooperative approaches to security and the moderation of great power rivalry through international law and treaty commitments. The economic order is founded upon the principles of free trade and non-discrimination, as well as multilateral arrangements for the management of the world economy. The human rights order consists of normative commitments to democracy, individual freedom, human rights, and freedom of movement. Together these make up the core of the postwar liberal international order. These pillars do not operate independently of one another, but are rather reinforcing and entwined.

The specific notion of a liberal international order and its role is by no means uncontested.[2] Four factors are relevant. First, the order is living. It has undergone significant changes over time, such as the expansion and integration of additional countries into the liberal order and the development of global governance institutions.[3]

Second, some countries—particularly in the developing world—see the liberal international order as an ideological agenda to protect the interests of the West.[4] There is a line of thought that China has a historical and psychological problem with the order because it was not "present at the creation."[5]

Third is the varying interlinkages between the three pillars of the order. Initiatives and institutions—such as the Truman Doctrine, Marshall Plan, and NATO—formed the foundations of the liberal international order by linking the complementing pillars of the order. Yet as Gideon Rose argues, the order was a product of an American desire to "revive and protect an American sphere of influence along liberal lines" from the Cold War era, and would only later "expand and flourish" at a global level once the Soviet threat had subsided.[6] This American preference for linking the pillars can also directly be seen in postwar U.S.-Japan relations. In the 1960 Treaty of Mutual Cooperation and Security between the United States and Japan, while the focus remains security-oriented, Article II makes clear the need to "encourage economic collaboration" and "[strengthen] free institutions" at the bilateral level.[7]

Fourth, creating healthy domestic liberal politics might require limitations on the liberal nature of a nation's international agenda. A well-functioning democracy with a healthy media and effective social security system does not necessarily entail public support for expanding free trade, open borders, and human rights intervention overseas. In fact, an expansive implementation of the liberal order makes it far harder to maintain domestic support and risks a popular backlash.[8] Furthermore, as Cas Mudde points out, "populism is an illiberal democratic response to undemocratic liberalism."[9] The demands of globalization, when combined with an overly zealous liberal foreign policy that spans both the security and economic realm, can come into conflict with domestic needs. This risks undermining the social cohesion and domestic order the liberal international order relies upon, by feeding populists who push for exclusivist and illiberal policies that polarize the public.

There has also been heated debate over the use of the concept of the liberal international order. In the academic community, Joseph Nye has said that the terms "liberal" and "American" should be discarded, proposing instead that we refer to the "open international and rules-based international order."[10] Even with this toned-down terminology, John Bolton, former national security adviser to President Donald Trump, reportedly banned his staff from referring to the "rules-based order."[11]

Regardless of the debate on the conceptualization of the liberal international order, it is clear that the foundations of the postwar international order are in crisis. Japan, a "frontline state," is playing and will continue to play a crucial role in determining the future of the Asia-Pacific regional order.[12] Although the subject of debate, China might stand to make strategic gains from the self-destruction of the American-led order.[13] In contrast, Japan would suffer the greatest of strategic losses.

Liberalism and democracy have become embedded in Japan's domestic governance. In the aftermath of Japan's surrender, as Kenneth Pyle has argued, "nowhere was American readiness to remake the world on clearer display than in Japan."[14] This American strategy meant that, for Japan, the character of the regional order and the viability of domestic institutions have been fused together for more than seventy years. Even before then, Japan's embryonic Taisho democracy and two-party politics had been inspired by the Anglo-American model of democracy. The ongoing erosion of the liberal international order thus directly weakens the foundations of postwar political governance in Japan.

Faced with the current crisis, the rationale for Japan to take on a leadership role to uphold and reform the order is no mere call from other liberal democracies for burden-sharing, but an essential part of Japan's own vital national interest.[15] This volume aims to set out the challenges for the liberal international order, propose a role for Japan to uphold and reform it, and identify constraints and limitations on Japan as it seeks to play a more active role.

Two of the leading figures of postwar U.S. diplomacy, Zbigniew Brzezinski and Henry Kissinger, gave contrasting but deeply thoughtful understandings of Japan's position. Brzezinski was keenly aware that Japanese prosperity depended "on circumstantial factors essentially not of their own making and often beyond their direct control."[16] Japan is geopolitically vulnerable as an archipelago off the Eurasian continent without its own resources. At the same time, for great powers, it is a geopolitical prize. For the United States, Japan is in the ideal strategic position for forward deployment into Eurasia. For China, Japan blocks its entry into the Pacific. A high prize can easily become a pawn. Yet as Kissinger wrote, "for nearly seven decades, this new orientation [taken by Japan since the end of the war] has proved an important anchor of Asian stability and global peace and prosperity."[17] But for the pawn to play the role of an anchor and take such an orientation, it would need to be embedded in the American-led liberal international order. Trump's America is upending this order, making this fundamental dilemma the most glaring it has been in the postwar period.

Challenges to the Liberal International Order: An Unfamiliar World

Where exactly do the biggest challenges lie for the order? Three new dynamics will have monumental impact on global geopolitics, the liberal international order in Asia-Pacific, and Japan's governance: the rebalancing of global power relations, rapid socioeconomic change driven by technological change and globalization, and demographics.

SHIFTING BALANCE OF POWER

The first significant force that shapes the threat to the liberal international order is the shifting global distribution of power—the relative decline of the United States concurrent with the "rise of the rest," including the monumental rise of China and the geopolitical gamechanger of North Korea's nuclear weapons and missiles.[18]

The United States: The Lost Superpower
The United States is no longer the dominant power that it used to be during and after the Cold War. The U.S. commitment and capacity to maintain, lead, and evolve the order, particularly in Asia, became increasingly uncertain after the global financial crisis in 2008, as the United States turned its focus to divisive domestic issues, such as growing inequality and identity politics. In a shift away from past presidents, Donald Trump has signaled his intention to abdicate America's postwar role as leader of the liberal order.[19] In the meantime, the populist and backlash politics in the United States, as well as in Europe, threaten to destroy the liberal order from within. Protectionist, zero-sum America First and economic nationalist policy under the Trump administration has weakened America's credibility as a global leader and alliance partner.

As a longtime beneficiary of the order, Japan has been accustomed to maintaining the status quo in Asia-Pacific through "leadership from behind" in the postwar period.[20] Following the diplomatic crisis between Japan and China in 2010, when a Chinese fishing boat collided with two Japanese coast guard vessels near the Senkaku/Diaoyu Islands, Japan sought Washington's commitment to protect the islands in the case of an attack.

Whether this status quo will continue is in question, as a governance gap opens up in the management of the U.S.-Japan alliance. The mutuality of the treaty has been under attack before and very explicitly under President Trump, who has depicted Japan as a freerider.[21] At present, the alliance between the United States and Japan remains best characterized as a "spear-and-shield" relationship, with the United States providing offensive capabilities and Japan providing defensive capabilities. Japan remains unable to take on any burden for the offensive "spear" element of the alliance, as its constitution puts constraints on a more robust Japanese role in regional security. Thus, Japan must take the steps that it can to secure American presence in Asia-Pacific and strengthen the U.S.-Japan alliance.

Japan's postwar strategy has been to promote the fusion of Asia with the Pacific via the U.S.-Japan alliance to ensure security and prosperity. Japan has promoted regional institutions that include the United States, such as the Asia-Pacific Economic Community (APEC), and opposed regionalization projects that exclude the United States, such as the East Asian Economic Caucus (EAEC). With American withdrawal from the Trans-Pacific Partnership (TPP), the Asia-Pacific fusion vision faces a new challenge. In Japan, there is deep-seated resistance to an Asian regional order without the United States. Without this counterbalance to China, the liberal international order could well unravel. Article II of the U.S.-Japan Security Treaty mandates that both countries coordinate their economic policy, showing the vital importance of economic statecraft to influencing wayward geo-economic behavior to achieve regional stability.[22] Japan must not only strengthen its alliance with the United States but also work to overcome its status quo–seeker mentality, taking on more of a leadership role so as to buy the United States time to return to multilateralism and reform global and regional governance.

China: Illiberal Innovator and Neighboring Superpower
China's economic stature has grown, and its military and paramilitary forces are undergoing modernization and rapid expansion. Its military budget, which was half of Japan's in 1989, overtook Japan's in 2001. By 2017, military expenditure by China was five times that of Japan.[23] China's buildup of arms has led to a destabilizing regional arms race. Japan increased its defense budget in 2018 for the sixth consecutive year in response, while Vietnam, the Philippines, Australia, and India have all been bolstering their military force.[24] Major power conflict between the United States and China would undoubtedly be the most disastrous calamity for the prosperity of Asia-Pacific. The direction of power relations between the United States and China is a critically important factor to peace and prosperity in the Asia-Pacific.

However, even given no military confrontation between the major powers, China has over "fifty shades of warfare," as observed by Sun Tzu, only the last of which is military combat.[25] A gradual chipping away from within at the legitimacy and authority of the rules and norms of the international order, or a new G2 great power relations deal between the United States and China, could result in the eventual destruction of the order.[26] Japan must recognize that wayward behavior short of war can slowly erode the economic, political, and normative foundations of the liberal international order and harm its national interests. China's threat to the order is different in kind from Russia's. Russia is not substantially integrated into the order—it is pounding liberalism and democracy from the outside. Thus the threats of China and Russia to the liberal international order should be viewed differently. For too long, Europe has been sleepwalking through China's corrosive "pick and choose" approach and preference for bilateral engagement, which it has only recently started to awaken to.[27]

As the RAND Corporation has recently argued, China is a "conditional supporter" of the postwar international order.[28] At the level of global governance, China shows signs of abiding by the rules of the international order as a responsible member. This can be seen in its contribution of some 2,500 troops to the UN Peacekeeping Forces. But in other instances, China makes hollow appeals concealing more blatant violations. Xi Jinping claimed global leadership on free trade at Davos in 2017, yet China has one of the most protective markets in the world, traffics in stolen intellectual property, and engages in market-distorting practices.[29]

Further analysis reveals that China's policies in its neighborhood are far more hostile and damaging for the liberal international order than its approach toward global issues such as nonproliferation, the global economy, and environmental issues. At the regional level, in the maritime sphere, China flouted the 2016 international legal rulings under the UN Convention on the Law of the Sea (UNCLOS) on the South China Sea, undermining the rule of law directly. On the economic front, China stands accused of using the Belt and Road Initiative to coerce countries in the Asia-Pacific, and alarms over its economic statecraft and debt-trap diplomacy are most explicitly mentioned by its neighboring countries. Such sentiment is exemplified by Malaysia's prime minister Mahathir's warning against a "new version of colonialism" during his visit to China in August 2018. As Thomas Wright argues, China's policy on regional issues is far more indicative than its policy on global issues—after all, major powers remain most attentive to and concerned by their immediate and regional environment.[30]

China has begun challenging the U.S.-led institutions and ideology with its system of state-led capitalism. Industrial policy, represented by Made in China 2025, shows China's ambitions to attain technological dominance. The concentration of economic and technological might is giving China greater claim to its status as a prominent geopolitical power, as well as confidence in its own illiberal model of governance.

Recent years have seen increasing emphasis on the Chinese state's desire to establish the country as an innovative leader in technology. But far from using technology to build a more open and free society, China's model might better be described as "illiberal innovation." Through deployment of technology—artificial intelligence (AI), big data, facial recognition, quantum computing, genomes, and so on—China is creating a new governance model of digital Leninism characterized by technologically driven social surveillance, political control, and one-party rule.[31]

It does not stop at domestic governance. China is creating its own digital sphere of influence in Southeast Asia, and gaining influence elsewhere, as companies with ties to the state, such as Huawei, Alibaba, and Tencent, come to control networks, logistics, and data.[32] This is in parallel with tactics to divide and trade across Southeast Asia to the effect of undermining the unity of the Association of Southeast Asia Nations (ASEAN) in favor of Chinese interests. China seeks to use the Belt and Road Initiative as a vehicle through which to strengthen and cement its technological infrastructure in global supply chains. In doing so, Chinese standards that fail to protect and value safety, fair competition, responsible governance, privacy, local dynamics, and human rights could come to dominate the rules of the technological sphere.

The uncertainty of U.S. commitment to Asia and the economic enticement of China has started to make its partnership vision a reality, as states in the region, such as the Philippines and Thailand, question their alignments as well as their system of governance. Japan is not in a dissimilar situation. Its security relies upon the United States, while its economy has become increasingly integrated with China's. China became Japan's largest trading partner in 2007 and represented 21.7 percent of Japan's trade in 2017.[33] Keeping Japan's alliance with the United States robust is insufficient. Japan must address both the swing toward illiberalism in Asia-Pacific and its own relationship with China.[34]

North Korea: An Existential Threat
North Korea is the most immediate national security issue for Japan, given the potential it has to strike a wedge in the U.S.-Japan alliance. North Korea is trying to disengage the United States from East Asia by terminating the development of long-range intercontinental ballistic missiles (ICBM), while keeping Japan exposed to its nuclear weapons and missiles. The unraveling of extended nuclear deterrence the United States has been providing for Japan would leave the rationale for and future of the alliance uncertain. The Treaty on the Non-Proliferation of Nuclear Weapons (NPT) is coupled with the U.S.-Japan alliance, and Japan's non-nuclear status comes as part of that package. North Korea is not just a regional problem. It is a global one, since it could destroy the global nonproliferation regime.

In order to uphold the nuclear nonproliferation regime, Japan has greatly contributed to International Atomic Energy Agency (IAEA) inspections and provided over 10 percent of its budget in 2016, hoping that it could enhance its security.[35] But in reality the number of states that have tested nuclear weapons has increased since the NPT entered into force, and North Korea has become a de facto nuclear weapon state.[36]

The summit between Trump and Kim Jong-un in Hanoi in February 2019 served to further confirm concerns over North Korea's ambitions and intentions. In Hanoi, negotiations seemingly reached an impasse and the summit was dubbed a "failure" in many quarters.[37] Despite Trump's claim that he has a "great relationship" with Kim Jong-un, little progress is being made toward denuclearization. In fact, satellite imagery suggests that after a period of moderate dismantlement of the Sohae Launch Facility following the Singapore Trump-Kim summit in June 2018, North Korea started to rebuild the launch pad in March 2019.[38] It seems clear that North Korea remains highly reluctant to reduce its missile and nuclear capabilities.

The weakening of trilateral cooperation between the United States, Japan, and South Korea also leaves Japan more threatened by North Korea. This has resulted jointly from Trump's dismissal of the importance of the U.S.–South Korea alliance, and a "compound fracture" in relations between Japan and South Korea. The former was evident in Trump's pledge to cancel military drills in June 2018, which surprised not only Seoul but also the Pentagon.[39] Trump's preference for a transactional approach— treating each interaction as if it were a discrete deal or agreement—goes directly against the orthodoxy of relationship-building foreign policy that had been the backbone of the U.S. approach to building and maintaining allies such as South Korea and Japan. Furthermore, Trump's and his administration's propensity to closely link national security concerns with economic issues poses a risk to trilateral cooperation, for instability in trade relations can have direct negative consequences for security.[40] At the same time, the rapid deterioration and "compound break" in relations between Japan and South Korea, most notably over the issue of compensation for conscripted workers, has narrowed the space for diplomatic negotiations and policy coordination.[41] For Japan, therefore, both its relationships—with South Korea and the United States—are under strain, which directly undermines the strength of trilateral cooperation.

Japan is ill-prepared for the serious threat posed by North Korea. Since 2017, the realization of the escalated threat from North Korea has resulted in some unprecedented suggestions to change Japan's long-held antinuclear posture. Foremost among these is former defense minister Shigeru Ishiba's suggestion that Japan acquire nuclear weapons to support the international order and ensure its national security.[42] Yet, political discussions about Japan acquiring nuclear weapons to enhance its national security mostly remain a taboo. The nuclear and missile threat of North Korea and the seeming unlikelihood of the denuclearization of the peninsula are demonstrative of Japan's great dilemma: whether it should begin to acquire nuclear capabilities by taking actions that might be perceived to be illiberal so as to ensure its own security and that of the region or to alternatively try to continue to make its non-nuclear identity compatible with reliance upon an extended U.S. nuclear umbrella.[43]

GLOBALIZATION AND TECHNOLOGICAL CHANGE IN THE ASIAN CONTEXT: LEAPFROGS, MISSED OPPORTUNITIES, AND SECOND CHANCES

A second force challenging the liberal international order is globalization and technological revolution. Globalization has lifted hundreds of millions out of poverty, but it has also disenfranchised and disempowered many. At the same time, the technological revolution of the future could result in mass disruption as technological breakthroughs in many areas are made simultaneously.

Japan failed to respond effectively to these twin forces as its economy stagnated across two Lost Decades—a period characterized by gradual economic decline, which saw a merry-go-round of short-lived governments that were willing to make changes but whose lack of political will or capital to implement tough economic reforms exacerbated stagnation. During this time, China and South Korea rose to economic prominence, catching Japan off guard and complicating regional diplomacy.[44]

Nevertheless, even during its two Lost Decades, Japan made many unrecognized gains and remained remarkably stable. This quiet steadiness is all the more noteworthy when viewed in the light of unstable politics in other advanced nations, such as the United States and the United Kingdom. Many nations traditionally in the lead face new kinds of problems but lack a model to draw upon for solutions. Since the Meiji restoration in 1868, Japan looked to Western civilization as the model for modernization at the expense of relations with Asian neighbors. ASEAN nations and India, with a joint population of 2 billion, are looking for liberal alternatives to the West and could be partners in building a free and open region with Japan. While Japan may not be a model, its relative success in politics and statecraft could become an opportunity for it to offer a different vision of society and globalization for Asia-Pacific. Its initiatives, policies, and approach may provide clues and references to the world as the frontrunner in tackling problems faced by other countries: deflation, depopulation, ageing, natural disasters, energy insecurity, ballooning national debt, and diminished horizons.[45]

Japan lost out on the opportunities presented by the development of the internet, digitalization, and smartphones. Former giants, such as Toshiba and Sharp, adopted their own "Galapagos" path of development, out of step with standardization elsewhere.[46] They were not willing to pay the price of success, burdened by the need to overcome legacy costs and cast away previous growth models. Japan could not meet the challenge of Silicon Valley.

The stakes are even higher with the technologies of the Fourth Industrial Revolution, such as AI, big data, blockchain, the Internet of Things (IoT), robotics, and nanotechnology. It is widely known that China is raising its game by becoming the first country to deploy 5G technology at a widespread level, and as a Department of Defense report has warned, this is likely to see China become dominant in "handset and Internet applications and services."[47] In this sphere, the rules of the game are yet to be defined. The dispute over 5G technology and Huawei is a symptom of this conflict, as both the United States and China seek to impose their own values and attain digital hegemony.[48]

The pervasiveness and omnipresence of technology in our day-to-day lives makes this competition qualitatively different. Whereas military competition and the arms race were concentrated in the realm of high-level politics, technology necessarily has a profound effect on individual lives across all spheres. The functioning of individuals, communities, societies, and states all rely on the seamless use of technology. It is dangerous because it appears benign and many people give little thought to the broader aggregated consequences of technology. All this has resulted in a technology arms race: the country that dominates technological infrastructure will gain an edge in the economic, military, and intelligence spheres[49] and at all levels.

If Japan stands still and is leapfrogged by other countries in technology, it will find its ability to develop and shape the rules of the technological order heavily compromised and weakened. There are already signs, with e-commerce and cashless payment systems, that Japan is not sufficiently alert to a second *Sputnik* moment and will be unable to muster a sufficient response to the challenge of other countries that are seeking to shape and define the rules of the Fourth Industrial Revolution.[50]

In this brave new technological world, Japan will also need to find ways to adequately respond to the social change and readjustment that will result from technological breakthroughs at an unprecedented speed and scale. Much like globalization, the dark side of technology lies in its ability to uproot daily lives and undermine social cohesion. Unless Japan can cushion those displaced by technology, vast populations could be left alienated, creating an environment that is conducive to populist fervor that undermines Japan's liberalism from within.

UNFAVORABLE DEMOGRAPHICS AND PUBLIC DEBT: EXPLOSIONS AND IMPLOSIONS

The third overarching trend affecting Japan's possible role and contribution in supporting the liberal international order is demographics. Japan's working-age population began to decline in 1995, followed by entry into a phase of absolute population decline in 2008. If current trends persist, by the end of the century Japan's population could decrease to as low as 50 million, of which 40 percent could be elderly. To remain a major power in the world, Japan arguably needs to maintain a population of no less than 80 million.[51]

Population is the lifeblood of economic vitality and international standing. The decline and ageing of the population was one of the primary undercurrent causes of Japan's two lost decades. The situation was made worse over twenty years by the continuing inability of right-wing ideology to muster comprehensive population policy and to avoid the priorities of youth being crowded out by the demands of an ageing society: healthcare, nursing, and pensions. As a result, Japan has begun to suffer a severe labor shortage. A new paradigm shift in the labor market could be brought about through innovation, such as responding to the labor demands through the introduction of automation and robots. But simply increasing productivity through technological innovation is unlikely to be enough to promote robust economic growth in Japan. The labor shortage has also been pivotal to the changing nature of trade politics by lessening fear of unemployment and weakening opposition to free trade, which has created conditions for an open door policy, such as support of TPP.[52] Another option to address the labor shortage is to tap into diversity by increasing social and economic inclusivity for women, the elderly, and foreigners. The Abe administration has attempted to increase participation of all three groups, which over many years could promote diversity, innovation, and growth.

In contrast to Japan, most of the Asia-Pacific is witnessing huge population growth, rivaled only by Africa, which has driven sustained high levels of economic growth. China and India are the two most populous countries in the world. Many of the nations in the region have young, technologically receptive markets. Japan has many opportunities to invest overseas to make up for the economic shortfall from the declining consumption of a shrinking population. There is a window of opportunity for Japan to share in Asia-Pacific's economic growth driven by favorable demographics, but its companies will also face the challenge arising from greater competition. In the longer term, the region as a whole will face rapid ageing due to improved healthcare and increasing lifespans, which will result in a reduction of the size of youthful populations. Such rapid ageing could be a destabilizing force for the region. Japan is a trailblazer in coping with the frontier challenges of an ageing society, and it could have much to offer its neighbors to help develop their welfare systems, deploy technologies, revitalize rural areas, and cope with degenerating mega-cities.

Japan's public debt, which stands at over 200 percent of GDP, is higher than its debt levels at the end of World War II, largely as a result of ever-increasing social spending.[53] Even if Japan can adapt effectively to population decline, public debt will inevitably continue to soar in the long term. The shift in the tax burden to a shrinking working population, combined with increasing healthcare costs to treat chronic diseases such as dementia, will put the youth of Japan under incredible financial and emotional strain. Furthermore, there are fears that household savings, vital to corporate investment, will lower as the elderly draw upon them. The generation gap in Japan is widening, as young people are realizing the unfair hand they have been dealt and the structural bias of Japanese politics toward the elderly.

Japan's appeal as a regional partner will be weakened as a consequence of its decline in population size, as other nations, such as Indonesia, overtake it.[54] The public debt, in combination with the "silver democracy" of elderly voters who hold increasing political power favoring social welfare spending, will prevent major increases in spending directed toward official development assistance (ODA) or the military. Comprehensive, effective policy to address ageing and depopulation is an urgent issue for Japan. It has far-reaching impact upon the regional order and the role that Japan can play within it.

Japan's Strategy for the Liberal International Order in Asia-Pacific: Rule Shaper for a Different Liberalism in Asia

Although Japan's limitations and the hostile regional and international environment are realities, Japan still has substantial capabilities and influence. Japan is still the second largest economy in the region and third largest in the world, and it is better positioned than Europe or the United States to prosper from Asia's boom. Even with a declining population, it dwarfs other mature regional democracies in size. Australia's population is one-fifth and South Korea's is under half of Japan's. Japan's stock of foreign direct investment in ASEAN still far exceeds that of China and even that of the United States.[55] It has a wealth of soft power assets and a tourism industry that is growing exponentially.

Emerging Asian democracies continue to see Japanese ODA and investment, as well as close government-to-government ties, as crucial for their development.[56] Japan offers an alternative to the interventionist approach of the United States and it has fought for the reform of international institutions such as the IMF and World Bank, supporting efforts to make them more representative. Japan understands that there is no single model of development that will benefit Asia-Pacific nations. This has meant that Japan has preferred a more pluralistic agenda while embracing the values of transparency, good governance, and accountability. The Asia-Pacific's variety of needs, cultures, history, development, and governance call for a plurality of reference architectures. The challenge is to work with a plurality of approaches without undermining liberal values that give the security and economic orders their ideational legitimacy. To be recognized as a reference country, Japan must work together with other countries to exchange experiences and build capacity. The Japan International Cooperation Agency's (JICA) ODA model of self-help aid through capacity-building has promoted responsible development and is a good starting point.[57]

It has been rare for the Bretton Woods institutions, the UN, or other powers besides the United States to take up responsibility for upholding the liberal international order. It is also unlikely that other powers will replace the United States in the near future. Japan may not possess the stature to be a "rulemaker," but it certainly may, in the words of German foreign minister Heiko Maas, aspire to be a "rule-shaper" in collaboration with other like-minded democratic nations.[58] German chancellor Angela Merkel identified Japan as a closer partner than geography would suggest.[59] In order to consolidate relations with "like-minded" democratic partners and foster strong ties with rising countries in the Asia-Pacific, Japan must both keep values of democracy and human rights central to its foreign policy and offer a new, less interventionist conception of the regional order.

FOREIGN POLICY OF THE ABE GOVERNMENT: SHIFT OF GEAR

To meet the challenges of the East Asian geopolitical environment and to protect the liberal international order, Japan has started to change under the government of Shinzo Abe in his second term in office. His administration has launched four major foreign policy initiatives to "shape the rules" of the liberal international order.

The most significant of these has been the decision of the Abe administration to increase Japan's contributions toward trade liberalization and international economic frameworks. Japan took leadership on the Comprehensive Progressive Trans-Pacific Partnership (CPTPP), which was signed on March 8, 2018, after the United States withdrew from the original TPP. Up until now, Japan's trade policy and domestic economic reform has almost always been reactive to *gaiatsu* (external pressure). This is the first time in postwar history that Japan has successfully taken the lead on multilateral trade liberalization. Ensuring American commitment to Asia, including a return to the TPP framework, is critical for Japan. TPP is not only a trade agreement but an Asia strategy for the United States and Japan.

The Abe government also signed an Economic Partnership Agreement (EPA) with the European Union (EU). As a background report by the European Parliament's Research Service noted, the EPA is crucial in playing "a leadership role in shaping the future of international trade."[60] Both the EU and Japan undoubtedly have a mutual awareness of the strategic need to contribute more to upholding the liberal international order and resist U.S. protectionism through the promotion of free trade. Building upon the EPA, the EU-Japan Strategic Partnership Agreement soon followed, with the aim of promoting cooperation in a wider field of areas beyond free trade.

Going further, Japan could even push for the entry of the EU into CPTPP to create a strategic high standard, antiprotectionist framework excluding the United States and China.[61] The Japanese government is also planning soon to conclude the Regional Comprehensive Economic Partnership (RCEP)—a free trade agreement between ASEAN nations, Australia, China, India, Japan, New Zealand, and South Korea. It shows that the world will not stand by without U.S. economic engagement.

Abe is also taking leadership on digital trade and technology in the age of the Fourth Industrial Revolution. While hosting the G20 summit in 2019, the prime minister announced the launching of the so-called "Osaka Track," an initiative that champions heightened protections for data flow between countries.[62] A group of twenty-four states signed a document supporting the framework.[63] Taking leadership on global data governance may only be a starting point, but it is nonetheless a step forward for a country that has traditionally lagged behind in technology and remains at risk of being leapfrogged by its neighbors in the Asia-Pacific.

The second initiative launched under Abe is the normalization in diplomatic relations with China. Relations plummeted in 2010 when the incident surrounding the Senkaku Islands occurred, and the wounds have taken time to heal, yet Abe has made serious efforts to rebuild diplomatic relations with China, as signified by his state visit to Beijing in October 2018. The improvement of relations is driven by both sides, as a form of mutual insurance against Trump's unilateral trade policy, which both countries see as a threat.[64] Japan hopes to influence standards on Belt and Road Initiative projects, while China hopes to include Japan to access its expertise and legitimize its infrastructure masterplan. Relations will not reach anything like a "mutually beneficial relationship based on common strategic interests," and as described by Abe's political ally Akira Amari, relations between Japan and China have, at best, gone "from minus to zero."[65] Even so, a stable relationship is welcomed by other Asian countries that do not want to be forced to take sides.[66]

Abe's China policy is not without challenges and risks, the biggest of which is collateral damage from the unpredictable nature of U.S.-China relations. A continuation or intensification of the trade war would put Japan in a compromised position, given that 21.7 percent of its trade last year and companies' supply chains are tied to China.[67] President Trump could put pressure on Japan to follow suit in coercing its companies to restrict China's access to technology and human resource.

Alternatively, Trump could make a U-turn on his special relationship with Abe if Japan signs multilateral and regional trade deals including China but not the United States. At the same time, the Japanese government is wary that its alliance with the United States could become subordinate to collusion in "new great power relations" between the United States and China, as was feared under President Barack Obama.

The third major initiative is the Free and Open Indo-Pacific (FOIP) strategy, launched in its seminal form under Abe in 2007. The FOIP strategic framework is intended to protect the sovereignty of nations in the Indo-Pacific and the free passage of the oceans.[68] FOIP connects the two oceans (Indian and Pacific) and two continents (Asia and Africa) under three pillars of economic prosperity of connectivity and trade, implementation of fundamental principles—such as rule of law and freedom of navigation—and initiatives to ensure security and peace. It centrally involves strategic collaboration with other partners, such as the United States, India, and Australia. While FOIP is not promoted explicitly as a containment strategy, and in principle remains open to China's involvement, its vision of creating a free, open, and rules-based region offers an important counterbalance to China's growing influence. While the concept still needs to be made operational, FOIP offers an alternative vision to the Belt and Road Initiative—China's infrastructure master plan for the Eurasian landmass (the belt) and the maritime domain below it (the road). It sends signals that regional players are willing to cooperate to counterbalance China's advances in Asia and come together when rules are violated. Although not often realized, FOIP's ultimate hidden (and original) agenda is not to contain China but to resist the temptation for the United States to form a G2 superpower club with China.

Meanwhile, on the security front, Abe bolstered Japan's independent national security through proactive contribution to peace. Japan's reinterpretation of its constitution to allow it the right to exercise limited collective self-defense, and its passage of security-related bills, are steps toward Japan taking on a larger role in regional and global peace and security. It still remains very restrictive, with stipulated conditions ensuring that collective self-defense is only exercised with minimum force and when there are no alternatives in response to a threat to the Japanese state or people.

Abe received severe criticism for enacting the security legislation in 2015. Even so, his politically risky moves toward establishing a national security state, alliance burden-sharing, and more autonomous national security have been vindicated as prudent by the heightened precariousness on the Korean Peninsula. This is the acceleration of a longer trend. Since the 1990s, jolted by the shock of complaints of "checkbook diplomacy" in the Gulf War, Japan has increased participation in UN peacekeeping operations, and Abe's proactive contribution to peace should be understood as part of that longer process.

Abe has sought to craft a crucial role for Japan to play as a "proactive stabilizer" in Asia-Pacific security affairs through a holistic package of economic, diplomatic, and security policy.[69] By strengthening its role in regional security through an expansion of its own capabilities and deepening cooperation with the United States and other like-minded stakeholders, the Abe administration hopes to create incentives for the United States to remain actively engaged in regional affairs, as well as offers its own vital contributions directly to the stabilization of regional security.

Constitutional revision, which would allow Japan to take on an even more substantial role in security in the Asia-Pacific, is what the Abe government sees as the next necessary step in that process. However, it is politically risky for Abe and an issue that does not fail to mobilize an otherwise apathetic public. Article 9, which renounces war and the maintenance of land, sea, and air forces, is under consideration for revisions that include the formalization of the Self-Defense Forces (SDF) and giving the Diet legal authority over the behavior of the SDF.[70] Abe has set constitutional revision as the central goal of his political agenda, aiming to revise it by 2020.[71] Yet it is a daunting task.

Challenges from Within: Strategy Begins at Home

As Japan supports the liberal international order and aspires to an ambitious foreign policy agenda, it is crucially important for Japan to get its domestic politics and statecraft in shape and manage the forces that give birth to populism.

DEFINITION OF POPULISM: ANTIPLURALISTIC, US-VERSUS-THEM DISCOURSE

Populism has become a recurring motif to describe liberal democracies in existential crisis. In 2016, the results of the Brexit referendum and victory of the U.S. presidential candidate Donald Trump, both understood as successful populist insurgencies, galvanized the world's attention. Since then, observers have been fretting about the menace of populists from Turkey's Recep Tayyip Erdoğan, Hungary's Viktor Orbán, and the Philippines' Rodrigo Duterte to Geert Wilders in the Netherlands, Marine Le Pen in France, and Matteo Salvini in Italy.

With the populist label being applied across so many contexts and movements with such emotive language, the term risks becoming a sloppily applied category. Some have understood populism to be an ideology.[72] In a now-dominant definition from Cas Mudde, populism is treated as a "thin-centered ideology" that divides society into two homogenous but antagonistic groups. Politics, in this worldview, is a battle between the "corrupt" elite and a "pure" people, with populists representing the "general will" of these people against a self-serving establishment.[73] Being a thin ideology, populism does not stand alone but combines with a host ideology: be it nationalism, socialism, market libertarianism (neoliberalism), or regionalism. Populists can therefore come in many guises; from the radical Right with "exclusionary" xenophobic or nativist attitudes and policies to Left-leaning parties, movements, and leaders (such as Podemos in Spain and U.S. presidential candidate Bernie Sanders) and even neoliberal populists, pitting economic globalization against inefficient government (such as Carlos Menem in Argentina or Junichiro Koizumi in Japan).[74]

Populism is, in essence, a rejection of pluralism. Pluralists believe that there is no single general will of the people, and politics should reflect the preferences of the many ideas and identities in society through consensus and compromise.[75] Populism can be identified by the use of a discursive method through which leaders appeal to the electorate as a representative of a homogeneous bloc of "virtuous" people against a "corrupt" and irresponsive elite.[76] Populists then use this phraseology in their efforts to delegitimize an opposition and to conduct attacks on liberal institutions that check the powers of the elite (be they courts, media, legislatures, or civil society) in the name of the people.

ABE'S PRAGMATISM: CROWDING OUT THE SPACE FOR RIGHT-WING POPULISM

Prime Minister Shinzo Abe has made important contributions to suppressing a populist uprising in Japan and strengthening Japan's role in upholding regional and global order. Journalist Leo Lewis commented that Abe has been forced to subsume his conservatism "to the practicalities of running an ageing country in a world where old certainties are under attack."[77] However, public support for him has never been strong in Japan. To a large extent, he has remained in power because of the lack of a better alternative rather than through his popularity. His wider international appeal, particularly in China and South Korea, was low because of criticisms of him as a nationalist and revisionist in the early period of his administration.

In reality, Abe has engaged in critical historical reflection—necessary for Japan to realize its current position—with straight acknowledgment that Japan tore down the previous international order. On the seventieth anniversary of the end of World War II, he stated:

> With the Manchurian Incident, followed by the withdrawal from the League of Nations, Japan gradually transformed itself into a challenger to the new international order that the international community sought to establish after tremendous sacrifices. Japan took the wrong course and advanced along the road to war . . . While taking silent pride in the path that we have walked as a peace-loving nation for as long as seventy years, we remain determined never to deviate from this steadfast course.[78]

A more accurate characterization of Abe is a "pragmatic nationalist" rather than an ethnic nationalist.[79] He has combined right-wing impulses and patriotic symbolism with a welfare state, exemplifying centrist politics. Abe's nationalism has tended to give the state priority over individuals, sliding into statism. The government has provided paternalistic, top-down support to manufacturing and agricultural industries, not leaving them at the mercy of market forces. He has engaged in economic *dirigisme*, such as jawboning the wage increase, supporting state-backed International Network Corporation of Japan's bid for Toshiba's memory chip business, potential intervention to lower monthly cellphone costs, and promoting bullet train sales overseas. This has helped to deter right-wing populists, while avoiding toxic aspects of populism itself, and softened the dislocating blow of global economic competition.

Abe entered government for the second time following a revolving door of fourteen prime ministers in twenty years. Had the high turnover of prime ministers continued, it is possible a virulent populist could have come to power. Despite various scandals and unpopular legislative moves that have unsettled the prime minister's approval rating, the continuity and pragmatism of Abe's policy, including attempts at historical reconciliation with the United States, South Korea, and China, has enabled the government to earn stability, helped along significantly by a lack of faith in better alternatives and the continued failure by the opposition to regroup. Abe's pragmatic nationalism stands in contrast to the idealistic wish-list policies of the preceding party in power, the Democratic Party of Japan (DPJ).[80] The opposition parties are in disarray. If the votes of disgruntled citizens that are currently being absorbed by the opposition parties have nowhere to go, then their dissatisfaction could well transform into populist impulses,[81] the most pernicious form of which arises when it merges with nationalism, or even ultranationalism. Abe's pragmatic nationalism has helped prevent the merge by absorbing, co-opting, reigning in, and staving off nationalistic instincts.

Effective policies for economic growth have been put in place by the Abe government. Abenomics—three arrows of robust monetary policy, fiscal stimulus, and structural reforms—certainly helped Japan to set out on the path to defeat deflation and overcome the Lost Decades. Yet it has failed to reach its inflation target for years, and primary balance of the fiscal budget has been delayed. Real wages growth has long been sluggish, with little improvement under Abe.[82] While the delayed arrival of globalization and resistance to technological deployment—in particular, in digitalization—helped Japan to mitigate an inequality gap, it came at the cost of innovation and a vibrant economy. Keeping some conservatism while ensuring it does not become an obstacle to creativity and productivity is a formidable challenge.

STRUCTURAL FACTORS: POPULISM BUFFERS, INNOVATION HAMPERS, FUTURE THREATS

Arguably, the structural factors of Japanese politics and society have been equally or more important than the Abe factor in making Japan populism-resilient and contributing toward sustaining the international order from within. In the longer term, such features of Japanese politics and society could be unsustainable for growth and stability.

Japan's social security budget has nearly doubled since 1990, in favor of pensioners and elderly care over education, family, and unemployment support. Abe has not departed from economic liberalism, and he continues to support the welfare state. He has even called himself a "liberal," which many would scoff at, but he is a fiscal liberal.[83] This reflects Japan's general tendency for a larger welfare state regardless of the party or leader in power. As Foreign Minister Taro Kono has noted, "In Japan, we have a party for big government and a party for bigger government."[84] There has been no acute economic and social dislocation equivalent to that experienced in Western nations following the Lehman shock in 2008. Instead, Japan has experienced a slow, steady, manageable expansion of income equality and despite the emergence of a "working poor" class in the cities and depopulation and decay in rural areas, such groups have been cushioned by an expanded welfare budget. It must be noted, however, that the lack of impetus to improve fiscal health and ward off primary balance deficit is inviting a future fiscal crisis.

Any future Japanese leader is facing the twin almost-existential challenges of demography and public debt. The decline of the working-age population is seriously affecting the sustainability of Japan's national power, growth, and productivity. Immigration is a necessary part of the solution. In reality, as of 2017, there were 2.47 million foreign residents in Japan, including 1.28 million foreign workers, nearly double of 2012.[85] The Abe government has a silent, de facto pro-immigration policy.[86] With a greater inflow of trade, capital, and people across its borders, Japan will need to find its own way to develop healthy nationalism, or civic nationalism, which does not seek to exploit the divisions of identity politics.[87] Japan's immigration policy has not included the acceptance of refugees and is proportionally far less generous than that of other developed nations, which is the second structural factor for Japan avoiding populist identity politics. This reluctance to welcome foreign immigrants for security and cultural reasons caps the degree to which immigrants can be allowed into Japan. Such sentiments—reflected in the decision to accept no more than thirty asylum seekers annually in the past few years—has undermined Japan as an exemplar and contributor to the liberal international order.

The third, rather important structural factor is that Japan differs from Europe and America in respect to the groups underrepresented in politics and to what tends to be left off the agenda. The forgotten demographic in the United States and United Kingdom are typically middle-aged, low income, high school graduates living in rural areas. But in Japan's case, it is the young families, women, and those working under nonpermanent contracts in the big cities who have been left behind. Political campaigns to mobilize these factions of society's underdogs have tended to be limited to the local level, seen, for example, in the efforts of Toru Hashimoto in Osaka. Tokyo governor Yuriko Koike's Party of Hope in the October 2017 election was another failed attempt to translate neoliberal populism to the national level. The elderly, rural, working class commands the most political power in Japan. The electoral system is weighted in such a way that one rural vote typically counts for more than two urban votes. The frustrated have an outlet for their demands in the political center itself.

But the lopsided voting system creates serious political inequality between rural and urban voters, which itself creates inequality between generations. Indeed, a high court ruling has deemed the gap in the weight of votes sufficient to be in a "state of unconstitutionality."

The fourth structural factor is that there is no clear elite in Japan parallel to Wall Street, Silicon Valley, or the Beltway in the United States. The elite is much more elusive in Japan, and this makes it harder for the people to resent them. This is likely to be due to actual differences in the society, as well as a matter of public perception.

The bureaucracy is probably the closest thing to a political elite in Japan. However, it is relatively small, modest, and poorly paid, by Organisation for Economic Cooperation and Development (OECD) standards, which restricts the extent it can be targeted to by populist rhetoric. Free trade is also not seen to benefit the business elites so much, perhaps because Japan has scant resources. In contrast to American and European media resentment against free trade elites, all five of the major newspapers in Japan, both conservative and liberal, supported TPP in their editorials.

Japanese themselves still perceive their society to be fundamentally middle class—the myth of *ichi oku sochuryu* (100 million, all in the middle class) persists. This is despite the fact that compared to its high-income counterparts, Japan has above average income inequality and a high rate of child poverty. The survival of this perception no doubt plays an important role in staving off populist strategies.

Furthermore, executives are not perceived to be sitting on big bonuses and paychecks. Japanese executives are paid much less than executives in the West.[88] Toyota's CEO was paid one-twelfth of what Fiat Chrysler's CEO received in 2015.[89] In 2010, Japan introduced legislation requiring companies to reveal the pay of executives earning over US$1.1 million. Bankers and financiers, principal targets of modern populism, are not perceived to be as greedy as elsewhere and were not let off so lightly in Japan's financial crisis in the late 1990s. The case of Katsunobu Onogi, the last president of Long-Term Credit Bank, which collapsed in 1998, is illustrative. He was thrown into prison after its collapse, accused of concealing the scale of its nonperforming loans, but was eventually acquitted. All the major banks that were bailed out by the government drastically cut salaries and bonuses for the top executives. Losing his pension, Onogi lived humbly. In contrast, many Wall Street bankers were able to move on to other executive positions and bonus schemes after the 2008–09 financial crisis.[90] The sense of fairness in Japanese society may have played its part in stemming populist revolt and averting the polarization of 99 percent against the top-earning 1 percent.

While Japan's stability and resistance to populism has been lauded, this has not come without problems of its own. Japan lacks the strong citizen engagement, open and diverse news media, and effective opposition parties that are characteristic of healthy democracies. The other side of the coin of so-called stability has been the lack of vigor and vibrancy in democracy in Japan, while factionalism and division have become pervasive in opposition parties since the fall of the Democratic Party of Japan in 2012, with "ideologically coherent and pragmatic policy platforms" lacking.[91] As Kaori Hayashi argues (chapter 10), it would not be an exaggeration to say that Japan suffers from a triad of silence and nonparticipation that includes "political disinterest, public apathy, and indifference to the media."[92]

Outline of the Book

This book attempts to lay out critical analysis and evaluation of Japan's policies under the Abe administration and to suggest what more Japan can do to protect and reform the liberal international order in the Asia-Pacific, factoring in political and socioeconomic limitations. By providing concrete ideas for the further role that Japan can play, we hope this volume will offer a comprehensive picture of the contributions that Japan does and can make to the regional order—and where it needs to do more.

The structure is split broadly into two parts: foreign policy and domestic statecraft. Despite both being deeply interconnected, the book is neatly separated along these lines. The first half of the book looks at the policies that Japan has adopted and could adopt in order to support stability and liberalism in the Asia-Pacific, given the multiple new challenges it faces today. This spans Japan's role in regional security, trade and economics, international organizations, diplomacy, and nuclear proliferation. The second half of the book focuses on how Japan can create a healthy functioning democracy and a domestic setting, free of antagonistic populism or nationalism, to support a more ambitious international agenda. The domestic statecraft issues covered in this book include state welfare, immigration, populist movements, the media, historical issues, and the constitution. All are critical to creating a participatory liberal democracy and setting the foundations for Japan to implement a more ambitious vision for the regional order.

Adam P. Liff (chapter 1) delves into Japan's role in the regional security order. Evaluating Japan's 2013 National Security Strategy as a positive step, he argues that Japan is on the right trajectory under Abe in the security realm, considering the logic of regional security in the Asia-Pacific and the new challenges posed by China's coercive behavior and "gray zone" operations. He reminds us of the domestic constraints placed on Japan's foreign policy and calls for Japan to work with countries based on behavior rather than regime type in implementing the "Free and Open Indo-Pacific" strategy.

Unlike in security affairs, where Japan remains under the microscope, since taking leadership on CPTPP, it has increasingly been seen as a champion of economic liberalization. Mireya Solís (chapter 2) gives a comprehensive, insightful analysis into the ailments facing the global and regional trading order and the reasons why Japan has stepped up to provide leadership for the first time on trade liberalization. She offers proposals on how Japan should cope with the trade policy of the Trump administration, while offering a route to constructively influence the development of China's economy. The good work of Japan on leading trade liberalization is shown to be dependent on the continuing importance of the correct domestic political foundation, such as the agriculture lobby, prime ministerial leadership, and future technological change.

Reform of the World Trade Organization to better reflect modern trading relations is proposed by Philip Y. Lipscy (chapter 3). This would provide Japan with an opportunity to take leadership in the reform of international institutions as a means to reinforce the liberal international order. Lipscy characterizes Japan as a "reformist status quo power," since Japan is uniquely placed, having peacefully transitioned to global influencer under the postwar system. He proposes that Japan support other countries seeking institutional reform of international organizations and take active leadership to strengthen and revive the institutions underpinning the liberal international order.

Maiko Ichihara (chapter 4) explores another aspect of Japan's diplomacy—its use of values. She argues that despite the notable uptick in the Japanese government's use of values diplomacy in the post–Cold War period, Japan has differed from the Western emphasis on democracy and human rights, instead favoring values that allow for more plurality in governance. Under the new challenge of China's influence in governance of developing countries, Ichihara urges policymakers to be more proactive in their approach to maintain the liberal international order through the deployment of values in diplomatic encounters, while continuing to place focus on the importance of good governance and a diverse range of values.

The final element of the foreign policy half of the book is the fragility of global nuclear nonproliferation and the persistent national security threat to Japan from North Korea's nuclear arms and missiles. Nobumasa Akiyama (chapter 5) argues that the non-nuclear proliferation model of "Atoms for Alliance" offered by the United States is in question, due to America's weakened position in the supply chain of nuclear technology and the proliferation cases of Iran and North Korea, especially at a time when there is a strong civil society movement to ban nuclear weapons. He argues that Japan's choice for not having its own nuclear weapons is a rational strategic choice rather than antinuclear sentiment based on Hiroshima and Nagasaki.

The role of Japan's welfare state and tight immigration policies toward stabilizing discontent from the public is analyzed by Akihisa Shiozaki (chapter 6). While acknowledging the important role of such policies to date in diffusing populist discontent, he warns that they could be unsustainable, given Japan's worsening fiscal condition, increasing intergenerational inequality, labor shortage, and the absence of an integration policy for immigrants.

A different angle on the drivers for populism in Japan is taken by Ken Victor Leonard Hijino (chapter 7), who inspects local populist movements in Japan, such as Toru Hashimoto and Yuriko Koike, who failed to transition their populism to the national level. He also offers fresh insights into identity politics in Okinawa. He makes the case that populism can be a useful corrective for Japanese democracy if engaged with properly. But he points out that populism should not be our sole concern, as nationalism, inequality, and disengagement are all potential threats for Japan's democracy and international agenda.

Nationalism is the main topic taken up by Thomas Berger (chapter 8), who contends that Japan is not a global outlier in its efforts to apologize for the dark aspects of its history, and has still managed to cooperate with China and South Korea when interests align. However, enduring reconciliation faces challenges because of political interests in China and South Korea. Regardless of the difficulties, he insists on the importance of Japan making efforts to address its history to avoid undermining its alliance with the United States and in its efforts to uphold the liberal international order.

Constitutional revision, one of the most controversial domestic political issues in Japan, is taken up by Kenneth Mori McElwain (chapter 9). The central feature of Japan's constitution is identified to be flexibility, with McElwain noting both the utility and the potential pitfall of this approach. Referring to results from a public survey of the Japanese public, commissioned as part of this project (see chapter 11 for details), McElwain offers original analysis of the effect of the changing geopolitical situation on voter support for amending Article 9.

Turning the focus to domestic statecraft, Kaori Hayashi (chapter 10) evaluates the role of Japanese media in fostering a robust democracy and avoiding polarization of attitudes through "fake news" and social media as seen in countries including the United States and the United Kingdom. The challenge for Japan is different from that of the West, as its version of liberalism is suffering from a triad of political disinterest, public apathy, and indifference to media. She proposes that the Japanese media industry leverage the crisis of the liberal order to transform the traditional and hierarchical media structure in the country into a more dynamic and diverse environment.

In chapter 11, Kenneth Mori McElwain and Adam P. Liff examine their findings from a public survey on attitudes toward Japan taking a more proactive role in international affairs. Based on a sample of over three thousand Japanese participants, they find that there is generally support for Japan playing a proactive role in upholding all three pillars of the liberal international order—security order, human rights order, and economic order.

This project benefited from the indispensable input of policymakers and the public. Over forty interviews with Japanese policymakers and experts were undertaken by the authors, and the views of the public were incorporated through the survey experiment. The authors did not merely endorse the increased internationalism and stability of Japan under the second Abe administration. We have aimed to provide proposals of what more Japan could do to support its own democracy and uphold regional peace and prosperity, while illuminating the limitations that Japan must work to overcome to achieve a greater role for the benefit of itself and the Asia-Pacific. The next few years will be critical in the battle to keep liberalism alive in the Asia-Pacific. Japan cannot single-handedly uphold the liberal order in the region, but it must do all within its power to shape a liberal order that works for the Asia-Pacific.

NOTES

1. Yoichi Funabashi, "Japan and the New World Order," *Foreign Affairs*, vol. 70, no. 5 (Winter 1991/1992); Yuichi Hosoya, "Japan's Strategic Position: Global Civilian Power 2.0," in *Reinventing Japan: New Directions in Global Leadership*, edited by Martin Fackler and Yoichi Funabashi (Santa Barbara, Calif.: Praeger, 2018).

2. See Patrick Porter, "A World Imagined: Nostalgia and Liberal Order," *Cato Institute Policy Analysis* 843 (June 5, 2018), for an argument about the misconceptions of the liberal order's causes and consequences. See Rebecca Friedman Lissner and Mira Rapp-Hooper, "The Liberal Order Is More than a Myth," *Foreign Affairs* (July 31, 2018) for a response, https://www.foreignaffairs.com/articles/world/2018-07-31/liberal-order-more-myth.

3. See G. John Ikenberry, "Liberal Internationalism 3.0: America and the Dilemmas

of Liberal World Order," *Perspectives on Politics*, vol. 7, no. 1, for five key dimensions that explain the different forms of the liberal international order.

4. Inderjeet Parmar, "The US-Led Liberal Order: Imperialism by Another Name?" *International Affairs*, vol. 94, no. 1 (January 5, 2018).

5. See Suisheng Zhao, "A Revisionist Stakeholder: China and the Post–World War II World Order," *Journal of Contemporary China*, vol. 27, no. 113 (2018), 643–58.

6. Gideon Rose, "The Fourth Founding," *Foreign Affairs*, vol. 98, no. 1 (January/February 2019).

7. "The Article II Mandate: Forging a Stronger Alliance between the United States and Japan," Asia Pacific Initiative and Center for Strategic & International Studies, November 28, 2018.

8. Jennifer Lind and William C. Wohlforth, "The Future of the Liberal Order Is Conservative," *Foreign Affairs*, vol. 98, no. 2 (March/April 2019).

9. Cas Mudde, "The Problem with Populism," *Guardian*, February 17, 2015. See later in this chapter for a definition of populism.

10. Joseph Nye, "China Will Not Surpass America Any Time Soon," *Financial Times*, February 19, 2019.

11. Mark Medish, "When Multilateralism Crumbles, so Does Our Rules-based Order," *Guardian*, February 21, 2019.

12. Janaka Oertel, Andrew Small, and Amy Studdart, "The Liberal International Order in the Indo-Pacific," German Marshall Fund, *Asia Program* (April 13, 2018).

13. Philip Stephens, "Donald Trump's Foreign Policy Is China's Gain," *Financial Times*, August 2, 2018.

14. Kenneth B. Pyle, *Japan in the American Century* (Harvard University Press, 2018), 107.

15. G. John Ikenberry, "The Plot Against American Foreign Policy," *Foreign Affairs*, vol. 96, no. 3 (May/June 2017); Takako Hikotani, "Trump's Gift to Japan," *Foreign Affairs*, vol. 96, no. 5 (September/October 2017).

16. Zbigniew Brzezinski, *The Fragile Blossom*: Crisis and Change in Japan (New York: Harper and Row, 1972), xii.

17. Henry Kissinger, *The World Order* (New York: Penguin Press, 2015), 189.

18. Fareed Zakaria, *The Post-American World* (New York: W. W. Norton, 2008).

19. In 2014, President Obama made a speech taken to be an expression of abdication of the United States's role as the global policeman. Some experts have pointed out the similarity in President Trump's and President Obama's policies, but the former's zero-sum, transactionalist worldview without room for multilateralism is qualitatively different.

20. Yoichi Funabashi, *Asia Pacific Fusion: Japan's Role in APEC* (Washington, D.C.: Institute of International Economics, 1995), 218–20.

21. Jesse Johnson, "Trump Rips U.S. Defense of Japan as One-Sided, Too Expensive," *Japan Times*, August 6, 2016; and Politico staff, "Full Transcript: First 2016 Presidential Debate," *POLITICO*, September 27, 2016.

22. "The Article II Mandate: Forging a Stronger Alliance between the United States and Japan," Asia-Pacific Initiative and Center for Strategic & International Studies, November 28, 2018.

23. Stockholm International Peace Research Institute, SIPRI Military Expenditure Database, https://www.sipri.org/databases/milex.

24. Mari Yamaguchi, "Japan Cabinet Approve Record US$46B Defence Budget," *Defense News*, December 27, 2017.

25. Graham Allison, *Destined for War: Can America and China Escape the Thucydides's Trap?* (New York: Houghton Mifflin Harcourt, 2017), 149–50.

26. Andrew S. Erickson and Adam P. Liff, "Not-So-Empty Talk: The Danger of China's 'New Type of Great-Power Relations' Slogan," *Foreign Affairs* (October 9, 2014), https://www.foreignaffairs.com/articles/china/2014-10-09/not-so-empty-talk.

27. Francois Godemont and Abigael Vasselier, *China at the Gates: A New Power Audit of EU-China Relations* (European Council of Foreign Relations, December 1, 2017); French president Macron noted in a May 2018 visit to Sydney that "it is important . . . not to have any hegemony in the Indo-Pacific region." See Jamie Smyth, "Macron Pledges to Counter China Power in Pacific," *Financial Times*, May 2, 2018.

28. Michael J. Mazarr and others, "China and the International Order," RAND Corporation, 2018.

29. Full text of Xi Jinping keynote at the World Economic Forum, https://america.cgtn.com/2017/01/17/full-text-of-xi-jinping-keynote-at-the-world-economic-forum.

30. Thomas J. Wright, *All Measures Short of War: The Contest for the Twenty-First Century and the Future of American Power* (Yale University Press, 2017), 33–34; see also K. Webb, "The Continued Importance of Geographic Distance and Boulding's Loss of Strength Gradient," *Comparative Strategy*, vol. 26, no. 4 (2007), 295–310, for an explanation on why geographic distance still affects foreign policy.

31. Yoichi Funabashi, "China's Embrace of Digital Leninism," *Japan Times*, January 9, 2018.

32. See Robert Kagan, "Backing into World War III," *Foreign Policy* (February 6, 2017), for explanation of the term "sphere of influence."

33. Statistics of Japan, Ministry of Finance, "Bōeki aite-koku jōi 10-kakoku no suii (yushutsunyū sōgaku: Nen bēsu)" [Shifts in the Top 10 Trading Partners of Japan (Annual Total Import/Export)], http://www.customs.go.jp/toukei/suii/html/data/y3.pdf.

34. Across Northeast and Southeast Asia, countries increasingly find themselves tied to China for trade and investment and the United States for security. See G. John Ikenberry, "Between the Eagle and the Dragon: America, China, and Middle State Strategies in East Asia," *Political Science Quarterly*, vol. 131, no. 1 (Spring 2016), 9–43. See also an analysis of this from the perspective of geo-economics by Asia-Pacific Initiative and Center for Strategic & International Studies in "The Article II Mandate."

35. Susan B. Epstein and Paul K. Kerr, "IAEA Budget and U.S. Contribution: In Brief," *Congressional Research Service*, https://fas.org/sgp/crs/nuke/R44384.pdf.

36. "Treaty on the Non-Proliferation of Nuclear Weapons (NPT)," United Nations Office for Disarmament Affairs, accessed October 16, 2019, https://www.un.org/disarmament/wmd/nuclear/npt/; "Treaty on the Non-Proliferation of Nuclear Weapons: Status of the Treaty," United Nations Office for Disarmament Affairs, accessed October 16, 2019, http://disarmament.un.org/treaties/t/npt; "North Korea Nuclear Timeline Fast Facts," *CNN*, May 6, 2019, https://edition.cnn.com/2013/10/29/world/asia/north-korea-nuclear-timeline---fast-facts/index.html; Hans M. Kristensen and Matt Korda, "Status of World Nuclear Forces," Federation of American Scientists, last modified July 2019, https://fas.org/issues/nuclear-weapons/status-world-nuclear-forces/; Kelsey Dav-

enport and Kingston Reif, "Nuclear Weapons: Who Has What at a Glance," Arms Control Association, last reviewed July 2019, https://www.armscontrol.org/factsheets/Nuclearweaponswhohaswhat; "A Brief History of Nuclear Weapons States," Asia Society, accessed October 16, 2019, https://asiasociety.org/education/brief-history-nuclear-weapons-states.

37. See Julian Borger, "Vietnam Summit: North Korea and U.S. Offer Differing Reasons for Failure of Talks," *Guardian*, March 1, 2019, for an example.

38. See Joseph Bermudez and Victor Cha, "After Hanoi Summit: Rebuilding of Sohae Launch Facility," Center for Strategic & International Studies, *Beyond Parallel* (March 5, 2019); Jack Liu and others, "North Korea's Sohae Satellite Launch Facility: Normal Operations May Have Resumed," 38 North (March 7, 2019), for reports on satellite imagery.

39. Erich Schmitt, "Pentagon and Seoul Surprised by Trump Pledge to Halt Military Exercises," *New York Times*, June 12, 2018.

40. Yoichi Funabashi, "Delinking Different Elements in Japan-U.S. Ties," *Japan Times*, April 7, 2017.

41. Yoichi Funabashi, "Poor Japan–South Korea Relations Weaken Trump's Hand with Kim Jong Un," *Washington Post*, February 25, 2019.

42. "Japan Should Be Able to Build Nuclear Weapons: Ex-LDP Secretary General Ishiba," *Japan Times*, November 6, 2017; Hugh White, "Japan's Tough Choice," *Strait Times*, October 31, 2017. See also Karl Gustafsson, Linus Hagstrom, and Ulv Hanssen, "Japan's Pacifism Is Dead," *Survival*, vol. 60, no. 2 (December 2018/January 2019), 137–58.

43. Tomohiko Satake, "Japan's Nuclear Policy: Between Non-Nuclear Identity and U.S. Extended Deterrence," ASPNet Policy Forum, May 21, 2009.

44. See Yoichi Funabashi, "Conclusion: Something Has Been 'Lost' from Our Future," in *Examining Japan's Lost Decades*, edited by Yoichi Funabashi and Barak Kushner (New York: Routledge, 2015).

45. Lully Miura, "Bridges Make Good Neighbors: Building Soft Power with ODA," in *Reinventing Japan*, edited by Martin Fackler and Yoichi Funabashi (Santa Barbara, Calif.: Praeger, 2018), 2–3.

46. "Galapagos Syndrome," a phrase that was coined by Nomura Research, refers to Japan's tendency to develop products and ideas in an inward-looking manner and in an isolated environment detached from the rest of the world, instead of seeking to export these products and ideas to an international audience. See Joseph Caron, "Conservatives' Insular Mind-Set Doesn't Fit Today's Global Reality," *Japan Times*, March 17, 2014, as an example.

47. See Defense Innovation Board, Department of Defense, "The 5G Ecosystem: Risks and Opportunities for DoD," April 2019.

48. Yoichi Funabashi, "The Battle over Huawei 'Spyware,'" *Japan Times*, February 13, 2019.

49. David Sanger and others, "In 5G Race with China, U.S. Pushes Allies to Fight Huawei," *New York Times*, January 26, 2019.

50. Jonathan Woetzel, Jeogmin Seong, and others, "China's Digital Economy: A Leading Global Force," Discussion Paper (McKinsey Global Institute, August 2017).

51. Inagawa Hidekazu, "Introduction," in *The Population Implosion: The 50 Mil-*

lion Shock, edited by Yoichi Funabashi (Basingstoke, U.K.: Palgrave Macmillan, 2018), 9–10.

52. Thanks to Yukiko Fukagawa for raising this point at the launch event for "The Article II Mandate" on November 29, 2018.

53. Kazumasa Oguro, "The Impact of Demographic Challenges on Macroeconomic and Public Finance," in *The Population Implosion: The 50 Million Shock*, edited by Yoichi Funabashi (Basingstoke, U.K.: Palgrave Macmillan, 2018), 84–87.

54. PwC, "How Will the Global Economic Order Change by 2050?" February 2017.

55. See Association of Southeast Asia Nations (ASEAN), "Foreign Direct Investment Statistics," https://asean.org/?static_post=foreign-direct-investment-statistics.

56. Japanese ODA is primarily given as loans, which is a major difference from most Western donors.

57. Hiromi Inami, "Bridges Make Good Neighbors: Building Soft Power with ODA," in *Reinventing Japan*, edited by Martin Fackler and Yoichi Funabashi (Santa Barbara, Calif.: Praeger, 2018).

58. "Speech by Minister for Foreign Affairs, Heiko Maas, at the National Graduate Institute for Policy Studies in Tokyo, Japan," https://www.auswaertiges-amt.de/en/newsroom/news/maas-japan/2121846.

59. Deutscher Bungestag, Plenarprotokoll 19/35, June 6, 2018.

60. Kristzina Binder, "EU-Japan Trade Agreement: A Driver for Closer Cooperation Beyond Trade," *European Parliamentary Research Service*, July 2018.

61. Thanks to Takashi Terada for raising this point at the launch event of "The Article II Mandate" by Asia-Pacific Initiative on November 29, 2018.

62. Satoshi Sugiyama, "Abe Heralds Launch of 'Osaka Track' Framework for Free Cross-Border Data Flow at G20," *Japan Times*, June 28, 2019, last modified June 29, 2019, https://www.japantimes.co.jp/news/2019/06/28/national/abe-heralds-launch-osaka-track-framework-free-cross-border-data-flow-g20/#.XaVjYugzZPY.

63. Ibid.

64. Jane Perlez, "Japan and China, Asian Rivals, Are Trying to Get Along," *New York Times*, October 24, 2018.

65. See Yoichi Funabashi, "Normalizing Japan-China Ties Poses Risks," *Japan Times*, December 11, 2018.

66. See Yoichi Funabashi, "Japan Must Ponder the Risks of Closer Ties with China," *Washington Post*, October 27, 2018.

67. See Funabashi, "Normalizing Japan-China Ties."

68. International Cooperation Bureau, Ministry of Foreign Affairs, "Priority Policy for Development Cooperation FY2017," 9.

69. See chapter 1 by Adam Liff.

70. As of November 2018. Information gathered from a presentation by Hakubun Shimomura at the Liberal Democratic Party (LDP) headquarters in Tokyo. It is more moderate than the LDP's 2012 proposal.

71. Tomohiro Osaki and Daisuke Kikuchi, "Abe Declares 2020 as Goal for New Constitution," *Japan Times*, May 3, 2017.

72. See Noam Gidron and Bart Bonikowski, "Varieties of Populism: Literature Review and Research Agenda," Weatherhead Working Paper Series No. 13-0004

(Cambridge, Mass.: Weatherhead Center, Harvard University, 2013). Kurt Weyland has argued instead that populism is "a political strategy by which a personalistic leader seeks or exercises government based on direct, unmediated, un-institutionalized support from large numbers of mostly unorganized followers," preferring direct forms of representation such as opinion polls, plebiscites, and referenda to mobilize the public rather than the indirect representation of the people through elected politicians, in Kurt Weyland and Raul L. Madrid, *When Democracy Trumps Populism: European and Latin American Lessons for the United States* (Cambridge University Press, 2019), 10.

73. Cas Mudde, "The Populist Zeitgeist," *Government and Opposition*, vol. 39, no. 4, 541–63.

74. *Populism in Europe and the Americas: Threat or Corrective for Democracy?* edited by Cas Mudde and Cristóbal Rovira Kaltwasser (Cambridge University Press, 2012).

75. Jan-Werner Müller, *What Is Populism?* (London: Penguin, 2017), 3.

76. As a discursive style, populism is measured by the frequency by which populist us-versus-them language is used by political elites or outsiders in campaigning or in rule.

77. Leo Lewis, "Deal with Brussels Liberates Abe from His Nationalist Tendencies," *Financial Times*, July 19, 2018.

78. "Statement by Prime Minister Shinzo Abe," Prime Minister of Japan and His Cabinet, August 14, 2015.

79. The term was used by Ezra Vogel, quoted in Jane Perlez, "Rivals Try to Get Along, Whether They Like It or Not," *New York Times*, October 25, 2018; Kevin Doak, "Japan Chair Platform: Shinzo Abe's Civic Nationalism," Center for Strategic & International Studies, *Japan Chair Platform*, May 15, 2013.

80. See *The Democratic Party of Japan in Power: Challenges and Failures*, edited by Yoichi Funabashi and Koichi Nakano (Abingdon, U.K.: Routledge, 2017).

81. Eiji Oguma, "Sensou no jyubaku, Seiji fushin, Nogarerarenu shakai" [Prisoner of Its Past War, Distrust of Politics, and a Society that Cannot Free Itself from Them], *Asahi Shimbun*, August 30, 2018.

82. Yuko Takeo, "Japan Is Growing but Wages Have Barely Budged. Why?" *Bloomberg*, March 5, 2018.

83. "Keizai Seisaku Henshitsu, 'Watashi Ha Liberal' Abe Shusho, Seiken Fukki 5 nen" [Changes in the Economic Policy, 'I Am a Liberal' 5 Years after Abe Returned to Power], *Asahi Shimbun*, December 26, 2017.

84. "Staying Power—Why the LDP Keeps Winning Elections in Japan: Pragmatism," *Economist*, October 12, 2017.

85. Ministry of Justice, "Heisei 29 Nen 6 Getsumatsu Genzai ni okeru Zairyuu Gaikokjinsuu ni tsuite" [Foreigners Residing in Japan in June 2017], http://www.moj.go.jp/content/001238032.pdf; Ministry of Health, Labor, and Welfare, "Gaikokujin Koyou Jyoukyou no Todoke Jyoukyou Matome" (Heisei 29 Nen 10 Getsumatsu Genzai) [Information about Reports on Foreign Workers], http://www.mhlw.go.jp/stf/houdou/0000192073.html.

86. In December 2018, a revision to the Immigration Control and Refugee Recognition Act was passed in Japan's upper house with support from Abe's party. See Shuhei Endo and Yusuke Matsukura, "Japan Ushers in Major Immigration Policy Change with Revision to Boost Foreign Workforce," *Mainichi Shimbun*, December 8, 2018, https://mainichi.jp/english/articles/20181208/p2a/00m/0na/013000c.

87. See Dani Rodrik, *The Globalization Paradox: Democracy and the Future of the World Economy* (New York: W. W. Norton, 2012); Lawrence Summers, "Voters Deserve Responsible Nationalism not Reflex Globalism," *Financial Times*, July 10, 2016; Jeff D. Colgan and Robert O. Keohane, "The Liberal Order Is Rigged," *Foreign Affairs*, vol. 96, no. 3 (May/June 2017).

88. "Bosses' Salaries in Japan—Paycheck," *Economist*, August 6, 2016.

89. "Toyota Chief Earned US$2.84 Million Last Year after Bonus Doubles," Reuters, June 24, 2015.

90. Gillian Tett, "A Japanese Lesson for Wall Street," *Financial Times*, October 6, 2017.

91. Mireya Solís, "Japan's Consolidated Democracy in an Era of Populist Turbulence" (Brookings, February 2019).

92. See chapter 10 by Kaori Hayashi.

PART I
FOREIGN POLICY

1

Proactive Stabilizer

JAPAN'S ROLE IN THE ASIA-PACIFIC SECURITY ORDER

ADAM P. LIFF

Since the early 1950s, the postwar Asia-Pacific security order and system of bilateral alliances centered on the United States have been a core determinant of Japan's security and foreign policy trajectory. Though the region has seen its share of conflict, the relative absence of direct great power war since 1945 facilitated Japan's rapid development and remarkably self-restrained security posture as it rebuilt from the ashes of World War II. Japan transformed from a militarist, imperialist power to a mature, peaceful democracy and economic superpower that, owing in significant part to U.S. security guarantees, chose to shun traditional great power politics, an indigenous nuclear deterrent, robust offensive weapons or power projection capabilities, and an international security role remotely close to its potential. In addition to mitigating regional military competition, the U.S. alliance-centered security order that took shape in those early years also facilitated newly democratized Japan's eventual enmeshment in international institutions and an open international trading system defined primarily by close economic and political ties with the United States and its allies.

Yet today, more than seventy years after Japan's postwar rebirth and a quarter-century after the Cold War's end, major geopolitical and geo-economic shifts challenge the regional and global status quo. Concerns abound about the rapidly shifting balance of power and the sustainability of what many policymakers and commentators now refer to as the "rules-based liberal international order" so fundamental to Japan's development, prosperity, security, and foreign policy. Such concerns transcend threats to the more conspicuously liberal elements of the postwar international order—especially the free and open trade system (see chapter 2 by Mireya Solís) and global governance and international institutions (see chapter 3 by Phillip Lipscy). In the security domain, the focus of this chapter, many observers see an array of challenges in China's rapidly growing power, influence, and coercive rhetoric and policies vis-à-vis its neighbors, all of which threaten to undermine key pillars of the regional order and pose larger threats to international law and rules-based norms and principles.

Beyond China, nuclear-armed North Korea's open affront to the nuclear nonproliferation regime and development of a nascent ICBM capability with a range that potentially includes Washington further exacerbates fears about the sustainability of the U.S.-centered alliance system (see chapter 5 by Nobumasa Akiyama). Add the Trump administration's apparent ambivalence about America's traditional leadership role and skepticism—if not transactionalism—with respect to alliances, free trade, international organizations, and democratic values, to the changing regional power balance and it becomes clear why many fear that the existing order faces an existential crisis. Exacerbating these concerns, major thought leaders, as well as current and former officials in the United States and its major treaty allies, have even identified Washington itself as a threat to the liberal international order's sustainability, either through passive "abdication" of leadership of an order it played an essential role in creating or active efforts to undermine it.[1] Some particularly heated rhetoric emanates from traditional U.S.–Asia-Pacific allies, where some experts are openly discussing the need for a "Plan B" if Donald Trump's America First posture and "mistrustful neglect" of alliances are not a temporary aberration, calling for deeper partnerships among U.S. allies to offset "U.S. withdrawal from some parts of the world stage," or even explicitly suggesting "get[ting] rid of" an alliance with the United States.[2] Further afield, European leaders have suggested they cannot depend on the United States, and advocated for the formation of a European army.[3]

In this context, many have called on other advanced liberal democracies and benefactors of the liberal international order to "step up" to sustain it, especially Japan—the world's third largest economy and a leading liberal democracy with significant existing influence and still greater potential.[4] Tokyo would also seem to have a clear national interest in doing so. All the aforementioned challenges threaten foundational pillars of Japan's economy and national security. Indeed, if the order were to collapse or the United States to "withdraw" or "abdicate" in the manner already suggested by some and feared by many, defining assumptions of Japan's foreign policy would be fundamentally undermined.

Though there are numerous calls for Japan to do more to champion the Asia-Pacific security components of the liberal order (see box 1-1), the associated discourse is often characterized by vague diagnosis and policy prescriptions. This chapter aims to begin addressing this gap by engaging with the following questions: What is the traditional logic of the postwar Asia-Pacific security order, how does it relate to the liberal international order and Japan's national security, and how has it evolved over time? What is the scope and nature of the contemporary challenges to it, especially from China and, to a lesser extent, the United States?[5] How has Japan's security policy evolved in response to associated challenges heretofore? And what more could it do?

By bolstering and rationalizing its own defense posture, strengthening ties with the United States, and deepening and expanding security and diplomatic links to other order-supporting countries within and beyond its immediate region, Japan has already developed and implemented a coherent and proactive national security strategy to mitigate risk. Given the rapid and seemingly fundamental shifts unfolding across the region and beyond, whether current strategy will be sufficient remains to be seen. The answer will undoubtedly depend significantly on developments beyond Tokyo's control—in particular, China's policies and the United States's own evolving strategy (or lack thereof). However, one thing is clear: during a period of rapid and potentially disruptive change, Japan has essential roles to play as a *proactive stabilizer* in the Asia-Pacific security order and constructive contributor to shaping its future evolution. By more actively and flexibly leveraging its considerable capabilities and strengthening ties with the United States and other regional partners, thereby further en-

> **BOX 1-1.** Defining the security components of the liberal international order[a]
>
> Though most academic commentary on the post-1945 liberal international order focuses on international organizations and free trade, in the security domain one can identify at least three security suborders:
>
> - the UN Charter–based nonaggression order rooted in law with powerful normative features, which includes commitments to territorial status quos, nonaggression, and the peaceful resolution of international disputes
>
> - a multilateral security order focused on areas of common interest such as security of the global commons, freedom of navigation and overflight (e.g., United Nations Convention on the Law of the Sea, UNCLOS), nonproliferation (e.g., Treaty on the Non-Proliferation of Nuclear Weapons, NPT), and antipiracy
>
> - the more traditional deterrence-focused aspects of U.S. security alliances and U.S. military power
>
> ---
>
> a. A recent RAND study generates a similar list. Michael J. Mazarr, Timothy R. Heath, and Astrid Stuth Cevallos, *China and the International Order* (Santa Monica, CA: RAND Corporation, 2018), 8. (www.rand.org/pubs/research_reports/RR2423.html).

couraging the continued engagement of the United States, Japan can help reinvigorate the liberal order—not only in terms of security—in the face of existing challenges and facilitate its necessary evolution as it inevitably must adapt to meet future ones.

The Logic and Evolution of the Postwar Asia-Pacific Security Order

Though often overlooked, central to any discussion about Japan's role in the rules-based liberal international order are security affairs—especially the U.S.-centered global alliance system that has underpinned it, albeit imperfectly, for nearly seventy years. In the Asia-Pacific, that system has been fundamentally baked into Japan's postwar national security, political, and economic DNA. The 1951 U.S.-Japan Security Treaty (revised in 1960) was effectively a quid pro quo, making termination of the U.S. occupation conditional on Tokyo agreeing to a security relationship with Washington. Motivated significantly by worsening anti-Communist sentiment during the Korean War, the treaty with Japan, as well as U.S. bilateral defense pacts with Australia, New Zealand, and the Philippines—and, incidentally, the reason no NATO-like collective security arrangement was possible—was also driven by American wartime allies' lingering mistrust of Japan.[6] In other words, from its inception, the alliance system's intent was in part to ameliorate regional security competition—even among nations aligned with the United States.

Given transparently exclusionary conditions for membership in the U.S.-centered "hub-and-spokes" system of bilateral alliances during the Cold War, the extent to which it was inherently "liberal" is debatable. At a minimum, however, its advocates have generally regarded it as sine qua non for achieving the more unambiguously liberal objectives of America's post–World War II grand strategy: facilitating Japan's and (Western) Germany's reemergence as peaceful, democratic powers, economically and politically integrated with North America and Western Europe; the expansion of a free and open trading system; nuclear nonproliferation; preventing war on the Korean Peninsula and across the Taiwan Strait; peacefully resolving disputes in a rules-based manner, with an emphasis on legitimate process rather than particular outcomes; making the world safe for democracy; and deterring, and ultimately defeating, the illiberal Soviet bloc. Furthermore, fundamental to the alliance-centered order within the Western bloc was the liberal and "open character of American hegemony . . . despite huge asymmetries of power," especially in the early postwar years, which meant that:

> America's partners were less fearful of domination or abandonment because they were reciprocally integrated into security alliances and multilateral economic institutions that limited the unaccountable exercise of power and created transgovernmental political processes for ensuring ongoing commitments and resolving conflict. . . . The open American polity provided points of access and "voice

opportunities," which in turn provided opportunities for the allies to become directly involved in making alliance policy. The array of binding institutions connected to democratic states provided the basis for both commitment and restraint.[7]

Indeed, U.S. alliances were part of a larger package of institutions designed to facilitate political and economic relations among wartime allies and erstwhile adversaries alike by providing a security guarantee where trust was lacking and, in key instances, antagonism remained powerful. In the words of John Foster Dulles, U.S. secretary of state (1953–59), the alliance system, especially in Europe, was about "cooperation *for* something rather than merely *against* something."[8] It was designed to make American power, according to scholar John Ikenberry, "more predictable, accessible, and usable," as well as "more certain and less arbitrary."[9] Though U.S. power and credibility are generally seen as essential to the functioning of the international order, the order's most conspicuously "liberal" institutions mutually reinforce other aspects, buttressing peace and prosperity.[10] Neither the security order itself nor the larger liberal international order is merely "a euphemism for U.S. hegemony."[11] Today, many states—large and small, of various political systems—have clear stakes in the order's preservation and fear the deleterious implications for their own security and prosperity if it were to collapse. This is why doubts about the U.S. ability and, more recently, willingness to actively champion it have raised such deep concerns.

Herein lies another important point. Though often treated as such, the liberal international order in practice has never been static, as discussed in the introductory chapter. Neither has the security order, whose characteristics, objectives, bounds, and membership have evolved and become significantly more inclusive, even arguably liberal, over time. During the early stages of the Cold War, U.S. allies in Asia shared more of a commitment to fighting Communism than championing liberal democracy, but this began to change in the late 1970s and 1980s, as key U.S. allies and partners democratized. The logic of the alliance system has also evolved significantly. Today, both Tokyo and Washington regularly refer to the U.S.-Japan alliance as the "cornerstone" of regional security and enabler of more liberal economic elements—which, in turn, has helped lift hundreds of millions across Asia out of poverty in recent decades. In the mid-1990s, even as they pursued "deep engagement" with China and other nonallies, U.S. leaders simultaneously reaffirmed the alliance system as a kind of insurance against geopolitical instability amid prescient concerns about looming power shifts and uncertainty. As Joseph Nye, then assistant secretary of defense for international security affairs, wrote in 1995, expected variables in the region's post–Cold War evolution included the "rise of Chinese power"; "eventual rejuvenation of Russia"; "evolving role of Japan"; and "tensions on Korean Peninsula." From this perspective, reaffirming the United States military's forward presence, alliances, and regional institutions served to "reduce the need for arms buildups and deter the rise of hegemonic forces." It was also seen not as a means to contain a rising China but as a necessary instrument to engage an illiberal regime; in particular, to make smaller and weaker regional states feel secure and confident in their interactions with China and less concerned about relative gains.[12] For many smaller regional countries, U.S. contributions to regional security were integral to facilitating their own engagement with China.[13]

This basic logic persisted across multiple U.S. administrations, as has a conviction that China is one of the U.S.-led order's greatest benefactors, "prospering as part of the open and rules-based system."[14] Concomitant with efforts to reaffirm and strengthen security alliances and partnerships in response to the region's strategic vicissitudes, the United States and its allies have simultaneously brought China and other formerly excluded countries into the more transparently liberal elements of the order: the free trading system—for example, the World Trade Organization (WTO), which China joined in 2001—and international institutions and treaties. By the 2000s, optimism was widespread and voices across the region called for the consolidation of a complementary regional security architecture focused on functional, action-oriented, and inclusive multilateralism,[15] aimed at tackling shared challenges and centered on regional institutions, which included the Six-Party Talks concerning North Korea's nuclear program, the Association of Southeast Asian Nations (ASEAN) Regional Forum, and the ASEAN Defense Ministers Meeting-Plus. Thus, for many advocates of liberal order, whether inherently liberal itself or not, the U.S.-led Asia-Pacific security order has been a prerequisite for more unambiguously liberal developments in other policy domains.

In short, since the collapse of the Soviet Union, what was originally an exclusionary system of anti-Communist bilateral alliances has itself evolved significantly—becoming more open and inclusive in the process—as it was complemented by nascent institutions and regimes aimed at expanding cooperation even further, especially on nontraditional security issues. By the 2000s, U.S. (and Japanese) leaders were actively seeking new security partners outside the traditional core of U.S. treaty allies, in key instances without regard for political system. Though not in all cases liberal or democratic internally, such as Singapore or Vietnam, these partners nevertheless appear committed externally to a more "principled and inclusive security network" focused on upholding liberal, rules-based principles grounded in international law, such as freedom of navigation and overflight, and peaceful resolutions of disputes.[16] Although there is no question that these deepening security ties are aimed partly at traditional balancing, it is important to stress that a major driver of both regional threat perceptions vis-à-vis Beijing and the resulting tightening of security ties has been specific Chinese *rhetoric and actions* in the East and South China Seas seen as illiberal and inimical to a rules-based order, rather than opposition to China's illiberal regime itself. This is an important distinction between the Cold War era and now. As a case in point, even a former Cold War adversary and domestically illiberal and Communist state like Vietnam now finds itself aligned with the United States. Further indicative of deepening complexity, even China itself has occasionally emerged as an important security partner for the United States in specific areas—such as antipiracy and counterproliferation.

Thus, there is no—nor has there ever been—*one* security order in the contemporary Asia-Pacific, much less a static one. Today, a conservative, sovereignty-centric and power-based order with the traditional deterrence effects of the U.S. alliance system at its core exists alongside (and, indeed, often overlaps and supports) a more liberal version of order based on shared interests, norms, laws, and principles. U.S. and allied military power has combined with the postwar order to contribute significantly to regional and global stability during periods of change, enabling many of the more liberal elements in this and other policy domains.[17] The post–Cold War surge of interest in nontraditional security issues exemplifies liberal strands, while more traditional balancing in response to security concerns—especially vis-à-vis China and North Korea—represent the conservative side.

Nevertheless, and regardless of its Cold War origins, the Asia-Pacific security order today can be said to have liberal characteristics in at least the following ways:

- it discourages aggression, while encouraging peaceful settlements of disputes based not on power ("might makes right") but on mutually acceptable processes, in accordance with the UN Charter;
- its rules and norms are not inherently biased against any particular country and are grounded in international law;
- the conditions for participation relate to foreign policy behavior, not regime type;
- those shared expectations are transparent, if contested;
- it contributes to the geopolitical stability that is *sine qua non* for the international order's more unambiguously liberal elements, including the open trading system and international institutions, to function effectively.

The "China Challenge" to Japan's National Security and the Asia-Pacific Security Order

Today, the Asia-Pacific security order faces manifold and deepening challenges, especially from North Korea (see chapter 5 for analysis) and China (the focus of this chapter).

Fifteen years ago, besides a possible Taiwan-related contingency, to most foreign observers China's military modernization and its rapidly increasing and relatively nontransparent defense budget were fairly abstract, prospective security concerns. Few paid much heed to the People's Liberation Army (PLA) development of large and capable arsenals of conventionally tipped ballistic missiles ranging across every U.S. military or Self-Defense Force (SDF) base in Japan, or other "anti-access/area-denial" capabilities intended to make the United States reconsider intervening in a regional conflict. Also generally overlooked were Beijing's controversial sovereignty claims in the East and South China Seas. Furthermore, concerns about China's subthreshold (not overtly military) coercion and "gray zone" operations in support of those claims were not a front-burner issue.

Yet much has changed, especially since 2010. Captured symbolically in China's supplanting of Japan that year as the world's second largest economy, the region's balance of power has been shifting rapidly. Between 2007 and 2018, Beijing's official military spending—widely considered to be underreported—increased from roughly US$45 billion to an expected US$175 billion. In other words, over a ten-year period, China and Japan went from having roughly the same official defense budget to the former spending four times as much. This largesse has accelerated the PLA's rapid modernization across the board, including the long-neglected PLA navy, which is now the world's largest, enjoys rapidly improving capabilities and operates with increasing frequency and intensity in the South and East China Seas, as well as farther afield.

Coupled with the illiberal nature of the Chinese Communist Party's rule, it is against this shifting geopolitical regional landscape and balance of power that Beijing's recent actions are seen as threats to the liberal international order and its security suborders in the Asia-Pacific. Particularly prominent has been Beijing's coercive gray zone operations in the East and South China Seas and its responses to widespread criticism that its activities undermine, if not flagrantly violate, international law—especially the UN Convention on the Law of the Sea (UNCLOS), which Beijing has ratified. More generally, China's rhetoric openly criticizing the U.S. alliance system as an anachronism and threat to regional stability, coupled with championing of alternatives, also raise concerns among those who see these alliances as public goods, security guarantors, and stabilizing forces during a period of rapid and unpredictable change.

THE COMPLEXITY OF THE CHINA CHALLENGE

Increasingly, the United States, Japan, and their security partners link the China challenge directly to concerns about the larger Asia-Pacific security order and advocate deepening ties with like-minded countries as a counterbalance. In October 2017, then secretary of state Rex Tillerson championed working with India to promote a "free and open Indo-Pacific" led by advanced democracies, stating that China's leaders were "undermining the international, rules-based order."[18] Beyond calling China and Russia "revisionist," the Trump administration's 2017 National Security Strategy expressed concerns about "adversaries and competitors . . . becoming adept at operating below the threshold of open military conflict and at the edges of international law"—a thinly veiled reference to their activities in the East and South China Seas and in Ukraine, respectively.[19] Its 2018 Nuclear Posture Review notes, "Since 2010 we have seen the return of Great Power competition. To varying degrees, Russia and China have made clear they seek to substantially revise the post–Cold War international order and norms of behavior"—a sentiment emphasized in a major, widely discussed speech on U.S.-China policy by Vice President Mike Pence that October.[20]

Such high-profile statements demonstrate that concerns about China as a "revisionist" threat to the liberal international order are now mainstream. Viewed holistically, however, China's posture toward the order—including free trade, international institutions, and some components of the security order—is complex and its record is mixed (as, it should be noted, is that of the United States). As a 2018 RAND report notes, "It is not entirely accurate to speak of China's interaction with 'the' international order." Beijing has been generally supportive of the global economic order while far more circumspect in political, such as human rights conventions and liberal democracy, and security elements. It has also been more supportive of the UN-centric order than more liberal aspects centered on the United States.[21] Indeed, one of the major challenges for policymakers is to recognize the seriousness of China's challenges, without falling victim to zero-sum, Manichean interpretations. The goal is to deter regional coercion and aggression while encouraging Beijing to more positively, proactively support a liberal order that has not only enabled but actively encouraged its peaceful rise.[22]

That China is not an unabashed, across-the-board revisionist makes it a particularly complicated challenge. To many, it has been far more supportive of the liberal international order at the global level, while at the regional level it is already seeking changes, sometimes through coercive and destabilizing means. Whether the latter is merely a prologue to greater revisionism on a global level remains an open question. But that also may not be the most important question to ask. As Thomas Wright cautions, "The most important piece of the liberal order is not the UN or international financial institutions, important as they are. It is healthy regional orders. . . . If those regional orders fall apart, so, too, will the global order."²³

FROM "RESPONSIBLE STAKEHOLDER" TO "REVISIONIST POWER"?

Those important caveats aside, China is widely seen as posing longer-term, more significant challenges today than many Japanese and U.S. policymakers anticipated hopefully ten or twenty years ago.²⁴ In the 1990s and mid-2000s, calls for a transformed Asia-Pacific order based on more inclusive, regional multilateralism, institutions, confidence-building, and functional cooperation were accompanied by growing optimism about China's own domestic and international transformation—what we might call the "Peaceful Rise" era. Beijing gradually opened its economy, pursued (relative) liberalization of its society, signed on to dozens of international treaties, expanded its participation in international organizations and UN Peacekeeping Operations, joined the WTO, and ratified major treaties, such as UNCLOS. In the United States, policies based on cautious optimism about China's evolution tempered by realism were reflected in the Clinton administration's "engage and balance" approach and, more famously, the George W. Bush administration's 2005 call for China to emerge as a "responsible stakeholder."²⁵

Yet the 2008–12 period precipitated a major shift in Japanese and U.S. perceptions about China's trajectory and intent, prompting calls for a policy course correction. It was first in the security suborder where China's approach became most conspicuously competitive and, from the allies' perspective, revisionist. By 2017, the United States National Security Strategy openly identified China and Russia as "revisionist powers . . . that use technology, propaganda, and coercion to shape a world antithetic to our interests and values," warning that a "geopolitical competition between free and repressive visions of world order is taking place in the Indo-Pacific region."²⁶

THE CORROSIVE EFFECT OF CHINA'S GRAY ZONE OPERATIONAL CHALLENGES

Over the past decade, and with apparent impunity, China's coercive rhetorical and physical assertion of its vast and controversial sovereignty claims in the South and East China Seas has had an indirect but deeply corrosive effect on the rules-based security order, not to mention openly threatening the national security of affected countries. Beijing has relied heavily on so-called gray zone operations, which are subthreshold aggressive activities that are difficult to deter without significant escalation risks, since they constitute neither a pure peacetime nor a traditional, armed attack situation.

For Japan, most provocative are the regular operations of the increasingly robust (and militarized) China Coast Guard (CCG) near the Senkaku Islands (Diaoyu in Chinese; below, the Senkakus).[27] Since September 2012, larger and more capable CCG vessels frequently enter the Senkakus' contiguous zone and conduct regular "presence" missions in the islands' territorial sea to coercively challenge Japan's decades-old effective administrative control.[28] Beyond the gray zone, China's "maritime advance" and increasing scope of its naval and air force operations place further pressure on Japan. For example, Japan's annual scrambles of Japan Air SDF fighters against approaching Chinese planes nearly tripled between 2012 and 2017, when the frequency reached a record high of 851.[29] Accordingly, nearly three dozen pages of Japan's 2017 defense white paper discuss concerns about Beijing's capabilities and operations, such as its "attempts to change the status quo by coercion."[30]

Beijing's East China Sea maritime gray zone operations appear intended to probe, or take advantage of, a perceived "seam" in Article V of the 1960 U.S.-Japan Mutual Security Treaty, which refers only to an "armed attack" situation. In addition to asserting its sovereignty claim, China's actions also seem aimed at undermining Washington's obligations by trying to establish a perception of "shared administrative control." They also may be intending to exploit political and legal constraints on Japan's Coast Guard (JCG) and Maritime Self-Defense Force (MSDF), as well as a general and longstanding reluctance on Japan's part to use kinetic force in situations outside of an armed attack against Japan.[31]

As these operations have been ongoing since late 2012, China appears to have concluded it can assert its claim coercively through these subthreshold operations with relative impunity.[32] Beijing's decision to limit its conspicuous coercion vis-à-vis the Senkakus to gray zone operations reveals how its activities are corrosive to the security order: not directly challenging it, but simultaneously undermining it in a manner that is also difficult to deter—by staying below the level of armed attack (*buryoku kōshi*, use of force) prohibited by the UN Charter. It further highlights the severity of the challenge that these activities take place while the PLA operates over the horizon, occasionally engages in provocative maneuvers and actions in international waters and Japan's contiguous zone, and is set to grow increasingly capable and active in the years ahead.

Further afield, the gray zone operations of the CCG and China's maritime militia in the South China Sea are additionally corrosive to rules in the maritime domain.[33] CCG vessels harass other countries' fishing boats operating in their exclusive economic zones.[34] The destabilizing activities of China's maritime militia have also gained increasing attention in Tokyo and Washington.[35] And, especially since 2013, Beijing's large-scale land reclamation and construction of civilian and military outposts are also widely judged as provocative and destabilizing.[36]

The contrast between Japan's self-restraint and China's—as well as, in all fairness, some other claimants'—activities in the South China Sea is stark. Although it does not officially acknowledge a dispute, since the 1970s Tokyo's policy toward the Senkakus has focused on *heion katsu anteiteki na iji oyobi kanri* (peaceful, stable management) characterized by three prohibitions: "No people, no development, no militarization."[37]

INTERNATIONAL LAW AND THE 2016 PERMANENT COURT OF ARBITRATION RULING

Following a tense 2012 standoff with China at Scarborough Shoal—a rock in the Philippines' exclusive economic zone about 120 miles west of Luzon—Manila filed a landmark case at the Permanent Court of Arbitration (PCA) in the Hague to challenge key aspects of China's claims in the South China Sea. The unanimous 2016 judgment was almost entirely in the Philippines' favor. It invalidated key tenets of Beijing's UNCLOS interpretation, criticized China's unlawful behavior, declared its island reclamation activities illegal, and stated that Beijing's claims to historic rights carried no validity under international law. China's Foreign Ministry dismissed the award "as null and void" and asserted that the judgment "has no binding force" and that "China neither accepts nor recognizes it" and "will never accept any claim or action based on those awards."[38] Coupled with China's various destabilizing activities in the South China Sea, including unilateral construction and militarization of artificial islands since

2014, such an unabashed and categorical rejection of the unanimous judgment of an international court has further deepened concerns in Tokyo, Washington, and across the region about Beijing's commitment to key pillars of the Asia-Pacific security order, especially concerning international law, freedom of navigation and overflight, and peaceful and noncoercive settlement of disputes. Provocative rhetoric from Beijing often suggests to many observers a "might makes right" mentality. Perhaps most notorious is the 2010 assertion of China's foreign minister, who, in response to criticism at the ASEAN Regional Forum of Beijing's policies, angrily declared that "China is a big country and other countries are small countries, and that's just a fact."[39]

China's rejection of the 2016 PCA ruling suggests not wholesale contempt of UNCLOS per se but an effort to seek carve-out exceptions and, in the words of scholar Isaac Kardon, to deter future legal "infringement on what China considers to be its sovereign prerogatives." Kardon sums up the implications thus, "If [arbitral] awards can be easily sloughed off, and further, denigrated as unlawful themselves, there may be a chilling effect on other attempts to launch arbitral processes . . . If fewer states believe that legal dispute resolution mechanisms can be used effectively, they will wither." He continues,

> The Chinese response to the South China Sea arbitration has set an important, if still uncertain, precedent for future practice. Backed up by impressive capacity and enabled by a less robust international legal environment *that lacks energetic American enforcement of key norms*, China is primed to externalize its distinctive approach.[40] [emphasis added]

As a testament to the post–Cold War Asia-Pacific security order being about much more than an exclusive grouping of U.S. allies and/or particular countries' narrow interests, concerns about China's actions and response to the ruling extend beyond Japan, U.S. allies, or other territorial disputants. As India's prime minister Narendra Modi noted at the 2018 Shangri-La Dialogue, "We should all have equal access, as a right under the international law, to the use of common spaces on the sea and in the air that would require freedom of navigation, unimpeded commerce, and peaceful settlement of disputes in accordance with international law."[41] Then U.S. defense secretary James Mattis was more direct: "China's policy in the South China Sea stands in stark contrast to the openness of our strategy. . . . China's militarization of artificial features in the South China Sea includes the deployment of anti-ship missiles, surface-to-air missiles, electronic jammers, and more recently, the landing of bomber aircraft at Woody Island. Despite China's claims to the contrary, the placement of these weapons systems is tied directly to military use for the purposes of intimidation and coercion. China's militarization of the Spratlys is also in direct contradiction to President Xi's 2015 public assurances in the White House Rose Garden."[42]

CHINA'S OPPOSITION TO U.S. ALLIANCES AND THE DECEPTIVE ALLURE OF PRC-PROPOSED ALTERNATIVES

As Beijing's behaviors appear to corrode key elements of the order in pursuit of narrow self-interest, it also appears—at least rhetorically—keen to undermine the U.S. alliance system, which it regularly disparages as "exclusive," "zero-sum," and reflecting a "Cold War mentality."[43] Even if one concedes that the alliance system is imperfect and may, inter alia, contribute to a security dilemma with China,[44] it is generally welcomed by regional states—especially those who feel insecure vis-à-vis Beijing—and has important stabilizing effects.

Some scholars identify the lofty rhetoric of Hu Jintao's "harmonious world" in 2005 or Xi Jinping's call for a "new type of international relations" and "a community with a shared future for mankind" based on "win-win" cooperation as China's "vision of the Asian political security order" and as "an alternative . . . to the U.S. vision."[45] Yet to refer to the status quo as "the U.S. vision" is misleading. A wide array of regional players publicly advocate for it, including both U.S. treaty allies and others who see it as fundamentally stabilizing—for example, Singapore. Furthermore, beyond lofty rhetoric and abstract, superficially attractive principles, China has offered no clear alternative to the U.S.-centered alliance system as a regional security guarantor. To be sure, Beijing has promoted its 1997 "New Security Concept" and 2014 "Asian Security Concept" as explicit foils to the U.S. alliance system and allegedly superior, enlightened pathways to "universal" security. Yet neither offers a clear plan for implementation or seems to acknowledge other states' legitimate traditional security concerns—especially with respect to Beijing. In contrast, major functions of the U.S. alliance system are "to ensure diplomacy is always the first line of resort and as a hedge if diplomacy should fail."[46] In short, it is not clear what an alternative, China-led security order would even look like. In fact, when it comes to Chinese discussions of "order," security often appears to be an afterthought. For example, a recent analysis of Chinese discourse on future international order barely mentions security affairs; instead, it focuses almost exclusively on international finance and economic integration.[47]

The U.S. Factor: The "Trump Effect" and Beyond

Despite the fact that much of the discourse on the modern-day crisis of the liberal international order focuses on post-2016 developments, the Trump administration is best understood as both a symptom and a cause, or catalyst, of a longer-term crisis.

In the 2016 primary campaign to be the Democratic presidential candidate, Bernie Sanders was vehemently opposed to the Trans-Pacific Partnership (TPP) and skeptical of free trade; and even Democratic nominee and former Obama administration's secretary of state Hillary Clinton also came out against TPP.[48] More specific to security, key drivers of concerns before Trump included the shifting power balance; the corrosive effect of China's irredentism, rhetoric, and policies in the East and South China Seas; and perceptions that Washington was unable or unwilling to confront China more directly. According to two American analysts at the U.S. Naval War College, the United States has "failed to halt China's bullying behavior," which "devalues Washington's commitments to its friends and shakes the foundations of the U.S. alliance system."[49] Beijing appears to have effectively exploited Washington's concerns about "reverse entrapment" in the 2012 Scarborough Shoal incident, its post–September 2012 operations around the Senkakus, and in the post-2014 construction and subsequent militarization of massive artificial islands across the South China Sea.[50] American allies' perceptions of Washington's ambivalence about its treaty commitments further undermine deterrence and reassurance. Examples include the Obama administration's reported unwillingness to openly declare the U.S.-Philippines defense pact's applicability to the South China Sea dispute and its public flirtation with Beijing's proposal for a "new type of great power relations" G2 model of diplomacy, despite evidence that China's goal was to sideline Japan and other "non-great powers."[51]

The United States's selective or incomplete support for certain organizations and regimes also undermines a core premise of a rules-based order: the fundamental principle that "great powers" must play by the same rules. Even if one limits the analysis to the Asia-Pacific, concerns are longstanding. Senate Republicans' refusal to ratify UNCLOS (though the U.S. navy does abide by it) weakens the normative power of the law of the sea, invites claims of U.S. hypocrisy, which China repeatedly exploits, and debones U.S. criticism of China for ignoring the 2016 PCA ruling. (This is not a partisan criticism. U.S. presidents of both parties have called for ratification of UNCLOS.) Even Admiral Harry Harris, then head of U.S. Pacific Command (now the Trump administration's ambassador in Seoul) and the U.S. military's most outspoken critic of China's actions in the South China Sea, stated flatly, "I think that in the twenty-first century our moral standing is affected by the fact that we are not a signatory to UNCLOS."[52]

Though Washington may be the most important actor in certain areas, of additional concern were factors largely beyond U.S. control, such as democratic backsliding across the region, and decreased emphasis on democracy promotion and human rights, as discussed in depth in chapter 4 by Maiko Ichihara. Philippines president Rodrigo Duterte's apparent decision to set aside the 2016 PCA ruling significantly weakened the impact of calls for China to abide by international law. As one former U.S. official noted, "Our rule was, we cannot want it more than the claimants do."[53] Outside of the Asia-Pacific, Russia's actions in Georgia in 2008, as well as its aggression in eastern Ukraine and illegal annexation of Crimea in 2014, also loom large as events that undermined the rules-based order and which the United States was unable to deter. In short, despite the focused attention the Trump administration receives, the alleged crisis of the security order significantly predates it.

Nevertheless, since Trump's election, related concerns have reached fever pitch. While most of Congress and the U.S. public support strong alliances, free trade, and U.S. active engagement in Asia, the rhetoric and policies of the current White House have further shaken confidence in American global and regional leadership, the U.S.-Japan alliance, and Washington's commitment to the liberal order. Publics are also responding. In June 2017, Pew found that after Trump's election global confidence in the American president to "do the right thing regarding world affairs" plummeted; in Japan it dropped precipitously, from 78 percent to 24 percent.[54] A spring 2018 Pew survey measured the median percentage of populations across twenty-five countries and found confidence in President Trump at a mere 27 percent.[55] This decreased confidence in U.S. leadership risks further undermining the liberal international order if leaders in the region judge that international politics must regress to power-based considerations, such as when smaller states lack confidence to challenge China—even rhetorically. Recent examples include ASEAN's reluctance to call out China's island construction or refer to the PCA ruling in summit declarations, and the Duterte administration's reluctance to raise the ruling with China on the apparent grounds that there is no "international police" to enforce it.[56]

Furthermore, Trump's rhetoric about and approach to allies in the context of America First and his self-proclaimed "nationalism" suggests, at best, a grudging appreciation of the utility of security alliances for deterrence against specific threats. Such narrow interpretation of the postwar security order's purpose and objective is a far cry from those of past leaders, who have seen alliances as the United States's most potent diplomatic and deterrence force multiplier; as a stabilizer during times of rapid change and uncertainty; as a way to make U.S. military power less threatening; as an empowering force for smaller, weaker countries; and as a facilitator of deeper political and economic ties among nations—to repeat the words of Allen Dulles, "cooperation *for* something rather than merely *against* something." These and other institutions are an imperfect but preferable alternative to Hobbesian self-help, and a useful means for ameliorating security dilemmas and/or arms races.

Specific to the U.S.-Japan alliance, qualitatively new threats and the relative decline in U.S. power have exacerbated longstanding Japanese insecurities. Even though this trend significantly predates 2016, the Trump administration's provocative rhetoric toward allies and international institutions, saber-rattling toward Pyongyang, and rhetorical ambivalence regarding U.S. global security commitments, in combination with North

Korea's continually advancing nuclear and missile capabilities despite Trump's shockingly premature claim after the June 2018 Singapore summit that "There is no longer a Nuclear Threat from North Korea" (sic), have exacerbated the uncertainties and tensions inherent in Japan's "alliance dilemma."[57] Meanwhile, Pyongyang's apparent ability to credibly threaten Los Angeles or Washington, D.C., with a nuclear-armed ICBM has raised new concerns about "decoupling" and the political undermining of U.S. extended deterrence[58]—leading even some moderate Japanese voices to call for a debate about nuclear weapons.[59] The Trump administration's open contempt for the WTO, its hardball with allies at multilateral summits (for example, the G7 in 2018), its unilateral withdrawal from TPP, its imposition of tariffs on steel and aluminum (and potentially auto) imports against Japan and other treaty allies on "national security" grounds, its willingness to link security guarantees to concessions on trade and accept Chinese and North Korean proposals to unilaterally freeze U.S.-ROK exercises—which the president himself called "provocative"—all deepen concerns about the viability of the United States as a champion of the liberal international order and the security order in the Asia-Pacific.

Even the U.S. intelligence community's own 2018 Worldwide Threat Assessment appears to contend (indirectly) that such developments are weakening the liberal order, playing into China's and Russia's hands, and exacerbating "U.S. allies' and partners' uncertainty about the willingness and capability of the United States to maintain its international commitments, which may drive them to consider reorienting their policies, particularly regarding trade, away from Washington," and that "forces for geopolitical order and stability will continue to fray, as will the rules-based international order."[60]

Nevertheless, there is clear desire among major countries for the United States to continue to play a leadership role in the world, including in the Asia-Pacific. For example, the aforementioned spring 2018 Pew survey found that across twenty-five countries, the median percentage of foreign publics that felt it "would be better for the world to have the United States as the leading power" was 63 percent. Only 19 percent preferred China.[61] Yet it is hardly only for the benefit of other countries that the United States has an interest in continuing its active engagement and global leadership. As Michael Mazarr, a political scientist at an American think tank, argues,

"Allowing the postwar order to melt away would sacrifice perhaps the greatest competitive advantage that a leading power has ever enjoyed."[62]

Japan as a Champion of the Asia-Pacific Security Order?

As the liberal international order in the Asia-Pacific confronts deepening challenges, and concerns amount over America's ability and willingness to champion it, calls for Japan to "step up" and play a more proactive and prominent role have spread.[63] During a visit to Japan in July 2018, for example, German foreign minister Heiko Maas highlighted what can go wrong when an order collapses—noting the two countries' wartime history—and called for Germany and Japan to "stand together" and "close ranks" as leaders of the postwar order; to "offset the U.S. withdrawal"; to "set boundaries against the methods of Trump"; and to form the core of a new "multilateralist alliance."[64] As Mireya Solís notes elsewhere in this volume, Japan has already emerged as an unabashed champion of regional and global free trade, reflected in the Trans-Pacific Partnership-11 and the EU-Japan economic partnership agreement, the largest free trade deal in history.

But what about Japan's role in the security order? Throughout the postwar period and especially since the 1990s, Japan's leaders have struggled to reconcile a desire to play a positive, constructive international role with constitutional, political, diplomatic, and other constraints on a more assertive posture in international security affairs. Most significant, Article 9 of Japan's "peace" constitution, which has never been revised, stipulates that it "forever renounces war as a sovereign right of the nation and the threat or use of force as means of settling international disputes" and commits that "land, sea, and air forces, as well as other war potential, will never be maintained."[65]

Though Japan's actual force structure and posture have shifted significantly in the decades since, Article 9 remains a salient practical and symbolic constraint on the SDF. In the postwar period, Japan's leaders have chosen to shun traditional great power politics, an indigenous nuclear deterrent, robust offensive weapons or power projection capabilities, and an international security role remotely commensurate with Japan's material potential. Though this remarkable and commendable self-restraint, coupled with Tokyo's alliance with the United States, has arguably helped ameliorate regional security competition, new challenges raise new questions about the continued viability of this posture and a rapid transformation of Japan's strategic environment. Nevertheless, important political, normative, and fiscal constraints still remain on how Japan's leaders are able to develop and employ the SDF and play a more proactive and robust role in regional security.

These factors all beg the following question: in light of the current crisis of order, what has Japan been doing and what more can it do?

BASELINING JAPAN'S REGIONAL DIPLOMACY AND SECURITY TRAJECTORY

Over the past decade, Japan has become unprecedentedly proactive in Asia-Pacific security affairs. Most recently, the Abe cabinet's 2013 national security strategy—Japan's first ever—links Japan's national security interests directly to Japan taking responsibility for "the maintenance and protection of international order based on rules and universal values":

> Japan's national interests are, first of all, to maintain its sovereignty and independence; to defend its territorial integrity; to ensure the safety of life, person, and property of its nationals; and to ensure its survival while maintaining its own peace and security grounded in freedom and democracy and preserving its rich culture and tradition.
>
> In addition, Japan's national interests are to achieve the prosperity of Japan and its nationals through economic development, thereby consolidating its peace and security. To this end, especially in the Asia-Pacific region, it is essential that Japan, as a maritime state, strengthens the free trade regime for accomplishing economic development through free trade and competition, and realizes an international environment that offers stability, transparency, and predictability.
>
> Similarly, the maintenance and protection of international order based on rules and universal values, such as freedom, democracy, respect for fundamental human rights, and the rule of law, are likewise in Japan's national interests.[66]

To achieve these goals in support of the order, the national security strategy calls for "strengthening and expanding Japan's capabilities and roles"; "strengthening the Japan-U.S. alliance"; and deepening security ties with like-minded countries within and beyond the Asia-Pacific.[67]

Strengthening and Expanding Japan's Capabilities and Roles to Bolster Territorial Defense

For years, Japan's defense posture has been undergoing a gradual evolution aimed at rationalizing SDF capabilities and deployments to more effectively deter or, if necessary, to rapidly and flexibly confront specific contemporary threats in both traditional and emerging domains, such as cyber, space, and the gray zone.[68] This shift has accelerated in response to Japan's rapidly changing security environment, motivated not only by North Korea but also the swiftly expanding capabilities, geographical and operational scope, and assertive—if not outright coercive—behavior of China's People's Liberation Army (PLA) and China Coast Guard (CCG).

In response to China's "maritime advance" toward the Western Pacific and operations in the East China Sea, one of Japan's priorities has been addressing a security vacuum surrounding its southwestern islands. For example, the SDF has set up surface-to-air and anti-ship missile units and radar sites on remote islands near the Senkakus. At the SDF's major southwestern bases, it has acquired more rapidly deployable platforms; increased the number of F15s; expanded intelligence, surveillance, and reconnaissance (ISR); and in 2018 even formed an Amphibious Rapid Deployment Brigade.[69]

Meanwhile, recognition that Japan's Coast Guard (JCG) is the first line of defense in a Senkakus gray zone contingency has prompted budget increases and other reforms. JCG's aggregate tonnage increased roughly 50 percent between 2010 and 2016. This has facilitated the creation of a dedicated Senkaku Territorial Waters Guard Unit and continuous JCG presence near the islands. JCG has also expanded patrols, improved aerial surveillance, created a direct video link to Kantei—the prime minister's office—and expanded cooperation with Japan's Maritime Self-Defense Force (MSDF)—albeit from a low base.[70]

Driven largely by perceived threats from China and North Korea, Japan has also carried out major institutional reforms aimed at facilitating more rapid, "seamless," "whole-of-government" coordination between Japan's political institutions and with its U.S. ally. Most significant, in 2013 the Abe administration created Japan's first ever national security council (NSC). The NSC further centralizes national security decisionmaking in the Kantei, bolsters interagency coordination and crisis management, and improves information-sharing across Japan's bureaucracies and intelligence community.[71] Japan is also acquiring new capabilities to further improve defense and deterrence, one example of which is Aegis Ashore, and considering others, including long-range land-attack cruise missiles and F-35Bs.

Strengthening the U.S.-Japan Alliance

A second core emphasis of Japan's national security strategy has been strengthening its alliance with Washington as the core pillar of Japan's defense posture and "cornerstone" of regional peace and stability.

In response to Japan's rapidly changing security environment, the 2015 U.S.-Japan Guidelines for Defense Cooperation emphasize "seamless, robust, flexible, and effective bilateral responses, synergy across the two governments' national security policies, and a whole-of-government alliance approach." It also established a standing "alliance coordination mechanism" to "strengthen policy and operational coordination" in all phases of a possible contingency—from peacetime to gray zone to an actual kinetic war.[72] More popularly known, the Diet passed major legislation that captured the practical consequences of the Abe cabinet's controversial 2014 reinterpretation of the constitution's Article 9 "peace clause" to allow exercise of the right of collective self-defense under "limited" conditions.[73] In effect, this moderately broadened the circumstances in which Japan's leaders may deploy the SDF if an armed attack against a third country "that is in a close relationship with Japan" occurs (so-called limited collective self-defense) and to use weapons to protect foreign military forces contributing to Japan's defense in peacetime—for example, during ISR operations or bilateral exercises. Though significant limitations persist,[74] it also creates new opportunities for Japan to cooperate with U.S. armed forces in contingency planning, exercises, and training, and to participate in international peace support activities, including inspections of suspicious ships and logistical support for the U.S. military. In summary, in recent years, Tokyo appears to be signaling its interest in a tighter and more "balanced" alliance, as well as its support for U.S. regional strategy more generally.

Promoting Security Cooperation with Asia-Pacific Partners and Beyond

In support of the U.S. and Japan's post-2000 emphasis on minilateralism among U.S. allies and expanding security ties with existing and new like-minded partners, a third emphasis of Japan's national security strategy has been to support an incremental shift from a system of U.S.-centered bilateral alliances to a regional network of mutually beneficial security ties centered on allies but inclusive of new security partners as well.[75] As well as having inherent utility from Tokyo's perspective, it is also part of Japan's efforts to highlight the allies' common values and vision for a rules-based order, and to encourage Washington to strengthen its commitment to Japan and the region. As Abe remarked in a major 2013 speech in Washington, "Japan must work even more closely with the United States, Korea, Australia, and other like-minded democracies throughout the region. A rules-promoter, a commons' guardian, and an effective ally and partner to the United States and other democracies, are all roles that Japan MUST fulfill."[76]

The Abe administration has built on past policies with a renewed emphasis on bolstering ties among maritime democracies as key champions of the liberal international order. It complements Abe's 2012 call for a "Democratic security diamond" focused on peace, stability, and freedom of navigation across the Pacific and Indian Oceans, which was in part a response to China's activities in the East and South China Seas.[77] The rhetoric promoting these initiatives is imbued with references to shared liberal values, peace, stability, and prosperity. In particular, Japan has championed the "Free and Open Indo-Pacific" as a "new foreign policy strategy,"[78] with the aim of "developing an environment for international peace, stability, and prosperity, and for sharing universal values."[79] Though the "strategy" has yet to be fleshed out, Japan has emphasized maritime security, humanitarian assistance, disaster relief, and peacekeeping operations,[80] in addition to other key tenets of the international order, including openness, security cooperation, and support for liberal democracy. Japan has also emphasized cooperation with the United States, Australia, and India (the so-called Quad).[81] In November 2017, the four democracies announced a plan to establish a coalition to patrol and exert influence on the waters from the Indian Ocean through the East and South China Seas to the Pacific.[82] The Trump administration has followed Japan's lead, incorporating the "Indo-Pacific" framing championed by Australian and Japanese strategists into its national security strategy and even renaming its Honolulu-based military command as Indo-Pacific Command.[83] In December 2015, Abe and Indian prime minister Narendra Modi announced the "Japan and India Vision 2025 Special Strategic and Global Partnership," which welcomed Japan's regular involvement in the prominent India-U.S. Malabar naval exercise to "help create stronger capabilities to deal with maritime challenges in the Indo-Pacific region."[84] Meanwhile, that same month Abe and Australian prime minister Malcom Turnbull "reaffirmed the two countries' special strategic partnership . . . based on common values and strategic interests including democracy, human rights, the rule of law, open markets, and free trade."[85]

Japan's more "proactive" regional security cooperation is also reflected in Tokyo's support of partner capacity building and defense technology transfers. For example, in 2016 Japan proposed a framework for ASEAN-wide defense cooperation.[86] It has also expanded defense technology cooperation with U.S. allies and partners, including agreements with France and the United Kingdom. Security cooperation with South Korea has also deepened, albeit in fits and starts and to a far lesser degree than its many advocates in Washington—and beyond—would prefer.

OUTSTANDING CONSTRAINTS

Relative to free trade, where Tokyo is widely seen as picking up a mantle dropped by Washington, efforts to adopt a more proactive leadership role in international security affairs face more stringent domestic obstacles. Despite significant reforms in recent years, persistent limitations on what Japan can—or is politically willing to—do in the security and military domain persist and must also be acknowledged.

ARTICLE 9 HAS (STILL) NOT BEEN REVISED. Since taking office again in 2012, and for years before that, Abe has repeatedly stated that revision of Article 9 is his government's "historic task." Yet, as of the time of this writing, this goal has proved elusive. Furthermore, his administration's only formal proposal for amendment called merely for adding a third clause asserting that the SDF "existence" is constitutional.[87] The proposal leaves untouched the existing clauses often pointed to by conservatives as major constraints on Japan's freedom of action, including the explicit renunciation of war, the "threat or use of force," and the maintenance of "war potential." Article 9 is the normative crux of Japan's defense policy, and barring a revision of its first and/or second clauses, significant limitations on SDF force development and employment are likely to persist. Beyond the article itself, the difficulty Japan's leaders face attempting to revise it is symbolic of a deeper resistance to deploying the SDF overseas, especially in operations that may require the use of lethal force.

SDF AUTHORIZATIONS TO USE FORCE OUTSIDE A "DEFENSE OF JAPAN" SCENARIO REMAIN LIMITED. Despite recent reforms, limitations on SDF involvement in collective self-defense or collective security operations—key concepts associated with the UN Charter and thus fundamental to the security component of the liberal international order—remain significant. As a sovereign state and UN member, Japan's "inherent right" of collective self-defense has been acknowledged for nearly seventy years. Nevertheless, its government has long judged that actual exercise would be unconstitutional. Although in 2014 the Abe cabinet reinterpreted Article 9 to enable the "limited" exercise of collective self-defense, the precondition on use of force is that the armed attack against another state must pose an existential threat *to Japan itself.* This conditionality limits the reinterpretation's practical implications.[88] It also means that the conditions under which Japan can defend the United States have expanded but remain limited.[89] Especially in the Trump era, any perceived imbalance of commitment—warranted or not, and regardless of Japan's significant contributions to the alliance, especially in terms of hosting U.S. bases on Japan's territory—may become a political target. Regarding collective security operations, Japan's ability to contribute to international security through nonkinetic means has expanded significantly since the Gulf War. However, it remains constrained in employing actual kinetic force or participating in associated combat operations.

Nevertheless, Japan's 2015 security legislation allows for an expanded set of roles and missions, such as more robust logistical support for U.S. military operations and more extensive bilateral planning and exercises. It also newly authorizes operations that somewhat resemble collective self-defense or collective security in various peacetime contingencies, such as protection of foreign militaries engaged in activities contributing to Japan's defense and use of small arms during UN peacekeeping operations.

While significant constraints on Japan's ability to use kinetic force all but ensure that Japan will not engage in unprovoked aggression—the most fundamental contribution any state can make to international peace, stability, and order—from another perspective, they may limit Japan's ability to deter unprovoked aggression by another state against a third party not clearly affecting Japan's security. To date, no SDF member has ever died in combat, and Japan's political leaders are widely seen as extremely casualty averse.[90] These factors carry implications for the SDF's role in regional security, such as a possible contingency in international waters in the South China Sea.

BUDGETARY CONSTRAINTS FRUSTRATE MORE ROBUST DETERRENCE AND DEFENSE POSTURES. Despite widespread global hype about the Abe government's "record high" defense budgets since 2013, Japan's 2017 defense budget was below 1 percent of GDP, and roughly the same as the 1997 figure in nominal yen terms. Without significantly increased investment, the more fundamental changes to SDF force structure or employment advocated by some face stiff budgetary headwinds. As it concerns gray zone challenges, JCG's budget has been increasing, but so has the severity of the challenge from China's own rapidly expanding and increasingly capable CCG. JCG is spread increasingly thin as the tempo and geographical scope of its patrols expand in response to China's operations. Even if normative and political obstacles to major SDF or JCG budget increases subside, structural factors—especially Japan's massive fiscal deficit and its aging and shrinking population and associated welfare burden—suggest fiscal constraints will worsen.[91]

THE GRAY ZONE CHALLENGE IS INTENSIFYING. Despite JCG's expanding budget and capabilities, especially near the Senkakus, the (even more) rapid growth of its Chinese counterpart—in hulls, capabilities, weaponry/armor, and mandate—is sobering.[92] That JCG remains thinly stretched has direct implications for its ability to play a more expansive role regionally. Furthermore, various legal and technical hurdles complicate closer coordination between the civilian JCG and the MSDF, such as deepening interoperability, expanding joint training/exercises, and increasing shared maritime domain awareness.[93] Japan also appears unsure how to deter less widely reported gray zone challenges, such as a foreign submarine in Japan's territorial waters.[94] Though Tokyo does not appear to define cybersecurity as a gray zone concern, other experts identify both cyber and space as additional domains in which Tokyo and Washington face major gray zone deterrence challenges, and where significant efforts are needed to deepen cooperation to improve situational awareness, stigmatize adversary operations, harden defenses, and prepare to impose costs.[95]

DIPLOMATIC OBSTACLES TO A MORE ROBUST REGIONAL SECURITY ROLE. Most prominently, historical issues perennially cloud Japan's political relations with China and South Korea, frustrating efforts to reduce tensions (see chapter 8 by Thomas Berger). Most significant, despite a clear and present danger presented by North Korea, efforts to encourage deeper trilateral security cooperation between Tokyo and Seoul have repeatedly been frustrated by political factors, despite the fact that both are close, democratic U.S. allies. When it comes to the prospect of Japan adopting a more robust regional security role, such political and diplomatic factors seem unlikely to disappear as variables anytime soon.[96] In Southeast Asia, by contrast, major countries, spanning the Philippines, Singapore, and Vietnam, welcome an expanded role for Japan, such as MSDF port visits and exercises, maritime domain awareness and capacity building, diplomacy, and investment.

It is also worth noting that some of Japan's proposed initiatives, such as bolstering security ties with maritime democracies, especially the Quad, face obstacles elsewhere. For example, India did not invite Australia to the 2018 Malabar naval exercises with the United States and Japan, even as an observer. Many commentators saw this as harming the efficacy of the Quad. To be fair, however, the Indian government noted that it has increased bilateral naval cooperation with Australia.[97]

DOMESTIC POLITICS. Setting aside fiscal and constitutional constraints, there is little unambiguous evidence of robust public support for crucial changes to Japan's security posture or regional role, such as fundamentally overturning longstanding principles like "exclusive defense" (*senshu boei*), or revising Article 9's first or second clause. Though resistance to change has attenuated somewhat in recent years, normative obstacles remain powerful, and pushing too far, too fast could backfire. The more than twenty-year effort—still unsuccessful—to relocate Marine Corps Air Station Futenma in Okinawa to an offshore location in Henoko is a case in point of the powerful role of local domestic opposition in alliance decisionmaking.

At an elite level, on contentious issues such as Article 9 revision and defense spending, there is also no clear consensus about the best way forward—even within Abe's Liberal Democratic Party (LDP). Furthermore, the fact that to get elected many LDP politicians depend on electoral cooperation with Komeito, the LDP's junior coalition partner with a pacifistic support base, gives Komeito significant leverage in intra-coalition debates on security policy, often enabling it to frustrate Abe and the LDP's ambitions.[98]

Nevertheless, a survey experiment of over three thousand Japanese respondents conducted as part of this project (see chapter 11 for further details) suggests that Japanese political leaders may have space to push the envelope—something Abe has already shown a determination to do since returning to office, without significant political headwinds affecting his ability to stay in power. The survey finds that citizens are concerned about Japan's rapidly changing security environment and U.S. commitments to Japan's and regional security. It also uncovered that they view the liberal international order as having been crucial to Japan's prosperity, peace, and stability in Asia-Pacific, and generally support Japan adopting a relatively more proactive leadership role in support of it. Specific to security affairs, the survey reveals strong support for Japan strengthening ties with Washington and other like-minded Asia-Pacific partners to balance China and deter North Korea, pursuing more robust defense capabilities aimed at bolstering deterrence, such as increased defense spending. (Respondents were rather ambivalent about Article 9 revision; see chapter 9 by Kenneth Mori McElwain.) Significantly, based on this survey experiment and generally speaking, the Japanese public's vision for Japan's role appears largely in harmony with U.S. policies.

WHAT MORE COULD JAPAN DO?

Despite these constraints, in recent years and in response to a rapidly changing region and world, Japan has already significantly expanded its ability to proactively contribute to the Asia-Pacific security order, both within and beyond a U.S. alliance context. Japan has major strengths, far beyond its economic wherewithal and capable SDF. It is significant—and in contrast to the United States today—that very few countries, perhaps only China, see Japan as a "threat" to international peace and stability, much less the liberal international order. It is widely popular internationally, enjoys a robust democracy and relatively healthy economy, and has proven remarkably immune to the populism reshaping politics across much of the Western hemisphere and parts of Asia (see chapters 6, 7, and 10). It has also picked up the mantle from the United States and emerged as a champion of free trade (see chapter 2).

Especially when evaluated while acknowledging the significant constraints Japan's leaders face domestically, the major pillars and direction of Japan's national security strategy appear sound. Recent policy shifts are aimed at becoming a proactive and stabilizing force, while minimizing disruptions to a regional status quo that has worked well for many countries. The strategy also reflects an explicit recognition that Japan's own national interests are inextricably linked to the liberal rules-based order. In contrast to an oft-heard critique of U.S. rhetoric and policies, Japan's approach is not disproportionately focused on military contributions (though the discourse often unhelpfully frames them as such) but comprehensive—including economic, diplomatic, and capacity-building cooperation with like-minded countries within and beyond the Asia-Pacific. Concerning China, the goal appears to be to cooperate where possible, while working together with like-minded countries—regardless of regime type, it should be noted—to discourage and deter destabilizing behavior, while promoting stabilizing, order-sustaining behavior.

To the extent concerns about Japan's ability to champion the liberal order exist, they primarily relate to disconnects between Japan's foreign policy objectives and the domestic constraints—budgetary and otherwise—its ambitious leadership faces. If concerns about U.S. leadership and commitment to the order persist and deepen, the urgency of addressing these issues will become only more severe. Alliance management and motivating Washington to stay maximally engaged must remain a top priority—throughout and beyond the Trump administration.

In the realm of traditional security, Japan should aim to ensure stability through a more "balanced" U.S.-Japan security relationship. Especially pressing is the need to strengthen deterrence by maximizing efficiencies and minimizing redundancies, thereby opening space for U.S. forces to focus more on regional security beyond Japan's territorial defense, and to undercut narrow criticisms from Washington and elsewhere of perceived "cheap-riding." To maximize its "deterrence bang" for a relatively limited "buck," Tokyo can exploit Japan's geography, in particular its vast number of islands, to emphasize asymmetric deterrence, while gradually increasing spending on defense and JCG. The United States and Japan must also coordinate closely if new SDF capabilities currently under consideration—for example, long-range cruise missiles, more robust amphibious capabilities, F-35Bs—come online. Concerning the gray zone challenge, both countries should consider developing declaratory policy on sub-threshold provocations to close the security treaty's Article V "armed attack" seam, which China's operations appear designed to exploit, and eliminate ambiguity concerning maritime militia involvement by bolstering ISR and intelligence cooperation and engaging in "naming and shaming" if it occurs.[99] Recognizing the scope of PLA-CCG cooperation and the reality that the latter is a paramilitary organization now under Central Military Commission control, Japan should bolster cooperation and contingency planning between JCG and the MSDF and enhance interoperability, joint training and exercises, and shared maritime domain awareness. Modifications to existing laws may be necessary, as may clarification of rules of engagement in gray zone scenarios, such as if a submerged submarine appears in Japan's territorial waters. In all cases, close coordination with Washington as well as anticipating and proactively engaging domestic political concerns will be crucial.

This sort of more traditional balancing and deterrence will better achieve its goals if coupled with a comprehensive regional diplomatic strategy of rhetorical and policy engagement aimed explicitly at supporting the regional security order in a maximally inclusive manner focused on opposing and deterring destabilizing *behavior*, rather than any particular country or regime type, per se. At the most general level, independently and in joint statements at bilateral and multilateral summits and international fora, Tokyo should repeatedly reaffirm commitments to norms and rules, and work to ensure that smaller states' voice and agency are protected. In Southeast Asia, in addition to continuing coast guard and other capacity building and occasional SDF presence missions, Japan should also adopt a more robust diplomatic posture toward multilateral security arrangements, including the ASEAN Regional Forum, ASEAN Defense Ministers Meeting-Plus, and so forth.

Recognizing that economics and security are interlinked, Japan should continue to champion an expanded and inclusive Comprehensive and Progressive Agreement for Trans-Pacific Partnership (CPTPP) and "leave the light on" for the United States to eventually return. Though the United States is Japan's most important partner, Tokyo should put more meat on the bones of the "Free and Open Indo-Pacific," and continue expanding security cooperation with any country that subscribes to the rules.[100] This is a good start. Though U.S. treaty allies and partners in the Asia-Pacific (especially Australia, India, Singapore, Indonesia, and the Philippines) and beyond (especially the United Kingdom, France, and Germany) are the logical place to focus, Japan should repeatedly and publicly emphasize that behavior, not regime type, is the condition for participation and inclusion. Patiently and repeatedly make it clear to Chinese leaders and the region that cooperation is welcome whenever and wherever interests align. The goal is balancing and deterrence of destabilizing behavior, not containment. Measures to bolster security ties with regional partners should be coupled with frequent and consistent diplomacy emphasizing that the target is China's behavior. At present, this signal is often lost. In this spirit, Tokyo should actively pursue economic, diplomatic, and security cooperation with China—especially on North Korea and counterproliferation—where possible, while maintaining realistic expectations, and work to ensure the effective implementation of the long overdue Japan-China air-sea contact mechanism, signed in 2018 after ten years of negotiations.

Japan's Role as a Proactive Stabilizer

Since the early Cold War, the Asia-Pacific security order and system of bilateral alliances centered on Washington have been a core determinant of Japan's security and economic well-being—a link recognized explicitly in Japan's own national security strategy. For years after the collapse of the Soviet Union, the Cold War–era system appeared capable of evolving to effectively confront a changing regional security environment. By 2019, however, such optimism has declined significantly. Rapid geopolitical and geo-economic shifts are widely seen as undermining key aspects of the regional and global status quo upon which Japan has depended for so long; in particular, the rules-based liberal international order essential to Japan's postwar foreign policy posture. In the security domain, leaders in Tokyo and Washington perceive China's rhetoric and coercive policies toward its neighbors to be corrosive of international law and rules-based norms and principles. Yet North Korea, a changing regional power balance, and doubts about U.S. policies and commitment to leadership—especially under the Trump administration—are also major concerns. They have further exacerbated worries about the liberal international order's sustainability and led to calls for Japan and other advanced liberal democracies and benefactors of the order to "step up."

As the world's third largest economy and a major diplomatic player in the Asia-Pacific and beyond, Japan has immense potential to shape, and a significant stake in, the future evolution of the Asia-Pacific security order and liberal international order more generally. Though Japan is not in any position to singlehandedly backstop the security order in the face of powerful headwinds, it has already shown itself capable of developing a coherent and proactive national security strategy in response to evolving contemporary challenges. In the midst of the region's rapid and potentially disruptive transformation, Japan has a crucial role to play as a *proactive stabilizer* in Asia-Pacific security affairs. By strengthening its role in regional security through an expansion of its own capabilities, SDF and JCG roles and missions, and deepening cooperation with Washington and other like-minded stakeholders, Japan will help keep the United States actively engaged in regional affairs and contribute directly to efforts to promote the stability that will be necessary to reinvigorate and reform the liberal international order more generally.

NOTES

1. Richard Haass, "America and the Great Abdication," *Atlantic*, December 28, 2017; Ivo H. Daalder and James M. Lindsay, "The Committee to Save the World Order," *Foreign Affairs,* vol. 97, no. 6 (November/December 2018).

2. Peter Jennings, "Trump Means We Need a 'Plan B' for Defense," https://www.aspi.org.au/opinion/trump-means-we-need-plan-b-defence; Uri Friedman, "A Top Adviser to the South Korean President Questions the United States Alliance," *Atlantic*, May 17, 2018; Iain Rogers, "Germany Seeks Japan Alliance to Counter Trump's America First," Bloomberg, July 25, 2018, https://www.bloomberg.com/news/articles/2018-07-25/germany-seeks-japan-alliance-to-counter-trump-s-america-first.

3. Jordan Fabian and Morgan Gstalter, "Merkel: Europe Can No Longer Rely on U.S. Protection," *Hill,* May 10, 2018; Jon Stone, "Emmanuel Macron Calls for Creation of a 'True European Army' to Defend against Russia and the U.S.," *Independent*, November 6, 2018.

4. G. John Ikenberry, "The Plot Against American Foreign Policy," *Foreign Affairs*, vol. 96, no. 3 (June 2017), 2–9; Takako Hikotani, "Trump's Gift to Japan," *Foreign Affairs*, vol. 96, no. 5 (September/October 2017); Daalder and Lindsay, "The Committee to Save the World Order"; Jeffrey W. Hornung, "The Fate of the World Order Rests on Tokyo's Shoulders," *Foreign Policy* (October 30, 2018).

5. See chapter 5 for an analysis of North Korea.

6. Michael J. Green, *By More Than Providence: Grand Strategy and American Power in the Asia Pacific Since 1783* (Columbia University Press, 2017), 278–91.

7. G. John Ikenberry, *After Victory: Institutions, Strategic Restraint, and the Rebuilding of Order After Major Wars* (Princeton University Press, 2001), 166.

8. Quoted in Ibid., 210; emphasis in original.

9. Ibid., 206.

10. Michael J. Mazarr, "The Real History of the Liberal Order," *Foreign Affairs*, August 2018, https://www.foreignaffairs.com/articles/2018-08-07/real-history-liberal-order.

11. Rebecca Friedman Lissner and Mira Rapp-Hooper, "The Liberal Order Is More than a Myth," *Foreign Affairs*, July 2018, https://www.foreignaffairs.com/articles/world/2018-07-31/liberal-order-more-myth.

12. Joseph S. Nye Jr., "The Case for Deep Engagement," *Foreign Affairs*, vol. 74, no. 4 (July/August 1995), 90–91.

13. Ja Ian Chong, "China–Southeast Asia Relations since the Cold War," in *East and Southeast Asia: International Relations and Security Perspectives*, edited by Andrew T.H. Tan (New York: Routledge, 2013), 89–98, 93.

14. Hillary Clinton, "America's Pacific Century," *Foreign Policy* (October 11, 2011).

15. Hitoshi Tanaka and Adam P. Liff, "The Strategic Rationale for East Asia Com-

munity Building," in *East Asia at a Crossroads*, edited by Jusuf Wanandi and Tadashi Yamamoto (Tokyo: Japan Center for International Exchange, 2008), 90–104.

16. Ash Carter, "America's Growing Security Network in the Asia-Pacific," http://www.defense.gov/News/Speeches/Speech-View/Article/716909/remarks-on-americas-growing-security-network-in-the-asia-pacific-council-on-for.

17. Michael J. Mazarr and Ashley L. Rhoades, *Testing the Value of the Postwar International Order* (Santa Monica, Calif.: RAND Corporation, 2018), 54.

18. Rex Tillerson, "Defining Our Relationship with India for the Next Century," https://www.csis.org/analysis/defining-our-relationship-india-next-century-address-us-secretary-state-rex-tillerson.

19. *National Security Strategy of the United States of America*, https://www.whitehouse.gov/wp-content/uploads/2017/12/NSS-Final-12-18-2017-0905.pdf, 27, 32.

20. *Nuclear Posture Review 2018*, https://media.defense.gov/2018/Feb/02/2001872886/-1/-1/1/2018-NUCLEAR-POSTURE-REVIEW-FINAL-REPORT.PDF, 6; "Vice President Mike Pence's Remarks on the Administration's Policy Towards China," Hudson Institute, https://www.hudson.org/events/1610-vice-president-mike-pence-s-remarks-on-the-administration-s-policy-towards-china102018.

21. Mazarr, Heath, and Cevallos, *China and the International Order*, 4.

22. Thomas J. Christensen, *The China Challenge: Shaping the Choices of a Rising Power* (New York: W. W. Norton, 2015).

23. Thomas J. Wright, *All Measures Short of War: The Contest for the Twenty-First Century and the Future of American Power* (Yale University Press, 2017), 33–34.

24. Aaron L. Friedberg, "Competing with China," *Survival*, vol. 60, no. 3 (May 4, 2018), 7–64; Kurt M. Campbell and Ely Ratner, "The China Reckoning," *Foreign Affairs*, vol. 97, no. 2 (March/April 2018); for a debate, see Wang Jisi and others, "Did America Get China Wrong?" *Foreign Affairs*, vol. 97, no. 4 (July/August 2018); Elizabeth C. Economy, "U.S. Policy Toward China: Dumping the Baby, the Bathwater, and the Tub," https://www.cfr.org/blog/us-policy-toward-china-dumping-baby-bathwater-and-tub.

25. U.S. Deputy Secretary of State Robert B. Zoellick, "Whither China: From Membership to Responsibility? (Remarks to National Committee on U.S.-China Relations)," http://2001-2009.state.gov/s/d/former/zoellick/rem/53682.htm. For an overview of this period, see Green, *By More than Providence*, chaps. 13–15.

26. "President Donald J. Trump Announces a National Security Strategy to Advance America's Interests," https://www.whitehouse.gov/briefings-statements/president-donald-j-trump-announces-national-security-strategy-advance-americas-interests/; *NSS 2017*, 45.

27. To minimize confusion, this chapter follows U.S. Board of Geographic Names convention and refers to the contested islands as "the Senkakus"; analysis in this section draws on Adam P. Liff, "China's Maritime Gray Zone Operations in the East China Sea and Japan's Response," in *China's Maritime Gray Zone Operations*, edited by Andrew S. Erickson and Ryan D. Martinson (Annapolis, Md.: Naval Institute Press, 2019).

28. Japan Coast Guard, "Senkaku Shoto Shuhen Kaiiki ni okeru Chugoku kosen nado no doko to Wagakuni no Taisho" [Activities of Chinese Government Vessels in the Waters Surrounding the Senkakus and Japan's Response], http://www.kaiho.mlit.go.jp/mission/senkaku/senkaku.html.

29. "Heisei 28nendo no kinkyu hasshin jisshi jyokyo ni tsuite" [About Circum-

stances Concerning Emergency Scrambles in 2016], http://www.mod.go.jp/js/Press/press2017/press_pdf/p20170413_01.pdf.

30. Japan Ministry of Defense (JMoD), *Defense of Japan 2017*, 110.

31. Liff, "China's Maritime Gray Zone Operations."

32. Ibid. On CCG militarization, see Ryan D. Martinson, *The Arming of China's Maritime Frontier*, China Maritime Studies Institute Report 2 (Newport, R.I.: Naval War College, June 2017).

33. Concerning gray zone operations in the South China Sea, see multiple chapters in *China's Maritime Gray Zone Operations*, edited by Erickson and Martinson.

34. Yuji Sato, "The Japan Coast Guard Protects the Senkaku Islands to the Last," *Discuss Japan*, no. 35 (October 18, 2016).

35. Conor M. Kennedy and Andrew S. Erickson, *China's Third Sea Force, the People's Armed Forces Maritime Militia*, China Maritime Report (Newport, R.I.: China Maritime Studies Institute, March 2017).

36. "South China Sea Photos Suggest a Military Building Spree by Beijing," *New York Times*, February 8, 2018.

37. Adam P. Liff, "'Self-Restraint' with Japanese Characteristics," *Asia Maritime Transparency Initiative* (Center for Strategic and International Studies, March 10, 2016).

38. "Full Text of Statement of China's Foreign Ministry on Award of South China Sea Arbitration Initiated by Philippines," *Xinhua*, July 12, 2016.

39. John Pomfret, "U.S. Takes a Tougher Tone with China," *Washington Post*, July 30, 2010.

40. Isaac Kardon, "China Can Say 'No': Analyzing China's Rejection of the South China Sea Arbitration," *University of Pennsylvania Asian Law Review*, vol. 13, no. 2 (January 1, 2018).

41. "Prime Minister's Keynote Address at Shangri La Dialogue," https://www.mea.gov.in/Speeches-Statements.htm?dtl/29943/Prime+Ministers+Keynote+Address+at+Shangri+La+Dialogue+June+01+2018.

42. "Remarks by Secretary Mattis at Plenary Session of the 2018 Shangri-La Dialogue," https://www.defense.gov/News/Transcripts/Transcript-View/Article/1538599/remarks-by-secretary-mattis-at-plenary-session-of-the-2018-shangri-la-dialogue/.

43. Adam P. Liff, "China and the U.S. Alliance System," *China Quarterly*, vol. 233 (March 2018), 137–65.

44. Thomas J. Christensen, "China, the U.S.-Japan Alliance, and the Security Dilemma in East Asia," *International Security*, vol. 23, no. 4 (Spring 1999), 49–80; Adam P. Liff and G. John Ikenberry, "Racing toward Tragedy?: China's Rise, Military Competition in the Asia Pacific, and the Security Dilemma," *International Security*, vol. 39, no. 2 (Fall 2014), 52–91.

45. Feng Zhang, "Chinese Visions of the Asian Political Security Order," *Asia Policy*, vol. 13, no. 2 (April 2018), 13–18.

46. Liff, "China and the U.S. Alliance System," 153–56.

47. Shiping Tang, "China and the Future International Order(s)," *Ethics & International Affairs*, vol. 32, no. 1 (2018), 31–43.

48. Mireya Solís and Jennifer Mason, "As the TPP Lives on, the United States Abdicates Trade Leadership," https://www.brookings.edu/blog/order-from-chaos/2018/03/09/as-the-tpp-lives-on-the-u-s-abdicates-trade-leadership/.

49. Ryan D. Martinson and Andrew S. Erickson, "Re-Orienting American Sea Power for the China Challenge," https://warontherocks.com/2018/05/re-orienting-american-sea-power-for-the-china-challenge/.

50. Zhang, "Chinese Visions of the Asian Political Security Order," 17–18.

51. Amy King, "Where Does Japan Fit in China's 'New Type of Great Power Relations?' The Asan Forum," http://www.theasanforum.org/where-does-japan-fit-in-chinas-new-type-of-great-power-relations/; Andrew S. Erickson and Adam P. Liff, "Not So Empty Talk: The Danger of China's 'New Type of Great Power Relations' Slogan," *Foreign Affairs*, October 2014, https://www.foreignaffairs.com/articles/china/2014-10-09/not-so-empty-talk.

52. Hannah Beech, "Why China Won't Listen to the United States on the South China Sea," *Time*, July 8, 2016, http://time.com/4397808/south-china-sea-us-unclos/.

53. Former U.S. government official, *Mt. Fuji Dialogue 2017* (Tokyo, Japan; held under Chatham House rules).

54. Richard Wike and others, "U.S. Image Suffers as Publics around World Question Trump's Leadership," Pew Research Center, June 26, 2017.

55. Richard Wike and others, "Trump's International Ratings Remain Low, Especially Among Key Allies," Pew Research Center, October 1, 2018.

56. "ASEAN Shuns Mention of China's New Islands, Arbitration Loss," Associated Press, November 16, 2017; "Palace: China's Acceptance or Rejection of Arbitral Ruling Irrelevant," *Philippine Star*, January 15, 2018.

57. "North Korea Reportedly Building More ICBMs," https://www.npr.org/2018/07/31/634201841/despite-denuclearization-pledge-north-korea-reportedly-building-more-icbms; Glenn H. Snyder, "The Security Dilemma in Alliance Politics," *World Politics*, vol. 36, no. 4 (July 1984), 461–95.

58. Mira Rapp-Hooper, "Decoupling Is Back in Asia," War on the Rocks, September 7, 2017, https://warontherocks.com/2017/09/decoupling-is-back-in-asia-a-1960s-playbook-wont-solve-these-problems/.

59. For example, Japan's former ambassador to the United States Ryozo Kato. Ryozo Kato, "What's at Stake in Allowing Japan a Nuclear Arsenal?" *Japan Forward*, February 15, 2018.

60. Daniel R. Coats, *Worldwide Threat Assessment of the U.S. Intelligence Community* (Washington, D.C., Office of the Director of National Intelligence, February 13, 2018), 4.

61. Wike and others, "Trump's International Ratings Remain Low."

62. Mazarr, "The Real History of the Liberal Order."

63. G. John Ikenberry, "The Plot Against American Foreign Policy," *Foreign Affairs*, vol. 96, no. 3 (June 2017), 2–9; Takako Hikotani, "Trump's Gift to Japan," *Foreign Affairs*, vol. 96, no. 5 (September/October 2017); Daalder and Lindsay, "The Committee to Save the World Order"; Jeffrey W. Hornung, "The Fate of the World Order Rests on Tokyo's Shoulders," *Foreign Policy* (October 30, 2018).

64. Peter Landers, "Japan and Germany Find Common Ground Opposing Trump on Trade," *Wall Street Journal*, July 26, 2018; Rogers, "Germany Seeks Japan Alliance."

65. The Constitution of Japan, https://japan.kantei.go.jp/constitution_and_government_of_japan/constitution_e.html.

66. Cabinet of Japan, *National Security Strategy*, http://japan.kantei.go.jp/96_abe/documents/2013/__icsFiles/afieldfile/2013/12/17/NSS.pdf, 4–5.

67. JMoD, *Defense of Japan 2014*, http://www.mod.go.jp/e/publ/w_paper/2014.html, 133–38.

68. The analysis in these sections draws on Adam P. Liff, "Japan's Security Policy in the 'Abe Era': Radical Transformation or Evolutionary Shift?" *Texas National Security Review*, vol. 1, no. 3 (2018), 8–34.

69. "Chuki Boueiryoku Seibi Keikaku (Heisei 26 nendo ~Heisei 30 nendo) Ni Tsuite" [Medium Term Defense Program (FY2014-2018)] http://www.mod.go.jp/j/approach/agenda/guideline/2014/pdf/chuki_seibi26-30.pdf; Bouei Hakusho (Defense of Japan, 2017), section 2, chapter 3, http://www.mod.go.jp/j/publication/wp/wp2017/html/n2230000.html.

70. Liff, "China's Maritime Gray Zone Operations."

71. Mayumi Fukushima and Richard J. Samuels, "Japan's National Security Council: Filling the Whole of Government?" *International Affairs*, vol. 94, no. 4 (2018), 773–90; Adam P. Liff, "Japan's National Security Council: Policy Coordination and Political Power," *Japanese Studies*, vol. 38, no. 2 (2018), 253–79.

72. JMoD, "Guidelines for Japan-U.S. Defense Cooperation," http://www.mod.go.jp/e/d_act/anpo/pdf/shishin_20150427e.pdf.

73. For the official overview, see "Outline of the Legislation for Peace and Security" in JMoD, Defense of Japan 2017, http://www.mod.go.jp/e/publ/w_paper/pdf/2017/DOJ2017_2-3-2_web.pdf, 241–55.

74. Adam P. Liff, "Policy by Other Means: Collective Self-Defense and the Politics of Japan's Postwar Constitutional Reinterpretations," *Asia Policy*, no. 34 (July 2017), 139–72.

75. For a nonexhaustive list of recent agreements beyond the United States, see Reference 46, "Situations Concerning the Conclusion of Agreements," in JMoD, Defense of Japan 2017.

76. Shinzo Abe, "Japan Is Back," policy speech, Center for Strategic and International Studies, February 22, 2013.

77. Shinzo Abe, "Asia's Democratic Security Diamond," *Project Syndicate*, December 27, 2012.

78. International Cooperation Bureau, Priority Policy for Development Cooperation, FY2017 (Tokyo: Ministry of Foreign Affairs, April 2017), 9.

79. Ibid., 3.

80. "Indo Taiheiyo Senryaku wa Nihon no Shori ka, Bukimi ni Hibiku Torampu shi no 'Beikoku Daiichi'" [Is the Free and Open Indo-Pacific Strategy a Victory for Japan? Uncanny, with President Trump's "America First"], *Sankei Shimbun*, December 5, 2017.

81. ICB, Priority Policy for Development Cooperation, FY2017, 9.

82. Cary Huang, "U.S., Japan, India, Australia . . . Is Quad the First Step to an Asian NATO?" *South China Morning Post*, November 25, 2017.

83. White House, National Security Strategy of the United States of America (2017), 45–47.

84. "Japan and India Vision 2025 Special Strategic and Global Partnership: Working Together for Peace and Prosperity of the Indo-Pacific Region of the World," Ministry of Foreign Affairs of Japan, December 12, 2015.

85. "Joint Statement—Next Steps of the Special Strategic Partnership: Asia, Pacific, and Beyond," Malcolm Turnbull, December 18, 2015, https://www.malcolmturn

bull.com.au/media/joint-statement-next-steps-of-the-special-strategic-partnership-asia-pacifi.

86. JMoD, "Vientiane Vision: Japan's Defense Cooperation Initiative with ASEAN," November 2016. For an overview of recent developments, see Catharin Dalpino, "Japan–Southeast Asia Relations: Both Push and Pull. Japan Steps Up in Southeast Asia," *Comparative Connections*, vol. 19, no. 1, 123–30; "Joint Statement of the Security Consultative Committee," Ministry of Foreign Affairs of Japan, August 17, 2017.

87. "Abe Shusho '9jo ni Jieitai Meiki' 'Kaiken 20nen shiko mezasu'" [Prime Minister Abe "Specify JSDF Existence in Article 9" "Aim for Constitutional Revision in 2020"], *Mainichi Shimbun*, May 3, 2017.

88. Liff, "Policy by Other Means," 150, 154–71.

89. Article V of the security treaty applies to "an armed attack against either Party in the territories under the administration of Japan," MoFA, Japan-U.S. Security Treaty, January 19, 1960.

90. For example, the SDF was recently recalled from a United Nations Peacekeeping Operation after the security situation deteriorated and without ever actually utilizing its new authority to use lethal force to come to the aid of other nations' personnel. Yuki Tatsumi, "Japan Self-Defense Force Withdraws from South Sudan," *Diplomat*, March 13, 2017.

91. Yoichi Funabashi, "Why Japan's Elderly Are Endangering Its Military," *National Interest*, December 16, 2015.

92. Liff, "China's Maritime Gray Zone Operations."

93. Céline Pajon, "Japan's Coast Guard and Maritime Self-Defense Force in the East China Sea: Can a Black-and-White System Adapt to a Gray-Zone Reality?" *Asia Policy*, no. 23 (2017), 112.

94. Ibid., 114.

95. Scott W. Harold and others, *The U.S.-Japan Alliance and Deterring Gray Zone Coercion in the Maritime, Cyber, and Space Domains* (Santa Monica, Calif.: RAND Corporation, 2017).

96. Eric Heginbotham and Richard Samuels, "With Friends Like These: Japan-ROK Cooperation and U.S. Policy," The Asian Forum, March 1, 2018, http://www.theasanforum.org/with-friends-like-these-japan-rok-cooperation-and-us-policy/.

97. Arzan Tarapore, "Sop to China or Signal to Australia?" *Indian Express*, May 11, 2018; Suhasini Haidar and Josy Joseph, "No Australian Presence in Naval Drills," *Hindu*, April 29, 2018.

98. Adam P. Liff and Ko Maeda, "Electoral Incentives, Policy Compromise, and Coalition Durability: Japan's LDP-Komeito Government in a Mixed Electoral System," *Japanese Journal of Political Science*, vol. 20, no. 1 (March 2019), 53–73.

99. Hideshi Tokuchi, "Gure Zon Jitai Sonae Isoge" [Prepare in Haste for the Gray-Zone State of Affairs], *Yomiuri Shimbun*, May 3, 2018.

100. Eric Sayers, "15 Big Ideas to Operationalize America's Indo-Pacific Strategy," War on the Rocks, April 6, 2018, https://warontherocks.com/2018/04/15-big-ideas-to-operationalize-americas-indo-pacific-strategy/; Yuki Tatsumi, "Is Japan Ready for the Quad? Opportunities and Challenges for Tokyo in a Changing Indo-Pacific," War on the Rocks, January 9, 2018, https://warontherocks.com/2018/01/japan-ready-quad-opportunities-challenges-tokyo-changing-indo-pacific/.

2

Follower No More?

JAPAN'S LEADERSHIP ROLE AS A CHAMPION OF THE LIBERAL TRADING ORDER

MIREYA SOLÍS

The construction and maintenance of an open, rules-based trading system has been a central plank of the postwar liberal international order. The architects of the multilateral trading system vowed to leave behind an era where rampant economic nationalism and tit-for-tat trade wars had undercut growth and fostered interstate frictions. Instead, the promise of the liberal trading regime was to structure trading relationships around rules and due process—not market power and unilateralism—and to maximize joint gains from trade, both to raise income levels across borders and to create bonds of interdependence among nations that would raise the costs of state conflict.

But the ambitions of the liberal trading order have never quite matched the realities of trade politics. The original General Agreement on Tariffs and Trade (GATT) was a small club of twenty-three nations. Its quest to become a truly multilateral regime presented the challenge of incorporating countries at different levels of development and/or operating with sharply different models of state regulation and intervention in the economy. Moreover, because protectionism morphs, the success of the liberalizing effort was predicated on the ability of the multilateral trading body to periodically update its rulebook to outroot unfair trading practices. Finally, while the postwar liberal order was founded on an "embedded liberalism" compromise permitting the coexistence of market opening and domestic welfare policies, it did not guarantee that governments would have the political will to address the distributional consequences of economic change brought about by both technological innovation and globalization.[1]

Hence, the arc of evolution for the liberal trading order has not been linear; rather, it has moved in fits and starts as these challenges always loomed large. However, the current crisis of the liberal trading order is of a different order of magnitude: it is existential. The absorption of China into the international trading regime not only brought large adjustment costs from incorporating a mammoth lower-wage labor force but also the distinctive nature of China's state capitalism has led many to question the ability of the liberal trading order to ensure a level playing field. China's expansive ambitions on international economic governance, as seen in its signature initiatives such as the Asian Infrastructure Investment Bank (AIIB) and the Belt and Road Initiative (BRI), have created concerns that China's economic clout as a creditor nation is being deployed for geopolitical gain: a connectivity agenda with both physical infrastructure and digital standards to create a Chinese sphere of influence in Asia. Confidence in the effectiveness of the policy of engagement toward China—with trade integration as a central pillar—is running low.

Large chunks of the Western industrial world also seem to have lost faith in the promised benefits of globalization. Populist movements calling for curtailed immigration flows and extolling the benefits of economic nationalism are gaining traction in core Western nations. Regardless of whether the populist backlash is driven by economic deprivation or cultural wars, it has jolted the liberal trading order.[2] This is particularly true of the trans-Atlantic duo, the United States and the United Kingdom, which played a leading role in designing the original Bretton Woods institutions. The Brexit vote seems highly likely to result in the United Kingdom's exit from the European Union (EU), on terms that remain to be decided. And the Trump administration has promised a fundamental reset of U.S. trade policy with bilateral trade deficit reduction as the guiding objective and tariffs as the weapon of choice. Populism has wounded the deepest economic integration project to date (the EU) and brought about a sharp reversal in the United States's international role: less a champion and more a disrupter of the open trade regime.

A liberal trading order cannot just be willed, it must be delivered, and state leadership is a sine qua non requisite. The question is, with China doubling down on its state-driven economic model to bring about high-tech self-sufficiency and a West in turmoil with deep social and political polarization, where will this leadership come from? At this critical juncture, Japan, a country that not long ago was known for its defensive trade policy, appears willing to rise to the challenge. The relaunch of the Trans-Pacific Partnership (TPP) after the American exit from the mega trade deal showcased a very different Japan, willing to step up and bring to fruition delicate negotiations among the remaining members. But the TPP rescue is just the end of the beginning, much remains to be done by Japan and like-minded coalitions of liberalizers to safeguard the World Trade Organization (WTO), fight protectionism, discipline China's unfair trading practices, and discourage an inward turn by the United States. Never before had Japan been so consequential to the fate of the liberal trading order.

What Ails the Liberal Trading Order?

The list of concerns stressing the trading regime is long, and many of the problems are not new, although the latest developments have ushered in a deep sense of foreboding with protectionism on the rise. First and foremost, we have witnessed the protracted weakening of the multilateral trading system and of the principle of multilateralism more generally.

DECAYING MULTILATERALISM

Just as the 1990s were a period of optimism on the spread of Western liberal democracy after the end of the Cold War, there was a major burst of confidence in the ability of the multilateral trading system to renew itself with the creation of the WTO in 1995. While GATT had delivered several rounds of trade liberalization in the postwar period, its limitations had become clear in the heady 1980s: huge pockets of the world economy were not under its purview (agriculture, textiles, services), protectionist loopholes had proliferated under the pretext of "voluntary" export restraints (VERs) and "voluntary" import expansions, and the enforcement mechanism was weak.[3] The newly minted WTO addressed these problems by significantly expanding its coverage, forbidding managed trade practices such as VERs, and creating an effective dispute settlement mechanism whereby a defendant could no longer block the implementation of an adverse ruling.

Despite this auspicious beginning, in its close to a quarter-century of existence, the WTO has a record of *zero* successful rounds of multilateral negotiations, with the Doha Round effectively dead. What went wrong? In essence, the WTO has been a casualty of its own design. Each institutional innovation that went into the creation of the WTO was on its own a positive step, but the combined effect was to render the organization a very ineffective negotiation forum. The democratization in decisionmaking with the elimination of the "green room" (where a smaller number of heads of delegations had informally participated in key negotiations) coupled with a membership surge made it harder to reconcile the preferences of a larger number of countries, each one of them enjoying veto power. The expansion of the WTO into behind-the-border issues and the principle of a single undertaking of the negotiation package meant that all members would be subject to far more extensive commitments. Because these rules had "teeth" through stronger enforcement, the negotiation stakes were much higher.[4]

These exacting conditions help explain why the WTO has delivered only one member-wide agreement (on trade facilitation), creating an incentive for governments to escape negotiation deadlock through two strategies. A strategy of plurilateralism allows a subset of countries inside the organization to negotiate agreements on select issues (for example, information technology or services). A strategy of preferentialism enables like-minded countries to ink free trade agreements (FTAs) that award liberalization benefits exclusively to members. The multilateral ideal of universal rules for all countries has been the casualty of this process.[5]

CHINA'S STATE CAPITALISM

China's entry into the WTO, its emergence as an export powerhouse, while integrating itself as an assembly platform for global supply chains, and its meteoric rise to become the second largest economy in the world, capable of financing—on its own terms—large swaths of infrastructure projects across the world, have created opportunities and challenges for the liberal trading order. On the positive side, the growing integration of China and other emerging economies into the world economy greatly contributed to the unprecedented expansion of the global middle class. Economist Homi Kharas notes that the pace-breaking increase of the global middle class (3.2 billion people today, triple what it was in 1985) means that, for the first time ever, the majority of the world's population will belong to middle income households.[6] This stunning outcome in raising living standards in many areas of the world, particularly in Asia, where half of the global middle class resides, is a major achievement of the liberal economic order.

But China's rise as a trading nation has been seen as a shock to the system; namely, the onslaught of cheap Chinese imports on jobs and wages of factory workers in the West and China's attempt to subvert the liberal trading order from within by cheating on the rules (for instance, intellectual property theft). Indeed, many people in the industrialized world feel that the "rise of the rest" has come at the expense of the middle class in the Western core. The animus against unfair competition from China has led many to criticize the decision itself to admit China into the WTO. This is the current view of the American government: "The United States erred in supporting China's entry into the WTO on terms that have proven to be ineffective in securing China's embrace of an open, market-oriented trade regime."[7]

The fundamental challenges that the rise of China presents today to the liberal trading order, however, have less to do with the terms of entry for China into the multilateral trading system and more to do with the paralysis in the WTO's rulemaking function and the decision of the Chinese leadership, post-WTO accession, to reassert state control over the economy. China's sticker price for WTO membership was steep: it agreed to commitments on non-market status for antidumping determinations and a China-specific safeguard allowing countries to impose import restrictions on Chinese products, as well as deeper tariff cuts than other developing nations and a ban on agricultural export subsidies that did not even apply to developed nations like the United States and members of the EU.[8] This was the most demanding accession package to date, and China has had a good record of compliance with adverse WTO rulings.[9] The WTO can only effectively discipline China if its unfair trading practices fall under the purview of WTO laws. But these have not been updated since the mid-1990s.

While the WTO's rulebook remained frozen, China established new institutions for state control over the economy in the years after its accession: a mammoth holding company to supervise assets of hundreds of state-owned enterprises (SOEs), an investment fund exerting top shareholding control over the financial sector, and a state planning body with wide powers, such as price setting for some core commodities, approving key infrastructure projects and administering competition law.[10] As Marc Wu has persuasively argued, "The China, Inc., challenge does not arise from the fact that the Chinese economic structure differs from market capitalism in its purest form. WTO rules, after all, accept different systems. Instead, the challenge stems from the fact that China, Inc., does not conform to *any* of the alternative economic forms envisioned under WTO rules."[11]

China's interventionist industrial policies have become a much greater concern for two reasons. One is that the Chinese government is attempting to retool its economic model. China no longer views itself as the assembly line for the world; rather, it aspires to become the hub for smart manufacturing and the knowledge economy. China's vision for high-tech state capitalism, as described in its policy document Made in China 2025, is to achieve self-sufficiency in frontier, advanced industries such as robotics, artificial intelligence, electric vehicles, and aerospace. China's quest for technological superiority is to be achieved through massive state funds, state-driven foreign direct investment to acquire critical technologies from abroad, investment restrictions to keep competitors at bay, and forced technological transfers from foreign companies seeking to invest in China. Through its Cybersecurity Law (that came into force in 2017), China has enshrined the notion of internet sovereignty, opposing the principle of freedom of data flows in favor of data localization requirements and awarding the government the discretion to demand access to source codes from foreign tech firms that could be used to bolster Chinese tech giants.[12]

The second reason is that China is implementing vast projects of regional integration, advancing its own economic standards and boosting its political influence as more countries come to depend on its development finance. The establishment of the AIIB marked a turning point for China's role in international economic governance. With the AIIB, China chose a multilateral route and, in its first years of operation, starting from 2016, the new bank has mostly cofinanced projects with other international development banks. It is, however, the Belt and Road Initiative that has created the most concerns about Chinese motives, the Chinese modus operandi, and the geopolitical consequences. China's blueprint is expansive: to dedicate more than a trillion dollars to build vast land and maritime corridors across Eurasia that are comprised of critical infrastructure, both physical (ports, railways, roads) and digital (fiber-optic networks). There is little transparency in the implementation of this mammoth undertaking, however, with China's policy banks providing loans, on a bilateral basis, that carry the risk of creating debt traps for recipient countries. Nadège Rolland, an expert on Chinese foreign and defense policy, explains that the BRI serves China's economic and geopolitical interests as an economic stimulus plan for the Chinese economy, which is slowing down, as a boost to inland provinces and as an outlet for some of its excess industrial capacity; but it also helps China assert its influence in regions where democratic governance is weak.[13] Andrew Small, another expert, sees in the BRI an instrument for China to achieve illiberal strategic goals: support authoritarian governments, create economic dependence for political advantage, and disseminate its own digital standards, all while undercutting the influence of the liberal West.[14]

A more illiberal and powerful China has led to a broader questioning of the policy of engagement, with influential voices deeming it a failure.[15] As the former high-level U.S. government officials Kurt Campbell and Ely Ratner themselves note, a faulty assumption has belied American engagement policy: that it could transform China to its own liking. On the economic front, it was mistakenly assumed that China's WTO membership preordained its transition to a market economy, when in fact the WTO was particularly ineffective in disciplining the distortions from China's revamped state capitalism as it suffered from rule paralysis.

Economist David Dollar's analysis of China's international economic role over the past four decades shows *both* successes and failures—rather than outright failure—in engaging with China.[16] On the positive front, China's export push is mostly a private sector story, of foreign firms setting up production facilities attracted by low labor costs. The Chinese private sector has grown rapidly, today representing the lion's share of its GDP. China's industrial takeoff has stimulated growth of other developing nations that export natural resources, and China has provided hefty amounts of development finance to cover sizable gaps in infrastructure finance. China has not set out to undermine the Bretton Woods institutions: it has acquired a larger voice in the International Monetary Fund (IMF), complies with adverse WTO rulings, and is supportive of the World Bank, seeking cofinanced projects with the AIIB (see chapter 3 by Phillip Lipscy for more details on Japan and China in international institutions). But the negatives of China's rise are also sizable. The large SOE sector continues to distort the economy; the Communist Party is influential even over ostensibly private enterprises; there has been almost no progress on strengthening rule of law and property rights; China has lagged in opening up more sectors to foreign direct investment; and the lack of discipline in its development finance is increasing the risk of another round of sovereign debt crises.

Because engagement has not been an outright failure, completely rejecting it in favor of a policy of containment is not advisable, either. While China's blueprints for high-tech dominance and a connectivity agenda for Eurasia sound grandiose, success of these endeavors is far from assured. China's state capitalism is its strength but also its weakness. China's master plan faces serious limitations due to the inefficient allocation of resources, the shortage of skilled human capital, and the lack of social adjustment measures to deal with job displacement from automation.[17] The BRI also faces significant headwinds as China may be hobbled by backing unfeasible projects and is already experiencing significant backlash among recipient nations for the very onerous terms of its infrastructure financing. Attempts to dial back the integration of the largest trading nation could be not only futile, they could compromise the stability of the world economy, jeopardize the expansion of the global middle class, and turn China into a purely revisionist power. A policy of conditional engagement and robust competition seems more effective: codifying and disseminating rules that tackle the externalities of Chinese industrial policies, demands for greater reciprocity in market access and investment, strengthening of multilateral mechanisms to enforce trade rules, and the supply of alternative blueprints and sources of capital in a large-scale connectivity agenda.

AMERICAN UNILATERALISM

A key challenge for the liberal trading order is that its chief architect—the United States—is getting cold feet. In the American body politic, the consensus in favor of championing a free and open trade system has frayed. Throughout the postwar period, Congress reauthorized trade promotion authority and passed trade liberalization agreements on a bipartisan basis. The temptations of managed trade (using unilateral measures to fix market outcomes) were evident in the 1980s as the United States sparred with Japan to curb Japanese auto exports, secure a market share for U.S. semiconductors in Japan, and reform institutions of Japanese capitalism (for example, tight *keiretsu* links) deemed to act as nontariff barriers. But the refounding of the multilateral trading system into the WTO was also predicated on a recommitment of the United States to a rules-based approach, agreeing to fix rules (not outcomes) and to rely on third party adjudication as the first instance to resolve a trade conflict (not unilateral measures).

Yet, U.S. trade leadership suffered an expanding domestic viability problem. The negotiation of the North American Free Trade Agreement (NAFTA)—the first preferential trade agreement with a developing country—was a wake-up call. The opposition of environmental groups and labor unions resulted in much reduced support among Democrats in Congress, making the reauthorization of Trade Promotion Authority and the ratification of trade agreements an increasingly fraught proposition. The China trade shock further shifted the trade policy debate in the United States with a much larger questioning of the payoffs of globalization among many sectors of the American public. Deindustrialization in the American Rust Belt and the significant contraction of U.S. manufacturing employment during the 2000s has been attributed to an onslaught of Chinese products manufactured with cheap labor. According to an estimate by economist David Autor and his colleagues, import competition with China was responsible for 985,000 industrial jobs lost during the 2000s.[18]

To put this number in context, four-fifths of jobs lost in manufacturing were a casualty of technological innovation (primarily automation), not trade, and the contracting share of manufacturing for total employment in the United States is consistent with the economy's long-term shift toward services.

It is, in fact, the other finding from this study that gives more clues as to why the United States lost its way on trade: the adjustment burden for displaced workers was much stiffer than reckoned before with long bouts of unemployment or exit from the workforce, drops in earnings potential, and meager support from trade adjustment assistance. This vulnerability is felt more keenly among some socioeconomic sectors (workers that perform routine tasks) and is concentrated geographically. For instance, Cullen Hendrix found that support for trade runs lowest in several battleground states that have experienced deindustrialization, such as Ohio, Michigan, and Pennsylvania.[19] The lack of political will to invest in workforce development and a robust safety net that creates social resilience to technology and trade shocks finally caught up with U.S. trade ambitions. The Trans-Pacific Partnership (TPP) trade agreement, the largest FTA ever negotiated by the United States, became a political orphan in the 2016 presidential campaign.

But the U-turn in trade policy under the Trump administration has been even sharper: taking the unprecedented step of withdrawing the United States from a signed trade agreement (the TPP), displaying hostility toward the WTO for allegedly undermining U.S. sovereignty, and renegotiating existing trade agreements (NAFTA, Korea–United States FTA) under the threat of termination. The American president and his advisers have elevated the reduction of bilateral trade deficits to a central objective in trade policy, are seeking the renationalization of the global supply chain, and have resorted to unilateral tariffs to gain leverage over partners and rivals alike. By reactivating the rarely used Section 232 of the Trade Expansion Act, which gives the executive branch the power to impose duties on imports, citing national security threats, the Trump administration made a feeble case to impose a 25 percent tariff on US$10.2 billion worth of steel imports and 10 percent tariff on US$7.7 billion of aluminum imports that primarily affected allied nations. Retaliation from affected countries and the added cost of inputs for downstream industries is estimated to lead to a loss of 400,445 jobs in the United States.[20] The conclusion from the U.S. Department of Commerce that automobile imports impair national security, used to justify a 25 percent tariff on US$208 billion worth of auto vehicle imports, is on even shakier ground. In-kind retaliation by affected countries could result in the loss of 624,000 jobs, according to one estimate.[21] Following a Section 301 investigation into China's unfair intellectual property and technology practices, the Trump administration moved to impose a 25 percent tariff on US$50 billion of Chinese imports, and after China retaliated for the same amount, the Trump administration imposed a 10 percent tariff on an additional US$200 billion of Chinese products.[22] The tit-for-tat tariff war that ensued has affected ever-larger swaths of bilateral trade flows. The Trump tariff shock could very well rival the China import shock in terms of American jobs lost.

The clashing trajectories of China and the United States may bring the WTO to its steepest crisis yet. Despite the modest negotiation outcomes, the WTO's role as central arbiter of trade disputes has been its strongest asset. However, the dispute settlement mechanism is under strain. Concerned about judicial overreach, the United States has blocked reappointments at the Appellate Body of the WTO, which is likely to have insufficient members to carry out its activities by the end of 2019. An enforcement arm facing atrophy is nevertheless poised to hear proliferating cases on the invocation of national security to tighten controls over trade flows, including one recently launched by South Korea against Japan.[23] Cases that test Article XXI of GATT on the national security exemption for WTO members will have far reaching consequences for the system, especially as the United States is increasingly resorting to these measures to justify tariffs. The United States has been adamant that its actions cannot be challenged at the WTO because a national security determination is self-judging; others disagree, fearing it will provide an easy out to open the floodgates of protectionism.

Why Is Japan Stepping Up to Sustain the Liberal Trading Order?

Integration into the world economy has been critical to Japan's reconstruction efforts after World War II and its continued economic prosperity today, as acknowledged by the Japanese public.[24] The success of Japan's export-led economic growth model hinged on unfettered access to overseas markets, and Japan's rise to the ranks of top foreign investors post–Plaza Accord brought tighter integration, with Japanese companies operating complex production systems across national borders. Yet Japan was a passive actor in the multilateral trading system, operating as a rule-taker, not a rulemaker. Even when Japan moved away from its exclusive focus on multilateralism and began negotiating preferential trade agreements, the results were a string of low-ambition deals with small economic partners. Japan's lackluster trade diplomacy owed much to its own domestic limitations: the need to play defensively because the powerful agricultural lobby effectively ruled out any major market opening initiative. But Japan's passiveness also reflected confidence that it could rely on the United States to fulfill its essential role as founder and guardian of the multilateral trading order.

No such reassurance exists today. The United States under the Trump administration has abdicated its traditional support for multilateralism and has circumvented the WTO process, launching a trade war with China. China, on the other hand, has had great ease in moving rhetorically to claim the role of champion of globalization, but it is not prepared to substantially open its domestic economy. Japan's systemic interest in the preservation of an open trading system undergirding a stable global economy and diminishing chances of state conflict has not changed. What is different is that the great power leadership vacuum means that Japan, as the third largest economy in the world, and in cooperation with others, must be strategic and proactive like never before to bring the global trading order to safe harbor.

In doing so, Japan is not only providing a public good but serving its national interest. Trade leadership helps Japan advance geo-economic and geopolitical interests. The global supply chain is essential to Japan's competitiveness. A Japan Bank for International Cooperation survey showed that the foreign production ratio (share of production activities carried out abroad) for Japanese companies across all sectors is 35.6 percent, but that it is much higher at 46.8 percent for firms in the automobile, electrical equipment and electronics, chemical, and general machinery sectors.[25] Japan's sharply adverse demographic trends—with an expected 30 percent drop in population levels in the next fifty years—will only enhance the importance of the network economy to the country's prosperity. However, the multilateral trading system has not codified the rules that enhance the operation of global supply chains: investment promotion and protection, liberalization of services essential to communications and transportation logistics, regulatory transparency, competition policy, and so on.[26] Closing this governance gap and avoiding a protectionist rollback in overseas markets are priorities for Japan.

Trade diplomacy also stands to deliver handsome geopolitical benefits for Japan. The U.S. exit from the TPP has taken place at a time when China is making a leadership bid in international economic governance with signature initiatives such as the AIIB and BRI. Japan is therefore confronted with a United States absent from the regional economic architecture and a hands-on China weaving closer ties throughout the region with its connectivity agenda. The prospect of an American void filled by China creates a compelling incentive for Japan to provide Asian countries with alternatives to Chinese-led economic integration. These will come through the supply of high-quality trade agreements, economic assistance, and infrastructure finance that create opportunities for joint liberalization gains and sustainable long-term economic development. The goal for Japan is not zero-sum competition with China. On the contrary, it is about promoting a constructive race to the top with China in regional economic integration standards, creating diversification avenues for developing Asian countries, and providing incentives for China to reform its domestic economy, especially if the TPP circle grows.

Japan's geopolitical interests are also served by re-anchoring the United States to the regional economic architecture. The region's worst fears about America's sustaining power materialized when President Trump made good on his campaign pledge and withdrew the United States from the Trans-Pacific Partnership on his third day in office. The economic leg of the promised U.S. rebalance toward Asia never materialized, and ditching a signed trade agreement dealt a severe blow to U.S. credibility as a reliable partner. Since the United States is Japan's closest ally and security guarantor, its diminished influence in the region deteriorates Japan's geopolitical environment and positioning. Ensuring that the United States remains a resident power in Asia is to Japan's advantage, and a proactive trade strategy has a role to play in this quest. Keeping the TPP alive and close to its original design leaves open the possibility of an eventual U.S. return to a regional trade architecture. Japan will certainly have to be patient, and it cannot really tackle the essential problem in restoring U.S. trade leadership: the need to deepen the American social compact.[27] But in the meantime, Japan can help disseminate economic standards the United States has long championed and can keep the TPP door open.

How Should Japan Provide Trade Leadership?

In fulfilling these objectives, Japan must ensure that its far more ambitious trade diplomacy is parallel to renewed efforts at domestic revitalization with a focus on social resilience to speed economic change.

LEADERSHIP ABROAD

The conclusion of high-quality trade agreements comprising ambitious liberalization goals and codifying cutting edge rules on trade and investment is a signal contribution for Japan and a budding coalition of liberalizers. These mega trade agreements can help stymie the tide of protectionism. The broader concern with the deterioration of the international trading regime, in fact, spurred Japan and the EU to overcome the roadblocks that had stalled trade negotiations, reaching a final deal in December 2017. Covering a third of world output and with a commitment to eliminate almost all tariff barriers, the aim of the Japan-EU trade deal, in the words of Cecilia Malstrom, the EU's chief trade negotiator, is to "send a powerful message in defense of open trade based on global rules."[28]

Japan's resurrection of the Trans-Pacific Partnership is to date its most transformative display of trade leadership. Prime Minister Shinzo Abe did not immediately rally behind the notion of a TPP without the United States, keenly aware that the American exit had put out of reach two of

Japan's core objectives going into that trade negotiation. The first objective had been to reach a compromise on long-divisive market issues between the United States and Japan. The second objective had been to forge a regional economic architecture with a shared vision between the United States and Japan on next-generation economic rules, at a time when Asia is experiencing a power shift with the rise of China. Nevertheless, Tokyo soon reassessed its calculus on the merits of pursuing a TPP without the United States. As noted above, the economic gains of enhancing the operation of supply chains and filling a vacuum that could be occupied by China were important motivations. But at the end of the day, the winning argument was that the only road to a TPP 12 (with a U.S. comeback) is through a TPP 11.[29]

Reviving the TPP presented the major challenge of reconciling two essential priorities: restructuring the balance of concessions for many of the TPP parties, who had agreed to sensitive provisions, expecting large economic payoffs from access to the American market, while at the same time maintaining the essence of the TPP with its high level of ambition to facilitate an eventual American reentry. This balancing act was achieved by agreeing to maintain tariff elimination targets and freeze twenty-two provisions on issues that mattered most to the United States. The thrust of the suspensions was to narrow down the operation of investor-state dispute settlement (by extracting investment agreements and investment authorizations) and to freeze intellectual property rules on data protection for biologics, copyright extension, and so on. Another important change was to ease the entry-into-force criteria by requiring ratification by only six members.

Against all odds, the remaining countries signed a revised Comprehensive and Progressive TPP (CPTPP) in March 2018, which entered into force a few months later. The CPTPP's influence was felt right away on three main fronts. It increased pressure on the United States as the costs of exclusion for American producers became more apparent. It spurred new interest among prospective new members such as South Korea, Thailand, Taiwan, Colombia, and the United Kingdom, signaling the potential of the CPTPP to become a more influential trade grouping. And it strengthened the hand of those who advocated for more ambitious outcomes in the negotiation of the Regional Comprehensive Economic Partnership (for example, Japan, Australia, and New Zealand), although those negotiations remained very challenging.

Japan, then, succeeded in filling the vacuum created by the U.S. exit from the TPP, but it has been more daunting to muster a response to U.S. protectionism that discourages the use of unilateral tariffs without escalating trade frictions or producing an overall deterioration in bilateral relations. Japan was disappointed when it did not receive an exemption from the steel and aluminum tariffs. While it refused to cave to the U.S. demand to impose voluntary export restraints (which are outlawed by the WTO), it did not impose any rebalancing measures, in contrast to the retaliatory response from all other affected parties. Nevertheless, Section 232 tariffs on automobiles could be a game changer in U.S.-Japan economic relations. The economic stakes for Japan are markedly higher. The value of auto exports at risk is four times as large as that of steel and, according to some estimates, Japan's GDP growth could take a hit with a reduction of 0.1 percent of GDP.[30]

In order to avoid the auto tariffs, at least temporarily, Prime Minister Abe agreed in September 2018 to initiate tariff negotiations on goods with the United States. The joint Abe-Trump statement underscored significant differences in negotiation objectives, with the American president alluding to the trade deficit and the Japanese prime minister referencing rules-based trade. But the statement also reflected a political compromise to enable the start of negotiations: the United States would seek market access outcomes that increase domestic production and job creation in the auto sector, and Japan would not go beyond the existing agricultural liberalization outcomes in its other economic partnerships.[31]

Bilateral talks moved at record speed. In October 2019, the United States and Japan signed two trade agreements: on the digital economy and on market access preferences. The digital economy agreement builds on TPP standards with some enhanced provisions and consolidates the U.S.-Japan partnership in an area where Japan has sought to carve international standards under the hallmark initiative of "data free flow with trust" for its 2019 G20 chairmanship. The agreement on goods liberalization, however, falls below TPP and WTO standards. The Japanese government agreed to match the agricultural market concessions of the original TPP, with some exceptions, rice being the most notable case. While the United States consented to modest tariff cuts on some industrial products, it pointedly excluded automobiles and auto parts from the deal. Japan remained steadfast in its rejection of auto export quotas, but in the end only received a vague assurance on auto tariffs in the leaders' joint statement (not the agreement itself) that no action against the spirit of the agreements will be undertaken as long as both parties faithfully implement their commitments. Defusing trade friction with its security guarantor is an important priority for Japan, but the lack of consistency in this mini-deal with the WTO-mandated standard for FTAs to liberalize substantially all trade is of concern, especially at this critical juncture for the multilateral trading system.

Japan has been more effective in its trilateral cooperation with the EU and the United States in codifying new rules that can address Chinese market-distorting policies. In dealing with China, the Trump administration's focus on bilateral trade deficits is a distraction, and the use of indiscriminate tariffs is imposing significant collateral damage as the vast majority of Chinese exports originate from foreign firms. Nor is it advisable to include in future U.S. trade agreements a non-market FTA clause, as featured in the revised NAFTA. This surprise clause, which was not vetted by domestic stakeholders,[32] creates new obligations: to notify the parties three months before launch of negotiations with a non-market economy (that is, China) and to submit for review at least a month before signing the full text of the trade agreement, including all side letters. The clause also provides that a party's entry into a trade agreement with a non-market economy allows the other members to terminate the existing agreement (in favor of a bilateral arrangement) if they so choose—even though NAFTA parties already have the option of six-month withdrawal upon notification. The purpose of the non-market FTA clause is political signaling: to discourage others from signing new trade agreements with China lest they risk losing preferential access to the American market. This symbolic win (since the United States does not gain veto power over other countries' trade relations with China) could, in fact, backfire. It provides an incentive for countries to conclude ongoing negotiations with China (Regional Comprehensive Economic Partnership [RCEP], for example) ahead of bilateral agreements with the United States in order to avoid getting caught in U.S. posturing.

Instead, a truly substantive effort to mitigate Chinese market-distorting policies must be multilateral and multidimensional. Japan has an important role to play in this. In rescuing the TPP, the remaining parties have maintained some of the most substantive disciplines to date in countering subsidies to state-owned enterprises and digital protectionism. Japan has also pushed for codifying digital economy rules at the WTO, and there is potential for pursuing a plurilateral e-commerce agreement.[33] One more measure that Japan is advocating is greater coordination among industrialized countries to tighten screening requirements for state-driven acquisitions of enterprises in critical technologies. The strengthening of foreign investment national reviews in the United States increases the chances of robust collaboration. With bipartisan support, the Foreign Investment Risk Review Modernization Act was passed in the summer of 2018. The most notable changes to the operation of the Committee on Foreign Investment in the United States (CFIUS) are its expanded purview over real estate transactions in close proximity to military installations, over minority investments in American business engaged in critical technologies, critical infrastructure, or sensitive personal data; plus the directive to exchange information and coordinate with allied nations.[34]

Trilateral cooperation shows promise in the areas of industrial subsidies and SOEs and forced technology transfers. The trade ministers from Japan, the United States, and the EU are producing unified positions on a new set of stronger disciplines on subsidies, on casting a wider net over SOEs that would have to abide by these standards, and on the need to root out investment and licensing policies that force companies to share their technologies.[35] Another avenue for coordinated action is to take China to court in the WTO in what legal expert Jennifer Hillman calls a "big, bold, multilateral case" that would build on different WTO rules to take a holistic approach countering Chinese intellectual property theft and discriminatory treatment of foreign enterprises.[36] The effectiveness of the WTO in this and other pressing endeavors will hinge, however, on its modernization. Japan should support the EU's initiative for WTO reform, which calls for broadening the negotiating agenda to rebalance the system and level the playing field, building a model of negotiation to advance individual issues by some members that could be incorporated into the WTO framework, and expanding the number and guaranteeing the independence of Appellate Body members.[37]

These are some of the building blocks of a conditional engagement approach where China can expect continued and improved market access abroad *provided* it reciprocates by correcting its trade distorting practices and offers reciprocal treatment to foreign products and companies. It also competes with Chinese standards of economic integration by generating an updated set of trade and investment rules to be disseminated through preferential and plurilateral agreements, and, where possible, to be adopted in the body of WTO law. The competitive effort extends as well to development finance and regional connectivity, where Japan has been in the lead in articulating a response to the BRI. Japan's strategy combines elements of competition and cooperation and has unfolded along three tracks. First, Japan has articulated its own model of development finance. In 2015, the Japanese government launched its Partnership for Quality Infrastructure with dedicated funds of US$110 billion for Asia, and later expanded the funding to US$200 billion globally. Not surprisingly, one of the selling points of this infrastructure finance push is that it offers a counterpoint to the practices of the BRI that have generated the most concern. The Japanese government has emphasized environmental and governance standards, local hiring, compatibility with development strategies, and financial sustainability. Second, Japan has sought partnerships with like-minded nations to flesh out an economic pillar to the Free and Open Indo-Pacific. This resulted in the launch of the Asia-Africa Growth Corridor with India and most recently a collaborative effort with Australia and the United States to finance infrastructure in the Indo-Pacific. Lastly, Prime Minister Abe has given the green light to project-specific cooperation with China in third countries, provided these infrastructure ventures meet standards on transparency, debt sustainability, and non-military use.[38]

Critical to Japan's newfound geo-economic leadership is domestic support for trade integration and political leadership to navigate pressing domestic socioeconomic challenges.

DOMESTIC FOUNDATIONS

Japan has not been gripped by the antitrade backlash that has figured prominently in the rise of populism in the West. This does not mean that there has been no opposition to market opening from sectors that are not prepared to face international competition or that there has been no questioning among different groups of society of the consequences of deeper economic integration. In fact, both these strands combined to produce one of Japan's most raging debates on trade: whether or not to join the TPP. For the agricultural sector, the prospect of eliminating all tariffs in a trade grouping comprising the largest exporters of farm products was anathema. In opposing the TPP, the agricultural lobby created a much larger coalition than before, including forestry and fishery cooperatives, consumer groups, and the Japan Medical Association, among others. Public opinion polls show that those critical of the TPP feared the devastation of Japanese agriculture, the endangerment of medical and food safety, and the "Americanization" of Japan. On the other hand, those who supported the TPP saw in trade an opportunity for economic growth and an avenue to tackle reforms to invigorate the economy and wanted Japan to have a voice in drafting the new trade framework. The robust public debate that ensued helped dispel the so-called TPP ghosts, namely unsubstantiated arguments that Japan would sacrifice its national health insurance and food sanitary standards because of the TPP, or that foreign corporations could use lawsuits to undo Japanese regulations. Throughout the TPP accession debate between 2010 and 2013, public opinion polls showed that support was larger than opposition.[39] Moreover, the survey experiment carried out for this project in 2018 (see chapter 11 for more details) underscored strong *net* support (+57 percent) for the new leadership role that Japan has undertaken as champion of the liberal trading order by actively promoting a relaunched TPP and other trade agreements.

Support for trade soured among many groups in the West as a reaction to the negative impact the rise of China had on Western factory jobs. But Japan has not experienced a similar trade shock from China. On the contrary, research by Mina Taniguchi (who replicated the Autor methodology for the Japan case) shows that Japanese local labor markets experienced *growth* as imports from China increased.[40] It is important to note that this effect was most marked when the share of intermediate components in the product mix was larger. In fact, there are critical differences in the respective trading relationships that the United States and Japan have with China that help account for the lack of a trade backlash in Japan. As Rei Naka and Yukiko Fukagawa show, Japan increased its imports from China more rapidly following its WTO accession, and imports from China occupy a larger share of total imports in Japan than in the United States.[41] Hence, the globalization of China clearly affected Japan. But these scholars point out that there are stark differences on the export side. Namely, China is a larger export market for Japan (21.6 percent of total exports) than for the United States (10.5 percent), and Japan exports a much larger share of intermediate products (64.6 percent) than the United States in their trade flows to China.[42] Trade complementarity between Japan and China helps explain the more muted appeal of protectionism in Japan.

An assessment of the domestic viability of Japan's international leadership bid should also highlight the constellation of domestic factors that enabled Japan to rise to the big leagues of international trade diplomacy to overcome its past profile as a passive trade negotiator. But it should also focus on the remaining domestic challenges in order to sustain a much larger burden in shoring up the liberal trading order. On the first dimension, at least three major factors combined during the second Abe administration for Japan to manage entry into the original TPP and successfully wrap up the talks. First, the return of political stability, leaving behind the revolving door of prime ministers, was essential for Japan to signal credibly to its counterparts that it could deliver substantial liberalization outcomes. Second, Japan was able to create a cohesive trade negotiation structure in government for the first time. The prime minister's office (Kantei) emerged as an effective control tower, capable of reconciling policy conflicts; Japan's lead negotiator Akira Amari had the full support of the prime minister; and the creation of a TPP headquarters diminished the perennial problem of bureaucratic sectionalism. Third, the organizational and electoral weakening of the agricultural lobby enabled the prime minister to extract the largest commitments to date on agricultural liberalization and to undertake some reforms of the agricultural cooperative system itself.[43]

For all these accomplishments, challenges remain in consolidating the domestic foundations of Japan's leadership of the liberal international order. For one, there is no reassurance that Japan's proactive trade strategy can outlast Prime Minister Abe. The question of what happens after Abe looms large, as there is concern that Japan could revert to the dynamic of political instability at the top, which in the past had prevented the country from implementing long-term strategies. Second, while Japan markedly improved itself in the TPP, it still came last in agricultural liberalization compared to the other participants (with a 95 percent tariff elimination ratio due to the political decision to keep tariffs on five "sacred" commodities). Looking ahead, Japan has not implemented key reforms to improve agricultural competitiveness (including eliminating subsidies to part-time farmers, reforms of the land transaction regime, and so on), and the pattern of TPP countermeasures replicated bad habits in disproportionately supporting public works in the countryside. Lastly, and perhaps most important for the future, the government has much to do in building social resilience to fast economic change, a theme also explored in chapter 6 by Akihisa Shiozaki. The expanding ranks of nonregular workers and growing income inequality are stern warnings of unsolved problems in need of attention. The Fourth Industrial Revolution, with its disruptive impact of automation, robotics, and artificial intelligence, will make investments in workforce development to facilitate mobility and lifelong skill acquisition even more imperative.

Conclusion

The viability of the liberal trading system is in question. The multilateral body charged with the task of abating old and new forms of protectionism and settling trade disputes among countries is in disrepair. The institutional handicap is greatly compounded by a void in great power leadership. China's appetite for reform waned in the aftermath of WTO accession; it embarked instead on new and more intricate forms of state intervention in the economy, which the multilateral body was ill prepared to address with an outdated kit of trade rules. China's bid for technological superiority predicated on self-sufficiency, and its ambitious plans to provide the hardware and software to connect large swaths of Eurasia, have raised concerns that its economic clout is deployed for the sake of an illiberal geopolitical project.

The United States strayed away from an embedded liberalism compromise and pursued globalization and technological change without recommitting to its social compact. Growing socioeconomic inequality and partisan gridlock have rendered trade politics in the United States more fractious and congressional votes on trade bills ever more uncertain. The notion that China's rise has come at the expense of the American middle class gained traction, and skepticism on the merits of engagement has grown due to unmet expectations of China's economic and political opening. The Trump administration has promised to take head-on the China challenge, but its first action on trade was to withdraw from the trade agreement that embodied the most substantial rules tackling unfair trading practices. Instead, President Trump has elevated the reduction of bilateral trade deficits to a core objective in trade talks and resorted to tariffs against both rivals and allies. The rapidly escalating U.S.-China trade war, the Trump administration's use of national security tariffs to obtain leverage in trade negotiations, and its demands for export quotas in violation of WTO disciplines all bode ill for the rules-based trading regime.

Economic nationalism, populism, and the revival of geopolitics present fundamental challenges to the liberal trading order and have compelled Japan to step up and supply trade leadership. Due to Japan's deep integration into the world economy, an open and stable trading system is essential for its economic prosperity. Japan has a paramount interest in avoiding a power vacuum in Asia, as the United States has disengaged from the regional architecture and China makes strides on its connectivity agenda. Japan is not seeking zero-sum competition with China, but rather a race to the top on trade liberalization, digital standards, and development finance that helps Southeast Asian countries and others avoid overdependence on China.

Japan's proactive trade diplomacy has yielded impressive results. In a few years, Japan has delivered ambitious mega-trade agreements in the Asia-Pacific and with the European Union, has been in the frontier of international governance for the digital economy, and has worked with likeminded countries to upgrade trade and investment rules and reform the WTO. But there have also been some missteps along the way. The timing of Japan's sudden decision to tighten export controls over key chemicals and to remove South Korea from its "white list" of preferred trading partners contributed to fears that economic interdependence can be a casualty to interstate frictions. And the bilateral mini-deal with the United States is not consistent with the WTO prescription that preferential trade deals can deviate from the most-favored-nation principle only if they substantially liberalize all trade.

Dealing with these concerns should be a high priority as Japan continues its bid for international trade leadership. Rather than test the WTO with one more case on the use of national security to justify trade restrictions, Japan and South Korea—both trade-dependent economies—will be better served with bilateral export-control talks that can restore trust on the proper operation of the system.[44] Furthermore, as the United States and Japan launch the second stage of trade negotiations, Japan must endeavor to strike a high-quality comprehensive agreement that makes no allowances for sectoral exclusions and U.S. unilateral tariffs. As Japan aims to shake off the image of a follower country and stakes its own path as a champion of rules-based trade, it should take to heart the lessons from the American experience: a liberal trading order is predicated on an effective and responsive liberal democratic polity. International leadership is as robust as its domestic foundations. Strong executive leadership that transcends the Abe era, investments in workforce development, and policies that build social resilience in the face of fast economic change are Japan's domestic challenges, but they will be of great import to the future of open trade.

NOTES

I appreciate comments from the editors Yoichi Funabashi and John Ikenberry, the Japan and Liberal International Order project participants, and my Brookings colleagues David Dollar and Ryan Hass. Jennifer Mason and Laura McGhee provided excellent research assistance.

1. John Gerard Ruggie, "International Regimes, Transactions, and Change: Embedded Liberalism in the Postwar Economic Order," *International Organization*, vol. 36, no. 2 (1982), 379–415.

2. Ronald F. Inglehart and Pippa Norris, "Trump, Brexit, and the Rise of Populism: Economic Have-Nots and Cultural Backlash," Harvard Kennedy School Faculty Research Working Paper Series RWP16-026 (Cambridge, Mass.: Harvard Kennedy School, August 2016).

3. Jagdish N. Bhagwati, *Protectionism* (MIT Press, 1988).

4. Llewelyn Hughes, Jeffrey Lantis, and Mireya Solís, "The Lifecycle of International Regimes: Temporality and Exclusive Forms of International Cooperation," *Journal of International Organizations*, vol. 5, no. 2 (2014), 85–115.

5. Mireya Solís, *Dilemmas of a Trading Nation: Japan and the United States in the Evolving Asia-Pacific Order* (Brookings, 2017), 33–34.

6. Homi Kharas, "The Unprecedented Expansion of the Global Middle Class: An Update," Global Economy and Development Working Paper 100 (Brookings, February 2017), 11.

7. United States Trade Representative (USTR), "2017 Report to Congress on China's WTO Compliance," https://ustr.gov/sites/default/files/files/Press/Reports/China%202017%20WTO%20Report.pdf.

8. Nicholas R. Lardy, *Integrating China into the Global Economy* (Brookings, 2002).

9. Philip Levy, "Was Letting China into the WTO a Mistake?" Snapshot, *Foreign Affairs*, April 2, 2018, https://www.foreignaffairs.com/articles/china/2018-04-02/was-letting-china-wto-mistake.

10. Mark Wu, "The 'China, Inc.' Challenge to Global Trade Governance," *Harvard International Law Journal*, vol. 57, no. 2 (2016), 292.

11. Ibid., 287.

12. Jack Wagner, "China's Cybersecurity Law: What You Need to Know," *Diplomat*, June 1, 2017.

13. Nadège Rolland, "China's Belt and Road Initiative: Five Years Later." Testimony before the U.S.-China Economic and Security Review Commission, https://www.uscc.gov/sites/default/files/transcripts/Hearing%20Transcript%20-%20January%2025%2C%202018_0.pdf.

14. Andrew Small, "Rival Economic Orders," in *Liberal Order in the Indo-Pacific*, German Marshall Fund Asia Program Report 13 (Washington, D.C.: German Marshall Fund of the United States, 2018), 9.

15. Aaron L. Friedberg, "Competing with China," *Survival*, vol. 60, no 3 (2018), 7–64; Kurt M. Campbell and Ely Ratner, "The China Reckoning: How Beijing Defied American Expectations," *Foreign Affairs*, vol. 97, no. 2 (March/April 2018).

16. David Dollar, "Four Decades of Reforming China's International Economic Role," paper prepared for the conference "Reform and Opening: Forty Years and Counting" (Philadelphia: Center for the Study of Contemporary China, University of Pennsylvania, 2018), 27–29.

17. Jost Wubbeke and others, "Made in China 2025: The Making of a High-Tech Superpower and Consequences for Industrial Countries," Merics Papers on China 2 (Berlin: Mercator Institute for China Studies, December 2016), 26–27.

18. David H. Autor, David Dorn, and Gordon H. Hanson, "The China Shock: Learning from Labor Market Adjustment to Large Changes in Trade," Working Paper 21906 (Cambridge, Mass.: National Bureau of Economic Research, January 2016).

19. Cullen S. Hendrix, "Protectionism in the 2016 Election: Causes and Consequences, Truths and Fictions," Policy Brief 16–20 (Washington, D.C.: Peterson Institute for International Economics, November 2016).

20. Joseph Francois, Laura M. Baughman, and Daniel Anthony, "Round 3: 'Trade Discussion' or 'Trade War'? The Estimated Impacts of Tariffs on Steel and Aluminum," Policy Brief (Trade Partnership, June 5, 2018).

21. Sherman Robinson and others, "Trump's Proposed Auto Tariffs Would Throw U.S. Automakers and Workers Under the Bus," *PIIE*, May 31, 2018, https://piie.com/blogs/trade-investment-policy-watch/trumps-proposed-auto-tariffs-would-throw-us-automakers-and.

22. Chad P. Bown and Melina Kolb, "Trump's Trade War Timeline: An Up-to-Date Guide," *PIIE*, September 20, 2019, https://piie.com/blogs/trade-investment-policy-watch/trump-trade-war-china-date-guide.

23. South Korea has lodged a complaint at the WTO regarding Japan's decision

in July 2019 to tighten export controls over three chemicals that Japan is a dominant supplier of and that are essential for semiconductor manufacture. The Korean government argues that the move to now require licenses for each export transaction was Japanese retaliation for the seizure of Japanese companies' assets mandated by a Korean Supreme Court ruling on individual cases of wartime labor compensation. The Japanese government has denied these developments are linked and has pointed instead to Korean breaches in export-control protocols. Japan and Korea have revoked each other's preferred status on export controls, and the Moon government announced it would not renew an intelligence information-sharing agreement. Both sides remain far apart on using the arbitration mechanism of the 1965 Treaty on Basic Relations between Japan and the Republic of Korea that normalized bilateral relations to address the labor compensation cases. For an excellent analysis of the Japan-Korea downward spiral, see Yoichi Funabashi, "Tokyo, Seoul and the Weaponization of History," *Japan Times,* October 10, 2019, https://www.japantimes.co.jp/opinion/2019/10/10/commentary/japan-commentary/tokyo-seoul-weaponization-history/#.XaC3ZC2ZM0o.

24. A survey experiment for this project (see chapter 11) showed strong *net* support of +48 percent for the proposition that free trade has contributed positively to Japan's economy.

25. Japan Bank for International Cooperation (JBIC), "Survey Report on Overseas Business Operations by Japanese Manufacturing Companies—Results of the JBIC FY2016 Survey: Outlook for Japanese Foreign Direct Investment (28th Annual Survey)," *Kaigai-Touyushi* (March 2017).

26. Richard Baldwin, "21st Century Regionalism: Filling the Gap between 21st Century Trade and 20th Century Trade Rules," *Policy Insight* 56 (Center for Economic Policy Research, May 20, 2011).

27. Solís, *Dilemmas of a Trade Nation,* 126–27.

28. Philip Blenkinsop, "EU, Japan Conclude World's Largest Free Trade Agreement," Reuters, December 8, 2017.

29. Interviews by the Japan and the Liberal International Order project team with high-ranking Japanese officials, Tokyo, August 2018.

30. Cited in Aurelia George Mulgan, "Deja Vu All Over Again in U.S.-Japan Trade," *East Asia Forum,* June 15, 2018.

31. The White House, "Joint Statement of the United States and Japan," September 26, 2018.

32. "Outside Advisory Panels Ask USTR to Remove NME Clause from USMCA," *Inside U.S. Trade,* November 9, 2018.

33. "Japan and the United States to Propose Digital Trade Rule to Counter China," *Nikkei Asian Review* (April 12, 2018).

34. James K. Jackson and Cathleen D. Cimino-Isaacs, "CFIUS Reform: Foreign Investment National Security Reviews," *Congressional Research Service,* August 22, 2018.

35. Office of the United States Trade Representative, "Joint Statement on Trilateral Meeting of the Trade Ministers of the United States, Japan, and the European Union," https://ustr.gov/about-us/policy-offices/press-office/press-releases/2018/may/joint-statement-trilateral-meeting.

36. Jennifer Hillman, "The Best Way to Address China's Unfair Policies and Practices Is Through a Big, Bold Multilateral Case at the WTO," testimony before the

U.S.-China Economic and Security Review Commission, https://www.uscc.gov/sites/default/files/Hillman%20Testimony%20US%20China%20Comm%20w%20Appendix%20A.pdf.

37. European Commission, "WTO-EU's Proposals on WTO Modernisation," WK 8329/2018 INIT, paper for Trade Policy Committee, July 5, 2018.

38. Tobias Harris, "China's Belt and Road Initiative: Five Years Later. Regional Reactions and Competing Visions," testimony before the U.S.-China Economic and Security Review Commission, https://www.uscc.gov/sites/default/files/transcripts/Hearing%20Transcript%20-%20January%2025%2C%202018_0.pdf.

39. Solís, *Dilemmas of a Trading Nation*, 170–71.

40. Mina Taniguchi, "The Effect of an Increase in Imports from China on Local Labor Markets in Japan," *Journal of the Japanese and International Economies*, vol. 51 (March 2019), https://papers.ssrn.com/sol3/papers.cfm?abstract_id=2531290.

41. Rei Naka and Yukiko Fukagawa, "Globalism at a Crossroads: Rising Protectionism and What It Means for East Asia," *Japan Spotlight* (May/June 2017), 53–58.

42. Ibid., 54.

43. Solís, *Dilemmas of a Trading Nation*, 128–64.

44. Bringing about an overall improvement of Japan-Korea relations is a daunting challenge given unresolved historical issues, different threat perceptions regarding North Korea and China, and the impact of domestic politics. As expert Jonathan Pollack admonishes, both sides are placing diminishing value in sustaining a well-functioning relationship. Solving the trade spat is one important step, but much more is needed. Japan's apprehension that the recent rulings of the Korean Supreme Court on individual cases of wartime labor compensation undermine the 1965 Treaty on Basic Relations between Japan and the Republic of Korea must be addressed. For a discussion of these issues, see "Stress Test: Japan in the Era of Great Power Competition," The Brookings Foreign Policy Interview series (October 21, 2019).

3

Reformist Status Quo Power

JAPAN'S APPROACH TOWARD INTERNATIONAL ORGANIZATIONS

PHILLIP Y. LIPSCY

International organizations are a centerpiece of the liberal international order. Despite their shortcomings, international organizations—such as the UN, IMF, and WTO—have played an integral role in facilitating cooperation and establishing rules and norms that underpin the order. However, like other aspects of the liberal order, international organizations have recently come under attack. Rising states, such as China, have criticized major international organizations like the IMF and World Bank for perceived Western domination.[1] The United Kingdom voted for Brexit in a 2016 popular referendum, an unprecedented challenge for the European Union (EU). U.S. President Donald Trump routinely disparages international organizations and withdrew from the UN Educational, Scientific, and Cultural Organization (UNESCO) as well as the Paris Agreement, the principal mechanism to address climate change under the UN Framework Convention on Climate Change (UNFCCC).

What can Japan do under these circumstances? Since its emergence as a major power in the early twentieth century, Japan has had a complicated relationship with international organizations. The country's exit from the League of Nations in 1933 starkly symbolized the failure of interwar experimentation with a rules-based order. As it rose from the ashes of World War II, Japan found itself marginalized in many postwar institutions. However, it played a constructive role in the postwar liberal order, seeking to rise peacefully by renegotiating and reforming international organizations to better reflect its priorities and ideas.

I argue that Japan can build on this history by acting as a *reformist status quo power,* supporting the liberal international order by proposing and implementing constructive reforms. Japan is ideally situated to play such a role. As a country that rose to international prominence as part of the postwar order without resorting to coercive means, Japan can act as an exemplar, advocating for peaceful power transitions within a rules-based order. Japan can also leverage its long diplomatic experience of renegotiating its status with international organizations to support similar efforts by other countries, mitigating potential sources of dissatisfaction. Most important, Japanese policymakers should take an active leadership role in strengthening the liberal international order by reforming institutions that have become ineffective or wasteful and proposing new institutions to tackle emerging challenges.

International Organizations in the Liberal International Order

International organizations occupy a central place in the liberal rules-based order established by the United States and its allies after World War II.[2] For sure, international organizations existed before World War II: the League of Nations was established in 1920, though U.S. nonparticipation and failure to constrain the military aggression of Italy, Japan, and Germany doomed it to failure.[3] It was in the era after World War II that international organizations truly came to occupy center stage in the world order. The United States played a crucial role, alongside its allies, in the creation of key institutions such as the UN, North Atlantic Treaty Organization (NATO), IMF, World Bank, and the General Agreement on Tariffs and Trade (GATT).[4] These international organizations became hubs for international cooperation and supported the liberal order by facilitating geopolitical stability, economic development, and free trade.

Figure 3-1 depicts the remarkable growth of international organizations since 1900. The figure is based on the narrow definition of international organizations adopted by the Correlates of War Project, which only includes formal international organizations with more than three member states.[5] As the figure shows, prior to the twentieth century, there were very few international organizations. Since World War II, there has been an explosion in the number and substantive importance of international organizations. International organizations now exist in essentially all significant areas of international cooperation—including security, economic issues, science and technology, the environment, human rights—and exercise important influence over policy outcomes.

Prior to the liberal international order, the international system was largely governed by the logic of military might. In order to gain recog-

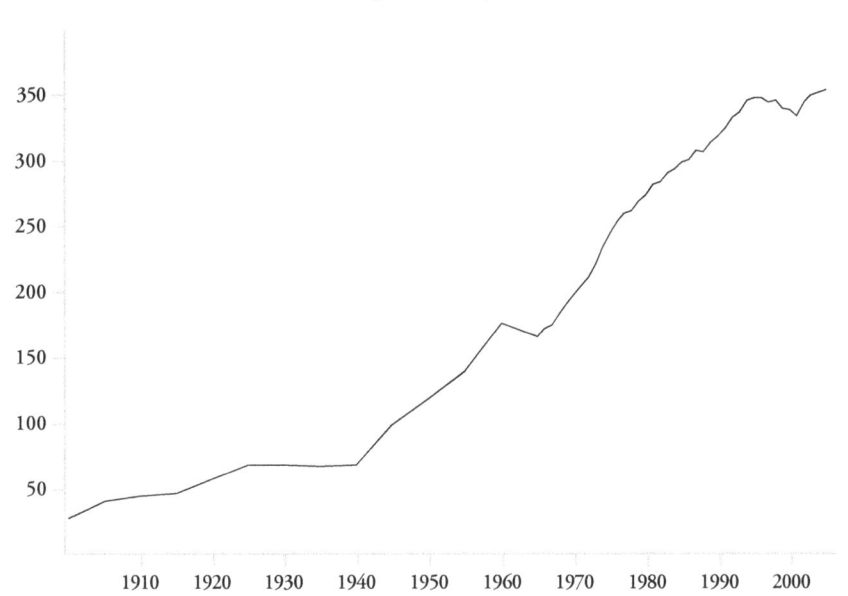

FIGURE 3-1. Number of International Organizations, 1900–2005

Source: Pevehouse, Jon C., Timothy Nordstrom, and Kevin Warnke. "The Cow-2 International Organizations Dataset Version 2.0." *Conflict Management and Peace Science*, vol. 21, no. 2 (2004): 101–19.

nition as a great power, Japan, much like other rising states, sought to mimic Western powers by building up its military strength and acquiring colonies. The advent of the liberal order transformed this logic in important ways.[6] International organizations play several important roles in the order.[7] Security institutions, such as NATO and the U.S.-Japan alliance, bind major liberal democracies into mechanisms of mutual constraint, increasing predictability and reducing the need for costly security competition.[8] More broadly, international institutions make it easier for countries to cooperate with each other by reducing transaction costs, clarifying rules and norms, and providing information.[9] Officials of international organizations are also actors in their own right, who create new norms, generate new opportunities for cooperation, and orchestrate cooperation among non-state actors.[10] International organizations can also facilitate peaceful power transitions by opening avenues for countries to increase their international influence and status without resorting to military coercion.[11] Joint membership in international organizations is associated with relatively peaceful international relations, constituting the so-called Kantian Triangle along with joint democracy and economic interdependence.[12]

Nevertheless, there are several important caveats about the role of international organizations in the liberal international order. First, despite the proliferation of international organizations, there are limits to their capacity to promote peace and shape international outcomes. Powerful countries frequently "go it alone" by leveraging their economic or military might, sidestepping the procedures and norms promulgated by international organizations like the UN.[13] The United States invaded Iraq in 2003 despite failing to secure authorization from the UN Security Council.[14] Russia annexed the Crimean peninsula in 2014 in violation of the territorial integrity norm despite widespread international condemnation.[15] China has asserted control over the South China Sea based on its concept of the Nine Dash Line, which has no basis in international law, despite its claims being ruled invalid by the Permanent Court of Arbitration in The Hague.[16]

Second, international organizations are bureaucracies, often prone to inefficiency and waste. Officials at major international organizations may prescribe misguided policies because of pathologies common in large organizations, such as thoughtless adherence to standard operating procedures.¹⁷ The IMF has been widely criticized for adopting a "one size fits all" approach to financial crisis response that ignores local institutions and conditions, a factor that became a major source of contention during the Asian Financial Crisis of 1997–98.¹⁸ International organizations are often criticized for "mission creep," expanding their purview into policy areas where they have limited competence, creating inefficiencies and wasteful duplication.¹⁹

Third, many critics see officials of international organizations as unaccountable international elites. International organizations like the IMF and the EU can intervene in the domestic affairs of member states, forcing economic reforms despite opposition from democratically elected national governments. This leads to charges of "democratic deficit" in international organizations, creating a tension between the democratic principles of the liberal order and its emphasis on international organizations.²⁰

Fourth, international organizations often resist change. This can lead to contestation between rising powers, which seek greater recognition of their newfound international power, and status quo states, which prefer to maintain their position of privilege. Such contestation has been a recurrent feature of international organizations under the U.S.-led postwar order. Despite numerous attempts, the UN Security Council has only been reformed once during its entire existence since 1945, and no permanent members have been added despite the rise of countries such as Japan and India. The IMF gives a greater share of voting power to countries that joined the institution early on at the expense of countries that joined later, including Japan.²¹ Addressing such rigidities has been an important theme of Japanese foreign policy toward international organizations under the liberal international order.

Japan's Role in International Organizations

Japan has had a complicated relationship with international organizations from the outset. In the aftermath of World War I, many Japanese officials—such as Fumimaro Konoe and Miyoji Ito—viewed the proposed League of Nations with suspicion, suspecting the organization was a Western scheme to keep rising powers like Japan in their place.[22] The Japanese delegation at the Paris Peace Conference was widely criticized as a "silent partner," for speaking up very little on issues that did not directly affect Japanese regional interests.[23] Japan's proposal to include a racial equality clause in the Covenant of the League of Nations received majority support among delegates but failed due to American and British opposition, deepening Japanese suspicions of Western intentions.[24]

Nonetheless, once the league was established in 1920, Japan became an important, constructive member. Japan was a permanent member of the league's council, alongside other great powers, like the United Kingdom and France. Japan also successfully negotiated for an undersecretary position for a Japanese national: Inazo Nitobe, whose portrait used to be featured on the 5000 yen bill, played an important role in the development of the International Committee on Intellectual Cooperation, which later became UNESCO. Another Japanese national, Mineichiro Adachi, became the president of the Permanent Court of International Justice in 1931. However, Japan also played a decisive role in the collapse of interwar experimentation with international organizations when it exited from the league in 1933 over its prerogatives in Manchuria. The image of the Japanese delegation storming out of the league came to symbolize the collapse of interwar idealism and the descent of the international order into aggression, cruelty, and barbarism.[25]

Japan's decision to turn its back on the interwar international order had lasting consequences. Joining the Axis alliance with Germany and Italy meant Japan was absent at the bargaining table when the core institutions of the liberal international order were formulated and negotiated. In contrast to the creation of the league, Japan's initial absence relegated the country to second-tier status in most postwar international institutions. Because many international institutions are path dependent, this meant Japan struggled to secure influence in the international order commensurate with its perceived status.[26] Former Japanese UN Ambassador Kiyoaki Kikuchi notes that Japan's status in the UN is low because it was a "latecomer," whose entry into the organization was delayed by World War II and Soviet opposition; even after membership, many countries saw Japan as a mere sidekick of the United States.[27]

Japan was subject to harsh treatment after it joined the GATT in 1955, when many existing member states prevented it from enjoying trade concessions by invoking the opt-out clause, Article XXXV.[28] Despite rising to become the world's second (now third) largest economy and ranking among the leading powers in terms of military capability,[29] Japan has been unable to secure a permanent seat on the UN Security Council. The UN Charter still includes anachronistic "enemy clauses," which technically allow military action without Security Council authorization against countries that fought on the losing side of World War II, including Japan.[30] While the clauses are generally considered obsolete, Russia has cited them in territorial disputes with Japan, and a country like China could plausibly invoke them to justify military action against Japan.

Despite these clear, persistent disadvantages, Japanese foreign policymakers have generally placed a high priority on international organizations. Upon joining the UN in 1956, the Japanese government proclaimed that its foreign policy would be based on three principles, and the first of these was to be "UN-centered."[31] Now Prime Minister Shinzo Abe noted that Japan's entry into the UN was a symbolic moment: Mamoru Shigemitsu, who oversaw Japan's UN entry as foreign minister, had been tried and imprisoned as a Class-A war criminal only a few years earlier.[32] Yasushi Akashi, former undersecretary general for humanitarian affairs and emergency relief coordinator, notes that in 1956, on the occasion of Japan joining the UN, "I was witness to the speech Foreign Minister Shigemitsu made at the UN General Assembly. It was a notable speech, well thought out, earnest, forthright. Perhaps in hindsight, Shigemitsu was perhaps a little bit too idealistic, judging from present-day reality of international affairs. But by and large, we can still adhere to the basic lines of Shigemitsu, and he really represented the convictions of many Japanese at that time as well as today."[33]

Although it quickly became apparent that UN-centrism was not a viable strategy for guaranteeing Japanese security, Japan has continued to emphasize its membership and contributions to international organizations in its foreign policymaking. Membership in major international organizations, such as the UN and Organisation for Economic Cooperation and Development (OECD), represented important milestones for war-ravaged Japan, and institutions like the World Bank are remembered fondly for their role in Japanese reconstruction.[34]

Elite support for international organizations remains robust. Former Japanese ambassador to the UN Mizuo Kuroda notes that "In the United States, if the UN does something they do not like, people defend their country by saying the UN should get out or we should stop paying our dues. For the Japanese, the UN ranks higher than Japan, so if something negative happens in the UN, the government is blamed for screwing up."[35] Similarly, former UN ambassador Kiyoaki Kikuchi notes that Japanese people tend to have "very strong respect for international organizations and see them as very powerful, important actors in international politics and economics," to a degree that if the UN secretary general makes a request, there is a feeling that it is almost impossible to say no.[36]

This elite support for international organizations is somewhat mirrored among the Japanese public, though many Japanese have limited knowledge of international organizations and do not hold strong opinions. For example, in a 1970 poll by the Cabinet Office, only 13 percent of respondents had any knowledge of Japan's activities in the UN, but 51 percent supported a UN-centered foreign policy while only 8 percent opposed (41 percent answered that they did not know).[37] In a more recent, 2016 global survey by Pew Research Center, Japanese favorability toward the UN was relatively low among countries surveyed, with 45 percent holding a favorable view, compared to 64 percent in the United States, 65 percent in Germany, 54 percent in China, and 40 percent in India.[38] In the survey administered by Adam Liff and Kenneth McElwain for this book (details of which can be found in chapter 11), respondents were asked to report favorability ratings for several major international organizations—the UN, G7, World Bank, IMF, WTO, NATO, Asian Development Bank (ADB), Asia-Pacific Economic Cooperation (APEC), Asian Infrastructure Investment Bank (AIIB)—along with China's Belt and Road Initiative (BRI). On average, the respondents reported positive feelings toward all of these organizations, except the China-led AIIB and BRI. However, most responses clustered very close to neutral for all organizations.[39] Japanese public sentiment toward international organizations might be best characterized as apathetic approval.

Limits to Japanese Leadership

Japan has generally been an active contributor to international organizations within the liberal international order. Japan has not only supported universalistic institutions at the core of the order, such as the UN and WTO but also played an active role in proposing and promoting new institutions, such as the ADB, APEC, and Chiang Mai Initiative Multilateralization (CMIM). However, Japanese leadership has also been limited in important respects.

First, Japanese contributions to international organizations have been limited by domestic political constraints. After much international criticism in the 1970s and 1980s, Japan increased its Official Development Assistance (ODA) contributions and became a large financial supporter of major international organizations. However, after the burst of asset price bubbles in 1991, the Japanese government has faced a tough budgetary environment, limiting further expansion of financial contributions. Japanese participation in peacekeeping operations has increased since the 1990s, but constitutional restrictions and public casualty aversion remain important constraints. An official of the Ministry of Foreign Affairs notes that there are realistic limits to what Japan can do on its own, given these constraints and Japan's economic weight in the world economy, which has declined from a peak of around 14–15 percent to 7–8 percent today: Japan cannot supplant the United States and must act in concert with other, like-minded countries.[40]

Second, Japan has been frequently criticized for a lack of initiative as an institution builder. Partly, this is because Japanese officials tend to approach international relations in a manner similar to Japanese domestic political norms, emphasizing consensus building behind the scenes rather than aggressively seeking the limelight. This has been variously dubbed "leadership from behind" or "stealth leadership."[41] For example, when Japanese policymakers floated the idea for an Asian Monetary Fund in 1997, they asked Thai officials to publicly propose the idea.[42] Similarly, Japanese officials asked Australia to be the public face of their idea for Asia-Pacific Economic Cooperation (APEC).[43] This is a stark contrast to Chinese and U.S. approaches to institution building, which emphasize their own countries' leadership. This reticent foreign policy approach can lead to distorted perceptions of Japan's international role. For example, Japan provides as much infrastructure investment to Asia as China does, but much more international attention has focused on China-led initiatives like the AIIB and BRI.[44] However, even accounting for its quiet diplomacy, Japan has still arguably been more of an institution taker than an institution builder.

Third, Japan is not immune to nationalist pressures that could threaten its engagement with the liberal international order. In particular, the Japanese government has adopted an aggressive approach toward UNESCO over wartime history issues. In 2015, over Japanese opposition, UNESCO included Chinese documents covering the Nanking Massacre in its Memory of the World list. In response, Cabinet Secretary Yoshihide Suga threatened to withhold Japanese funding from the agency.[45] Since Japan was the second largest contributor to the UNESCO budget, Japanese policymakers saw an opportunity to exercise leverage over the institution's portrayal of Japanese wartime atrocities. The Abe cabinet was said to have contemplated withdrawing from UNESCO entirely if the institution accepted documents related to comfort women.[46] The halting of UNESCO funding brought significant international criticism, but Japan secured an important concession through its threat: UNESCO altered its rules so that new applications for the Memory of the World list would be suspended in cases where "two or more parties involved in the 'memory' dispute the facts or recognition of history."[47] This effectively gave Japan a veto over the inclusion of historical materials documenting Japanese wartime atrocities.

A Japanese Ministry of Foreign Affairs official notes that Japan's approach toward UNESCO reflects long-term changes in foreign policy thinking and is unlikely to be the last instance where Japan uses similar tactics: "There may be a psychological change in Japanese foreign policy. Before, even when we had something to say, there was a tendency to keep quiet, but now we say what we want to say. This can be attributed to our track record and pride of having made many contributions since the end of World War II. There is also a sense of urgency: can we really survive in international society by adopting a Japanese sense of quiet virtue rather than speaking up?"[48] This proactive approach may provide greater opportunities for leadership and give Japan more say over outcomes in international organizations. However, there is also a risk that the loudest, nationalist voices in Japan will be magnified and make it difficult for Japan to support institutions that underpin the liberal international order.

Japan as a Reformist Status Quo Power

What is the best way for Japan to engage with international organizations moving forward? Many observers see the rules-based liberal order as being in an existential crisis. China has expressed dissatisfaction with the status quo in existing international institutions and created its own institutions such as the AIIB and New Development Bank (NDB). The EU is under severe distress with the mishandling of the Euro crisis and Brexit. President Trump has questioned and criticized bedrock institutions of the liberal order, such as NATO and the WTO, and he has withdrawn the United States from the Paris Agreement and UNESCO.

Under these circumstances, Japan faces several choices. First, Japan could follow the Trump administration's transactional approach by seeking "better deals" from international institutions, even if this means undermining the broader order. Japan's approach to UNESCO is one illustration of this approach: rather than supporting a neutral, technocratic process consistent with the institution's rules and norms, Japan prioritized appeasing domestic nationalist impulses. Although there is a difference in degree, Japan's approach in this instance is largely akin to the Trump administration's approach toward international organizations. Japan's climate change policy under the UNFCCC is also largely consistent with this path: although the Japanese government is not openly skeptical of climate change like the Trump administration, it has done little and relies heavily on accounting gimmicks in its international commitments, such as manipulating the base year to exaggerate emissions reductions.[49]

Second, Japan can adopt a holding position in defense of the status quo, based on the assumption that the Trump administration represents a temporary anomaly and the United States will eventually reassume its traditional leadership role. If this assumption is correct, Japan could strategically invest diplomatic and financial resources to support the status quo in areas where the United States chooses to step back. However, there are several problems with this approach. There are limits to Japan's ability to replace the United States in the liberal international order, even on a temporary basis. The Japanese economy is only about a quarter of the size of the U.S. economy. Japan's capabilities are even more limited when it comes to security institutions, where the country faces both material and legal restrictions. In addition, there are no guarantees that U.S. policymaking will return to the status quo ante. Although Trump is a unique president, he was propelled into office by American voters who sympathized with his message of "America First" and promises to reevaluate fundamental pillars of the liberal international order. Both the Republican and Democratic parties in America have isolationist and protectionist wings: there are no guarantees that the next U.S. president will return to the traditional mold.

The third path holds the greatest promise: to act as a reformist status quo power. The liberal order is not under crisis only because of recalcitrant politicians in select countries. As Jeff Colgan and Robert Keohane argue, the international order has come to be seen as "rigged" in favor of global elites at the expense of regular citizens.[50] There are nontrivial problems that require diplomatic effort and innovative solutions. What is needed is a process of reform that strengthens the liberal order by making concrete reforms to remedy shortcomings and gaps that have emerged over the past seventy years. Japan can play a central role in such reform efforts by leveraging its status as a country that has both supported and benefited from the order while seeking reforms to remedy its shortcomings.

There are three primary ways Japan can contribute to the liberal international order as a reformist status quo power. First, Japan can serve as an important exemplar of how the international order allows countries to increase their prosperity, influence, and international stature without resorting to traditional means of exerting influence—namely, power-based coercion and conquest. Second, Japan's track record of seeking reforms in the international architecture holds important lessons for other rising countries. Japan can leverage its position as a country that is both a status quo power and a reformist within the existing order. Third, Japan can play an active role in seeking pragmatic reforms to liberal international order institutions in order to assure its long-term viability.

JAPAN AS AN EXEMPLAR

A crucial question for the future of the liberal international order is how it will accommodate and adjust to newly rising states such as China, India, Indonesia, and Brazil. Long-range economic forecasts see these countries growing rapidly and enlarging their position in the world economy in the coming decades.[51] Although economic forecasts are necessarily uncertain, there is no question that an important shift is underway in the world economy away from the West and toward developing countries, particularly those in Asia. Can the liberal international order integrate these countries peacefully and effectively, as responsible stakeholders? Will the order come under strain as these countries become dissatisfied and seek to challenge the privileged position of the United States and its allies?

Japan has an important role to play in resolving these questions. Japanese policymakers can do more to leverage Japan's historical experience as a rising country that succeeded by choosing to work within the institutions, rules, and norms of the postwar order. Japan did not participate in the creation of the order, and it struggled to achieve membership, influence, and status. U.S. policymakers played a dominant role in the creation of the order, and the country is often seen as drawing various privileges by virtue of a rigged system.[52] Japan symbolizes how the order can flexibly accommodate new, rising states and elevate their influence and status.

Consider Japan's postwar policy toward East Asia. As the result of rapid economic growth after 1945, Japan emerged as one of the leading economic powers of the postwar world. Although the United States and Japan maintained close diplomatic relations during the Cold War, basic tensions in the two countries' policies toward Asia paralleled more serious differences in the prewar era. Japan saw itself as the leader of East Asia, envisioning a "flying geese" model of economic development that placed Japan at the head of a rapidly developing and increasingly integrating region.[53] The United States continued to view East Asia from a global perspective, emphasizing the role of universalistic international organizations such as the WTO and IMF and espousing economic liberalization and free market capitalism.

By the 1980s and 1990s, many scholars foresaw Japan's emergence as a potential competitor to the United States in both the economic and geopolitical realms.⁵⁴ Analogously, in the wake of the Cold War, realist scholars such as Kenneth Waltz famously predicted that Japan would increase its military capabilities and perhaps acquire nuclear weapons as it reemerged as a great power and reasserted its authority over the region.⁵⁵ However, rather than pursuing zero sum conflict by building up its military forces, acquiring nuclear weapons, or seeking to displace the United States economically, Japan sought to achieve its objectives by working within the basic framework of the postwar international order. This included policies toward universalistic institutions, particularly attempts to increase Japan's voice and alter the developmental approach of the Bretton Woods institutions to be more accommodating toward East Asian approaches, as well as the creation of regional frameworks that enhanced Japan's stature in the region, exemplified by the ADB.

One example of Japan drawing on its historical experience under the liberal international order is the concept of human security. Sadako Ogata, former UN high commissioner for refugees, notes that Japan played a central role in enshrining the concept of human security as a core mission of the UN. Human security broadens traditional notions of security, which focus on the nation state and external military threats, to a holistic notion that places individuals at the core and includes dimensions such as economic security, food security, and environmental security. Ogata observes that this concept was rooted in Japan's unique postwar experience and geopolitical circumstances, which limited the options for military solutions and necessitated a focus on nonmilitary aspects of security.⁵⁶

SUPPORTING RENEGOTIATION

Japan is also well positioned to provide advice and guidance to rising countries seeking to renegotiate their status within the international order. Japan has struggled for seven decades, since the end of World War II, to enhance its position in international organizations, both through renegotiation efforts and the creation of organizations like the ADB and failed Asian Monetary Fund. Much as Japan has sought to share insights with the international community from its postwar developmental model, struggles with deflationary stagnation, and lessons from the Fukushima nuclear disaster, Japanese policymakers can serve as advisers and mentors to other states that seek to establish their place in the contemporary order.

This exercise has two distinct benefits. First, it will reinforce support for the existing order by potentially mitigating sources of frustration and discord. Japan can contribute know-how based on its own experience: What renegotiation strategies have been successful, and under what circumstances? When was creating new international organizations more effective than seeking to work within existing organizations? What are the institutional settings that have proven particularly difficult and hence require new strategies and approaches?

Second, this approach will potentially help Japan secure greater international support for reforms in areas where it has struggled in the past, such as the UN Security Council and the international financial architecture. UN Security Council reform is an important priority for Japan, which has real consequences for Japanese foreign policymaking. Former Japanese ambassador to the UN Yoshio Hatano notes that the UN Security Council has become the critical organ of the UN as it increasingly deals with multifaceted issues that were traditionally the purview of other UN organs. This makes Japanese membership in the UNSC essential.[57] Hatano also attributes Japanese mishandling of its contribution to the Persian Gulf War in 1991 to Japan's lack of a permanent seat on the UN Security Council, which meant Japanese officials could not participate in closed-door discussions concerning the war.[58] An official of the Ministry of Foreign Affairs notes that when Japan rotates off from the Security Council as a nonpermanent member, the country is literally removed from the Security Council email list, shutting down an important source of information. In addition, Japan must invest diplomatic resources every time there is an election for nonpermanent members, which often requires the country to barter away other priorities, such as representation in other international organizations.[59]

By coordinating renegotiation policies and strategies, like-minded countries may be better able to link their efforts across institutional settings, exerting greater leverage for reform. For example, while Japan is dissatisfied with its lack of permanent membership in the UN Security Council, it is largely satisfied today with its status in the Bretton Woods institutions. This is reversed for China, which has a permanent seat on the UN Security Council but suffers from underrepresentation in the Bretton

Woods institutions. Rather than seeking institutional changes separately, linking efforts across institutional settings could foster larger coalitions for reform: in most international organizations, major changes require supermajorities of supporting states. A Japanese leadership role in such an initiative would be less provocative and alarming than if it emerged as a foreign policy initiative of states already seen as threatening and revisionist, such as China or Russia.

LEADING REFORMS

The ascent of Donald Trump raises important questions about U.S. leadership of the liberal international order. To date, Japan has responded proactively, rallying international support for certain elements of the liberal order, such as its resuscitation of the Trans-Pacific Partnership (TPP), commitment to high-quality development assistance, and international cooperation on universal healthcare. However, like most European countries, Japan's role thus far has been largely limited to a defensive stance. For the most part, Japanese officials have sought to protect the status quo in the hopes that normalcy will eventually return to the United States.

A more proactive agenda is necessary, and Japan can step up to play an active leadership role. There is an important precedent for this: Japan played a crucial role as a reformist status quo power in the 1980s, when the U.S. administration under Ronald Reagan grew increasingly skeptical of the UN. U.S. criticisms of the UN at the time echo skepticism expressed by the Trump administration today: U.S. policymakers felt that many UN agencies were dominated by antagonistic developing countries, and financial resources contributed by the United States were often used without accountability. In 1984, the United States withdrew from UNESCO, citing the organization's ideological bias and corruption. In 1986, Congress passed the Kassebaum-Solomon Amendment, which would reduce U.S. contributions to the UN budget unless the United States was given greater say over the budgetary process.

In this context, Japan acted as a mediator and took an active leadership role in UN financial and administrative reforms. In 1984, Japanese opposition was an important factor in slowing salary and pension increases for UN staff. In 1985, Japanese Foreign Minister Shintaro Abe, the father of future Prime Minister Shinzo Abe, proposed the Group of High-Level Intergovernmental Experts to discuss UN reform.[60] Japan not only proposed the reform framework but took an active role in rallying support among General Assembly members and UN staff, many of whom were skeptical about reform. The reforms rationalized the operations of the UN by reducing high-level positions and restraining administrative bloat. Former Japanese ambassador to the UN Yukio Takasu, who was directly involved in these efforts as a Japanese official, notes that after the reforms, "It became a consensus that there would be no annual increases in the regular UN budget. This decision was a remarkable breakthrough."[61]

Japan also played a major role in reforming UNESCO and restoring U.S. membership. Koichiro Matsuura, who served as director-general of UNESCO from 1999 to 2009, undertook significant administrative reforms of the organization, such as reducing the number of staff positions and reining in the budget. Matsuura also personally lobbied the U.S. government, nongovernmental organizations, and media to create support for U.S. reentry. Matsuura notes that his lobbying efforts included getting First Lady Laura Bush on his side by designating her as the UNESCO Honorary Ambassador for the Decade of Literacy, after which President George W. Bush became a reliable supporter of the organization.[62] Matsuura's efforts directly contributed to President Bush's announcement that the organization "has been reformed" and that the United States would resume its membership.[63]

Japan is in an ideal position to play a similar role today, channeling American skepticism toward international organizations in a productive direction by implementing constructive reforms. Yukio Takasu notes that reforming international organizations often requires a major crisis: the 1986 UN administrative and financial reform reflected fears that without serious change, the UN could become unviable.[64] American threats to disengage from the liberal international order—exemplified by the rise of Trump—present such a crisis. Japan can support U.S. reengagement by facilitating practical reforms to the liberal order. Takasu notes that "the United States is interested in UN reforms, and tends to say very proactive things in general terms. However, the United States does not usually propose specifics, because there are too many players in the U.S. government . . . It is therefore Japan's role to make proposals that are technically sound and likely to gain acceptance."[65]

There are other areas where the Trump presidency may present opportunities for reform. Although Trump's rhetoric may be over the top, Japanese government officials agree with many of his criticisms of international organizations. For example, the Trump administration has attacked the WTO appellate body for overreach and has refused the appointment of new judges, leading to widespread condemnation.[66] However, a Japanese Ministry of Foreign Affairs official notes that many U.S. allies, including Japan, fundamentally agree with the Trump administration's critique of the appellate body: the organ often oversteps its mandate by issuing sweeping judgments that become international precedent. Hence, Trump's strongarm tactics may present an opportunity for countries like Japan to step in and initiate pragmatic reforms to modernize the WTO.[67]

Another Foreign Ministry official notes that the Trump administration presents an important opening for Japan to influence American policy. In the past, Japanese policy proposals would often be dismissed or set aside by U.S. policy officials in various agencies. However, under the Trump administration, career bureaucrats and political appointees have often been sidelined, enabling Japanese officials to make policy proposals straight to the top levels of the White House. The official notes that this has given Japan almost unprecedented input into the formulation of U.S. foreign policymaking, symbolized by the Free and Open Indo-Pacific Strategy, which was a Japanese initiative that the Trump administration adopted wholeheartedly.[68] This policy influence stems in large measure from the close personal relationship between Trump and Abe, who converse frequently on the phone, sometimes for over an hour at a time. Trump also relies on Abe to mediate his relations with other global leaders, particularly in the G7.

Japan thus finds itself in a unique position of influence at a time of global turbulence. Japan holds significant sway with the United States and is also well positioned to leverage American skepticism toward international organizations in a constructive direction. Japan's history as a reformist status quo power gives it credibility to propose and muster support for pragmatic reforms of the international organizational architecture. If Japan can use this opportunity to implement meaningful reforms, it may also provide an impetus for U.S. reengagement with the liberal international order, much as Japanese reforms of UNESCO brought the George W. Bush administration back into the fold.

What are the priorities for reform? The liberal order is not simply under threat because of rising states and U.S. policy instability. The order has created the seeds of its own destruction. Since the 1980s, the economic emphasis of the order has shifted from what John Ruggie described as "embedded liberalism"[69] to what Susan Strange called "casino capitalism."[70] Rather than lifting all boats, unfettered globalization has exacerbated inequities and undermined social safety nets, leading to lamentations that the "international order is rigged."[71] Global capital flows and deregulatory policies have exacerbated financial instability and crises, particularly among democratic states that constitute the core of the order.[72] Policies of international institutions, such as the IMF, have been biased by the political interests of influential states, contributing to global economic imbalances.[73] The order has failed spectacularly to make meaningful progress on international climate change, one of the most pressing concerns for humanity.[74] The liberal international order needs more than just defense and protection. It is in urgent need of reform.

Conclusion

Japan can play a greater role as a *reformist status quo power*, strengthening the liberal international order through reforms of the international organizational architecture. Defending the status quo is not enough: the order is under stress in part because it has failed to serve the interests of diverse stakeholders in the international community. Japan has an impressive track record of supporting practical reforms in international organizations, renegotiating its status to acquire greater voice, and creating new institutions. With the liberal order in crisis, Japanese officials must build on this track record to facilitate major reforms to strengthen the foundations of the order.

I will close by identifying and discussing several issue areas where Japanese leadership could make a difference in addressing new challenges that threaten to undermine the liberal order. First, the international system needs better mechanisms to deal with financial instability in large, advanced industrialized countries, which are beyond the scope and capacity of IMF intervention. After World War II, there was a long period of relative financial stability thanks to the suppression of global capital flows and interventionist policies among major states.[75] Financial crises became more common after the 1970s, but they mostly affected developing countries that could turn to the IMF. However, starting with Japan's 1990s "Lost Decades" crisis, financial instability has spread to large, developed countries, culminating in the 2008 U.S. subprime crisis and the Euro crisis. The international system lacks effective mechanisms to manage and respond to large-scale financial crises in major economies, instead relying on ad hoc measures that have often proven ineffective.

The early success of the liberal international order was underpinned by the Bretton Woods system, which stabilized the financial systems of the largest, most advanced economies of the world.[76] In a liberalized international economic order, democratic countries are particularly vulnerable to financial crises: financial instability is not only harmful economically, but it can also destabilize democratic rule and undermine the basic underpinnings of the liberal order.[77] New institutions and frameworks are needed to strengthen the international financial architecture against future instability. Plausible steps include greater international coordination to regulate cross-border capital flows, peer review systems to strengthen domestic financial regulation, and institutions to monitor and preempt asset price bubbles.[78] Many of these measures can be developed within or in coordination with existing institutions, such as the IMF and Bank for International Settlements.

Second, international cooperation on mitigating climate change remains woefully inadequate.[79] Unmitigated climate change is an existential threat to humanity and requires significant multilateral efforts to reduce greenhouse gas emissions and adapt to rising temperatures. Japan took a proactive role in early climate change cooperation, helping to build international support for the 1997 Kyoto Protocol. However, since then, Japan has become a laggard, exiting from the second commitment period of the Kyoto Protocol and falling to the bottom of international climate change rankings.[80] The Abe government has invited international criticism for unambitious greenhouse gas emissions targets and for promoting coal-fired power plants.[81] This is an area where Japan should act as a leader, not a straggler.

An important policy priority should be to establish an international framework for the application of green border adjustment taxes.[82] Existing climate change agreements under the UNFCCC rely on country-level emissions reduction targets, but these have achieved limited success. One important reason for this is the fact that energy-intensive production tends to be internationally footloose: aggressive regulatory measures in one country tend to encourage international relocation, resulting in "carbon leakage."[83] Green border adjustment taxes could potentially mitigate this problem by accounting for cross-national variation in the stringency of mitigation policies.[84] In addition, such taxes provide a productive way to channel protectionist impulses in countries such as the United States, where President Trump rode to victory promising to renegotiate "unfair" trade agreements. A carefully designed, multilateral framework for green border adjustment taxes could strengthen the liberal order by rebuilding public support for free trade while reducing incentives to freeride on mitigation efforts in other countries.

Finally, there are important opportunities for new institutions and agreements to address emerging issues that do not neatly fall under the scope of existing arrangements. Cybersecurity has emerged as a major challenge in recent years, but international cooperation remains limited, and there is ample room for cooperation on rules-setting and coordinated countermeasures. International responses are also lagging behind the rapid advancement of artificial intelligence and robotics, which will require cooperation on a variety of issues such as standards, best practices, and the permissibility of military applications. Potential economic disruption from accelerating automation also presents a major economic challenge across all major economies, which will benefit from greater international cooperation.

NOTES

1. Phillip Y. Lipscy, *Renegotiating the World Order: Institutional Change in International Relations* (Cambridge University Press, 2017).

2. For an overview of the liberal international order, see, among others, G. John Ikenberry, *Liberal Leviathan: The Origins, Crisis, and Transformation of the American*

World Order (Princeton University Press, 2011); Stewart Patrick, "World Order: What, Exactly, Are the Rules?" *Washington Quarterly*, vol. 39, no. 1 (Spring 2016); G. John Ikenberry, "The End of Liberal International Order?" *International Affairs*, vol. 94, no. 1 (2018), 7–23.

3. George Scott, *The Rise and Fall of the League of Nations* (London: Macmillan, 1974); Martyn Housden, *The League of Nations and the Organization of Peace* (Harlow, U.K.: Pearson, 2012); Leland M. Goodrich, "From League of Nations to United Nations," *International Organization*, vol. 1, no. 1 (1947); Inis L. Claude Jr., *Swords into Plow Shares: The Problems and Progress of International Organization* (New York: Random House, 1984).

4. Stephen D. Krasner, *International Regimes* (Cornell University Press, 1983); Robert Keohane, *After Hegemony: Cooperation and Discord in the World Political Economy* (Princeton University Press, 1984); G. John Ikenberry, *After Victory: Institutions, Strategic Restraint, and the Rebuilding of Order after Major Wars* (Princeton University Press, 2000).

5. The formal criteria are as follows: (1) an IGO must consist of at least two members of the COW-defined state system; (2) an IGO must hold regular plenary sessions at least once every ten years; (3) an IGO must consist of at least three members of the COW-defined state system. See Jon C. Pevehouse, Timothy Nordstrom, and Kevin Warnke, "The Cow-2 International Organizations Dataset Version 2.0," *Conflict Management and Peace Science*, vol. 21, no. 2 (2004).

6. G. John Ikenberry and Charles A. Kupchan, "Socialization and Hegemonic Power," *International Organization*, vol. 44, no. 3 (1990), 283–315.

7. Among others, see G. John Ikenberry, "Institutions, Strategic Restraint, and the Persistence of American Postwar Order," *International Security*, vol. 23, no. 3 (1999), 43–78; Ikenberry, *After Victory*; Ikenberry, *Liberal Leviathan*.

8. Daniel Deudney and G. John Ikenberry, "The Nature and Sources of Liberal International Order," *Review of International Studies*, vol. 25, no. 2 (1999), 179–96.

9. Keohane, *After Hegemony*, 85–109.

10. Michael N. Barnett and Martha Finnemore, "The Power of Liberal International Organizations," in *Power in Global Governance*, edited by Michael N. Barnett and Raymond Duvall (Cambridge University Press, 2004); Kenneth Abbott and others, *International Organizations as Orchestrators* (Cambridge University Press, 2015).

11. Lipscy, *Renegotiating the World Order*, 266–89.

12. Bruce Russett and John R. Oneal, *Triangulating Peace: Democracy, Interdependence, and International Organizations* (New York: W. W. Norton, 2001).

13. Lloyd Gruber, *Ruling the World: Power Politics and the Rise of Supranational Institutions* (Princeton University Press, 2000); Erik Voeten, "Outside Options and the Logic of Security Council Action," *American Political Science Review*, vol. 95, no. 4 (2001), 845–58.

14. Ewen MacAskill and Julian Borger, "Iraq War Was Illegal and Breached UN Charter, Says Annan," *Guardian*, September 16, 2004.

15. Mark W. Zacher, "The Territorial Integrity Norm: International Boundaries and the Use of Force," *International Organization*, vol. 55, no. 2 (2003), 215–50.

16. Ankit Panda, "A Year Later, the South China Sea Award Stands as Evidence of China's Rule-Breaking Behavior," *Diplomat*, July 17, 2017.

17. Michael N. Barnett and Martha Finnemore, "The Politics, Power, and Pathologies of International Organizations," *International Organization*, vol. 53, no. 4 (1999), 699–732.

18. Paul Blustein, *The Chastening* (New York: Public Affairs, 2003); Phillip Y. Lipscy and Haillie Na-Kyung Lee, "The IMF as a Biased Global Insurance Mechanism: Asymmetrical Moral Hazard, Reserve Accumulation, and Financial Crises," *International Organization*, vol. 73, no. 1 (2019).

19. Jessica Einhorn, "The World Bank's Mission Creep," *Foreign Affairs*, vol. 80, no. 5 (September/October 2001).

20. Andreas Follesdal and Simon Hix, "Why There Is a Democratic Deficit in the EU: A Response to Majone and Moravcsik," *JCMS: Journal of Common Market Studies*, vol. 44, no. 3 (2006); Giandomenico Majone, "Europe's 'Democratic Deficit': The Question of Standards," *European Law Journal*, vol. 4, no. 1 (1998).

21. Phillip Y. Lipscy, "Explaining Institutional Change: Policy Areas, Outside Options, and the Bretton Woods Institutions," *American Journal of Political Science*, vol. 59, no. 2 (2015), 341–56.

22. Hatsue Shinohara, *Kokusai Renmei: Sekai Heiwa He No Yume to Zasetsu* [The League of Nations: Failure of the Dream of World Peace] (Tokyo: Chuo Koron Shinsha, 2010), 57–60.

23. Ibid., 62.

24. Margaret MacMillan and Richard Holbrooke, *Paris 1919: Six Months that Changed the World* (New York: Random House, 2007), 316–21.

25. Thomas W. Burkman, *Japan and the League of Nations: Empire and World Order, 1914–1938* (University of Hawaii Press, 2008).

26. Lipscy, *Renegotiating the World Order*, 63–119.

27. Kiyoaki Kikuchi, "Kikuchi Kiyoaki Taishi" [Ambassador Kiyoaki Kikuchi], in *Oral History: Nihon to Kokuren No 50nen* [Oral History: 50 Years of Japan and the UN], edited by Yasushi Akashi and others (Kyoto, Japan: Minerva Shobo, 2008), 178–79.

28. Judith L. Goldstein, Douglas Rivers, and Michael Tomz, "Institutions in International Relations: Understanding the Effects of the GATT and the WTO on World Trade," *International Organization*, vol. 61, no. 1 (2007).

29. See, for example, the Composite Index of National Capability as developed by J. David Singer, Stuart Bremer, and John Stuckey, "Capability Distribution, Uncertainty, and Major Power War, 1820–1965," in *Peace, War, and Numbers*, edited by Bruce Russett (Beverly Hills, Calif.: Sage, 1972).

30. Hitoki Den, "U.N. Charter's Anachronistic Enemy State Clauses," *Japan Times*, January 19, 2017.

31. Sadako Ogata, "The Changing Role of Japan in the United Nations," *Journal of International Affairs*, vol. 37, no. 1 (1983), 34.

32. Shinzo Abe, *Abe Shinzo Taironshu: Nihon Wo Kataru* [Abe's Dialogues: Describing Japan] (Tokyo: PHP Kenkyujo, 2006).

33. Interview with Yasushi Akashi, August 16, 2018.

34. Glenn D. Hook and others, *Japan's International Relations: Politics, Economics and Security* (New York: Routledge, 2005), 319.

35. Mizuo Kuroda, "Kuroda Mizuo Taishi" [Ambassador Mizuo Kuroda], in *Oral History: Nihon to Kokuren No 50 nen*, 168.

36. Kikuchi, "Kikuchi Kiyoaki Taishi," 177.

37. Cabinet Public Relations Office, "Kokusai Rengou ni Kansuru Yoron Chosa [Opinion Poll about the UN]," https://survey.gov-online.go.jp/s45/S45-07-45-05.html.

38. Jacob Poushter, "Favorable Views of the UN Prevail in Europe, Asia, and U.S.," Pew Research Center, September 20, 2016, http://www.pewresearch.org/fact-tank/2016/09/20/favorable-views-of-the-un-prevail-in-europe-asia-and-u-s/.

39. Respondents were asked to express favorability toward each institution on a scale from 0 to 10, where 0 indicated least and 10 greatest favorability, and 5 was neutral. Based on one-sample t-tests, opinions of the listed organizations were all significantly above the neutral level with 95 percent confidence, with the exception of the AIIB and BRI, which were significantly below the neutral level with 95 percent confidence. However, responses closely clustered around the neutral level: the highest mean favorability rating was for the G7 (5.5) and the lowest for the BRI (4.1).

40. Interview with Ministry of Foreign Affairs official, August 13, 2018.

41. Alan Rix, "Japan and the Region: Leading from Behind," in *Pacific Economic Relations in the 1990s: Cooperation or Conflict?* edited by Richard Higgott, Richard Leaver, and John Ravenhill (Boulder, Colo.: Lynne Rienner, 1993); Reinhard Drifte, *Japan's Foreign Policy in the 1990s: From Economic Superpower to What Power?* (New York: St. Martin's Press, 1996).

42. Phillip Y. Lipscy, "Japan's Asian Monetary Fund Proposal," *Stanford Journal of East Asian Affairs*, vol. 3, no. 1 (2003), 83–104.

43. Yoichi Funabashi, *Asia-Pacific Fusion: Japan's Role in APEC* (Washington, D.C.: Peterson Institute for International Economics, 1995).

44. Sean Creehan, "If You Build It, They Will Come: Why Japan May Fund More Infrastructure than China," Federal Reserve Bank of San Francisco, October 12, 2017.

45. Kiyoshi Takenaka, "Japan May Halt Funds for UNESCO over Nanjing Row with China," Reuters, October 13, 2015.

46. "'Seijika' Shita UNESCO: Ianhu Shiryo ga Kioku Isan ni Toroku sareru nara Nihon Dattai ["Politicized" UNESCO: Japan May Leave if Documents about Comfort Women Are Registered to Memory of the World]" *Sankei Shimbun*, October 18, 2017.

47. Nozomi Matsui, "'Memory of the World' to Change Rules after Asian Controversies," *Asahi Shibun*, October 19, 2017.

48. Interview with Ministry of Foreign Affairs official, August 15, 2018.

49. Trevor Incerti and Phillip Y. Lipscy, "The Politics of Energy and Climate Change in Japan under Abe: Abenergynomics," *Asian Survey*, vol. 58, no. 4 (2018).

50. Jeff D. Colgan and Robert O. Keohane, "The Liberal Order Is Rigged," *Foreign Affairs*, vol. 96, no. 3 (May/June 2017).

51. PwC, "The World in 2050. The Long View: How Will the Global Economic Order Change by 2050?" https://www.pwc.com/gx/en/issues/economy/the-world-in-2050.html; https://www.mri.co.jp/news/press/teigen/027615.html.

52. For example, the exorbitant privilege associated with the status of the US$ as a reserve currency, Barry Eichengreen, *Exorbitant Privilege: The Rise and Fall of the Dollar and the Future of the International Monetary System* (Oxford University Press, 2011).

53. Saburo Okita, "Special Presentation: Prospect of Pacific Economies," in *Pacific Cooperation: Issues and Opportunities: Report of the Fourth Pacific Economic Cooperation*

Conference (Seoul, Korea: Korea Development Institute, 1985); Kiyoshi Kojima, "The 'Flying Geese' Model of Asian Economic Development: Origin, Theoretical Extensions, and Regional Policy Implications," *Journal of Asian Economics*, vol. 11 (2000); Kaname Akamatsu, "Waga Kuni Yomo Kogyohin No Susei" [The Trend of the Wool Industry of Japan], *Shogyo Keizai Ronso*, vol. 13 (1935), 129–212.

54. Miles Kahler and Jeffrey Frankel, "Introduction," in *Regionalism and Rivalry: Japan and the United States in Pacific Asia*, edited by Miles Kahler and Jeffrey Frankel (University of Chicago Press, 1992), 8.

55. Kenneth N. Waltz, "The Emerging Structure of International Politics," *International Security*, vol. 18, no. 2 (1993), 56, 65.

56. Sadako Ogata, "Ogata Sadako: Moto Kokuren Nanmin Koto Benmukan" [Sadako Ogata: United Nations High Commissioner for Refugees], in *Oral History*, 52.

57. Yoshio Hatano, "Hatano Yoshio Taishi" [Ambassador Yoshio Hatano], in *Oral History*, 199.

58. Ibid., 201.

59. Interview with Ministry of Foreign Affairs official, August 16, 2018.

60. Wakamizu Tsutsui, "Japan's Role in the International Organizations with Particular Reference to the United Nations," *Archiv des Völkerrechts*, vol. 25, no. 1 (1987), 34.

61. Yukio Takasu, "Takasu Yukio: Kokuren Kaikaku Tanto Taishi" [Yukio Takasu: Ambassador to the United Nations], in *Oral History* , 133–34.

62. Koichiro Matsuura, "Matsuura Koichiro Unesco Jimukyokucho" [Director-General of UNESCO Koichiro Matsuura], in *Oral History*, 104.

63. George W. Bush, "Remarks by the President in Address to the United Nations General Assembly," https://georgewbush-whitehouse.archives.gov/news/releases/2002/09/20020912-1.html.

64. Yukio Takasu, "Takasu Yukio: Kokuren Kaikaku Tanto Taishi," 151.

65. Ibid., 144.

66. For example, Simon Nixon, "Trump Puts the WTO on the Ropes: President Sows Crisis by Invoking National Security for Tariffs and Blocking Trade-Judge Appointments," *Wall Street Journal*, July 11, 2018.

67. Interview with Ministry of Foreign Affairs official, August 14, 2018.

68. Interview with Ministry of Foreign Affairs official, August 16, 2018.

69. John Gerard Ruggie, "International Regimes, Transactions, and Change: Embedded Liberalism in the Postwar Economic Order," *International Organization*, vol. 36, no. 2 (1982), 379–415.

70. Susan Strange, *Casino Capitalism* (Manchester University Press, 1997).

71. Colgan and Keohane, "The Liberal Order Is Rigged."

72. Carmen M. Reinhart and Kenneth S. Rogoff, *This Time Is Different: Eight Centuries of Financial Folly* (Princeton University Press, 2009); Phillip Y. Lipscy, "Democracy and Financial Crisis," *International Organization*, vol. 72, no. 4 (2018).

73. Randall W. Stone, *Controlling Institutions: International Organizations and the Global Economy* (Cambridge University Press, 2011); Lipscy and Lee, "The IMF as a Biased Global Insurance Mechanism."

74. David Victor, *Global Warming Gridlock* (Cambridge University Press, 2011);

Robert O. Keohane, "The Global Politics of Climate Change: Challenge for Political Science," *PS: Political Science and Politics*, vol. 48, no. 1 (2015).

75. Reinhart and Rogoff, *This Time Is Different*.

76. Michael D. Bordo, "Bretton Woods International Monetary System: A Historical Overview," in *A Retrospective on the Bretton Woods System: Lessons for International Monetary Reform*, edited by Michael D. Bordo and Barry Eichengreen (University of Chicago Press, 1993).

77. Lipscy, "Democracy and Financial Crisis."

78. See discussion of IMF reform in [https://link.springer.com/article/10.1007/s11558-016-9246-z]

79. Keohane, *After Hegemony*.

80. Phillip Y. Lipscy, *The Institutional Politics of Energy and Climate Change*, book manuscript (2018).

81. Incerti and Lipscy, "The Politics of Energy and Climate Change in Japan under Abe."

82. Roland Ismer and Karsten Neuhoff, "Border Tax Adjustment: A Feasible Way to Support Stringent Emission Trading," *European Journal of Law and Economics*, vol. 24, no. 2 (2007).

83. Rahel Aichele and Gabriel Felbermayr, "Kyoto and Carbon Leakage: An Empirical Analysis of the Carbon Content of Bilateral Trade," *Review of Economics and Statistics*, vol. 97, no. 1 (November 2011).

84. Robert Keohane and David Victor, "The Regime Complex for Climate Change," *Perspectives on Politics*, vol. 9, no. 1 (2011).

4

Universality to Plurality?

VALUES IN JAPANESE FOREIGN POLICY

MAIKO ICHIHARA

A commitment to values such as democracy, human rights, liberty, freedom of speech, independent judiciaries, and the rule of law has been a core tenet of the U.S.-led postwar liberal international order. Despite the blow delivered by the United States in its interventionist war in Iraq with the universalist agenda of democracy promotion, values are still a critical component of the order.

However, the values pillar of the liberal international order is under existential threat, particularly in the Asia-Pacific. In formerly and currently fragile democracies spanning from Indonesia to the Philippines and Thailand, the rise of populism has caused increased human rights abuses of certain religious or ethnic groups.[1] Civic space has shrunk in these countries, with tightened control over the funding sources of domestic nonprofits and over the activities of international nonprofit and media.[2] Democracy in Hong Kong and Taiwan is increasingly challenged by the authoritarian Chinese government.[3] China, for its part, managed to develop without adopting the values of liberal democracy, and its new form of techno-authoritarianism is perceived increasingly as a viable option for other nations. In view of these phenomena, Asia-Pacific has become the region facing the most serious deterioration of democracy in the last few years.[4]

Japanese diplomacy has placed an increasing focus on values since the middle of the 2000s, in what I have analyzed as a means to strengthen Japan's relations with the United States and other democracies in face of the threat from China, based on Japan's unique understanding of democracy support.[5] Yet other liberal democracies remain skeptical about Japan's commitment to values.[6] What kind of values has Japan supported in its diplomacy after World War II? In the context of increasing populist politics in the developed world, and fragile democracies in the Asia-Pacific shifting to authoritarianism, how has values diplomacy developed under Prime Minister Shinzo Abe? What should Japanese diplomacy do to support the development of liberal democracies in the Asia-Pacific? This chapter intends to answer these questions.

Values, norms, and morals have been used interchangeably in existing studies on foreign policy, and thus the existing literature on values and foreign policy tends to focus on liberal values. Scholars such as Thomas Berger and Peter J. Katzenstein, who wrote some of the most important works on the impact of values and norms on Japanese foreign policy during the Cold War, argue that pacifist and antimilitarist norms had a major impact,[7] and Yasuhiro Izumikawa reinterprets the antimilitarist norms by inserting the perspective of antitraditionalist norms.[8] Bhubhindar Singh has also focused on the shift in Japanese foreign policy from a reactive to proactive stance after the end of the Cold War, noting a change in the types of norms themselves to international state norms.[9]

Apart from these norms, however, not much analysis has been conducted as to what values have been reflected in Japanese foreign policy. Although there are studies of Japan's values diplomacy since the 2000s, the focus of these works is mostly on alignment behaviors with other democracies in Japanese security policy, and not the types of values espoused.[10] In addition, existing studies on values in Japanese diplomacy tend to focus on the period since the end of the Cold War and have not analyzed the continuity/discontinuity of values in Japan's diplomacy throughout the postwar era.[11] It is imperative to examine which values have affected Japan's diplomacy in what direction to understand the future direction of values diplomacy for Japan.

In this chapter, I argue that the liberal values that have influenced Japanese diplomacy have shifted over time, and while these values functioned to constrain Japanese diplomacy during the Cold War, they began functioning to lead Japan to take more proactive diplomatic initiatives after the end of the Cold War. And with trials and errors of values diplomacy, Japan has shifted to an incremental and pluralistic approach over time.

Based on this current trend, this chapter argues that Japan can promote liberal values with this incrementalist and pluralistic approach. Japan is uniquely positioned to operate in the diplomatic space between the value-laden approach of Western democracies and the realities of governance in the Asia-Pacific. It can use its influence in governments around the Asia-Pacific to help promote the agenda of liberal democracies in a way that is appropriate for the country in question. Finally, I suggest that without substance, Japan's values-oriented diplomacy could crumble, and Japanese policymakers should do more to ensure that a mismatch between rhetoric and action does not end up undermining Japan's diplomatic efforts.

World War Experiences, Ideological War, and Liberal Values during the Cold War

During the Cold War, liberal values such as pacifism, antimilitarism, democracy, civil liberties, and antinuclearism were reflected in Japanese diplomacy. These values were nurtured as reflections on the experiences of the world wars and were further strengthened by Japan's postwar position in the free camp as an ally of the United States. However, Japanese diplomacy did not proactively support other countries for such causes, and instead, these values functioned to constrain Japanese foreign and security policies.

Japan's defeat in World War II, the loss of more than 3 million people from the Sino-Japanese War to the end of World War II,[12] and a sense of guilt for invading other Asian countries fostered the emergence of pacifism and strong suspicion of the military as an institution in the postwar period. Pacifists and antimilitarists sought to set bounds on Japan's security policy in order to prevent the Japanese government from initiating any more wars, calling for Japan's complete disarmament, neutrality between the United States and Russian camps, abolition of the U.S.-Japan alliance, and legal constraints on Japan's use of military force.[13] Facing the need to reconcile with these antimilitarist demands, pragmatic mainstream conservatives represented by Prime Minister Shigeru Yoshida led the Japanese foreign and security policies toward the Yoshida doctrine, which limited Japan's military capabilities while relying on the U.S.-Japan alliance for security[14] (see chapter 8 by Thomas Berger for more detail).

Concurrently, the wartime experience led the Japanese to respect norms of democracy and civil liberties. As political scientist Masao Maruyama argues, the "system of irresponsibility" deprived individuals of civil liberties and free thought under the ultranationalism of the two world wars. Even public officials did not have a sense of responsibility under such a system, which led to the multilayered oppression Maruyama called the "transfer of repression."[15] Postwar intellectuals in Japan called for civil liberties in order to make individuals think for themselves and assume a sense of responsibility. Antitraditionalists took a stance against those intending to build the nation on values such as obedience to authority, self-sacrifice, and collectivism, instead seeking to promote the values of liberal democracy.[16] Calls for freedom of the press, freedom of assembly, and freedom of speech were being heard even before the U.S. Occupation installed democracy in Japan.[17]

The emergence of domestic liberal democratic norms coincided with Japan's regional role in the ideological war between the United States and the Soviet Union. As the Cold War structure permeated into Asia, the United States renewed its recognition of Japan as a bulwark against communism and positioned the U.S.-Japan alliance at the center of its Cold War strategy in Asia. Japan was thus deeply incorporated as a member of the free camp, and Japanese diplomacy accordingly revolved around the U.S.-Japan alliance as one of the three pillars of Japan's foreign policy, alongside diplomacy as a member in Asia and the UN-centered approach.[18] Given the ideological nature of the Cold War, shared values were deeply embedded in the alliance as a cohesive package.

Within these bipolar dynamics, Japan sought to connect the United States with Southeast Asian countries that were in the nonalignment movement and were thus keeping a certain distance from the United States. This bridging role aimed to stabilize and develop the region, and to prevent the spread of communism. Such measures were enacted in response to formal and informal requests from the United States to play a proactive supporting role for U.S. policies toward Asia. Japan's unique dual positions—as a member of the free camp and a member of the Asia-Africa group of the UN—made such diplomatic measures possible and also satisfied two of the pillars of Japanese diplomacy: U.S.-Japan alliance and diplomacy as a member in Asia. Although the role fits with Kent Calder's observation of Japan as a reactive state,[19] it served Japanese economic interest as well, since Japan used economic cooperation as the primary tool to achieve the bridging function. But although political stability and economic development were the desired result of such diplomatic moves, these values were not necessarily liberal ones.

The third pillar of Japan's diplomacy, the UN-centered approach, served more as a justification of Japanese security and foreign policies than as a vehicle for multilateral initiatives, although Japan did support multilateralism. Japan's active involvement in the UN is well known. Japan has been appointed a number of times as a nonpermanent member of the UN Security Council, the Economic and Social Council, and the International Court of Justice. However, Japan was not a proactive player or contributor to the UN system during the Cold War; rather, its membership in the UN lent it legitimacy for foreign and security policies. The Japanese government positioned, for example, the legitimacy of the U.S.-Japan alliance in relation to the right to collective self-defense acknowledged in the UN Charter and explained the alliance as an interim measure that effectively defended Japan before the UN defends the country.[20]

One value that appeared contrary to the system of values in the U.S.-Japan alliance was antinuclearism. The antinuclear public sentiment due to the atomic bombings of Hiroshima and Nagasaki was further strengthened by the victimization of the *Lucky Dragon* fishing boat in the U.S. thermonuclear bomb test on Bikini Atoll in the Marshall Islands in 1954. The Japan Socialist Party embodied this public antinuclear position, and to conciliate the public sentiment against nuclear weapons, the Eisaku Sato administration announced in 1967 its three non-nuclear principles: no possession, no production, and no introduction of nuclear weapons on Japanese territory. However, the policy had to be reconciled with the reality that Japan needed the U.S. nuclear umbrella for its security (see chapter 5 by Nobumasa Akiyama).[21]

These liberal values—pacifism, antimilitarism, democracy, civil liberties, and antinuclearism—functioned to constrain Japan from having full-fledged military capabilities but were not promoted abroad. Even after Japan gained more policy autonomy alongside the weakening American presence in Asia in the 1970s, Japan did not proactively promote peace, democracy, civil liberties, or non-nuclear policy—unlike West Germany, which began assisting the democracy of neighboring countries around this time.[22] Strong sovereignty norms in Asia and Japan's sense of guilt about its past wars caused Japan to hold well back from political interference.

Restrained Activism in Support of Liberal Values after the Cold War

After the end of the Cold War, Japan began promoting liberal values through its diplomacy, albeit in a restrained manner. In addition to the increased perception of democracy as the ultimate political regime type, as discussed by Francis Fukuyama,[23] there were two triggers: the Tiananmen Square incident and the Gulf War.

As a wave of democratization spread across Eastern Europe, the Chinese government's brutal crackdown on pro-democracy protests in 1989 posed a stark contrast and became the biggest challenge for Japan's liberal values. While Western European countries such as France and West Germany quickly condemned the Chinese government and applied sanctions, in Japan domestic opinion about the desirable response was split. Upholding the principle of noninterference, embracing the sense of guilt about its wartime behavior toward Asian neighbors, and sensing the need to avoid isolating China and losing channels for engagement, Japan was slow to react. At the same time, voices demanding that the Japanese government condemn the crackdown and apply pressure emerged in the Ministry of Foreign Affairs (MOFA), the Diet, and the business community, in addition to the general public. Japan's reaction ultimately reflected this split: although it eventually froze new loan projects and terminated high-level interaction with China, it worked to persuade G7 member countries to lift sanctions early and swiftly normalized its own relations with China. The prolonged decisionmaking compared to other G7 countries was, as some in MOFA noted, due to the lack of a valid policy on human rights diplomacy.[24]

Universality to Plurality? 139

The Tiananmen Square incident thus led to the creation of the Official Development Assistance (ODA) Charter, which stated: "Full attention should be paid to efforts for promoting democratization and introduction of a market-oriented economy, and the situation regarding the securing of basic human rights and freedoms in the recipient country."[25] Since then, Japan has used diplomatic persuasion and economic sanctions in response to grave incursions on democracy and human rights. Examples of cases where Japan has applied economic sanctions include the crackdown on pro-democracy forces in Togo in the 2000s; the coups d'état in Haiti, Guatemala, Gambia, Niger, Zambia, Sierra Leone, Côte d'Ivoire, and Guinea from the 1990s to the 2000s; and human rights abuse in countries such as Kenya, Malawi, Sudan, and Sierra Leone in the 1990s.[26] In addition to negative sanctions, Japan has assisted democracy abroad through foreign aid, mainly to support elections, central and local state institutions, and the rule of law.[27]

Experience of diplomatic defeat in the Gulf War further prompted Japan to expand its international cooperation. While Japan made a massive financial contribution of US$13 billion to the coalition force, the country did not dispatch personnel, due to pacifistic constraints. However, international criticism for the lack of manpower support and feeble acknowledgment of Japan's financial contribution led to awareness on the part of Japan that if it desired international recognition, it would have to make more substantial contributions in addition to financial support.

This gave rise to opposing views about the form such contributions should take. Ichiro Ozawa proposed that Japan should become a "normal country" by expanding its international contribution in the security domain.[28] Along the lines of this proposal, despite extensive opposition from pacifists, the Peacekeeping Operations (PKO) Cooperation Act was passed in 1992, and since then Japan has dispatched the Self-Defense Force (SDF) to peacekeeping operations in countries such as Cambodia, East Timor, Haiti, Iraq, Israel, Mozambique, Nepal, Sudan, Syria, and South Sudan.

Bhubhindar Singh argues that the expansion of Japan's roles in the security realm can be understood in terms of the change of dominant norms from peace state to international state norms.[29] Whether international state norms are liberal invites scrutiny because behind such a norm shift lies the understanding that Japan needed to shift from an "abnormal," unique peace state to a "normal" nation, meaning a sovereign, autonomous actor in international relations, as argues Linus Hagström.[30] Thus problematized, Japan's stance has resonance with autonomist rather than with liberal values.

However, the rise of international state norms within Japan was not unbounded, and pacifism constrained the dispatch of SDF in UN PKOs. Heated debate continued on the extent to which SDF should be allowed to use weapons for defense, in addition to the situations in which they should be deployed. On the one hand, Japan's desire to expand its participation in UN PKOs over time has loosened the conditions of weapons use for the protection of the lives of SDF personnel. On the other hand, the imperative to make SDF activities constitutional has caused obfuscation of the local conditions of conflict in such countries as South Sudan and Iraq. The obfuscation was used in an attempt to mislead the public that Japan can expand its contribution to the UN PKOs while still satisfying the requirements of its pacifist constitution and government interpretations of it. This not only damages Japanese democracy by reducing accountability and transparency but could also expose dispatched SDF personnel to great danger. There remains a constitutional limitation on what Japan can do internationally as a "normal country" without damaging its liberal values domestically.

Another line of thought about desirable contributions on the part of Japan came from Yoichi Funabashi in a perspective that provided greater emphasis on liberal values. Asserting that Japan should be a "global civilian power," Funabashi proposed fine-tuned international contribution in fields where Japan has positive experience, through politico-economic rather than military forms.[31] In other words, it was a proposal for a "middle power diplomacy" that would buttress the international order while seeking a certain degree of diplomatic autonomy.[32]

A number of diplomatic initiatives have been taken along this line, reflecting such liberal values as environmental protection, poverty reduction, democracy, market economy, and human security. Notable examples include the launch of the Tokyo International Conference on African Development (TICAD); the expansion of ODA for such issues as environmental protection, the improvement of basic human needs, democracy, and economic structural adjustment; Japan's massive financial support of Asian countries that were hit by the Asian financial crisis; and Japan's initiatives on human security, such as the UN Trust Fund for Human Security, the Commission on Human Security, and the Friends of Human Security Forum. While there might have been pragmatic aims—for example, to expand the scope of the security concept to include human security in order to show that Japan has roles to play as a member of the UN Security Council[33]—the global civilian power/middle power diplomacy helped Japan reflect plural norms in its diplomacy. Although much of the focus in Japanese foreign policy under prime ministers Koizumi and Abe has tended to be placed on expansion in the security realm, diplomatic initiatives have more often been taken along the line of a global civilian power.

It must be noted, however, that there is a gradation in the reflection of liberal values in such diplomatic initiatives. This can especially be seen in Japan's interpretation of human security, which mainly focuses on freedom from want rather than freedom from fear. While countries such as Canada and Switzerland emphasize human rights and provide support to tackle conflicts and political violence with the emphasis on freedom from fear, Japan's approach instead focuses on assistance for economic development and natural disasters. While both of these approaches intend to liberate people from the causes of their "unfreedom," to use the phrase of Amartya Sen,[34] Japan's emphasis is more on values in relation to basic human needs, whereas Canada's and Switzerland's emphasis is more on political values such as democracy and human rights. Although satisfying basic human needs would be a first step toward increasing people's political awareness and thus attaining greater political development, Japan's support for liberal values takes a longer-term approach compared to these Western countries.

Structural Change, International Order, and the Impact of Values since the 2000s

Japan's restrained and long-term approach to supporting liberal values was forced to upgrade due to the change in the international power structure in the 2000s. With the relative decline of U.S. power after the prolonged Iraq War and financial crisis of 2007–08 on the one hand, and the rise of China on the other, the unipolar characteristic of the post–Cold War international order was weakened. In East Asia, in addition, Japan was surpassed by China in terms of both military expenditure and GDP, in 2007 and 2010 respectively, and this power shift in the region prompted Japan to seek ways to differentiate its own diplomacy from that of China to maintain its external influence.[35] Whereas Japan established strategic mutual relations with China in October 2006, due to the importance of maintaining good relations with the country, values diplomacy was placed at the core of diplomatic initiatives starting in November of that year.[36]

Perception of the need for differentiation was further strengthened with the rising tension over territorial issues, which, in the understanding of Japanese MOFA officials, was partially a negative repercussion of the poor handling of U.S.-Japan relations during the Yukio Hatoyama administration in 2009–10.[37] After a Chinese fishing boat hit a Japanese Coast Guard patrol vessel in the sea near the Senkaku Islands and heightened tensions between the two countries over the islands in 2010, Japanese domestic discourse on China worsened and justified competitive diplomacy vis-à-vis that country.[38]

The first two decades of the twenty-first century have also been a time of increased skepticism about the U.S. commitment to liberal values. While the weakened hegemonic position of the United States itself—which has supported international public goods based on liberal values such as open economies, multilateralism, and the rule of law throughout the post–World War II period—is a cause for concern about the maintenance of the liberal international order, it is the aggressive damaging of such values that has most worried critics. The U.S. unilateral war against Iraq under the George W. Bush administration was a serious blow to the perception of U.S. commitment to not only multilateralism but also democratic values because the administration used promotion of democracy as a pretext for its military attack.[39] The Trump administration has further begun to inflict damage on nearly every aspect of liberal values. It has damaged multilateralism and its associated values by withdrawing from frameworks such as the Trans-Pacific Partnership (TPP), the Paris Agreement, and the Intermediate-Range Nuclear Forces (INF) Treaty. It has also weakened U.S. commitment to free trade values by taking a protectionist stance. Furthermore, the administration has attacked democracy and civil liberties both domestically and internationally; it has damaged the human rights of immigrants, Muslims, and women; it has undermined media freedom and has even contributed to the spread of disinformation itself; it has been undermining checks and balances; and externally, the administration has attempted to largely cut the budget for international democracy support, shown a lack of interest in such support, and praised authoritarian leaders.[40] Barry Posen described the arrival of the Trump administration as the country's turn to an "illiberal hegemon."[41] This fundamental change in the balance of the international order necessitates that its beneficiaries assume new roles to sustain the liberal order.

The structural change poses other questions: will the challenger provide international public goods if it becomes a hegemon, and what kind of international order will that entail? China is already making attempts at great power diplomacy, seeking to influence the formation of the international order. With the Belt and Road Initiative (BRI), China has used its economic power to build infrastructure internationally, developing ports along the Indian Ocean based on its String of Pearls strategy to secure a maritime sea lane to transport natural resources to China. In her speech at Chatham House in July 2016, Fu Ying, chair of the Foreign Affairs Committee of China's National People's Congress Strategy, quoted Xi Jinping's words spoken at the ninety-fifth anniversary celebration of the founding of the Communist Party of China, held in the same month: that China accepts international institutions such as the UN but is willing to revise an international order that reflects Western values and is constructed around the U.S.-centered alliance networks (analyzed in chapter 1 by Adam Liff).[42] While for many years China's diplomacy seemed aimed at defense of its long borders, the paradigm shift in China's foreign policy from *tao guang yang hui* (remaining low key) to Xi Jinping's "China Dream," which aims for "the great rejuvenation of the Chinese nation," changed China's diplomatic posture to more proactive great power diplomacy.

Neoliberal institutionalism argues that international regimes remain even after the decline of hegemons, due to cost-benefit calculations on the part of beneficiaries that such international regimes can mitigate collective action problems.[43] However, neoliberal institutionalists overlook that regimes reflect the norms of hegemons. While the United States has committed to liberal democratic norms, China, as the potential next hegemon, has a nonliberal interpretation of democracy and human rights. The Chinese government does not believe in the institutionalization of democracy comprising universal suffrage and civil liberties and understands human rights in terms of "relative human rights," with the focus not on civil liberties but on social rights.[44] Claiming the responsibility to assure its citizens' social rights through cyberspace, the Chinese government has developed an extensive surveillance network, and this "digital Leninism" deprives citizens of civil liberties.[45] Authoritarian governments have an affinity with the Chinese understanding of democracy and human rights. If China embarks on construction of the international order reflecting Chinese interpretation of these concepts, commitment to the liberal values of democracy, freedom, human rights, and the rule of law—and therefore an essential pillar of the liberal order—will be greatly weakened.

Furthermore, despite its global presence as a major donor, China is not a member of the OECD Development Assistance Committee (DAC), which inhibits existing donors from urging China to abide by foreign aid norms. Thus positioned, Chinese loans lack transparency and need not comply with the rules on foreign aid conditionality set by the OECD DAC. Such loans have caused labor, environmental, and human rights issues in recipient countries. Interest rates are also set high, and a number of countries that have implemented infrastructure projects with loans from China are facing difficulty in repaying their debts. In this situation, the Sri Lankan government ended up leasing the Hambantota Port, constructed with loans from China, to China for ninety-nine years. According to research conducted by the Center for Global Development, twenty-three out of sixty-eight countries researched are "at risk of debt distress," and eight countries (Djibouti, Kirgiz, Laos, Maldives, Mongolia, Monte Negro, Tajikistan, and Pakistan) are particularly at risk.[46] While it might be a learning process for China, and the contents of its projects have been improving in recent years, Malaysian prime minister Mahathir Mohamad has expressed concern about being dominated by new colonialism,[47] and U.S. vice president Mike Pence stated in October 2018 that China might have the intention of using "debt diplomacy" for the expansion of its influence.[48]

While the liberal international order faces threats from such multiple fronts, European countries' actions for the support of the order are constrained by the spread of populism throughout Europe. As a beneficiary of the liberal order and a sizable power, Japan has responsibility to take an ever more proactive stance to support the liberal order, particularly in Asia-Pacific.

Universal Values and Diplomacy of the Abe Administration

Being aware of the necessity of proactive diplomacy to support the liberal international order, values such as democracy, human rights, and the rule of law have been brought to the forefront of Japanese diplomacy as "universal values" since the mid-2000s, especially under the Abe administrations, although the emphasis and wordings have changed over time. In the prefatory note to the *Diplomatic Bluebook 2006*, Taro Aso, then foreign minister of the Koizumi administration, mentioned Japan's own postwar nation-building efforts as having been based on universal values of freedom, democracy, basic human rights, and the market economy and showed a resolve to promote these values around the world based on Japan's own experience.[49] This resolve was expressed in November 2006 as a commitment to support the stability and prosperity of countries that share these values to create an "Arc of Freedom and Prosperity" in the wider Asian region, enjoying strengthened ties with other democracies such as the United States, India, and Australia. Aso positioned this values diplomacy as the fourth pillar of Japanese diplomacy.[50]

A number of new diplomatic moves appeared around 2007, in alignment with this initiative. Japan began developing security cooperation with Australia and India, as two major regional democracies, concluding joint declarations on security cooperation with them. Japan proposed and led the first quadrilateral security dialogue between Australia, India, Japan, and the United States (the Quad). More direct moves for democracy support appeared as well, and Japan contributed US$10 million to the UN Democracy Fund (UNDEF). Democracy assistance was positioned as one of the priority issues for ODA in 2007, resulting in expanded ODA provision for good and democratic governance (see figure 4-1). Enthusiasm toward values diplomacy had reached an unprecedented level.

However, the initiative was perceived to represent a containment strategy creating an arc surrounding China, and suspicions were raised by China. Criticism arose domestically and even from the United States, with

U.S. secretary of state Condoleezza Rice warning that this initiative "could send an unintended signal to China."[51] The initiative was "a bit premature diplomatically,"[52] and thus disappeared from the diplomatic scene after the administrations of Abe (2006–07) and Aso (2008–09).

When values diplomacy returned to the forefront of Japanese diplomacy with the inauguration of the second Abe administration in December 2012, Abe asserted that values diplomacy is strategic diplomacy.[53] The National Security Strategy of 2013 stated one of the objectives of Japan's diplomacy as "improve the global security environment and build a peaceful, stable, and prosperous international community by strengthening the international order based on universal values and rules, and by playing a leading role in the settlement of disputes, through consistent diplomatic efforts and further personnel contributions."[54] For this purpose, the strategy aims to strengthen cooperation with countries that share universal values and to support democracy in developing countries with ODA.[55] Each of these aims is examined in greater detail below.

SECURITY COOPERATION

Japan has accordingly rapidly expanded security cooperation with other democracies, and universal values of democracy, human rights, the rule of law, and free trade have been used as banners to display the strong bond between these countries. In addition to weakening asymmetry in the U.S.-Japan alliance, Japan has expanded security cooperation with American allies and friends. Development of security cooperation has been distinctive with Australia and India, and in addition to bilateral frameworks, quadrilateral security dialogues were resumed in 2017.[56] Japan has conducted joint military drills with democratic countries, including Australia, India, and South Korea, with the United States as the hub, and collaboration with the United Kingdom and France has also been accelerating. Emphasizing the shared values of freedom, democracy, human rights, and the rule of law, Japan seems to be intending to promote "we-feeling" among these countries to constitute a security community of democracies.[57] Just as a high-ranking Japan International Cooperation Agency (JICA) official positively evaluated Japan-India working together as "collaboration between democracies in Asia based on a commitment to the rule of law,"⁵⁸ Japan is trying to buttress the alignment based on shared interests with shared values.

Learning lessons from the Arc of Freedom and Prosperity initiative, however, it has also been imperative for Japan not to give the impression that its new approach is a containment strategy against China. Prickling China is not, in fact, desirable for any of the cooperating parties, due to high economic interdependence with it. Efforts have been made to demonstrate the inclusiveness of these security cooperation moves. For example, Sri Lanka and the Maldives participated as observers in the U.S.-India-Japan joint military drill, Malabar, in 2018, after being reassured that such collaboration does not intend to force countries like them to reject their relations with China.⁵⁹

In addition, maritime security, freedom of navigation, and the rule of law have gradually been brought to the forefront starting around 2014, replacing universal values as banners for such security cooperation. These values are deemed important, given China's increasing militarization in the South China Sea, which is challenging the maritime status quo and the international order that has been maintained based on international law. Although positioning these values at the core of Japanese diplomacy could indeed encourage pushback from China, these are values that can be shared not only by democratic but also nondemocratic countries. The apolarity of these values not only makes them acceptable for nondemocratic countries that have territorial disputes with China, it also potentiates their justifiability for China itself.

ODA

Reflecting the centrality of values in Japan's foreign policy, stronger commitment has been shown in Japan's foreign aid for the support of universal values as well. For example, the very first section of the first chapter of the ODA White Paper 2012 emphasized Japan's commitment to democracy support,⁶⁰ and the Development Cooperation Charter of 2015 positioned "sharing universal values and realizing a peaceful and secure society" as one of the priority issues.⁶¹

While an emphasis on these values is similar to that made in Western countries, the approach to attaining the goal is different. Japan eschews taking a direct approach to advance political reforms for the promotion of liberal values. While Western assistance in support of universal values (and this is especially true for Northern European countries) is largely given to political parties and civil society for democracy assistance, Japan's corresponding assistance has been provided mostly for state institutions and the rule of law. According to the ODA data from OECD DAC for "151: I.5.a. Government & Civil Society-General, Total," Japan has expanded aid to public sector policy and administrative management since the mid-2000s, followed by the expansion of rule-of-law assistance in the 2010s (figure 4-1).

The values Japan promotes with its ODA are mostly related to good governance, such as rule of law, trust, and capacity, in addition to market economy. Japan directs most of its energies to assistance to state institutions for the purpose of helping to bring good governance, and it often positions good governance and democracy as short-term and longer-term purposes of aid projects, respectively. A high-ranking official stated in an interview that "while fundamental values should ultimately prevail, it would be counterproductive to impose principles on developing countries without being conscious of differences in their political, economic, and social situation. In this sense, governance assistance will lead to democracy assistance in the long term."[62]

While it differs from the Western approach of providing substantial assistance for opposition political parties and civil society actors, and thus tends to be understood by Western commentators as the absence of values diplomacy supporting liberal democracy in Japan, this approach is based on a stern belief that improvement of the political system and human rights conditions in the short term is not only impossible but such attempts could actually aggravate the situation. While this approach makes it difficult to push for positive change, it is reasonable when considering the importance of able state institutions, especially at the time of democratization. According to Edward Mansfield and Jack Snyder, in contrast to the absence of wars between democracies, democratizing states are prone to wars. One of the reasons for this difference lies in the weakness of state institutions in democratizing countries.[63] Given the absolute undesirability of causing wars, it would seem sensible to support freedom in a stable manner, nurturing the capacity of state institutions that will then be able to maintain governance during democratization.

FIGURE 4-1. Gross disbursements of Japan's ODA for democracy and governance (2000–16)

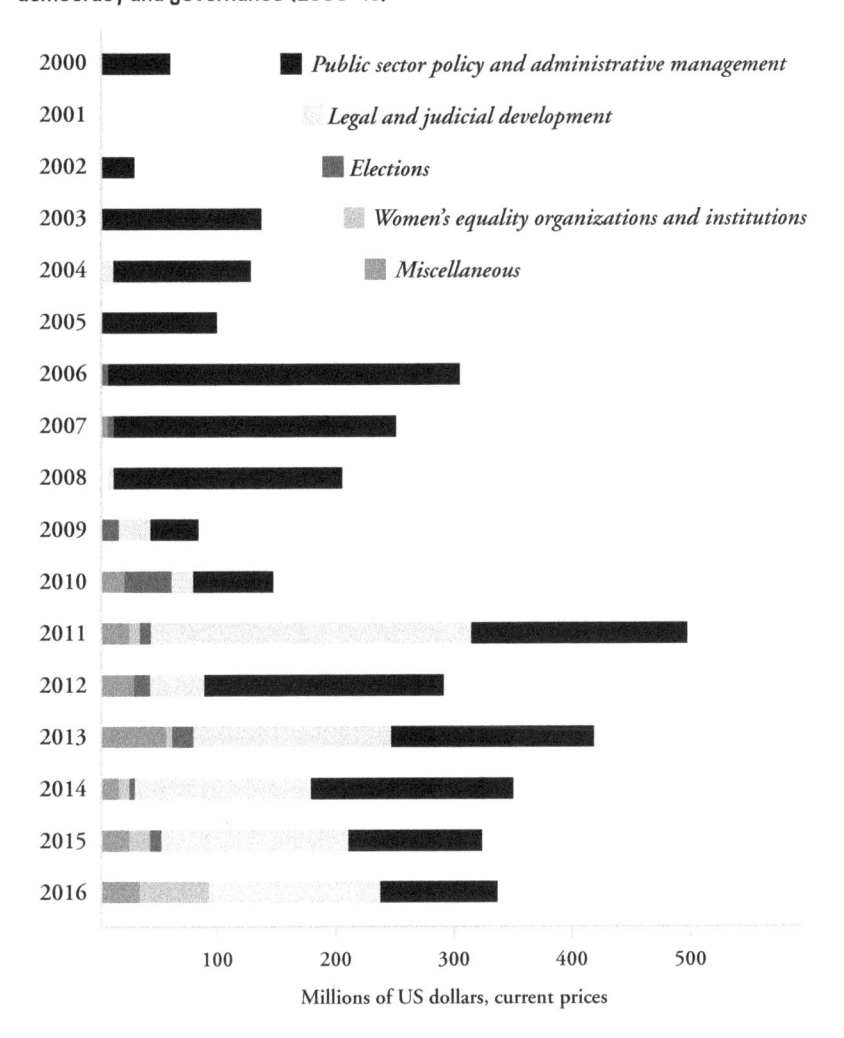

■ *Public sector policy and administrative management*
Legal and judicial development
■ *Elections*
Women's equality organizations and institutions
■ *Miscellaneous*

Millions of US dollars, current prices

Note: Miscellaneous includes "Public finance management," "Decentralisation and support to subnational government," "Anti-corruption organisations and institutions," "Domestic revenue mobilisation," "Democratic participation and civil society," "Legislatures and political parties," "Media and free flow of information," "Human rights," and "Ending violence against women and girls."

Source: "151: I.5.a. Government & Civil Society-General" in OECD, Creditor Reporting System (data extracted on March 23, 2018).

Behind Japan's reticent attitude toward values lies an understanding among government officials that the recent setback in democracy is a backlash against U.S. democracy promotion. A Japanese high-ranking official stated that "there is a regret in the world that we did too much and thus it did not go well after the Arab Spring," recognizing that too much assistance for pro-democracy factions has caused political chaos.[64] The official finds issues with the approaches America has taken and states that "most American-style democracy promotion activities failed. The U.S. understands freedom as the absence of repression and thus incites people to fight. They provide money to the oppressed and try to provide weapons. Japan instead wants to construct a community with these people."[65] Japan considers it desirable to assist the creation of better societies in a stable manner rather than cause instability. Although U.S. democracy promotion is somewhat misunderstood in the sense that the United States Agency for International Development (USAID) has, in fact, assisted state institutions more than civil society, the large amount of such assistance compared to what is given by other countries understandably causes a strong impression of America's positioning.[66]

JICA has placed importance on capacity-building of state institutions and trust-building between local government officials and citizens for the sake of good governance. The diverse sectors where Japan has provided capacity-building to date span from law and police to tax, border control, intellectual property, and economic policy-planning, among others. Projects with the aim of trust-building include, for example, Japan's police assistance to Bekasi, Indonesia. The project created a community police system in Bekasi and trained local police to nurture friendly relations with people in the community for trust-building. In Bangladesh, JICA has assisted improvement of the administrative service provided by city offices, in order to strengthen citizens' trust. Japan intends to provide good governance assistance to improve the quality of administrative service providers and, ultimately, for the betterment of administrative service as a whole, thereby helping to build trust between citizens and the state. Japan considers that such assistance can form the basis for political reform measures undertaken in a stable manner.

Japan has also put considerable effort into promoting the rule of law—ODA allocation for legal and judicial development saw dramatic expansion in the 2010s (figure 4-1). Japan's legal assistance, which includes the goal of helping to develop liberal economic systems, began in 1994, and while most legal assistance projects have focused on civil and commercial law sectors, recent projects are increasingly positioning the assistance as a tool to help bring democracy in the long run. In addition, while the Japanese government used the term "legal assistance" until the early 2010s, it started using the term "rule of law assistance" beginning with the second Abe administration to reflect that foreign aid policies were now integrated as a part of diplomacy and that Japan intends to support the rule of law and not just legal technicalities.[67]

In the Japanese understanding, assistance in the field of commercial law equates to support for a prerequisite of democratization. This stems from belief in the modernization argument made by scholars such as Seymour Martin Lipset.[68] It should be noted that this is not an understanding unique to Japan. The U.S. anti-Communist stance in the early Cold War period similarly posited that economic stability and development would help prevent the intrusion of communism into societies, and likewise help democracy to take root.

In 2017, Japan launched the Free and Open Indo-Pacific (FOIP) initiative based on Abe's keynote speech at the Tokyo International Conference on African Development (TICAD) VI, held in Kenya in 2016. While "free" and "open" are terms closely related to democracy, Japan underscores the values of rule of law, freedom of navigation, and free trade, rather than democracy per se.

In so doing, Japan intends to avoid giving the impression that FOIP is a containment strategy against China, unlike the Arc of Freedom and Prosperity strategy—and, in a sense, this message is directed to Southeast Asian countries more than to China itself. Having strong economic ties with both China and Japan, Southeast Asian countries hope to maintain excellent relations with both regional giants. When Japan was emphasizing democracy and human rights, these countries felt they were forced to choose between Japan and China. In order not to lose Southeast Asian countries to China, Japan intentionally weakened its emphasis on democracy. Thus, FOIP is Japan's reassurance policy, especially toward Southeast Asian countries. A high-ranking MOFA official stated in an interview that "Japan and the United States are not playing an Othello game with China over the countries in Southeast and Southwest Asia. These countries would like to avoid falling into a situation in which they have to choose one of the two, Japan and the United States on the one hand, or China on the other. Although the Cold War U.S.-Soviet relations had some characteristics like an Othello game, our game with China is not like this."[69]

When Japan launched the Arc of Freedom and Prosperity initiative in 2006, it did pay attention to not sending the wrong signals regarding its intentions toward China. However, due to a lack of tangible moves on the part of Japan to provide a persuasive explanation, understanding of the initiative as a containment strategy against China was solidified. Learning lessons from the past, in his policy speech in January 2018, Abe expressed the intention to promote the new initiative alongside Japan-China cooperation, saying, "We will also work with China to meet the growing infrastructure demand in Asia. Japan and China share significant responsibilities for the peace and prosperity of the region, and maintain an inseparable relationship. We will fulfill the expectations of the international community by deepening our friendly relationship in a stable manner from a broad perspective."[70]

Cooperation with China is seen as an opportunity to push China to adhere by international standards while gaining understanding from loan recipient countries of the importance of responsible investment screening based upon such standards.[71] It was with this intention that Japan agreed with China in May 2018 to seek to create cooperative projects between their respective business sectors in third countries.[72] In seeking out third-country cooperation, Japan underscores the necessity of observing the four conditions of openness, transparency, economic efficiency, and financial health of the target countries—conditions accorded high regard in FOIP.[73] By tying such projects to values of good governance that are shared among members of the OECD, Japan intends to "have China observe international standards such as transparency and financial health and consolidate these standards in Asia."[74]

A delicate handling is necessary, however. A high-ranking MOFA official showed recognition in an interview that China is trying to seek support from Japan for its BRI projects.[75] Given that the swing in U.S.-China relations has repercussions for the Japan-China balance, China has approached Japan when experiencing difficult times with the United States.

Even though this might appear to be an opportunity for augmented economic relations between the two Asian countries in this triangle, Japan must maintain its four conditions in third-country cooperation. It should be careful not to hug China too tight and thereby forgo the opportunity to influence Chinese projects to raise their governance standards. It is imperative to use this opportunity to encourage China to become a responsible superpower.

In recent years, a multilateral approach to assistance for universal values has been gaining greater importance. In addition to Japan's historic roles for the support of free trade, as exemplified by the conclusion of the Comprehensive and Progressive Agreement for Trans-Pacific Partnership (CPTPP) in January 2018 and by the Japan-EU Economic Partnership Agreement (EPA) signed in July 2018, Japan and the EU have concluded a Strategic Partnership Agreement (SPA). The SPA aims to "contribute jointly to the promotion of shared values and principles, in particular democracy, the rule of law, human rights, and fundamental freedoms," and clearly states that the two parties will cooperate and coordinate for this purpose.[76] Actual moves based on the SPA remain to be seen, but Japan will need to coordinate its understanding and emphasis on liberal values with the EU perspective in order to engage in any meaningful cooperation.

In sum, Japan became more proactive in emphasizing liberal values such as democracy, human rights, the rule of law, and market economy after the end of the Cold War, and particularly during the Abe administrations. Such a values diplomacy proceeded according to trial and error, and emphasis on those values that cannot be shared by nondemocratic governments has waned in the late 2010s. Figure 4-2 shows the results of a correspondence analysis performed on statements by foreign ministers (available on the MOFA website), from 1995 to 2016, using KH Coder. Focusing on terms denoting liberal values that appeared more than five times throughout the target period, it analyzed which terms of liberal values were used in what year and whether the usage of the term was unique to the year. Terms and years plotted close to each other show correspondence. Terms that are plotted far from the coordinate origin of the two dimensions (0, 0) are used particularly often in specific years, whereas terms near the coordinate origin are used across years. The analysis shows that such terms as *minshuteki* (democratic), *minshushugi* (democracy), and *heiwa* (peace) have been mentioned

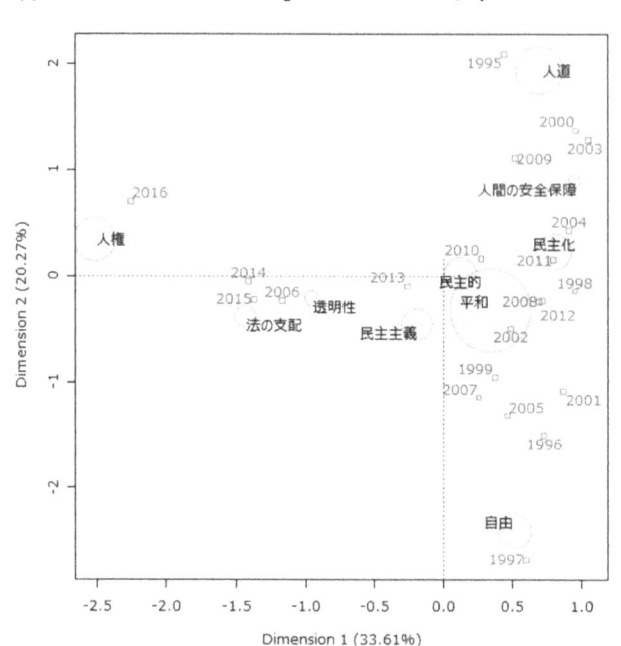

FIGURE 4-2. Appearance of Terms Relating to Liberal Values, by Year

Source: Created by the author. From left to right, 人権 means "human rights," 法の支配 means "rule of law," 透明性 means "transparency," 民主主義 means "democracy," 民主的 means "democratic," 平和 means "peace," 自由 means "freedom/liberty," 民主化 means "democratization," and 人間の安全保障 means "human security."

frequently and have appeared continuously over the years. By contrast, such terms as *jindo* (humanitarianism), *jinken* (human rights), *jiyu* (freedom/liberty), *toumeisei* (transparency), and *hou no shihai* (rule of law) are used in specific years. In the actual statements that mention "humanitarianism," "human rights," and "freedom/liberty," these terms appeared in relation to humanitarian crises in Chechnya, Bosnia, and North Korea in 1995 (in the case of "humanitarianism"), human rights violation by North Korea and related moves on the side of Japan at the UN in 2016 (in the case of "human rights"), and Cambodian elections, Hong Kong's reversion to China, and negotiations of the World Trade Organization over financial services (in the case of "freedom/liberty"). On the other hand, although "transparency" and the "rule of law" were not used in conjunction with any specific incidents, these terms began being used around 2014. It supports the argument that the discourse on values has changed over time in Japan.

Limitations in Japan's Values Diplomacy and Policy Recommendations

Michael Blaker once pointed out the risk-aversive tendency of Japanese foreign policy,[77] and scholars such as Kent Calder argue that Japan does not take proactive moves but remains reactive in its foreign policies.[78] While these arguments might, to a certain extent, explain Japan's diplomacy vis-à-vis values, Japanese officials have their own beliefs about the appropriate approach to the promotion of liberal values. For one thing, Japan has diversified the values that it promotes, with the intention not to upset the established order in the short term, to avoid causing or worsening humanitarian disasters. For another thing, they intend to ensure that Japan's values diplomacy is not anti-China, to maintain good relations not only with China but also with Southeast Asian countries.

Although such an approach does indeed have a positive dimension, it also has drawbacks and limitations. More than anything, Japan's emphasis on stability could reinforce the status quo in recipient countries, with the (unintentional) result of buttressing authoritarian governments and violations of liberal values.

Although there are multiple fronts where Japan can build cooperation with European countries for the promotion and protection of liberal values, such as Japan-EU SPA and G7, Japan's stability-emphasized and state-centric approach is likely to be an obstacle for developing SPA-based cooperation with the EU. Although Japanese officials often take a critical view of U.S. assistance for opposition forces, it is Northern European countries that are more enthusiastic supporters of political parties and civil society. In addition, unlike the great powers that heavily reflect their pragmatic interests in foreign aid, Northern European countries assist democracies abroad more normatively. The discrepancy between Japan and European countries in the approach taken toward promotion of liberal values is likely to function as a limitation for such cooperation. European diplomats often lobby for democracy and human rights more actively than the United States, and from their point of view, Japan does not lobby hard enough to governments in Southeast Asia. Japan's reticent approach of avoiding causing changes counters European normative belief in the support for democracy and human rights, and thus could hamper building coalitions and cooperation with European democracies.

Japan often hedges in relation to values in order to avoid damaging its relations with non-democracies or illiberal democracies, which not only makes cooperation with the EU on this front difficult, but also weakens Japan's messages on pro-liberal values. Cambodia's general election of July 2018 is a recent example. By closing independent media, expelling international nonprofits, and dissolving the biggest opposition party, Prime Minister Hun Sen of Cambodia facilitated conditions to conduct the election without competition. Even though Japan did not simply walk away from this issue and instead continued persuading Hun Sen behind the scenes to give amnesty to members of the Cambodia National Rescue Party (CNRP, a dissolved opposition party) and to engage in dialogue with them,[79] the election was conducted undemocratically. But although Japan suspended the dispatch of election observers, which was a sign that it did not intend to endorse the election, it sent a mixed message to Cambodia after the election: while Japan's foreign minister Taro Kono told the foreign minister of Cambodia, Prak Sokhonn, that Japan regretted the election and urged Cambodia to engage in democratic political processes,[80] the secretary general of Japan's Liberal Democratic Party (LDP), Toshihiro Nikai, sent a letter to Prime Minister Hun Sen, which stated that he "sincerely congratulated the overwhelming victory" of Hun Sen's party in the general election.[81] The intention would have been to send a strategic signal that, while the Japanese government cares about democracy, the LDP values maintaining good relations with Cambodia. However, this move was not sensible in that it not only endorsed such an outrightly undemocratic election but also disaffirmed Japan's belief in the democratic election process. While it is understandable that Japan chose not to pressure Cambodia, to avoid pushing the country into the arms of China, it should have maintained a consistent message.

In order to overcome these limitations, this chapter recommends that Japan take a slightly more proactive approach for the maintenance of the liberal international order, while continuing to pay attention to the importance of good governance and diversity of values.

Given the strong sovereignty norms, great sensitivity will continue to be important for values diplomacy. Therefore, Japan should take a gradual and low-key approach to promote the values of good governance and the rule of law for the consolidation of and transition to democracy in the long run. In the Asian region, where political tensions have increased, support for the expansion of transparency, accountability, participation, and the rule of law should be continued. Although these are aspects emphasized in FOIP, it would be better not to stress a prominent and overarching initiative of this sort, but maintain a low-key tone. Thus, it would be sensible to gradually reduce the usage of the FOIP label.

I also urge Japan to promote the values of human security, human rights, and democracy through multilateral frameworks. After the Iraq War, views on promoting democracy suffered serious damage, and the failure of the Arab Spring in bringing democracy to the Middle East (with the exception of Tunisia) drew a gloomier picture of prospects for supporting democracy bilaterally. Furthermore, due to recent tightened control over nonprofits, it has been increasingly difficult to provide meaningful support for actors trying to embed democratic values domestically through bilateral channels. As one of the most active supporters of the concept of human security, Japan has contributed a total of US$413.63 million for human security in the twenty years since 1998.[82] Japan is the fifth largest contributor to the UNDEF, having provided US$10.2 million in total since the fund's establishment in 2005.[83] The country should continue providing assistance through such multilateral frameworks.

In its diplomacy, Japan should also utilize values that do not necessarily originate in the West. One such value would be neutrality. In countries under competitive authoritarianism, to use the phrase of Steven Levitsky and Lucan Way,[84] election-related institutions that are supposed to be neutral, such as election administration committees, lean toward governing parties. It would be therefore desirable to include content that values the neutrality of such institutions in Japan's capacity-building training.

Japan's stability-focused and state-focused approach should be balanced with a slightly more proactive approach to promote freedom. To this end, Japan's grant assistance for grassroots projects, which is the program that supports Japanese and local civil society organizations, should be broadened to include organizations in political issue areas. This will help promote greater transparency of governance, which is one of the targets in the FOIP strategy.

While Japan has provided various forms of legal assistance since the mid-1990s, in some countries human rights abuses violate laws created with support from Japan. In those cases, Japan should support the Japan Federation of Bar Associations (JFBA) to urge enforcement of such laws and the protection of human rights. As a civil society organization, JFBA has a greater free hand in its activities.

There has been an increased awareness about interrelations between democracy and the environment, and a greater emphasis has been placed on the importance of civic participation for environmental protection. The World Resources Institute created the Environmental Democracy Index in 2015 and annually evaluates and promotes civic participation for the environment.[85] Japan should partner with civil society organizations in the environmental field to support environmental protection in developing countries. This would be an activity that champions not only the value of environmental protection but also the values of freedom of speech, human rights (right to a healthy environment), and democracy.

The expansion of assistance in the area of disaster relief and disaster risk reduction, based on the value of human security, would be desirable as well. Out of its dense experience and knowledge in disaster risk reduction, Japan has taken the initiative in hosting all the meetings of the World Conference on Disaster Risk Reduction since 1994. A continued commitment to disaster relief and risk reduction assistance, reflecting the values of humanitarianism and human security, is one area in which Japan should elevate its activities.

Last but not least, expansion of the income gap due to globalization is one of the gravest causes of degradation of the liberal international order today. Thus, an approach that tackles income disparity is necessary. This is a domain of human security, and Japan needs to pay attention to values such as community, income disparity, and solidarity.

Conclusion

As a whole, various liberal values have influenced Japan's diplomacy in the postwar era, and the types of values have diversified over time. While pacifism/antimilitarism, civil liberties/antitraditionalism, and antinuclear values were the core liberal values that directed Japan's diplomacy as constraining and regulative norms, the values of international contribution, multilateralism, human security, democracy, and human rights joined in the post–Cold

War era as constitutive norms and fostered the creation of Japanese foreign policy. With the change of the international power structure furthered in the twenty-first century, the necessity of buttressing the liberal international order led Japan to emphasize such values as freedom of navigation, the rule of law, and free trade. The chronological shift shows that, while the dominant values in the twentieth century aimed mostly at the support of domestic social progress in Japan, in the twenty-first century Japan began seeking greater roles in the international scene based on values for international social progress. At the same time, Japan underwent trial and error in its values diplomacy and came to grasp the constructiveness of a nonconfrontational and nonantagonistic approach. This led Japan to emphasize values of good governance—such as the rule of law, openness, transparency, economic efficiency, and financial health—as values that are acceptable for all, rather than democracy and human rights, which can be rejected outright by authoritarian leaders. The values in Japan's diplomacy were gradually diversified and became less confrontational. Japan has thus shifted from a somewhat more universalistic approach to a pluralistic approach over time.

However, the situation concerning the liberal order has changed drastically in recent years. China has expanded external assistance in the fields of governance and law in the last decade. According to Zeng Aiping, China began sharing its governance experience with African countries in the late 1990s, and this was officially positioned as one of the priority issues in the Forum on China-Africa Cooperation in 2006. Most of the projects involve training and mutual official visits whose purpose is to apply a Chinese governance model to African countries.[86] Legal training has also expanded in recent years, and centers for legal training have been established at institutions such as the China Law Society and Southwest University of Political Science & Law.[87] Furthermore, in June 2018, China established the First and Second International Commercial Courts of China in Shenzhen and Xi'an, respectively. These courts aim to cover international commercial disputes across countries and regions related to the BRI[88] and seek commercial conflict resolution based on Chinese laws.[89]

Such active export of China's governance model has led to "competition over governance" between China on the one hand and traditional donors, including Japan, on the other. The spread of the Chinese governance model could expand "rule by law"—arbitrary application and creation of laws by the authorities—instead of governance based on the "rule of law."[90] Now that the Trump administration has abandoned America's role as supporter of the liberal international order, Japan, together with Europe, has to proactively defend the liberal order.

Given the unconventional nature of challenges facing the liberal international order today, and due to Japan's clear responsibility in supporting that order, a greater—yet fine-tuned—activism is required.

NOTES

The author wishes to thank Yoichi Funabashi and G. John Ikenberry for their invaluable comments and research support, Atsushi Sugii and Minhee Jeong for their research assistance, and API staff members and interns. Special thanks also go to all of the interviewees for their valuable inputs. This work was supported by JSPS KAKENHI grant no. 15K17012.

1. See, for example, Vedi R. Hadiz and Richard Robison, "Competing Populisms in Post-Authoritarian Indonesia," *International Political Science Review*, vol. 38 (September 2017), 488–502; Pasuk Phongpaichit and Chris Baker, "Thaksin's Populism," *Journal of Contemporary Asia*, vol. 1 (2008), 62–83; Alfred W. McCoy, "Philippine Populism: Local Violence and Global Context in the Rise of a Filipino Strongman," *Surveillance & Society*, vol. 15 (2017), 514–22.

2. See, for example, Douglas Rutzen, "Civil Society Under Assault," *Journal of Democracy*, vol. 26 (October 2015), 28–39; Thomas Carothers and Saskia Brechenmacher, "Closing Space: Democracy and Human Rights Support Under Fire," Carnegie Endowment for International Peace (February 20, 2014).

3. See, for example, Maiko Ichihara, "The Changing Role of Democracy in Asian Geopolitics," Carnegie Endowment for International Peace (September 14, 2017).

4. Economist Intelligence Unit, "Democracy Index 2017" (2018), 25.

5. Maiko Ichihara, *Japan's International Democracy Assistance as Soft Power: Neoclassical Realist Analysis* (New York and London: Routledge, 2018).

6. See, for example, Steven Lewis-Workman, "International Norms and Japanese Foreign Aid," *Asian Perspective*, vol. 42 (2018), 85–120; *Japan's Foreign Aid: Old Continuities and New Directions*, edited by David Arase (New York and London: Routledge, 2005).

7. See, for example, Thomas U. Berger, *Cultures of Antimilitarism: National Security in Germany and Japan* (Johns Hopkins University Press, 1998); Peter J. Katzenstein, *Cultural Norms and National Security: Police and Military in Postwar Japan* (Cornell University Press, 1998).

8. Yasuhiro Izumikawa, "Explaining Japanese Antimilitarism: Normative and Realist Constraints on Japan's Security Policy," *International Security*, vol. 35 (Fall 2010), 123–60.

9. Bhubhindar Singh, *Japan's Security Identity: From a Peace-State to an International-State* (Abingdon, U.K.: Routledge, 2013).

10. Following the discussion of Thomas Wilkins, this paper uses the term "alignment" as security cooperation that is informal, unlike alliances. Thomas S. Wilkins, "'Alignment,' not 'Alliance'—The Shifting Paradigm of International Security Cooperation: Toward a Conceptual Taxonomy of Alignment," *Review of International Studies*, vol. 38 (January 2012), 53–76. On values diplomacy as a whole, see, for example, Yuichi Hosoya, "The Rise and Fall of Japan's Grand Strategy," *Asia-Pacific Review*, vol. 18 (May 2011), 13–24; Yuichi Hosoya, "Japan's Two Strategies for East Asia," *Asia-Pacific Review*, vol. 20 (November 2013), 146–56; Daniel Kliman and Daniel Twining, *Japan's Democracy Diplomacy*, German Marshall Fund of the United States (July 2014); Ryo Sahashi, "Security Partnerships in Japan's Asia Strategy," Center for Asian Studies (February 2013); Christopher W. Hughes, "Japan's Response to China's Rise," *International Affairs*, vol. 85 (July 2009), 837–56.

11. Ichihara, *Japan's International Democracy Assistance as Soft Power*; Junichiro Shiratori, "'Kachi' wo Meguru Mosaku. Reisen-go Nihon Gaiko no Shin-kyokumen" [Search for "Values": A New Phase of Post–Cold War Diplomacy], *Kokusai anzen hosho*, vol. 45 (March 2018), 68–85.

12. The estimate is from *Hikiage to Enjo 30nen no Ayumi* [Thirty Years of the Salvaged and Foreign Aid], edited by Koseisho Engokyoku (Tokyo: Ministry of Health and Welfare, 1977), 399.

13. Berger, *Cultures of Antimilitarism*; Katzenstein, *Cultural Norms and National Security*.

14. Richard J. Samuels, *Securing Japan: Tokyo's Grand Strategy and the Future of East Asia* (Cornell University Press, 2008), 38–59.

15. Masao Maruyama, "Cho-kokkashigi no Ronri to Shinri" [The Logics and Psychology of Ultra-Nationalism], *Sekai* (May 1946), 206–18.

16. Joji Watanuki, *Nihon Seiji no Bunseki Shikaku* [An Analytical Perspective on Japanese Politics] (Tokyo: Chuo Koronsha, 1976), 181–211; Ichiro Miyake, *Seitou Shiji no Bunseki* [The Analysis of Support for Political Parties] (Tokyo: Shobunsha, 1985); Izumikawa, "Explaining Japanese Antimilitarism," 130–31.

17. Eiji Oguma, *"Minshu" to "Aikoku." Sengo Nihon no Nashonarizumu to Koukyousei* ["Democracy" and "Patriotism": Nationalism and the Public Nature of Postwar Japan] (Tokyo: Shinyosha, 2002), 68–69.

18. Mentions of the three pillars appeared in MoFA, *Japan's Diplomatic Bluebook* (Tokyo: MoFA, 1957).

19. Kent E. Calder, "Japanese Foreign Economic Policy Formation: Explaining the Reactive State," *World Politics*, vol. 40 (July 1988), 517–41.

20. Pan Liang, "Reisen-ki Nihon no Kokuren Gaiko: Chansu to Jirenma no Hazama de" [Diplomacy of Japan in the United Nations in the Cold War–Era: Between Chances and Dilemmas], *Gaikoshiiryokanpo*, vol. 27 (December 2013), 51–52.

21. Akira Kurosaki, "'Hikaku' Nihon no Kakugunshuku, Fukakusan-gaiko: Hibakukoku no Kyozo to Jitsuzo" ["Non-Nuclear" Japan's Diplomacy of Nuclear Disarmament and Non-Proliferation] in *Nihon no Gaiko* [Japanese Diplomacy], vol.2, *Gaiko-shi Sengo-hen* [Diplomatic History after the War], edited by Sumio Hatano (Tokyo: Iwanami shoten, 2013), 245–71.

22. Thomas Carothers, *Aiding Democracy Abroad* (Washington, D.C.: Carnegie Endowment for International Peace, 1999), 30–37.

23. Francis Fukuyama, *The End of History and the Last Man* (New York: Free Press, 1992).

24. "Seifu, Tai-chu Kankei wo Saiken" [Government Reconsiders Relations with China], *Nikkei Shimbun*, June 11, 1989.

25. MoFA, "Japan's Official Development Assistance Charter," http://www.mofa.go.jp/policy/oda/summary/1999/ref1.html.

26. Koichi Sugiura, *Minshu-ka Enjo: 21seiki no Kokusai Kankei to Demokurashi no Kousa* [Support for Democracy: Where Twenty-First Century International Relations and Democracy Were Linked] (Tokyo: Horitsu bunka sha, 2010), 202–03; Yasutami Shimomura, "Nihon no Kaihatsu Enjo Seisaku ni Okeru 'Kainyu-do' no Hendo" [Changes in the "Levels of Intervention" in the Japanese Aid Policy], paper submitted to the Japan Association of International Affairs Annual Conference, October 14, 2016.

27. Ichihara, *Japan's International Democracy Assistance as a Soft Power*.

28. Ichiro Ozawa, *Reform Plans for Japan* [in Japanese] (Tokyo: Kodansha, 1993).

29. Bhubhindar Singh, *Japan's Security Identity: From a Peace-State to an International-State* (Abingdon, U.K.: Routledge, 2013).

30. Linus Hagström, "The 'Abnormal' State: Identity, Norm/Exception, and Japan," *European Journal of International Relations*, vol. 21 (March 2015), 122–45.

31. Yoichi Funabashi, "Japan and the New World Order," *Foreign Affairs*, vol. 70 (Winter 1991/1992), 58–74; Yuichi Hosoya, "Japan's Strategic Position: Global Civilian Power 2.0," in *Reinventing Japan: New Directions in Global Leadership*, edited by Martin Fackler and Yoichi Funabashi (Santa Barbara, Calif.: Praeger, 2018), 197–215.

32. On middle power diplomacy, see, for example, Yoshihide Soeya, *Nihon no 'Middle Power' Giko: Sengo Nihon no Sentaku to Koso* [Japan's "Middle Power" Diplomacy: The Vision and Choices of Postwar Japan], (Tokyo: Chikuma shobo, 2005).

33. Nobumasa Akiyama, "Gaiko-seisaku to Ningen no Anzenhosho. Kiro ni Tatsu Ningen no Anzenhosho" [Human Security at the Crossroad: In the Context of Japanese Diplomacy], in *Funso to Ningen no Anzenhosho: Atarasii Heiwa Kouchiku no Apurochi wo Motomete* [Conflict and Human Security: Seeking a New Approach for Peace-Building], edited by Hideaki Shinoda and Yuji Uesugi (Tokyo: Kokusai shoin, 2005), 263–64.

34. Amartya Sen, *Development as Freedom* (Oxford University Press, 1999).

35. Interview with a high-ranking MoFA official, July 19, 2018.

36. Yoshihide Soeya, "Nihon Gaiko no Tenkai to Kadai: Chugoku tono Kankei wo Chushin ni" [Prospect and Issues in Japanese Diplomacy: Centering around Relations with China], *Kokusai Mondai*, vol. 588 (January/February 2010), 5–6.

37. Interview with a special adviser to Prime Minister Abe, July 10, 2018.

38. See, for example, Soeya, "Nihon Gaiko no Tenkai to Kadai," 4–6.

39. See, for example, Tony Smith, *A Pact with the Devil: Washington's Bid for World Supremacy and the Betrayal of the American Promise* (London: Routledge, 2007).

40. Thomas Carothers, "Democracy Promotion Under Trump," Carnegie Endowment for International Peace (September 6, 2017); Frances Z. Brown and Thomas Carothers, "Is the New U.S. National Security Strategy a Step Backward on Democracy and Human Rights?" Carnegie Endowment for International Peace (January 30, 2018); Thomas Carothers and Frances Z. Brown, "Can U.S. Democracy Policy Survive Trump?" Carnegie Endowment for International Peace (October 1, 2018).

41. Barry R. Posen, "The Rise of Illiberal Hegemony: Trump's Surprising Grand Strategy," *Foreign Affairs*, vol. 97 (March/April 2018), 20–27.

42. "Full Text: Fu Ying's Speech at Chatham House in London," *China Daily*, July 8, 2016.

43. See, for example, Robert O. Keohane, *After Hegemony* (Princeton University Press, 1984), chapter 6.

44. Rosemary Foot, *Rights beyond Borders: The Global Community and the Struggle over Human Rights in China* (Oxford University Press, 2000); Andrew Nathan and Robert Ross, *The Great Wall and the Empty Fortress* (New York: W. W. Norton, 1998), 100–22.

45. See, for example, Andrew Browne, "China Uses 'Digital Leninism' to Manage Economy and Monitor Citizens," *Wall Street Journal*, October 17, 2017.

46. John Hurley, Scott Morris, and Gailyn Portelance, "Examining the Debt Implications of the Belt and Road Initiative from a Policy Perspective," http://www.cgdev.org/sites/default/files/examining-debt-implications-belt-and-road-initiative-policy-perspective.pdf.

47. Lucy Hornby, "Mahathir Mohamad Warns against 'New Colonialism' during China Visit," *Financial Times*, August 20, 2018.

48. "Vice President Mike Pence's Remarks on the Administration's Policy Toward China," http://www.hudson.org/events/1610-vice-president-mike-pence-s-remarks-on-the-administration-s-policy-towards-china102018.

49. MoFA, *Diplomatic Bluebook 2006*.

50. MoFA, "Arc of Freedom and Prosperity: Japan's Expanding Diplomatic Horizons," http://www.mofa.go.jp/announce/fm/aso/speech0611.html.

51. Yoshifumi Sugita, "Nichi-bei-go Senryaku Taiwa Koso ni Hiteiteki Kenkai" [Negative Opinion about the Japan-U.S.-Australia Strategic Dialogue Concept], *Yomiuri Shimbun*, August 10, 2007.

52. Interview with a high-ranking MoFA official, July 19, 2018.

53. Kantei, "Policy Speech by Prime Minister Shinzo Abe to the 183rd Session of the Diet," https://japan.kantei.go.jp/96_abe/statement/201301/28syosin_e.html.

54. National Security Strategy (provisional translation), http://www.cas.go.jp/jp/siryou/131217anzenhoshou/nss-e.pdf, 5.

55. Ibid, 32.

56. Ankit Panda, "US, Japan, India, and Australia Hold Working-Level Quadrilateral Meeting on Regional Cooperation," *Diplomat*, November 13, 2017.

57. For security community, see, for example, Karl W. Deutsch and others, *Political Community and the North Atlantic Area: International Organization in the Light of Historical Experience* (Princeton University Press, 1957); *Security Communities*, edited by Emanuel Adler and Michael Barnett (Cambridge University Press, 1988).

58. Interview with a high-ranking JICA official, July 25, 2018.

59. Interview with a special adviser to Prime Minister Abe, July 10, 2018.

60. MoFA, *Japan's Official Development Assistance White Paper 2012*.

61. MoFA, "Cabinet Decision on the Development Cooperation Charter," http://www.mofa.go.jp/mofaj/gaiko/oda/files/000067701.pdf, 6.

62. Interview with a high-ranking MoFA official, July 19, 2018.

63. Edward D. Mansfield and Jack Snyder, "Democratization and the Danger of War," *International Security*, vol. 20 (Summer 1995), 5–38.

64. Interview with a cabinet official, July 11, 2018.
65. Ibid.
66. Ichihara, *Japan's International Democracy Assistance as Soft Power*, chapter 3.
67. Interview with a high-ranking MoFA official, July 26, 2018.
68. Seymour Martin Lipset, "Some Social Requisites of Democracy: Economic Development and Political Legitimacy," *American Political Science Review*, vol. 53 (March 1959), 69–105. On Japanese understanding of democratization, see Ichihara, *Japan's International Democracy Assistance as Soft Power*, chapter 5.
69. Interview with a high-ranking MoFA official, July 19, 2018.
70. Kantei, "Policy Speech by Prime Minister Shinzo Abe to the 196th Session of the Diet," https://japan.kantei.go.jp/98_abe/statement/201801/_00002.html.
71. Interview with a high-ranking MoFA official, July 26, 2018.
72. MoFA, "Nicchu Kyodo Kisha Happyo ni okeru Abe-souri Hatsugen" [Prime Minister Abe's Statements at the Japan-China Joint Press Conference], http://www.mofa.go.jp/mofaj/a_o/c_m1/cn/page4_004094.html.
73. Interview with high-ranking MoFA officials, July 26, 2018.
74. "Nicchu no Daisangoku Keizai Kyoryoku ha Zeka Hika?" [Is the Third Country Cooperation of Japan and China Good or Bad?], *Sankei Shimbun*, September 20, 2018.
75. Interview with a high-ranking MoFA official, July 19, 2018.
76. MoFA, "Strategic Partnership Agreement between the European Union and Its Member States, of the One Part, and Japan, of the Other Part," http://www.mofa.go.jp/mofaj/files/000381942.pdf.
77. Michael Blaker, *Japanese International Negotiating Style* (Columbia University Press, 1977), 11–12; Michael Blaker, "Japan's Diplomatic Style," in *Japan's Foreign Policy after the Cold War: Coping with Change*, edited by Gerald L. Curtis (Armonk, N.Y., and London: M. E. Sharpe, 1993), 27.
78. Calder, "Japanese Foreign Economic Policy Formation," 517–41.
79. Interviews with high-ranking officials of MoFA and the cabinet, July 10 and 26, 2018; Masatoshi Sugiura, remarks at Cambodia Now: After the "General Election" of July 2018, held by the Cambodia Citizens Forum, Tokyo, October 13, 2018.
80. MoFA, "Japan-Cambodia Foreign Ministers' Meeting," http://www.mofa.go.jp/s_sa/sea1/kh/page3e_000895.html.
81. "Kambojia chugoku-keisha masu. 'Kyouken' yotou ga zengiseki kakutoku. Jinken towazu shien koutsugou" [Cambodia Increasingly Approaching China], *Yomiuri Shimbun*, August 18, 2018, 9.
82. MoFA, "Human Security: Records" (in Japanese), http://www.mofa.go.jp/mofaj/gaiko/oda/bunya/security/statistic.html.
83. UNDEF, "Contribution Table," http://www.un.org/democracyfund/contribution-table.
84. Steven Levitsky and Lucan A. Way, *Competitive Authoritarianism: Hybrid Regimes after the Cold War* (Cambridge University Press, 2010).
85. The World Resource Institute, Environmental Democracy Index, https://environmentaldemocracyindex.org/.
86. Zeng Aiping, "China-Africa Governance Exchanges and Experiences," in *FOCAC 2015 A New Beginning of China-Africa Relations*, edited by Garth Shelton, Funeka Yazini April, and Li Anshan (Africa Institute of South Africa, 2015), 80–106.

87. Ibid.; Legal and Judicial Information Center for China-ASEAN Countries, "China-ASEAN Legal Forum," http://www.china-aseanlawinfo.org/List/FullText?articleId=802b160b-24b8-4c4c-8707-bea9578f1d43&subjectId=002002&language=en-US.

88. Ik Wei Chong, "China Establishes International Commercial Courts to Resolve International Commercial Disputes," *Mondaq Business Briefing*, August 30, 2018.

89. Information from a Japanese lawyer, September 21, 2018.

90. Andrew J. Nathan, "China's Challenge," *Journal of Democracy*, vol. 26 (2015), 156–70.

5

Atoms for Alliance Challenges

JAPAN IN THE LIBERAL INTERNATIONAL NUCLEAR ORDER

NOBUMASA AKIYAMA

The liberal international order is now under serious challenge. Some of the most serious challenges in the international strategic environment center around nuclear weapons.

Intensified strategic competition among the United States, Russia, and China is forcing a transformation to the foundation of the power structure of the contemporary international order. The termination of the Intermediate-Range Nuclear Forces Treaty (INF Treaty) and ongoing disagreement between the United States and Russia over the agenda for negotiations for a follow-on treaty of the new Strategic Arms Reduction Treaty (START), along with the withdrawal from Anti-Ballistic Missile (ABM) Treaty in 2001, may bring into collapse the arms control regime between the United States and Russia, which has institutionally supported strategic stability between the two countries.

The rapid modernization of China's nuclear forces with sophisticated and more resilient missile capabilities and the development of antiaccess and area-denial (A2/AD) capabilities—which limit U.S. future presence by targeting U.S. and its allies' land- and sea-based military assets in the

Asia-Pacific region—would bring the U.S.-China strategic relationship into a new dangerous stage of competition. So far, the United States and China have not established any formal platform for nuclear arms control dialogue and negotiation. However, as hinted at by the Trump administration in the announcement of the withdrawal from the INF Treaty, there are rising concerns in the United States over China's nuclear buildup—and a sense of urgency for coping with it.[1]

In Ukraine and the South China Sea, Russia and China, respectively, are trying to change the existing international status quo, in part by casting their longer and longer "nuclear shadows" over their neighbors. Unrestrained behavior by major nuclear powers indicate the resurgence of nuclear weapons in shaping international politics. Along with the decline of arms control regime, such behavior may also lead strategic competitions among major powers into a "rule-less" arms race competition and increase the risk of actual use of nuclear weapons.

Outside of major world powers, the nuclear proliferation cases of North Korea and Iran overshadow the successes of the nuclear nonproliferation regimes. North Korea's nuclear program has been a major source of threat and instability for Asia and the entire international community. A series of moves in 2018 seemed to open a window of opportunity to solve this long-outstanding problem, yet doubts are strong whether this process will lead to the complete, verifiable, and irreversible denuclearization of North Korea. Meanwhile, the failure of the negotiations may cause another stalemate in the process, which would prolong the possession of nuclear weapons by North Korea. It would decrease the prospect for nuclear threat reduction and could deteriorate the security environment in East Asia, which would affect strategic calculations of regional players, including China and Japan.

If North Korea's nuclear problem is not properly solved, it also undermines the credibility of the global nuclear nonproliferation regime. A proper solution should not give unbalanced "rewards" to North Korea in return for an unproven nonproliferation commitment it once made. Excessively favorable conditions (both in economic and security aspects) for denuclearization may eventually encourage other potential nuclear aspirants.

U.S. withdrawal from the Joint Comprehensive Plan of Action (JCPOA) for Iran's nuclear problem and sanction snapbacks have a great implication for the rule-based nuclear nonproliferation regime. It is certainly true that Iranian behaviors, such as threatening its neighbors with missiles, supporting nonstate actors, and intervening in other states, are destabilizing factors for regional security, and it is in the interest of America as well as the international community to reduce such threats. However, actions by the United States as unilateral as withdrawing from JCPOA without any clear Iranian violation of its commitments in the agreement, and no proper consultations with other parties to the agreement, weakens the habit of and trust in rule-based and dialogue-based solutions of international disputes, which reinforce the resilience of the international nonproliferation regime.

These challenges raise concerns regarding the sustainability of the liberal international order: first, how will the resurgence of rivalries among great nuclear powers, coupled with setbacks to the arms control regime and much less self-restraint on the part of great powers, affect the current power alignment and relatively stable relationships among major powers, which have backstopped the liberal international order? The second question is, how could resolutions and evolutions of ongoing nuclear proliferation problems, namely North Korea and Iran, affect the credibility of nonproliferation norms, diplomatic approaches to solutions, and U.S. leadership, all of which are offered through the current nuclear nonproliferation regime and liberal international order?

Along with the crises mentioned above, the Fukushima nuclear disaster placed Japan into an even more awkward position and poses difficult questions, the answers to which are yet to be found. Japan has been a (self-claimed) model student of the multilateral nuclear nonproliferation regime and has fully enjoyed the right to peaceful use of nuclear technology. It also is highly cooperative with the International Atomic Energy Agency (IAEA) in implementing safeguards at the highest level and receiving thorough inspections at nuclear facilities. Furthermore, Japan's security has benefited from the nuclear nonproliferation regime and, consequently, it has made commitments to uphold it. However, Japan is now losing its leverage and legitimacy as a "model" of the global nuclear nonproliferation regime. After the Fukushima nuclear accident, the Japanese civilian nuclear power sector has been struggling to come back, as it has to meet new safety guidelines as well as regain public confidence. The suspension of Japan's civilian nuclear program, while retaining its nuclear fuel cycle policy, has put Japan in a difficult position, having accumulated a plutonium stockpile of approximately forty-seven tons.

Another challenge in global nuclear governance is the deep divide of the international community over nuclear disarmament. The rise of humanitarian concerns over nuclear weapons has created a global trend toward banning nuclear weapons, completely incongruous with the reemerging role of nuclear weapons in major power politics. The Treaty on the Prohibition of Nuclear Weapons (TPNW)—which Japan decided not to sign—was adopted by the approval of 122 states at the United Nations (UN) in 2017. It marked a historic moment for the movement toward legally banning any activities related to nuclear weapons.

This process was led by International Campaign to Abolish Nuclear Weapons (ICAN), an international civil society network and the 2017 Nobel Peace Prize laureate, and a group of states who emphasize the catastrophic humanitarian consequences resulting from the use of nuclear weapons. This approach is supported by many states, but it is unlikely to gain universal support—or it may even be impossible—since there are states whose security relies on nuclear weapons, or states under threat from nuclear weapons, that criticize this approach for not taking into account the reality of their security environment. This divide is particularly critical for Japan. On the one hand, its security relies on U.S. extended nuclear deterrence, and on the other hand, it is destined to promote nuclear disarmament as a national manifesto, given its experiences of humanitarian catastrophe in the two nuclear devastations in Hiroshima and Nagasaki.

Japan, which has been a beneficiary of the liberal international order and would be seriously affected by the deterioration of the global nuclear governance, must commit to and take possible actions for upholding the global nuclear governance based on rules and U.S. superiority. As these crises force Japan to rethink its strategic calculations, what should and can Japan do, including regarding its own nuclear policy, in order for global nuclear governance to remain favorable to Japan's strategic interests? This paper will discuss Japan's responses to the crises and its possible role in upholding the liberal international order from the perspective of global nuclear governance, the sustainability of which will greatly contribute to a better international environment and Japan's national interest.

The Relationship between the Liberal International Order and Nuclear Weapons

The relationship between the liberal international order and nuclear weapons bears careful scrutiny. There are two ways that nuclear weapons affect the shaping of the liberal international order. First, the distribution of nuclear weapons has been one of the determinants of the power structure of contemporary international politics. Power distribution, which is the foundation of U.S. superiority, underpins the formation and maintenance of the international order of a liberal nature.

Second, the global nuclear nonproliferation regime has contributed to the establishment and consolidation of the U.S.-led liberal international order. By controlling the spread of nuclear weapons, it fixes the distribution of power and provides a foundation for major nuclear countries to maintain superior political power. The global nuclear nonproliferation regime also features characteristics of the rule-based liberal international order. Although the nuclear nonproliferation regime is a universal, inclusive institution that does not distinguish liberal, democratic states from others in membership, its norms and rules induce rule-based (democratic) behavior by states. Further, major powers and even states outside the regime are also shaped to behave in a self-restrained manner in accordance with norms of the regime.

U.S.-provided incentives that motivate non-nuclear weapon states, mainly allies and partners of the United States, help to keep their commitment to the existing nonproliferation agreements. This U.S. incentive program consists of a security incentive of offering extended nuclear deterrence and a civil nuclear cooperation benefit, for commitment to the rule-based nuclear nonproliferation regime. It can be described as "atoms for alliance."

NUCLEAR WEAPONS AND POWER DISTRIBUTION IN INTERNATIONAL POLITICS

Nuclear weapons are "revolutionary" in their implications for international relations.[2] Facing the devastating impact of the use of nuclear weapons, they raise greatly, perhaps prohibitively, the cost of war between major nuclear powers. The power of nuclear weapons casts some doubts on the role of international liberalism in shaping the world order and the nature of U.S. hegemony in it, highlighting the geopolitical elements of international politics.

Daniel Deudney, an American political scientist, argues, "The fact that nuclear weapons are so widely thought to have importantly shaped world politics over the nearly seven decades of their existence poses the possibility that many of the effects widely attributed to hegemony or to the liberal aspects of American hegemony may, in fact, be the result of nuclear weapons or nuclear weapons deterrence rather than hegemony."[3] Harvard professor Graham Allison takes a view that at least the first forty-five years out of the seven decades of postwar "long peace" were the byproduct of dangerous nuclear confrontation between the Soviet Union and the United States, under American liberal leadership but without clear design.[4]

Despite such realist geopolitical views on the role of nuclear weapons that de-emphasize the role of multilateral institutions and political leadership of the United States in the international order, the power structure of international politics through the distribution of nuclear weapons has been consolidated and managed by the multilateral nuclear nonproliferation regime and the U.S.-Soviet (Russia) arms control regime. Commentators like Deudney and Allison underestimate the role that those institutions have played in the maintenance of the international order spearheaded by the United States.

The nuclear relationship between the United States and the Soviet Union, and later Russia, is often characterized by "mutual assured destruction" (MAD), a strategically interlocking state forcing two powers to act with self-restraint. MAD is "institutionalized" by and managed through the bilateral comprehensive arms control regime and provides strategic stability.

Strategic stability has been supported by various arms control agreements, which set the arena for strategic competition between the United States and the Soviet Union. The ABM Treaty limited the sphere of strategic competition mainly within offensive domain. They later controlled the size of their arsenals at strategic nuclear (START and its follow-on treaties), regional nuclear (INF Treaty), and conventional (Treaty on Conventional Forces in Europe [CFE]) levels and relied on verification and inspection mechanisms under "trust but verify" principles in order to minimize the risk of cheating. Strategic stability, which has been maintained under the regime, in fact, was and is a balance of power in pro forma standard. It shaped the modality of strategic competition and posed the constraints on Russia in ways of playing the game. It eventually constrained Russia's competitiveness and ensured the superiority of the United States as a gap in the research and development and production capabilities widened between them.

THE GLOBAL NUCLEAR NONPROLIFERATION REGIME AS A CONSTITUTIVE PART OF THE LIBERAL INTERNATIONAL ORDER

The flip side of the coin of strategic competition between the United States and the Soviet Union/Russia was a collaborative relationship, or a marriage of convenience for nuclear nonproliferation. Two confronting nuclear great powers found that containing nuclear proliferation was in their mutual interest. Indeed, they collaborated in building the nuclear nonproliferation regime through establishment of the IAEA (1957) and the Treaty on the Non-Proliferation of Nuclear Weapons (NPT, 1968) in the midst of intensifying arms races during the Cold War.

The NPT sets the rights and obligations for the signatories of the NPT, regarding nuclear disarmament, nonproliferation of nuclear weapons, and peaceful use of nuclear technology. The safeguards mechanism of the IAEA ensures the compliance of the nonproliferation obligations under the NPT. The universally shared norm of nonproliferation, which no one—at least officially—challenges, provides the foundation for individual policies or policy frameworks by groups of like-minded countries. In principle, the rule-based regime also sets the rules of the game of dealing with nonproliferation, as seen even in the most critical noncompliance cases of North Korea and Iran.

The nuclear nonproliferation regime provides a sound normative basis for the U.S. leadership to be effective by preventing the world's multipolarization, as it limits, with authority and legitimacy, others' quest for power through acquisition of nuclear weapons.

Some features of the global nuclear nonproliferation regime share characteristics with the liberal international order. First, the nuclear nonproliferation regime provides a foundation for rule-based relationships among states. Compliance by non-nuclear member states with the treaty's nonproliferation obligation is ensured by the safeguards and verification of the IAEA. In cases of noncompliance, the IAEA tries to solve the problem according to a standard procedure set in its statute. Serious noncompliance cases will be brought to the UN Security Council, which discusses measures to bring noncompliant states back in compliance by imposing sanctions. In the meantime, solutions are sought through negotiations at ad hoc groups of stakeholders, such as the six-party talks for North Korea's nuclear problem and E3+3 for Iran's nuclear problem.

Second, the fact that, with the adherence by 191 member states, the NPT is nearly universal demonstrates the openness of the regime. The very fact that there are globally only nine nuclear-armed states—the United States, Russia, the United Kingdom, France, and China under NPT; India, Pakistan, North Korea, and Israel outside of NPT—demonstrates that the norm of nuclear nonproliferation set out by the global nuclear nonproliferation regime has been well accepted by the vast majority of the international society, despite the discriminatory nature of the NPT, which legally distinguishes nuclear status. The nuclear nonproliferation regime has contributed to the maintenance of a relatively stable distribution of power in international politics.[5]

Meanwhile, Ikenberry argues that as more actors participate in and benefit from the order, disrupting or changing the order becomes more costly.[6] As membership grows, the order (or regime) loses flexibility in adapting to new strategic environments and coping with new challenges. While the global nuclear nonproliferation regime has gained universality in its membership, it faces the dilemma of losing effectiveness in decision-making because of its high level of participatory multilateralism. For that reason, supplementary subregimes for enforcement and problem-solving mechanisms outside of the formal regime become necessary.

Third, the history of the establishment of such supplementary subregimes for the nuclear nonproliferation regime shows that strong U.S. leadership has played an essential role in making the global nuclear nonproliferation regime more functional. The very initial concept of the regime stems from President Dwight D. Eisenhower's 1953 "Atoms for Peace" speech, which advocated the idea of sharing the peaceful use of nuclear technology while containing the proliferation of nuclear weapons and minimizing the risk of nuclear catastrophe.[7] Further, the United States took the lead in establishing various policy instruments, such as export control regimes and other relevant international frameworks for monitoring and regulating the transfer of nuclear-related sensitive technology and materials, which supplement the IAEA and the NPT. They include Nuclear Suppliers Group (NSG), the Wassenaar Arrangement (WA), and Proliferation Security Initiative (PSI). They are groups of like-minded countries that regulate the supply-side of technology transfer without enforcement mechanisms. PSI and UNSCR 1540 are mechanisms to prevent clandestine nuclear transfers, mostly undertaken in the nuclear black market.

In the second nuclear age, after the end of the Cold War, following the collapse of the Soviet Union in 1989, the end of bipolar world politics increased states' incentives to acquire nuclear weapons to ensure their security without guarantees from two superpowers, as their commitment to security diminished in some regions, such as South Asia and the Middle East. The risk of nuclear proliferation increased as a result of the emergence of so-called nuclear tipping points, which could cause proliferation to cascade.[8]

According to Benjamin Frankel, "Bipolarity inhibits the spread of nuclear weapons while multipolarity induces their proliferation." Frankel predicted that in the post–Cold War era, "nuclear arms proliferation will likely intensify," and "the owners of these weapons will likely brandish them more openly to advance their political objectives." He warned that their "inherent complexity . . . dooms multipolar systems to instability, making them susceptible to crisis and war." Thus, the "end of bipolarity means that superpower guarantees—the most effective instrument to moderate the effects of systemic characteristics—will be reduced and weakened."[9]

After the end of the Cold War, while the threat of a large-scale nuclear war has faded with the collapse of the Soviet Union, nuclear proliferation by so-called rogue states—such as Iraq, North Korea, and Iran—have become the most serious proliferation risk and threat to the international community. In addition, the 9/11 terrorist attacks in 2001 raised awareness of the threat of nonstate actors, such as terrorist organizations, involved in the proliferation and use of weapons of mass destruction. There is concern that these actors behave with logic different from the conventional patterns associated with national security, and conventional nuclear deterrence may not work against them.

The United States took the initiative in establishing new nonproliferation policy tools, such as UN Security Council Resolution (UNSCR)

1540, the Proliferation Security Initiative (PSI), G8 Global Partnership, and others, in order to cope with these new proliferation challenges. These policy frameworks were established based on U.S.-led multilateral coordination. In order to make these initiatives effective in ensuring compliance with rules and norms of the nonproliferation regime, they emphasize verification and enforcement, with which these initiatives can be characterized as "effective multilateralism."[10] An "effective multilateralism" approach, unlike conventional norms oriented by principles of universality and formality, brings together a coalition of the willing, whose policies resonate with one another, sacrificing universality at least in the short term and prioritizing effective implementation. Even though they seek broader participation, the most responsive partners of the U.S. initiatives have been liberal democratic states in Europe and Asia. These subregimes have also contributed to fixing the supply and hence distribution of nuclear weapons—principal sources of their power in world politics.

Particularly, the success of the global nuclear nonproliferation regime can also be highlighted with the non-nuclear choices by Japan and Germany, who were the main proliferation concerns in the 1960s and 1970s because of their industrial and financial capabilities, as well as given their strategic environments with nuclear-armed neighbors. Had they chosen nuclear options, they could have constituted major challenges to the liberal international order and U.S. leadership in it.

The fixed distribution of power, achieved by constraining nuclear proliferation primarily by the means of preventing relatively large liberal democracies from acquiring nuclear weapons, had an important role in making the liberal international order function. What made such a rule-based nonproliferation regime sustainable were the incentives and disincentives provided by the United States.

ATOMS FOR ALLIANCE

A critical missing piece of the existing nonproliferation regime is a mechanism to address national security concerns of states. A national security concern is an important driving motive for states to choose nuclear armament. In particular, if there are nuclear-armed regional rivals, states tend to seek nuclear deterrence. When the enforcement mechanism within the regime is not effective and strong enough to dissuade states from violating the regime rules, and the political and security impact of nuclear weapons is too big for many states to follow the norms of the regime spontaneously, compliance must largely rely on additional incentive and disincentives. If, as Ikenberry describes, "the liberal order was a sort of full-service security community, reinforcing the capacity of Western liberal democracies to pursue policies of economic and social advancement and stability,"[11] such full-service in the context of the global nuclear governance is provided by the United States in the manner of a comprehensive package of incentives for inducing compliance with and disincentives for preventing breakout from nonproliferation commitments under the regime.

The incentive package for allies and partners of the United States to induce compliance can be described as "atoms for alliance," which includes both security assurance (extended nuclear deterrence) and the offer of cooperation in exchange for the peaceful use of nuclear technology and a nonproliferation commitment in accordance with the United States's nonproliferation strategy. Japan and West Germany, during the Cold War, can be identified as good success examples of the nuclear nonproliferation regime's "atoms for alliance" package, which composes the following: (1) cooperation in peaceful nuclear use by providing technology and material as an incentive for recipient states to commit to nonproliferation obligations and norms; (2) stringent nonproliferation measures, including safeguards requirements added on top of IAEA safeguards, as a condition for nuclear cooperation; and, most important, (3) the provision of security assurances, including extended nuclear deterrence.

The first and second elements are set through bilateral nuclear cooperation agreements (or "123 Agreements"). While the United States as a supplier state provides nuclear technology and material for peaceful purposes to recipient states, it monitors recipient states' activities and checks against the conversion of provided materials and equipment for military use. The United States retains the right of withdrawing cooperation and technology in case of violations of rules set by the multilateral and bilateral agreements regarding peaceful use and nuclear cooperation. The third element is provided through bilateral alliance mechanisms for Asian allies and through NATO for European allies. The provision of security assurance to deter nuclear attack (or extended nuclear deterrence) is the most distinctive element of the "atoms for alliance" package. It addresses national security concerns of partner states and lessens their motivation for going nuclear.

Challenges to the Liberal International Nonproliferation Order

Global nuclear governance has brought benefits of long-term maintenance of power distribution at the international system level and suppression of a possible power shift at the system level. It contributed to stability and predictability in the international order and established the platform for U.S. liberal hegemony. At the regional level as well, the United States's commitment to regional security has inhibited nuclear proliferation in Europe and East Asia. On the other hand, in South Asia, where U.S. influence was limited and its strategic involvement was inadequate, nuclear competition among regional rivals arose.

However, global nuclear governance has been continuously challenged by proliferation crises. Two of the most critical nuclear proliferation challenges that the current liberal international order faces are nuclear developments in North Korea and Iran. Both cases present the challenging nature of proliferation problems, showing that the global nonproliferation regime alone cannot provide solutions, and these problems are deeply embedded in regional security dynamics, which the global nuclear nonproliferation is not designed to deal with.

What is common to the cases of North Korea and Iran is that the motives to pursue nuclear weapons—such as gaining advantage in the regional security order, deterrence against political pressure from the international community, especially from the United States, and the threat of forced regime change—are factors that cannot be dealt with within the framework of the nuclear nonproliferation regime. The sanction and incentive mechanisms that the global regime is equipped with are not effective enough for these violating states to return to compliance.

REGIONAL SECURITY-NONPROLIFERATION NEXUS IN IRAN'S CASE

Iran's case poses the most tangible potential risk of a cascade of nuclear proliferation in the region, due to a more complex and war-torn regional security environment. With Iran playing a role in a number of conflict flashpoints in the Middle East, the regional security order is rather fluid and unstable. Furthermore, Israel, which is the most serious security threat for Iran, is believed to have a nuclear arsenal.

The JCPOA was negotiated between Iran and EU3+3 (France, Germany, and the United Kingdom plus the United States, Russia, and China). No immediate regional security stakeholder who needed to be reassured was officially involved. The JCPOA has succeeded in containing the risks of nuclear proliferation in Iran at least for the time being (and so far Iran remains committed to the agreement except for a few minor breaches even after the United States's unilateral declaration of withdrawal from the agreement).[12] But it failed to provide assurance to regional stakeholders, including Saudi Arabia and Israel, both of which see Iran as their greatest strategic rival and security threat in the region. The JCPOA does not address their security concerns, including Iran's involvement in regional conflicts and missile capabilities. President Trump mentions that one of the reasons for the withdrawal is "to counter the totality of the regime's malign activities" in various places in the Middle East.[13]

U.S. withdrawal from the JCPOA and sanction snapbacks for reasons other than noncompliance with the agreement have great implications for the rule-based nuclear nonproliferation regime. U.S. unilateral withdrawal from the agreement also diminishes the credibility of U.S. leadership vis-à-vis allies and partners rather than restores leadership and provides solutions. Such unilateral action by the United States to withdraw from JCPOA without any clear violation by Iran of any commitments in the agreement, and no proper consultations with other parties to the agreement, weakens the habit and trust of rule-based and dialogue-based solution of international disputes, which reinforce the resilience of the international nonproliferation regime. Instead, U.S. unilateral snapback sanctions and pressure on Europe, Japan, India, and other partners to discontinue their business with Iran may strengthen the influence of Russia and China in the Middle East. It may further accelerate the rebalancing in the Middle East, allowing the rise of Russian and Chinese influence in the region. It could eventually lead to the realization of global rebalancing, which is already underway.

REGIONAL STRATEGIC IMPLICATION OF NORTH KOREA'S DENUCLEARIZATION PROCESS

In contrast, the Six-Party Talks included all major regional stakeholders of security dynamics in the Northeast Asia region—China, Japan, North Korea, Russia, South Korea, and the United States—and it attempted to act as a forum for addressing both North Korea's nuclear issues and regional security concerns, linking regional security dynamics with the global nuclear nonproliferation regime.

However, it did not work. There were divergent views, including on the imminence of North Korea having a nuclear deterrent, and differing policy priorities among stakeholders regarding how North Korean threats should be dealt with. North Korea was also not convinced of U.S. commitment of the guarantee of regime security and thus retained its nuclear weapons program. Following a missile launch to which the UN Security Council responded with the threat of sanctions, North Korea withdrew from the Six-Party Talks in 2009, and the talks have since then been discontinued.

The long stalemate of negotiation on North Korea's nuclear problem was broken by the inter-Korean summit by President Moon Jae-in of South Korea and Supreme Leader Kim Jong-un of North Korea, which was held in April 2018. At the meeting, the Panmunjom Declaration for Peace, Prosperity, and Unification of the Korean Peninsula was agreed upon and signed by the two leaders. It was followed by the U.S.-North Korea summit meeting held in Singapore on June 12, 2018, where the president of the United States and the leader of North Korea met for the first time and signed a joint statement.

Given that some of North Korea's top priorities have been to establish a direct dialogue with the United States and to receive a credible guarantee of security and regime survival, for Kim, directly engaging the president of the United States at the summit meeting in Singapore was a great achievement. The joint statement signed by President Trump and Supreme Leader Kim covered some principles for improving the bilateral relationship between the United States and North Korea, and building a lasting and stable peace regime on the Korean Peninsula, with the formal end of the Korean War possibly on the agenda if a further summit is held. It also mentions how "reaffirming the April 27, 2018, Panmunjom Declaration, the DPRK commits to work toward complete denuclearization of the Korean Peninsula."[14] President Trump, in his press conference after the summit meeting, added that the United States would "stop" a joint military exercise with South Korea and indicated possible withdrawal of U.S. troops from South Korea in the future.

However, this process of negotiation between the United States and North Korea did not produce an agreement on the details of a roadmap for "denuclearization." It is also unclear whether North Korea had fully committed to the denuclearization of North Korea (and not the Korean Peninsula) in the sense of eliminating nuclear weapons stockpiles and weaponization capabilities as well as delivery capabilities.

Views on prospects for the denuclearization process after the Singapore summit were divided. In Japan, skeptical views on North Korea's intention to denuclearize prevailed, and the government of Japan sought clearer commitments while insisting on maintaining maximum pressure with stringent sanctions.[15] In the current nuclear forces of North Korea, medium-range missiles that are capable of delivering nuclear warheads pose credible threats to Japan. If the DPRK denuclearization process does not progress or continues in an incomplete state, North Korea's nuclear threat to Japan will thus remain unchanged. If the United States compromises in this regard—for example, only demanding that long-range intercontinental ballistic missiles (ICBMs) are no longer developed—leaving uncertainties in North Korea's nuclear and missile capabilities, then the implication would be that Japan needs to coexist with the missile threat from North Korea and it would leave a gap between the severity of threat posed by North Korea to Japan and to the United States. If the United States compromises in its demand for denuclearization and chooses to coexist with a nuclear North Korea, the absence of extensive dialogue on how the regional security environment should be shaped and how reassurance is provided would pose questions about the effectiveness and credibility of nuclear deterrence in the alliance.

The most realistic scenario, at least for the time being, is for China to keep North Korea as a buffer zone to avoid direct confrontation with the United States on land. If North Korea's nuclear weapons serve this objective—or, in other words, if North Korea's nuclear weapons can guarantee regime survival—China has a good reason not to put significant support behind the denuclearization of North Korea. If nuclear weapons would contribute to the greater autonomy of North Korea and its departure from China's security interests, China would prefer to move forward with the denuclearization of North Korea.

If denuclearization genuinely happens in North Korea as a result of the U.S.-DPRK negotiations, it would reveal that the real concern in the U.S.-Japan alliance is China's modernized nuclear forces and air and sea power superiorities in the region. In this case, the furthering of U.S.-China strategic stability dialogues will also become important, and the role of the United States vis-à-vis its allies will become even more crucial. The formula of give and take—that is, the deal between security assurance to North Korea and North Korea's concrete actions that contribute to nuclear threat reduction—must be carefully considered to prevent undermining the credibility of U.S. commitment to extended deterrence in Asia. The United States must also take into consideration the signals it sends to China on how it seeks to shape the East Asian security environment. Give-and-take would send a clear signal to North Korea that although the United States and its allies are flexibly engaged in the denuclearization process, the final goal of nuclear threat reduction or denuclearization would never be abandoned, and its civilian nuclear programs (if they remain) must be put under appropriate, multilaterally acceptable safeguards and verification measures.

In due course, close trilateral coordination between the United States, Japan, and South Korea will be vital to avoid the gap of threat perceptions among the three countries and a split in their strategic vision of East Asia, the difficulties of achieving which are discussed in chapter 8 in this volume.

Both cases of Iran and North Korea combined indicate that nonproliferation problems cannot be resolved and a deal cannot be sustainable if security concerns of relevant stakeholders are not properly addressed. As the global regime is not designed to address such specific security concerns, solutions for noncompliance cases would be better sought through ad hoc consultative bodies, such as the Six-Party Talks, despite the same difficulties that these bodies would face in reaching and keeping the deals once agreed upon.

WIDENING GAP OVER NUCLEAR DISARMAMENT

In the past several years, strategic confrontation between the United States and Russia has been deepening, and the two countries have disagreements over the issues to be dealt with in the succession agreement of the new START Treaty (scheduled to expire in 2021). As the strategic environment deteriorates, nuclear weapon states put much less importance on nuclear disarmament. At the Second Preparatory Committee of the 2020 NPT Review Conference Investigation Committee, which was held from the end of April to the beginning of May 2018, the United States, which underpins nuclear disarmament for the improvement of the security environment, submitted a working paper titled "Creating Conditions for Nuclear Disarmament (CCND)."[16] This working paper demonstrated the harsh position of the Trump administration that nuclear disarmament cannot be advanced unless the conditions stated in the working paper are fulfilled. Nuclear weapon states other than the United States show growing reluctance in supporting nuclear disarmament. It seems that momentum for nuclear disarmament has become lost among nuclear weapon states.

Contrary to that, new momentum for the enthusiastic promotion of nuclear disarmament has risen from a different source, which emphasizes the humanitarian catastrophic consequences resulting from the use of nuclear weapons and calls for a legal ban. The humanitarian approach to nuclear disarmament is trying to establish a norm to prohibit nuclear weapons through consolidating norms on nonuse of nuclear weapons, appealing to the moral imperative to prevent catastrophic human, environmental, and social consequences of nuclear weapons. Driven by the strong imperative of the humanitarian approach, the TPNW was adopted at the UN in 2017. Frustrated with the stagnation in nuclear disarmament and the lack of commitment by nuclear weapon states, non-nuclear weapon states—in particular, unallied countries—and civil society have been advocating nuclear disarmament through strongly appealing to the inhumanity of nuclear weapons, ultimately leading to the processes of creating the TPNW. ICAN, a global network of nonprofits, was awarded the Nobel Peace Prize for a great contribution in gaining support from global civil society toward this effort.

Unallied states that are enthusiastic about nuclear disarmament criticize nuclear weapon states that show a reluctance to work toward nuclear disarmament by attaching security conditions to nuclear disarmament, indicating, in effect, that they are not willing to engage in nuclear disarmament. These unallied states add that nuclear disarmament is essentially a legal obligation under Article 6 of the NPT and there should be no security condition attached to such an obligation.

According to a report released in April 2018 by the Group of Eminent Persons for the Substantive Advancement of Nuclear Disarmament, sponsored by the Ministry of Foreign Affairs of Japan, "This divide has deepened and become so stark that groups with different thoughts have been unable to engage meaningfully with each other on key issues." Therefore, it is necessary to build a "bridge" between two groups and restore civility in the discussions on nuclear disarmament.[17]

Non–nuclear weapon states that are in alliance with the United States and whose security depends on U.S. extended nuclear deterrence are put in a difficult position between the two camps. In particular, Japan greatly struggles to reconcile two diverging thoughts and trends on nuclear disarmament. While that country, surrounded by nuclear-armed states such as North Korea, China, and Russia, sees that security conditions must be considered in nuclear disarmament, it also holds close the legacy of Hiroshima and Nagasaki and thus is destined to advocate nuclear disarmament.

Further, because it is a leading country in the peaceful use of nuclear technology, preserving the cohesiveness and effectiveness of the NPT is an important policy objective for Japan. The nonproliferation regime ensures the legitimacy of Japan's nuclear energy program with the full nuclear fuel cycle. But the deep divide over nuclear disarmament may lead frustrated TPNW-supporting states to disengage or possibly dissociate from the NPT.

Japan, as well as other states caught in the midst of this divide, are moving toward "bridge-building" to search for common ground. However, such efforts will not be able to lead to a quick-fix resolution, although such efforts will be necessary to uphold the nonproliferation regime under the NPT.

POWER SHIFT IN NUCLEAR MARKET

In global nuclear governance, technological capabilities and the market as a channel for technology diffusion also matter. Capacity to supply technology and material and to shape the market is a source of greater power in the politics than shaping the norms and rules. In that respect, it also should be noted that the market structure—in particular, competitiveness of supplier states—is another element that affects the effectiveness of the nuclear nonproliferation architecture. The retreat of the United States and Japan in the nuclear market can also be seen as a potential factor in bringing about structural change in the liberal international order.

Historically, in the course of the development of the regime, the U.S. dominance in the world nuclear market (except the Eastern Bloc market, where the Soviet Union dominated) helped the United States take the lead in developing the nuclear nonproliferation architecture. The original concerns of the United States and the Soviet Union in nuclear proliferation, which drove them to collaborate in developing the international nuclear nonproliferation institutions such as IAEA and NPT, were the potential risks of industrialized countries, including West Germany and Japan, pursuing nuclear armaments. They had technical competence and other resources, which were necessary to develop and operate nuclear programs.

The international nuclear market structure has shifted from U.S. dominance, held up until the 1970s, to multisupplier. There has been a decline in U.S. competitiveness with the rise of other suppliers, including Western Europe and Russia, which, in turn, meant a decline in U.S. leverage in shaping other states' behavior in the nuclear domain. And that is why the multilateral nonproliferation regime required cooperation among states and strategic restraints by the United States to establish an order based on rules and norms by ensuring spontaneous compliance with such rules and norms.

Such structural changes did not appear critical before the Fukushima nuclear accident. Driven by growth in developing economies and rising needs for addressing global warming issues, demand for nuclear energy was increasing, and international nuclear industry was about to flourish. This trend was called "nuclear renaissance." However, the Fukushima nuclear accident sounded a very serious alarm about safety concerns of nuclear power. Some countries—including existing nuclear energy countries, such as Germany, and potential nuclear energy aspirants—reviewed their energy policy and reversed it to forgo nuclear energy. The higher safety requirement also raised the cost of building nuclear power plants, and the international nuclear business stagnated.

Meanwhile, Russia and China have been increasing their shares in the international nuclear market, with nearly two-thirds of new reactors under construction worldwide estimated to be using their designs.[18] They have state-enterprise business models and enjoy an advantage (through financing and deal packages and other concessional conditions) in the international nuclear market. The rise of Russia and China in the international nuclear market sharply undermines the competitiveness of U.S., Japanese, and Korean companies. But the implications go beyond business. The lack of competitiveness in nuclear cooperation means that the United States and its partners are losing leverage in enforcing rules or cooperation in nuclear nonproliferation activities.

123 Agreements were a very effective tool for the United States to bring partner states into U.S.-led nonproliferation policy frameworks and to pressure them to accept nonproliferation commitments such as forgoing nuclear fuel cycle activities in exchange for receiving the assurance of fuel supply (the so-called gold standard of the 123 Agreements). They have different approaches to nuclear nonproliferation than the United States and its partners. For emerging nuclear power countries, Russia and China offer different models for developing a nuclear program with much less emphasis on nuclear nonproliferation and security obligations. In addition, as a result of the increased number of supplier-states and subsequent expansion of the membership of NSG, it has become more difficult for the NSG to make decisions by consensus. This is indicative of how diminishing U.S. power in the market leads to a decline of power over setting rules and enforcing compliance.

Japan as a Role Model for Global Nuclear Governance?

Maintaining and upholding a global nuclear governance stemming from the idea of liberal internationalism would serve Japan's security interests. In this context, engaging great powers—including the United States, Russia, and China—in their arms control dialogues and putting their strategic competition into a certain framework of arms control would be beneficial. An ability to keep the credibility of the global nuclear nonproliferation regime and manage threats from actual proliferation cases is directly linked to threat reduction for Japan. It is clear that Japan should have a vision of how best to contribute to achieving the objective of upholding the global nuclear governance, which would help ensure an international environment beneficial to Japan's pursuit of its national security and economic interests.

In the meantime, as a country that has the largest civil nuclear program with fuel cycle programs, or "latent nuclear capability," Japan also needs to address proliferation concerns that may arise from its nuclear policy.

CRITICAL CONSIDERATIONS FOR JAPAN'S NON-NUCLEAR CHOICE

With regard to the question of how plausible nuclear armament will be for Japan, there are several aspects to be considered: technical competency for breakout capability or latent nuclear weapon capability (most important, capability of producing weapon-usable fissionable materials and a space program); security drivers in the context of regional security dynamics; political and security cost-benefit analyses; availability of alternative measures for enhancing security, including credible extended nuclear deterrence provided by the United States; the risk of drastic changes to the international economic and political environment triggered by Japan's decision to pursue nuclear armament; and domestic political and social factors, including the policy preference among political leaders and public opinion.

Wohlstetter and others argue that if non–nuclear weapon states can have and use nuclear weapons in a short period of time, and the breakout time is extremely short, it has the same deterrent effect as actually holding nuclear weapons.[19] Before the Fukushima nuclear accident in 2011, Japan operated fifty-four nuclear power plants and pursued a full-scale commercial nuclear fuel cycle, including enrichment, reprocessing, and fast reactor programs, which are not yet officially abandoned. Some in the international community believe that combined with a sophisticated space program and other cutting-edge technologies, this gives Japan breakout capabilities. In this respect, Japan has very strong latency.

Apart from technical capability, Japan's political and policy commitment to nuclear nonproliferation has been very affirmative. Although there have been some voices calling for Japan to opt for nuclear armament, they have failed to gain support either from the public or the policy community. As history has shown, this commitment has remained resilient to Japan's changing external strategic environment.

There were several moments and periods in postwar history when the strategic environment surrounding Japan seriously deteriorated and prompted some interest in nuclear armament. First was the success of China's first nuclear test in 1964, a critical game changer in the East Asia strategic environment. Another was the drastic shift by President Nixon in U.S. policy toward Asia, otherwise known as the Guam Doctrine, in 1970, combined with U.S. rapprochement with China. It suggested the retreat of U.S. military presence and responsibility in Asia and could have been seen as diminishing the credibility of U.S. commitment to the defense of Japan. Despite such drastic changes in the security environment in East Asia, Japan remained against going nuclear. In 1968, Prime Minister Eisaku Sato declared the basic outline of Japan's nuclear policy, which has been long embodied in the so-called four nuclear principles. It included: (1) three non-nuclear principles, namely, the Diet's 1971 resolution not to possess, produce, or allow the introduction of nuclear weapons; (2) reliance on the extended nuclear deterrence of the United States; (3) the peaceful use of nuclear power; and (4) nuclear disarmament. This basic nuclear policy combined a reflection of strong public antipathy to nuclear weapons with the reality of the security environment surrounding Japan and its economic needs at that time, backed by the U.S.-Japan alliance. Japan chose to strengthen the alliance with the United States to address its security concerns rather than to seek independent military capability.

Another moment of significant change in the strategic environment for Japan was North Korea's successful intermediate-range missile test, which flew over Japan in 1998. It was a demonstration by North Korea of its capability to directly attack any point in Japan. Even after North Korea conducted six nuclear tests between 2006 and 2017, the overwhelming majority of Japan's public and security community did not choose to advocate for its own nuclear deterrent. The options Japan took were the strengthening of missile defense capability, UN Security Council sanctions, and making the policy consultation and coordination mechanism with the United States more robust, which was expected to reaffirm political commitments of both sides to the alliance.

Currently, even though North Korea's denuclearization process has not made substantial progress—a situation still far from satisfactory for Japan—it seems unlikely that whether Japan should pursue nuclear armament will be a subject of a major debate at home. So long as two conditions are met—namely, that the United States remains committed to extended deterrence and its role in Asian security and that Japan properly manages its strategic relationship with China—there would be no other major reason for Japan to go nuclear.

These conditions are actually intertwined. There may be a risk of being trapped by a stability-instability paradox if or when China establishes military superiority both in air and over sea in the South China Sea and East China Sea, in addition to antiaccess and area-denial capabilities vis-à-vis U.S. forward deployment, and either as a result of such superiority or as its cause, some may start to wonder if the United States would retreat from the region. (China's behavior in the South China Sea is similar to what is characterized as "hybrid warfare" in the context of Russian assertiveness in its neighborhood. The existence of nuclear weapons would further strengthen China's position in a scenario of hybrid warfare. See chapter 1 by Adam Liff for more details on gray zone challenges.) In this scenario, Japan's security may be perceived as deteriorating and unstable while the U.S.-China relationship may establish stability for mutual noninterference.

Indeed, a formula for a stable strategic relationship between two countries with incorporation of U.S. allies' security interests would become highly complicated, as is clear from the fact that China has pursued not the nuclear parity but an asymmetric way of nuclear deterrence vis-à-vis the United States. The strategic stability of the U.S.-China relationship should be defined differently from the strategic stability between the United States and Russia. But it does not necessarily mean that no arms control would be required to stabilize the U.S.-China strategic relationship.

As seen in the U.S. announcement of its possible withdrawal from the INF Treaty and the long stalemate of negotiation for the follow-on treaty of the new START, the arms control regime now faces serious challenge. Further, in the context of the relationship with China, there is an argument that the termination of the arms control regime between the United States and Russia is not necessarily bad, because it will lead the United States to gain freer hands to shape its strategic relationship and deal with

China. Some U.S. officials indicated that a decision to withdraw from the INF Treaty was made with this implication. Yet it is not self-evident whether strategic competition with China can dominate in the absence of arrangements to regulate the modality, size, and domains.

However, if a habit of arms control and its institutionalization are absent, the world may enter uncharted waters of strategic competition with escalating arms races, which would force regional security players in Asia to live with greater uncertainty and potential instability. It is also important to make sure that such unbound, ruleless strategic competition would not become the new normal prescribing strategic relationships among states.

U.S.-JAPAN DIVERGENCE IN FUEL CYCLE POLICY AND NONPROLIFERATION COMMITMENT OF JAPAN

With regard to compliance with nonproliferation obligations of the global regime, Japan has been identified as a role model, or *yutosei* (honor student), of the global nonproliferation regime under the "atoms for alliance" incentive structure. In other words, while Japan has a full-scale nuclear fuel cycle, a significant nuclear power program, and a sophisticated space program, which all constitute the latent nuclear capability, it accepted the full scope of IAEA safeguards and ratified the Additional Protocol (AP) to the Comprehensive Safeguards Agreement (CSA). It is always issued a "broader conclusion" by the IAEA for the implementation of CSA and AP, which is the indication that its nuclear material is for peaceful purposes, with no indication of diversion.

On top of these, the special relationship between Japan and the United States through Atoms for Alliance has played a significant role in shaping Japan's nuclear policy in the context of both civilian nuclear program and deterrence against security threats posed to Japan. Under the U.S.-Japan nuclear cooperation agreement, Japan has enjoyed U.S. cooperation in various civil nuclear activities, such as construction of nuclear power plants, and establishing advanced nuclear research activities, including nuclear fuel cycle technology. At the same time, the United States keeps on providing security assurances to Japan, including extended nuclear deterrence.

The "atoms for alliance" model had three implications, two positive and one negative. First was the political merit of demonstrating the correctness of U.S. nonproliferation policy in line with the norm structure of the multilateral regime. Second, the incentive structure of the "atoms for alliance" model was shown to help achieve the success of non-nuclear policy to states partnering with the United States. And finally, the United States had to emphasize that the "honor student" was an exception and would not make a general example of non-nuclear weapon state's nuclear activities. As the United States was tightening its nonproliferation policy, it had to manage the risk associated with its "atoms for alliance" relationship with Japan.

Since the late 1970s, the differences in perception of the nuclear fuel cycle between Japan and the United States became a source of friction. The United States ceased its national commercial fuel cycle policy, indefinitely deferring the reprocessing of spent nuclear reactor fuel, and basically stopped its international cooperation in fuel cycle, which was also reflected in its nonproliferation policy.

The Carter administration tried to stop the operation of the reprocessing plant at Tokai-mura, based on the right of advance consent stipulated by the U.S.-Japan nuclear cooperation agreement—that is to say, on the necessity of America's consent for the reprocessing of nuclear fuel originating in the United States. The intention of the United States in its policy toward Japan was to establish a new multilateral standard by changing Japan's policy. After negotiations with Japan, however, in 1977, the United States agreed to allow Japan to operate the reprocessing plant in exchange for certain concessions. The United States failed to establish a new norm that civilian reprocessing activities should not be pursued.[20]

Japan's reprocessing activities once again became a focal issue when Japan and the United States negotiated for the extension of the bilateral nuclear cooperation agreement during the 1980s, which was to expire in 1988. The central issue was whether the United States would continue to provide Japan with "advance consent arrangement" introduced in 1982, which recognized the independence and flexibility of friendly countries in their civilian nuclear activities using material and technology provided by the United States. Even within the U.S. government, there was a divide between the group that placed importance on the U.S.-Japan alliance and the group that placed importance on the principle of nuclear nonproliferation. Eventually, at a meeting attended by undersecretary-level representatives from the National Security Council (NSC), the Department of State, the Department of Energy, the Department of Defense, and the Nuclear Regulatory Commission, it was decided by a narrow margin to recognize an "advanced consent arrangement" for Japan. It is said that the biggest reason for this was because President Ronald Reagan personally made the U.S.-Japan alliance a priority.[21]

For a special security relationship with Japan and its strategic significance, managing the nuclear relationship with Japan required the United States to simultaneously meet contradicting policy goals in its nuclear nonproliferation policy. At the bilateral level, the United States showed flexibility in acknowledging Japan's plutonium policy. The United States had to make a concession to the principle of its global nonproliferation, which was to minimize the production of weapon-usable fissile materials, in particular plutonium, worldwide.

As a result, the United States had to fulfill the following requirements in its nonproliferation policy: (1) balance the maintenance of the special relationship with Japan as an ally providing security advantages with the merits of preventing Japan from having nuclear weapons and thus sustaining the nonproliferation order; (2) minimize contradiction between the tailored (privileged) approach to alliance management (that is, bilateral agreements that take into account the variances in regulations among allies) and regulations founded on universal norms of the multilateral regime; and (3) the need for compromise and cooperation toward the establishment of partnerships with other countries to ensure the effectiveness of nuclear nonproliferation amid the decline of U.S. influence and the limits of the multilateral regime.

In 1988, thirty years since the revision of the U.S.-Japan Nuclear Cooperation Agreement, the agreement was automatically extended, as neither side requested a review of the deal. Now the agreement will continue unless either side expresses its intention to terminate it. Although this situation is seen by some Japanese experts as legally unstable, it is not a likely scenario that either side will choose to withdraw, which means physically remove, all materials and equipment provided through bilateral cooperation.

However, through the process of discussing and negotiating the automatic extension of the agreement, it has become clear that the daunting task for Japan to lower the international community's proliferation concerns is to minimize its plutonium stockpile and hold its nuclear fuel cycle program to greater accountability and transparency. Currently, due to the stalemate over the nuclear fuel cycle program, plutonium stockpile and spent fuel for reprocessing have been accumulated unnecessarily.[22]

Just before the extension of the agreement was announced, the government of Japan released its Fifth Strategic Energy Plan, in which it made a pledge to reduce the stockpile of plutonium extracted from spent nuclear fuel.[23] As of the end of 2017, the plutonium stockpile has reached 47.3 tons, with 36.7 tons stored in Britain and France and 10.5 tons at home. The goal of reducing the unused plutonium stockpile was apparently made in view of a concern expressed by the United States during its negotiation with Japan.[24]

Japan needs to redesign its nuclear energy policy based on the reality on the ground. In particular, its back-end management policy must be reformulated, reflecting new developments such as the abandonment of Monju, a prototype fast reactor. In the meantime, further transparency measures are necessary, such as more concrete plans for reducing the plutonium stockpile.

Conclusion

As U.S. primacy wanes with the rise of emerging (or reemerging) powers such as China and Russia, which do not share and respect liberal democratic values, there is an argument as to whether the reliance on liberal democratic values in maintaining global nuclear governance is self-reinforcing or self-defeating.

The answer is, both.

Global nuclear governance provides a foundation for U.S. leadership in the liberal international order. The nonproliferation regime based on norms and rules (which coincide with important elements of the liberal international order) covers almost the entire international community. Mechanisms that sustain the universal nuclear nonproliferation mostly emerged from liberal internationalism. Incentives that the United States prepared for engaging its partners, such as extended nuclear deterrence, played a significant role in encouraging allies and partners to choose against nuclear armament. Further, liberal democratic partners of the United States are reliable partners in promoting nonproliferation measures that are effective in countering proliferation risks in the second nuclear age. This will continue to be true for the foreseeable future.

In the meantime, disincentives such as stringent conditions for nuclear cooperation and provision of nuclear technology set by the NSG, or other nonproliferation measures, caused a sense of inequality at the global level. The divide over nuclear disarmament added to further frustration for non-nuclear weapon states on which nonproliferation measures are imposed. Resentments have arisen among "follower" states that aspire to, yet have forgone, nuclear programs due to restrictions on transferring nuclear technology. In other cases, since the benefits of nonproliferation have been spread so thinly, many states see them as given almost exclusively to the United States and its partner states. As technology diffuses, more nonproliferation measures need to be taken qualitatively as well as quantitatively. Even though U.S. leadership will remain critical, there will be a mismatch between policy resources that the United States and its partners have and policy needs for maintaining an effective global nonproliferation regime. Managing this gap will be a challenge.

Another challenge is how to engage existing and emerging major players, such as Russia, China, and India, who do not fully associate themselves with regulative norms of the liberal international order and play a rather traditional power-based, less rules-based, mercantilist game. Japan and the United States need to jointly consider how to manage the decline of U.S. power and leverage in the liberal international order in the nuclear domain, namely the international nuclear market, making concessions to accommodate the rise of Russia and China.

As the Iran and North Korean cases suggest, "one size fits all" solutions to noncompliance problems, which can be provided through the global nonproliferation regime, are not sufficient. While relying on universal norms set by the regime, individualized packages for comprehensive solutions, which take into account individual strategic and security factors, are needed. In that case, whether the package is reliable or not depends mainly on U.S. commitment to the solution. In other words, when the U.S. commitment becomes less credible and deliverable, stakeholders may consider departing from the deal.

The flip side of this coin is that even though other stakeholders may strongly wish to keep the deal, U.S. departure is likely to ruin it. In the case of JCPOA, the United Sates has said it would withdraw and expressed an interest in reinstating sanctions. Given this, efforts by European members to salvage JCPOA have been insufficient to keep European businesses in Iran, as corporations are afraid of losing their business in the U.S. market. However, sanctions enforced by the United States and followed by European and Asian partners such as Japan, South Korea, and Australia may not dissuade China and Russia from continuing cooperation with Iran.

Finally, if the end of credible extended nuclear deterrence by the United States ever arrives, the gravest risk may come from an inside collapse of the "atoms for alliance" mechanism, largely for political reasons. If political confidence between Japan and the United State fades, and such a situation becomes the new normal, any allies or partners of the United States must consider a hedging strategy. Indeed, in Germany and Australia, there are appeals to consider their own nuclear armament.[25]

In Japan, President Trump's "America First" attitude and his reluctance to continue the forward deployment of U.S. forces prompted concern over continued commitment by the United States to the defense of Japan and the credibility of extended deterrence. While NATO and the U.S.-ROK alliance face struggles, the U.S.-Japan alliance seems to enjoy relative stability. Although the two countries have major differences in their positions over trade issues, the security relationship, including coordination for North Korea issues, has been well managed by the two leaders and their security policy teams. However, despite efforts by "alliance managers" in the policy community, this stability largely depends on the political climate, including the domestic political agenda.

In this context, options for Japan's own nuclear weapons have not attracted much support by the public. It is partly due to the legacy of Hiroshima and Nagasaki. The Japanese public in general still holds very strong antinuclear feeling. Even prominent politicians' reference to nuclear armament did not generate public debate.[26]

At the same time, it is also noted that Japanese security experts have negative assessment on the indigenous nuclear capability of Japan. Some argued for nuclear sharing with the United States, possibly with the deployment of Dual Capable Aircraft (DCA), and training Japanese pilots for dual missions.[27] But nuclear sharing arguments were received by the security policy community with great misgivings.[28] In NATO-type nuclear sharing with DCA and joint decision mechanisms, the United States continues to maintain the ultimate decision-making power on whether and when nuclear weapons are used. This would not provide Japan with autonomy in the decision about the use of nuclear weapons, which would not be reassuring.

There is general consensus within the Japanese security community that the only way to increase Japan's security in such an uncertain strategic environment is to unwearyingly continue to engage with the United States. This will involve the further sharing of common strategic goals and increasing the complementarity of both countries' roles in alliance, and will also serve as a reminder of the importance of preserving multilateral institutions to maintain U.S. leadership, which cannot be replaced by any other means in sustaining the liberal international order. In a sense, the reality is that such a rational strategic calculation, rather than antinuclear sentiment based on the legacy of Hiroshima and Nagasaki, provides a foundation for Japan's non-nuclear choice and a robustness for Japan's commitment to the upholding the U.S. leadership in the liberal international order.[29]

Ikenberry views the current crisis of the liberal international order as a crisis of authority, but not a crisis of liberal internationalism.[30] If an additional perspective may be put in, it should be the lack of resources available to the United States in the maintenance of the international order (even if not a particularly liberal one) in the nuclear domain when liberal internationalism diminishes. The United States has provided extended nuclear deterrence and vast technological, industrial, and financial superiority and has helped shape the international nonproliferation regime. This means that the United States will face "strategic insolvency," which Mazarr describes as a crisis in managing the gap between the U.S. strategic objectives and its capability to manage international systems.[31] If the United States stops observing multilateral rules and gives up its leadership with self-restraint, incentives for other countries to comply with rules and norms will decline. As a result, the cost for the United States to pressure other countries to follow or return to norms and rules will increase. Since emerging powers such as China and India, along with Russia, are rising, the relative loss of military, economic, and technological superiority will affect psychological superiority, which might discourage other states from endorsing or associating themselves with U.S.-led global institutions, like the nuclear nonproliferation regime. The loss of nuclear governance under U.S. superiority without substitution would be a nightmare situation, which all liberal democracies should make every effort to avoid.

NOTES

1. Adam Taylor, "How China Plays into Trump's Decision to Pull Out of INF Treaty with Russia," *Washington Post*, October 23, 2018.

2. Bernard Brodie, *The Absolute Weapon: Atomic Power and World Order* (New York: Harcourt, Brace and Co., 1946); Robert Jervis, *The Meaning of the Nuclear Revolution: Statecraft and the Prospect for Armageddon* (Cornell University Press, 1989).

3. Daniel Deudney, "Hegemony, Nuclear Weapons, and Liberal Hegemony," in *Power, Order, and Change in World Politics*, edited by G. John Ikenberry (Cambridge University Press, 2014).

4. Graham Allison, "Myth of the Liberal Order," *Foreign Affairs*, vol. 97, no. 4 (July/August 2018), 124–33.

5. Woosang Kim and Scott Gates, "Power Transition Theory and the Rise of China," *International Area Studies Review*, vol. 18, no. 3 (2015), 219–26.

6. G. John Ikenberry, *After Victory: Institutions, Strategic Restraint, and the Rebuilding of Order after Major Wars* (Princeton University Press, 2001), 69–79.

7. Dwight D. Eisenhower, *Address by Mr. Dwight D. Eisenhower, President of the United States of America, to the 470th Plenary Meeting of the United Nations General Assembly*, December 8, 1953.

8. William J. Perry and James R. Schlesinger, *America's Strategic Posture: The Final Report of the Congressional Commission on the Strategic Posture of the United States* (Washington, D.C.: United States Institute of Peace Press, 2009), x.

9. Benjamin Frankel, "The Brooding Shadow: Systemic Incentives and Nuclear Weapons Proliferation," in *The Proliferation Puzzle: Why Nuclear Weapons Spread*, edited by Zachary S. Davis and Benjamin Frankel (London: Frank Cass, 1993), 36.

10. Andrew K. Semmel, "Effective Multilateralism: The U.S. Strategy for Dealing with Global Nuclear Proliferation," https://2001-2009.state.gov/t/isn/rls/rm/56942.htm.

11. G. John Ikenberry, "The End of Liberal International Order?" *International Affairs*, vol. 94, issue 1, (January 2018), 7–23.

12. Francois Murphy and Robin Emmott, "Iran Is Complying with Nuclear Deal Restrictions: IAEA Report," Reuters, August 30, 2018.

13. White House, "President Donald J. Trump Is Ending United States Participation in an Unacceptable Iran Deal," https://www.whitehouse.gov/briefings-statements/president-donald-j-trump-ending-united-states-participation-unacceptable-iran-deal/.

14. White House, "Joint Statement of President Donald J. Trump of the United States of American and Chairman Kim Jong Un of the Democratic People's Republic of Korea at the Singapore Summit," https://www.whitehouse.gov/briefings-statements/

joint-statement-president-donald-j-trump-united-states-america-chairman-kim-jong-un-democratic-peoples-republic-korea-singapore-summit/.

15. "Government Officials Say Japan Will Keep Maximum Pressure on North Korea ahead of Summit," *Japan Times*, May 28, 2018.

16. United States of America, "Creating the Conditions for Nuclear Disarmament," working paper delivered at the second session of the Preparatory Committee for the 2020 Review Conference of the Parties to the Treaty on the Non-Proliferation of Nuclear Weapons, April 18, 2018, https://s3.amazonaws.com/unoda-web/wp-content/uploads/2018/04/1806176E.pdf.

17. Group of Eminent Persons for Substantive Advancement of Nuclear Disarmament, *Building Bridges to Effective Nuclear Disarmament: Recommendations for the 2020 Review Process of the NPT*, https://www.mofa.go.jp/files/000349264.pdf.

18. Maria Korsnick, "Nuclear Power Is Critical Infrastructure," https://www.nei.org/News- Media/Speeches/Nuclear-Power-is-Critical-Infrastructure.

19. Albert Wohlstetter, Gregory Jones, and Roberta Wohlstetter, "Why the Rules Have Needed Changing," part I of *Towards a New Consensus on Nuclear Technology*, vol. 1 (Los Angeles: Pan Heuristics, 1979), 36–37.

20. Shinsuke Tomotsugu, "1970 nendai no Beikoku Kaku Fukakusan Seisaku to Kaku Nenryo Saikuru Seisaku-Higashi Ajia Takokukan Saishori Koso to Tokaimura Shisetsu o Meguru Gaiko Kosho Kara no Kosatsu" [Nuclear Nonproliferation Policy and Nuclear Fuel Cycle Policy of the United States in the 1970s—Plan for Multinational Reprocessing in East Asia and Observations from the Diplomatic Talks Around the Tokaimura Plant], *Ningen Kankyo Gaku Kenkyu* [Human Environmental Studies Research], vol. 7, no. 2 (2009).

21. Interview with former high-ranking official of the Department of Energy during the Reagan administration, October 3, 2011, Washington, D.C.

22. Robin Harding, "Japan Plutonium Stockpile Fuels U.S. Unease," *Financial Times*, June 25, 2018.

23. Government of Japan, Fifth Strategic Energy Plan, http://www.meti.go.jp/english/press/2018/pdf/0703_002c.pdf.

24. "Reducing Japan's Plutonium Stock," *Japan Times,* July 7, 2018.

25. Ulrich Kuhn, Tristan Volpe, and Bert Thompson, "Tracking the German Nuclear Debate," https://carnegieendowment.org/2018/08/15/tracking-german-nuclear-debate-pub-72884; Stephan Frühling, "A Nuclear Armed Australia—Contemplating the Unthinkable Option," *Defending Australia: Australian Foreign Affairs*, no. 4 (October 2018).

26. For example, Shigeru Ishiba of the ruling Liberal Democratic Party, the contender against Prime Minister Shinzo Abe in the party leadership election in 2018, suggested a need for discussion on possible deployment of U.S. nuclear forces in Japan, "Beigun kaku no kokunai haibi giron o" [Discuss the Deployment of U.S. Nuclear Forces in Japan], *Sankei Shimbun*, September 6, 2017.

27. Masahiro Matsumura, "The Time for 'Nuclear Sharing' with Japan Is Drawing Near," *Japan Times,* September 27, 2017.

28. Masashi Murano, "Deterring North Korea," *Diplomat*, May 24, 2017.

29. Nobumasa Akiyama, "Japan's Nuclear Disarmament Dilemma," in *The War*

That Must Never Be Fought, edited by George P. Schultz and James Goodby (Stanford, Calif.: Hoover Institution, 2015), 436–69.

30. G. John Ikenberry, "The Future of Liberal World Order," *Japanese Journal of Political Science*, vol. 16, no. 3 (September 2015), 450–55.

31. Michael J. Mazarr, "The Risks of Ignoring Strategic Insolvency," *Washington Quarterly*, vol. 35, no. 4 (2012), 7–22.

PART II
STATECRAFT

6

Japan's Homogenous Welfare State

DEVELOPMENT AND FUTURE CHALLENGES

AKIHISA SHIOZAKI

Japan in Insulation from the Populist Tsunami

As discussed in previous chapters, over the recent years, many advanced industrial economies throughout Europe and the United States have been increasingly exposed to, and have sometimes succumbed to, unprecedented political tsunamis of antielitism, antiglobalism, and economic nationalism. Large crowds of voters rallied in support of the "Vote Leave" campaign in the 2016 U.K. Brexit referendum, or the "America First" slogan by Donald Trump during his presidential campaign; many of them voicing strong fear of the growing number of immigrants and deep anger at the globalizing economy, both considered serious threats to the jobs and safety of average citizens.

While its Western allies were falling prey to these populist challenges, Japan, on the contrary, appears to have remained strikingly insulated from such trends. Ever since the Liberal Democratic Party (LDP) regained power from the Democratic Party (DPJ) in 2012 in a landslide electoral victory, Prime Minister Shinzo Abe has been enjoying a remarkably long term in government, surpassing his first-time predecessor Prime Minister Junichiro Koizumi and potentially becoming the longest-serving prime minister in the nation's history. Japan's political stability is particularly interesting, since Abe has been pursuing policies largely in support of maintaining and strengthening the liberal international order, which the conventional leaders of the order have turned their backs on. The most symbolic of these policies was his strong efforts to broker the Trans-Pacific Partnership (TPP) free trade agreement, and then TPP-11, after the United States dropped out from the pact three business days into Trump's presidency (see chapter 2 by Mireya Solís for more details).

Why has Japan not suffered the populist backlashes that have flooded its Western allies? In this chapter, I first provide an overview of the key theories describing the rise of populism and examine their relevance in Japan, with particular focus on the effect of two key domestic policies that differentiate Japanese society from its Western peers. These are (1) Japan's egalitarian welfare state policies, which have placed effective controls on widening income disparity, largely through the nation's universal pension and healthcare coverage; and (2) Japan's historically tight immigration policies, which have strictly limited the number of foreign workers and residents in Japan. I examine how Japan's policies in these areas compare with those of the nations that have recently been exposed to strong anti-globalist and nationalist pressures. I argue that Japan's broad redistribution policies and strict immigration policy have diffused the accumulation of public rage against foreign workers and the government's liberal trade programs and have thus allowed the nation to step up as a primary defender of the liberal international order. While these findings should offer useful insights for other nations struggling with the rise of populist movements, I conclude by noting the serious challenges facing Japan in sustaining these policy conditions, which are likely to weaken the effectiveness of these safeguards in the future.

The Usual Suspects behind the Rise of Populism

In this book, populism is defined primarily as a discursive method that seeks to mobilize voters by appealing to them as the "pure" people against a "corrupt" and irresponsive elite (see introduction chapter). While there is populism outside of the West—for example, in Latin America—I will focus on comparing the situation in Japan with populism affecting the more economically advanced democracies, both for reasons of scope and the comparable level of social and political institutional development. The literature explaining the rise of such populism in Europe and the United States has focused on a broad range of economic, cultural, and institutional conditions that determine the electoral success of populist parties. Some of the major causal factors will be introduced below.

ECONOMIC INSECURITY AND GLOBALIZATION

First and foremost, populism is often understood as a reaction to a syndrome of economic changes caused by globalization, technological advances, and the shift to a knowledge economy. These changes have been accompanied by a reduction in manufacturing jobs, a general decline in job security, sluggish income growth, growing income inequality, and a widening economic gap between urban and rural areas, among other things. The resulting economic deprivation and anxiety about the future have driven frustrated voters—"the least secure strata"—who feel "left behind" to embrace populists and lash out at the establishment.[1]

A corollary to the theory of economic deprivation breeding populism is that of regional inequality: regions that face diminishing economic prospects, primarily rural areas with lower population densities, have been found to be more supportive of populism than wealthier urban areas. Evidence from presidential elections in the United States, France, Turkey, and the U.K. Brexit referendum back a global trend where poorer, depopulating rural areas provide the strongest support for the antiestablishment option.[2]

In the 2016 U.S. presidential primaries, candidate Bernie Sanders surprised the nation with his strong campaign, winning twenty-three primaries and caucuses and approximately 43.1 percent of the pledged delegates, making an impressive showing against Hillary Clinton in the Democratic run-up. Enjoying strong backing from supporters of the Occupy Wall Street movement,[3] a political movement criticizing the concentration of wealth among the top 1 percent elites, Sanders's campaign focused primarily on income and wealth inequality. "In recent years, over 99 percent of all new income generated in the economy has gone to the top 1 percent," claimed Sanders in a speech at the Brookings Institution, and argued such disparity was placing undue burden on the American middle class.[4]

In the U.K. Brexit referendum, *Politico* reported the correlation between wealth inequality and voter outcome, showing that "some of the poorest regions in the country had the largest majorities in favor of Brexit."[5] Professor Danny Dorling of Oxford University calls the United Kingdom "the most unequal society in Europe," inviting attention to the fact that the United Kingdom is an outlier among European nations, since the income threshold for the top 1 percent of earners is 6.3 times median U.K. household income, a ratio significantly higher than any of the other large European countries (where the ratio lies within a range of 4.2 to 4.9).[6] A report by Oxfam concluded that massive inequality in the United Kingdom contributed to the vote to leave, stating "whatever your views on Brexit, the referendum brought divisions within our country to a head, with many people expressing distrust and disconnection with political processes and voting for change in the hope that it would improve their economic position."[7]

IMMIGRATION

Another pervasive explanation for the rise of populism is that an influx of immigrants, when perceived as a threat to the native population's jobs and traditions, triggers a reaction against an establishment. Rather than actual immigration statistics, it appears that a growing perception of the threat of immigration, exacerbated by populist rhetoric and contingencies such as terrorist attacks linked to immigrants, feed support for populist parties.

Trump's election campaign platform in 2016 was unique in many aspects, compared to conventional presidential candidates, but perhaps most notably in its stark opposition to immigration. His campaign promise to build "a great, great wall" between the United States and Mexico—and to demand that Mexico pay for it—became his signature campaign issue. Trump called for the deportation of the 11 million undocumented immigrants residing in the United States, pledged to triple the number of Immigration and Customs Enforcement agents, and attempted to cut federal support to so-called sanctuary cities (municipalities with policies limiting cooperation with federal immigration agencies) through an executive order. He demonized "immigration" as the reason why American workers were losing their jobs and social benefits and promised to fundamentally overturn such policies. Trump proposed a temporary ban on all Muslims entering the country, stating that he would "suspend immigration from areas of the world when there is a proven history of terrorism against the United States, Europe, or our allies,"[8] and indeed enacted such policy shortly after assuming office. Trump's call for tighter immigration policies resonated with his support base. Results from the 2017 Chicago Council Study Survey of American Public Opinion and U.S. Foreign Policy found that 80 percent of Trump supporters see immigration as a critical threat, far above the average among all of the U.S. public, which stands at 37 percent.[9] Furthermore, a survey conducted by the Pew Research Center in 2016 showed that 70 percent of voters considered "immigration" a "very important" topic in determining their vote.[10]

A similar debate took place in the U.K. Brexit referendum, where "immigration" was viewed as a decisive factor that influenced many frustrated "leave" voters. Under New Labour leadership from 1997 to 2007, Britain had adopted a pro-immigration policy, welcoming a significant number of foreign workers. However, according to a study by Ipsos MORI in 2016, 48 percent of British adults chose "immigration/immigrants" as the most important issue facing Britain, far surpassing other important policy considerations, such as healthcare and education.[11] The survey results appear to demonstrate how U.K. voters were largely concerned that immigration had placed too much pressure on public services of the nation. Local workers had feared their wages were being pushed down by low-skilled immigrants and felt that immigration, according to Britain's *Daily Mail*, "is seriously bad news for the low-paid who find their wages nailed to the floor."[12] Accordingly, a study by the Resolution Foundation shows that communities in which the proportion of non-native U.K. residents increased most in the decade before the referendum were more likely to vote "leave."[13]

EDUCATION

Across different contexts, one of the key predictors of voting for the populist option appears to be education. In the United States, the Resolution Foundation has found that controlling for other factors, such as income levels and growth, unemployment, race, age, and proportion of non-native residents, low education levels strongly correlated to swings in support for Trump and the Republican Party during the 2016 election.[14] Similarly, in the United Kingdom's referendum, areas that had a lower share of population with university degrees were more likely to vote for Brexit.[15] Analyses of recent elections in the Netherlands and France have also confirmed that education was a stronger predictor for populist support than the usual suspects: percentage of immigrants, income, or unemployment.[16] The logic is that those with lower education levels perceive globalization and immigrants as a threat rather than an economic opportunity. Such anxiety drives less-educated voters to embrace populists, who both inflame such fears and offer simplistic solutions to "take back the country" for the people from the educated elites.

POLITICAL INSTITUTIONS AND CIVIC ATTITUDES

Certain institutional features of a political system can also block or enable underlying support for populists. Electoral systems with more proportional rules ensure that even small populist parties will be able to gain a foothold in parliament, which gives them legitimacy and, consequently, a sufficient voice in government to appease their movements, or, conversely, enough power to veto policies proposed by the ruling party. Thus, electoral rules partly explain why many European parliaments with proportional electoral systems have seen smaller populist parties gain ground, while in the United Kingdom and the United States, with their majoritarian first-past-the-post systems, dominance of the two traditional parties continues. Populists have also claimed victory, or have come surprisingly close to doing so, in one-shot electoral contests, which do not require building a sustained national party organization. The obvious examples are the presidential campaign of Donald J. Trump and Marine Le Pen as well as the Brexit referendum.

Besides these institutional features, public attitudes toward the political system itself, including commitment to democratic process and liberal values, will affect the appeal of antiestablishment rhetoric.

THE JAPAN CASE

Japan has been blessed with a set of unique socioeconomic conditions that have allowed the nation to avert, so far, the divisive, angry populism jolting other Western liberal democracies. Comparatively low levels of income and inter-regional inequality, low levels of immigration, an egalitarian system of high-quality public education, and electoral institutions that disadvantage small and new challengers at the national level have all contributed to this. In particular, the nation's political leadership follows a long history of investing in the "homogenous welfare state" by (1) controlling the widening income disparity between the cities and villages through distributive welfare state policies such as universal pension and healthcare coverage; and (2) avoiding the influx of unskilled foreign workers by maintaining Japan's historically tight immigration policies. We now turn to examining these historic efforts and their relevance to buffering the disruptive effects of populist temptations.

Japan's Egalitarian Distribution Policies

In many countries, income and wealth inequality have been recognized as primary drivers of public rage toward the elites and pro-globalist policies. They give rise to a strong sense of unfairness among the voters, casting doubt toward the governments' economic and social welfare policies as being unfairly biased toward the elites.

However, Japanese voters have shown surprising resistance to such temptations. Japan, despite nearly three decades of sluggish growth and prolonged periods of deflation, remains a relatively wealthy and equal society. Unemployment levels are among the lowest in the OECD, with particularly low levels of youth unemployment. Sustained political protest against economic inequality in Japan has been limited. Most of the new types of protest movements in recent years have focused primarily on opposition to nuclear power, constitutional reform, and national security issues rather than questions of economic justice. Membership and support for the Japanese Communist Party, the party most clearly committed to combating poverty and economic inequality, has not increased and has stayed low in the past twenty years. Although experiencing a small bump in support in 2014, the party has fallen back down to below 10 percent of all votes cast in recent Lower House elections in 2017.[17]

Most Japanese do not identify themselves as one of the "elites," or the "have nots," but consider themselves to belong to the "middle class." This aspect of Japanese society is best summed up in the phrase *ichioku sochuryu*

("100 million, all middle class"), an expression widely recognized during Japan's postwar recovery driven by its rapid economic growth and liberal social policies. By the 1970s, more than 90 percent of the population saw themselves as "middle class" despite the existence of relatively large income gaps between the cities and villages at the time, sharing the vision of a rising egalitarian welfare state. Such a shared self-image of the nation extends to this day. Government surveys have found that 92.4 percent of the population still identify as middle class (upper-middle, middle-middle, or lower-middle) in 2017.[18] The same poll reveals that the proportion identifying as lower class has stabilized at around 5 percent.[19]

Despite public perception, however, income disparity among Japanese citizens has actually steadily grown over the years. As shown in figure 6-1, Japan's "market income" Gini coefficient (before taxes and transfers) marked 0.5704 in 2014, the highest since Japan started measuring this

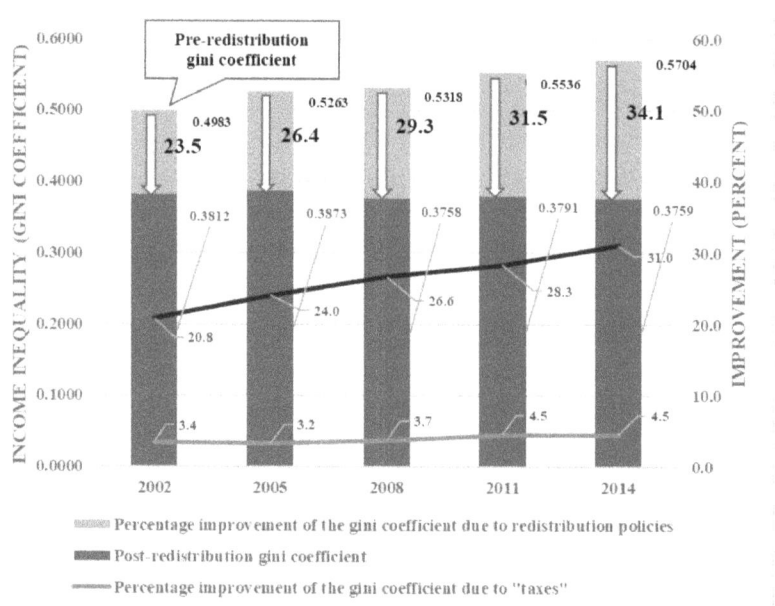

FIGURE 6-1. Income inequality and redistribution in Japan

Source: Ministry of Health, Labor, and Welfare in Japan, "Heisei 26 nen: Shotoku sai bunpai chōsa hōkoku-sho" [2014: Income Redistribution Research Report], www.mhlw .go.jp/file/04-Houdouhappyou-12605000-Seisakutoukatsukan-Seisakuhyoukakanshitsu /h26hou.pdf, 6.

index, pointing to a steadily increasing trend of income inequality since the 1980s.[20] The poverty ratio, defined as the proportion of the population with an income less than the median equivalent disposable income,[21] has also steadily grown over the years,[22] largely due to an increase in the number of singleperson households within the elderly population. Among the working age population, over the past twenty years, the number of households exceeding an annual income of 10 million yen (approximately US$89,000) has decreased, and the number of such households earning less than 5 million yen (approximately US$44,000) has substantially increased.[23]

However, the Japanese government has been successful in managing the social backlash, potentially arising from such economic disparity, through effective redistribution policies. As can be seen above, despite widening market income disparity, Japan has been able to maintain its "disposable income" Gini coefficient (after taxes and transfers) to be generally stable over the past decade. Largely due to its aging demographics, the nation's "market income" inequality has steadily widened, since citizens beyond the average retirement age of sixty-five are more likely to face wider variety in their working conditions and income. Nonetheless, the gap appears to be largely offset by effective redistribution efforts made through social welfare and taxes.

The Ministry of Health, Labor, and Welfare (MHLW) estimates that more than 90 percent of such redistribution effect derives not from taxes but from social welfare benefits largely consisting of pension payments and medical insurance. For example, as shown in table 6-1, an average household with a household income at 4.3 million yen is estimated to receive approximately 1.1 million yen in pension distribution, 0.5 million yen in medical coverage, and 0.1 million yen in long-term care annually. When combined, social security accounts for roughly 30 percent of the 33.5 percent Gini coefficient improvement through redistribution.[24] However, such income redistribution is targeted heavily toward the "elderly" households above sixty-five years old, which enjoy roughly 70 percent more social welfare benefits than the average household and more than three times more benefits compared to a single-mother household.

Japan's level of economic inequality on various measures is moderate compared to the United States and the United Kingdom. Both Japan's "market income" and "disposable income" Gini lie slightly above the OECD average, but are still below the United States and the United Kingdom. Income con-

TABLE 6-1. Status of redistribution (breakdown by household category)

	Average	Elderly Household	Single-Mother Household	Others
Market income	429.2	100.4	236.7	592.7
Redistribution	70.7	265.0	48.4	−23.1
Income (postredistribution)	499.9	365.4	285.1	569.6
Tax and social insurance contributions	111.5	43.5	44.8	145.9
Social welfare total	182.3	308.5	93.3	122.8
Pension	108.4	211.0	21.9	60.4
Medical	51.4	69.9	19.7	43.0
Long-term care	13.1	24.4	0	7.9
Others	9.3	3.1	51.7	11.5
Gini (market income)	0.6	0.8	0.4	0.4
Gini (disposable income)	0.4	0.4	0.3	0.3
Gini improvement (%)	33.5	52.9	37.4	17.5

Source: Ministry of Health, Labor, and Welfare, 2017 Income Redistribution Research Report, 10.

centration among the top 1 percent in Japan is 10.4 percent (2010), which is almost half the level of concentration in the United States (see figure 6-2).[25] Japan's concentration of wealth at the top 1 percent of households is also limited to 9 percent of the nation's total wealth and marks considerably lower than comparative Western industrial countries.[26] Mizuho Research Institute observes that Japanese corporate executives receive large performance-based bonuses less often than their American and European counterparts, which results in a smaller concentration of income and wealth.[27]

In sum, similar to other developed economies, income disparity continues to grow in Japan on a market income basis. However, due to the nation's universal pension and healthcare system, the government appears to have managed to effectively redistribute wealth from the working population to the elderly.

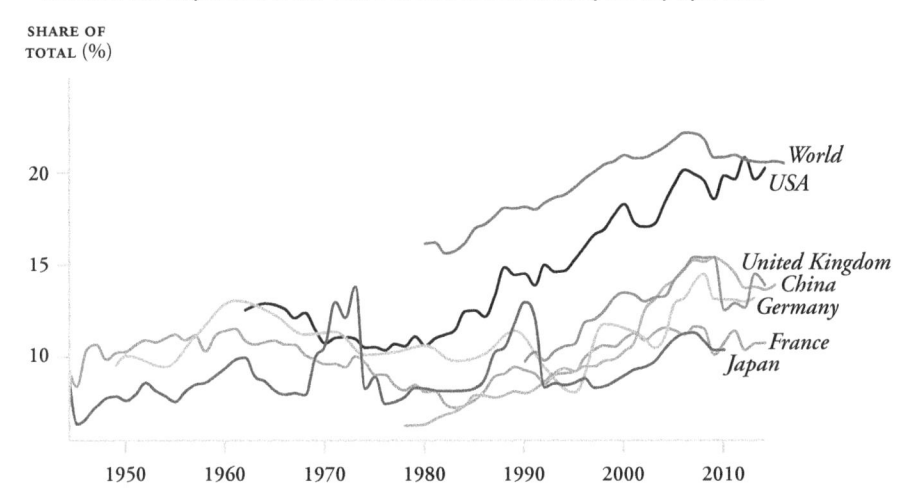

FIGURE 6-2. Comparison of the share of total wealth held by the top 1 percent

SHARE OF TOTAL (%)

[Line chart showing top 1% national income share from 1950 to 2010 for World, USA, United Kingdom, China, Germany, France, and Japan. USA and World rise to about 20% by 2010; UK, China, Germany around 13-14%; France and Japan around 10-11%.]

Source: World Inequality Database, "Top 1% National Income Share," https://wid.world/world/#sptinc_p99p100_z/US;FR;DE;CN;WO;JP;GB/last/eu/k/p/yearly/s/false/5.497/30/curve/false/country.

THE DEVELOPMENT OF THE EGALITARIAN WELFARE STATE

In the early stages of its postwar recovery, Japan was quick to introduce two key components of its social welfare: universal healthcare coverage and universal pension coverage. A brief look at the historic development of these welfare systems provides an excellent portrait of the continuous struggle among Japanese administrations to ease public discontent against increasing economic disparity, while managing the nation's fiscal limitations and conservative political forces.

Japan was one of the first nations in the world to introduce comprehensive coverage of pensions and health insurance in 1961. In 1956, Nobusuke Kishi announced that the Liberal Democratic Party (LDP) sought to establish comprehensive coverage of health insurance and pensions in order to stabilize people's livelihoods. At the time, the LDP was facing strong pressure from the opposing Japan Socialist Party (JSP), who were advocating the extension of pension coverage from civil servants and workers in large companies to also include small businesses, farmers, fishermen, and the self-employed.[28] Kishi's pledge developed into an LDP campaign promise during the 1956 Upper House election to provide universal health insurance coverage by 1960, as well as to explore the establishment of elderly pensions and widow-children pensions.

Under Prime Minister Hayato Ikeda's "Income Doubling Plan," carried out during the 1960s, strong emphasis was placed on economic growth policies, largely through increase in jobs and wages. However, Ikeda was mindful of the side effects of the growing income disparity, and he increased pension payments and reduced the financial burden of medical insurance on the individual, focusing on sectors that would not share in the rapid postwar economic growth. By the mid-1960s, however, the Japan Communist Party (JCP) and Kōmeitō attracted urban salaried workers who were not sharing in the fruits of double-digit GDP growth under the Income Doubling Plan, introducing a new era characterized by fragmentation of the opposition. As LDP's conservative policies under Prime Minister Eisaku Sato started to wane in popularity, an increasing number of progressive local governors and mayors put pressure on the national government by introducing social welfare packages beyond national standards. To name just one example, Tokyo Governor Ryokichi Minobe introduced free medical care for people over seventy in 1969.

Feeling pressure from these local political movements, in 1973 Prime Minister Kakuei Tanaka announced *fukushi-gannen* ("the first year of the welfare era"). He drastically expanded pension and healthcare coverage, including the implementation of free medical care for people over seventy, an increase in the level of employee pensions and national pensions, and an increase in reimbursement provisions under the National Health Insurance. During the rapid economic growth of the 1960s and 1970s, many young workers moved to the rapidly industrializing cities, leaving behind their parents in their villages, which did not prosper from the rapid economic growth. Tanaka's social welfare reforms, combined with large public spending in rural areas, were largely aimed to serve as "social subsidies,"[29] addressing rising "rural versus urban" inequalities and "intergenerational inequalities" simultaneously. The paradox of the ruling conservative party introducing a generous social welfare system in Japan derived from the wide spectrum of the LDP's constituencies and the opposition's shift to radicalism, thus allowing the LDP to "erode social democracy."[30]

The 1980s saw a resurgence of the conservative camp, crystallized in the policy proposals announced in 1983 by the Second Provisional Council for Administrative Reform, better known as the *Rincho*. The *Rincho* vocally supported welfare retrenchment, introducing the concept of the *kokumin futan ritsu* (people's burden rate), calculated as the proportion of total tax revenues and social security contributions to national income. Resonating with earlier domestic discussions over the *igirisu-byo* (British disease), a theory claiming Britain's long-term decline and stagnation at the time were attributable to its strong trade unions, large public sector, and the welfare state, the *Rincho* argued that while the ratio would inevitably increase from the then-level of 35 percent, the ratio should be kept much lower than the European level of 50 percent.

Today, the MHLW takes pride in its social welfare system, suggesting that Japanese citizens are getting a rather good deal in terms of their social welfare package. On the one hand, Japan's total public social expenditure, comprising cash benefits, direct in-kind provision of goods and services, and tax breaks with social purposes, has been on the rise and amounted to 23.1 percent of its GDP in 2013, exceeding that of the United States (18.8 percent) and the United Kingdom (21.9 percent), and the average among the OECD countries (21.1 percent) at the time.[31] On the other hand, Japan's people's burden rate amounted to 42.6 percent in 2015, still below the 50 percent ceiling suggested by *Rincho*. Although this is higher than the United States (33.3 percent), it remains lower than the United Kingdom (46.5 percent), Germany (53.2 percent), Sweden (56.9 percent), and most other European nations.[32] Thus, the MHLW claims that the Japanese people are receiving "mid-level" social expenditure while only bearing "low level" national burden compared to other OECD countries.[33]

HOW SUSTAINABLE IS THE JAPANESE WELFARE STATE?

So, should the Japanese social welfare system be recognized as a role model by other nations for effectively combating the spreading hostility against economic inequality to weather the strong pressures of populism? At least two issues stand out to challenge the system's sustainability: soaring costs and intergenerational tension.

The first challenge is the sustainability of the rapidly increasing social welfare budget. While the current cost of social welfare of 121 trillion yen

(US$1.08 trillion) already accounts for 33 percent of the national budget, a May 2018 forecast by the government predicts that the total cost of social welfare benefits will rapidly increase up to around 140 trillion (+16 percent, US$1.25 trillion) by 2025 and around 190 trillion (+57 percent, US$1.69 trillion) by 2040.[34] A large source of this cost increase will be increasing payouts for public medical insurance and long-term care; public medical insurance benefits, currently at 39 trillion yen (US$346 billion), are expected to grow to around 68 trillion yen (US$604 billion) by 2040 (+74 percent), and long-term care benefits currently at 11 trillion yen (US$97 billion) are expected to grow at an even faster pace to 26 trillion yen (US$231 billion) by 2040 (+141 percent). While the government points out that such costs will be around 24 percent of the nation's GDP, not only is this still relatively high, the projections are based on an ambitious baseline model that sees Japan achieve no lower than 1.7 percent growth until 2028.[35] This appears quite ambitious, in light of Japan's sluggish recovery from deflation and its aging demographics. During this period, Japan is expected to lose approximately 15 million of its working-age population (fifteen to sixty-four), while the number of elderly citizens over sixty-five will steadily rise to 35.3 percent in 2040,[36] thus making it even more challenging to finance the increasing social welfare budget through economic growth.

However, when asked about one's preference regarding the appropriate balance between the level of social welfare benefits and the tax burden, 53.5 percent of Japanese citizens said either that "increasing social security levels and increasing the burden is unavoidable" or that "maintaining social security levels and increasing the burden due to the declining birthrate and aging population is unavoidable." In comparison, only 13.1 percent said that social security levels should decrease.[37] These figures indicate that the Japanese public may still have some leeway in accepting paying higher costs in the form of taxes and contributions in order to sustain the current level of social welfare benefits.

The second major challenge will be the rising frustration among the youth against intergenerational inequality. Income redistribution under Japan's current welfare system has been heavily skewed toward cross-generational redistribution and cross-geographic redistribution, providing generous subsidies to the senior population living in the rural areas, while taxing the young and working generations living in the cities. As shown earlier in table 6-1, while an average senior household enjoys a lavish net redistribution benefit of 2.7 million yen each year through various social welfare programs, a single-mother household receives only 0.5 million yen, and a standard working-generation household experiences a net redistribution loss of 0.2 million yen.[38] The postredistribution disposable income of a single-mother household remains at only two-thirds of an elderly household, which has led to a daunting poverty rate for single-parent households (50.9 percent in 2013), by far the highest among OECD nations.[39] Compared to its Western peers, Japan spends a larger budget, proportionate to its GDP, on its elderly population in the form of pension and long-term care, while spending a smaller budget on its younger generations in the form of family support, housing, labor mobility, and unemployment. A policy report by a group of young Ministry of Economy, Trade, and Industry (METI) bureaucrats published in 2017 called into question the sustainability of the nation's elderly-focused redistribution policies, stating, "as the population ages, how long can the Japanese society stand to continue treating all elderly citizens as the 'weak,' and continue pumping unlimited wealth into medical insurance, long-term care, and pensions?"[40]

Such signs of growing frustration among the younger generations have had little political impact so far, due to the overwhelming political voice of the elderly generation to protect its vested interests—a notable feature of Japanese politics, which many scholars call "silver democracy." The political voice of the younger generation has long been discounted in the Japanese electoral scene, due to the outpacing increase of elderly voters, as a result of Japan's aging demographics, and the low voter turnout among the younger generation. For example, in the 2016 general election, while the turnout for voters in their sixties was 72 percent, only 34 percent of voters in their twenties cast their votes.[41] The low youth voter turnout, combined with the increasing number of the elderly population, has amplified the political presence of the elderly generation, making it increasingly difficult for politicians to support policies that would deprive the elderly generation of their status quo welfare benefits. Prime Minister Abe, during his first term, learned this lesson the hard way, when the LDP's medical insurance reform bill aiming to increase contribution by those older than seventy-five faced fierce opposition from the elderly generation. Yoshihide Suga, then the minister for internal affairs and communications, has been quoted as saying that this was the most significant reason for the devastating defeat in the 2007 Upper House election.[42]

However, as discontent among the younger generation toward intergenerational inequality continues to mount, and as an increasing number of younger voters start to voice their frustration through electoral action, the government may be forced to revisit its "silver" social welfare policies. A point of particular concern is the mounting frustration among the "nonworking" middle-aged generation currently in their forties and fifties, otherwise referred to as the "missing workers."[43] Born in the late 1960s and 1970s as second-generation baby boomers, many among this generation suffered the most from the decline of the Japanese economy in the late 1990s and failed to find a permanent job in their youth, which caused many of them to go from part-time job to part-time job during the past two decades. Researchers estimate that among those in their forties and fifties, in addition to the 720,000 "unemployed," there are more than a million "missing workers" who have given up searching for a job (therefore not showing up in the unemployment statistics) and who have mostly remained single and continue to live with their parents.[44] Shiro Yamasaki, a former MHLW senior bureaucrat, warns that, "as most of their parents start to retire from work and become economically feeble, the sense of insecurity and frustration among this generation is likely to accumulate and become a big source of social instability."[45]

The LDP recognizes these serious challenges to the sustainability of the nation's "silver" welfare policies, heavily skewed toward benefiting the elderly generation, and is carefully pursuing a fundamental policy shift to address such intergenerational imbalances. In his opening policy speech on October 24, 2018, Prime Minister Abe highlighted the administration's strong commitment to transform Japan's social welfare system into an "all-generation social welfare model" over the next three years, with a particular focus on making childcare and higher education free for all children, while also lightly touching upon the planned raise of the nation's consumption tax from 8 percent to 10 percent in 2019.[46] This initiative dates back to early discussions during the Fukuda and Aso administrations in the late 2000s, on the need for an integrated reform of tax and social welfare, to dilute the heavy concentration of social welfare expenditure aimed toward the elderly and offer more to younger generations, and at the same time shift the burden of social welfare from an age-based system to a system where all citizens would be asked to contribute based on their ability to pay. Learning from the past failed attempts to raise taxes or cut back on elderly welfare, Japanese political leaders will continue to carefully explore creative political rhetoric and appropriate pacing of this difficult policy shift.

Japan's Restrictive Immigration Policy

While many industrialized societies have recently suffered sharp surges of nationalistic hostility rising against migrants, Japan's historically restrictive immigration policy has allowed the country to remain remarkably distant from such tensions.

A survey by Ipsos MORI across twenty-five countries in 2017 found that 48 percent of all respondents believe there are too many immigrants in their country, while only 21 percent disagree.[47] Japan stands out as an outlier, with only 15 percent believing "there are too many immigrants in our country," which is half as many as in Poland (30 percent), the second lowest. The survey further describes that hostility against immigration generally stems from two factors globally: (1) fear of immigrants placing excessive pressure on public services; and (2) fear of immigrants making it more difficult for people to get jobs. Again, Japanese citizens scored lowest in their level of concern about immigrants placing pressure on public services and the third lowest in their level of concern regarding the fear of losing jobs, underscoring their relative confidence over the inflow of immigrants (see figure 6-3).

These figures come as no surprise, given that Japan has the lowest percentage of foreign population among major industrialized countries. The percentage of foreign population in Japan, consisting of people who hold the nationality of another country, amounted to only 1.6 percent in 2013, by far the lowest among any of the G7 countries.[48] Figure 6-4 presents a historic perspective of how the G7 nations have invited foreign nationals over the past decades, where Japan stands out, displaying remarkable consistency in maintaining its tight immigration controls, while other nations, such as the United Kingdom and Italy, have significantly increased their foreign popula-

FIGURE 6-3. Opinion polls on immigration

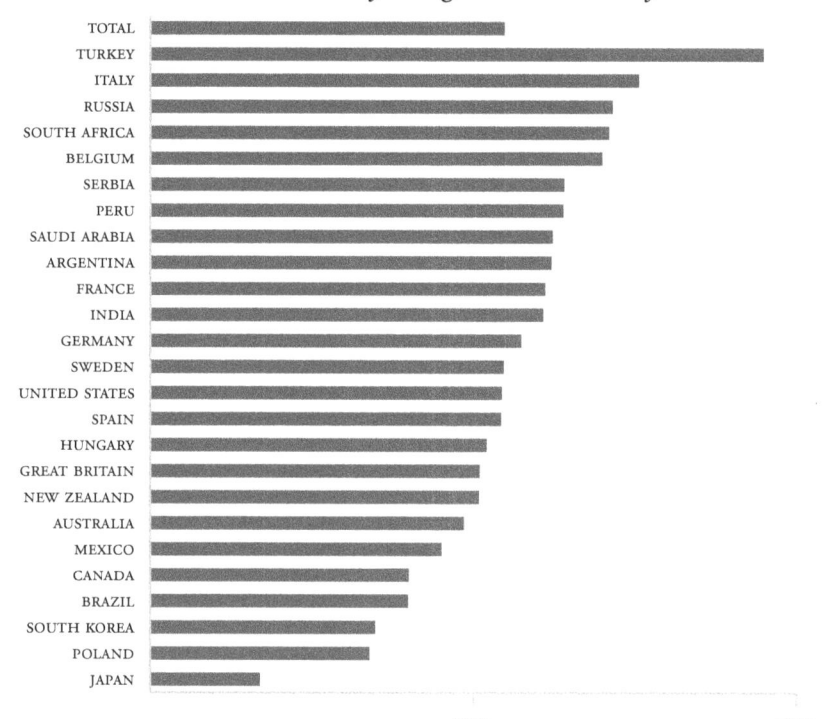

"There are too many immigrants in our country"

TOTAL	
TURKEY	
ITALY	
RUSSIA	
SOUTH AFRICA	
BELGIUM	
SERBIA	
PERU	
SAUDI ARABIA	
ARGENTINA	
FRANCE	
INDIA	
GERMANY	
SWEDEN	
UNITED STATES	
SPAIN	
HUNGARY	
GREAT BRITAIN	
NEW ZEALAND	
AUSTRALIA	
MEXICO	
CANADA	
BRAZIL	
SOUTH KOREA	
POLAND	
JAPAN	

50%   75%

"Immigrants have placed too much pressure on public services"

TOTAL	
TURKEY	
SOUTH AFRICA	
ITALY	
GREAT BRITAIN	
BELGIUM	
SWEDEN	
UNITED STATES	
INDIA	
FRANCE	
HUNGARY	
SPAIN	
NEW ZEALAND	
ARGENTINA	
SERBIA	
GERMANY	
AUSTRALIA	
CANADA	
RUSSIA	
PERU	
SAUDI ARABIA	
POLAND	
SOUTH KOREA	
BRAZIL	
MEXICO	
JAPAN	

50%　　　75%

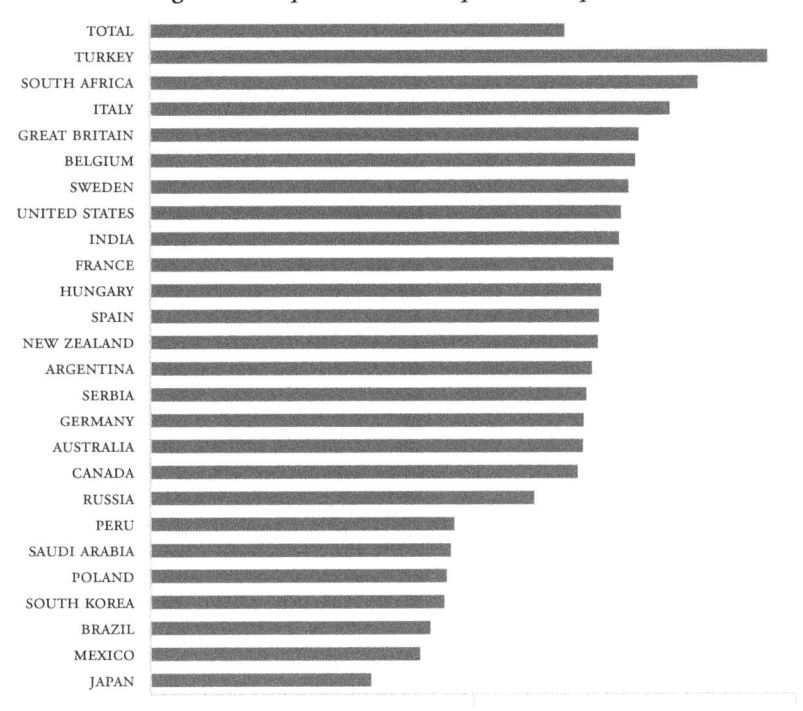

"Immigrants have made it more difficult to get jobs"

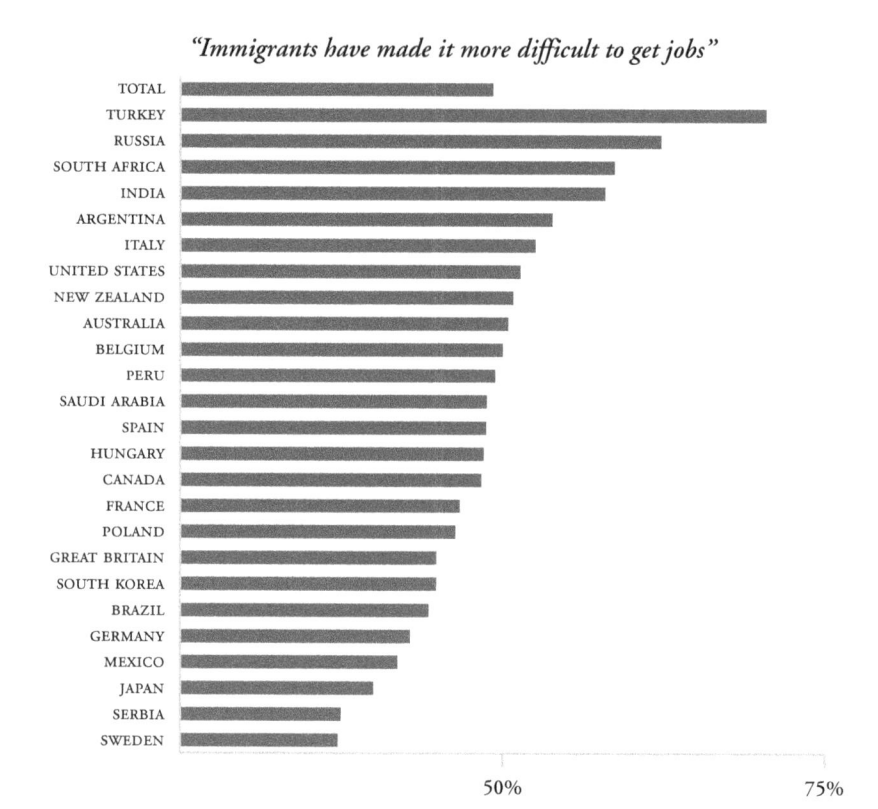

TOTAL	
TURKEY	
RUSSIA	
SOUTH AFRICA	
INDIA	
ARGENTINA	
ITALY	
UNITED STATES	
NEW ZEALAND	
AUSTRALIA	
BELGIUM	
PERU	
SAUDI ARABIA	
SPAIN	
HUNGARY	
CANADA	
FRANCE	
POLAND	
GREAT BRITAIN	
SOUTH KOREA	
BRAZIL	
GERMANY	
MEXICO	
JAPAN	
SERBIA	
SWEDEN	

Source: Ipsos MORI, "Global Views on Immigration and the Refugee Crisis," https://www.ipsos.com/sites/default/files/ct/news/documents/2016-09/Global_Advisor_Immigration.pdf, 4.

tion over the years. The threat of foreign workers and immigrants stealing jobs and freeriding public services are likely less visible to the average Japanese citizen simply due to the smaller size of the foreign population. It has begun to rise with the latest Ministry of Internal Affairs and Communication press release in July 2018, announcing that the percentage of foreign-born population in Japan has risen to 1.96 percent, still very distant from peers such as the United Kingdom, which is at around 14.3 percent.[49]

Japan's asylum and refugee policies have also been repeatedly criticized as extremely restrictive. While the government has ratified the 1951 Refugee Convention, recognizing the rights of the displaced and the obligation of states to protect them, the number of refugees admitted in Japan are dismally small. In 2017, the total number of forcibly displaced individuals worldwide grew to 68.5 million at a record high, and the Total Protection Rate (TPR), calculated as the proportion of asylum-seekers accorded refugee status or a complementary form of protection by the total number of substantive decisions, was recorded at 49 percent globally. However, the UNHCR was not shy about expressing its frustration at Japan in its 2017

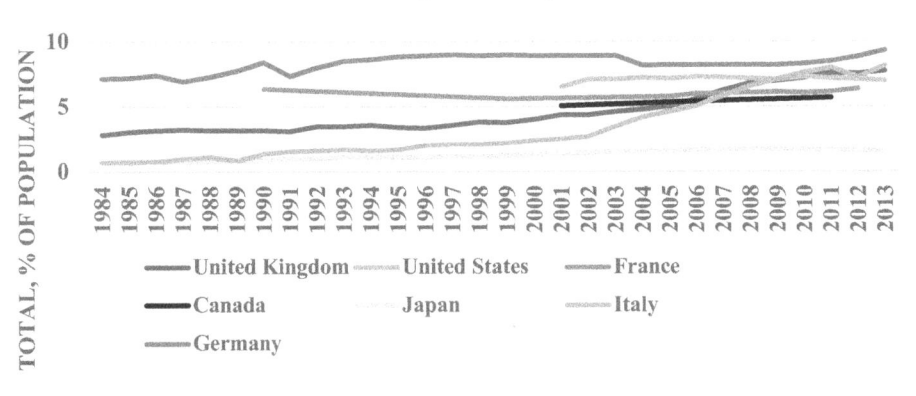

FIGURE 6-4. Increase in numbers of foreigners residing in G7 nations

Source: Organization for Economic Cooperation and Development (2019), "Foreign population" (indicator), https://doi.org/10.1787/16a914e3-en.

report by noting that "Japan stands out as having a particularly low TPR with under 100 positive decisions out of 12,900 decisions made, resulting in a TPR of under 1 percent."[50] According to an article by Rei Shiba, when inquired about the reason for the low TPR, Japan's Ministry of Justice responded, "The number of asylum applications from the top five refugee nations shown in the UNHCR's Global Trends report (Syrian Arab Republic, Afghanistan, South Sudan, Myanmar, and Somalia) are actually very small . . . We suspect that the majority of the asylum seekers are not true refugees, but their true intent is to work in Japan."[51] The Ipsos MORI survey reveals a general lack of social attention and interest toward refugee issues in Japan, where 33 percent of Japanese respondents answered, "Do not know" when asked about whether they agree or disagree with the statement "We must close our borders to refugees entirely—we cannot accept any at this time." In the face of rising numbers of asylum applications, the Ministry of Justice announced in January 2018 that it was planning to introduce stricter standards for accepting asylum seekers.

ACHIEVING ECONOMIC PROSPERITY WITHOUT RESORTING TO HIRING FOREIGN WORKERS

Japan's long-standing hesitance toward accepting immigrants goes back to the strict *sakoku* (country closure) policies during the Edo era (1603–1868), which kept Japan secluded from the rest of the world for over two centuries. During this period, nationals and non-nationals were prohibited from leaving or entering the country, with the exception of limited trade relations with the Netherlands, China, and Korea conducted through the ports of Nagasaki and Tsushima. While foreign trade and travelers brought significant economic gains and information, the shogunate was concerned that the expansion of Catholicism within Japan through the influence of Catholic traders and missionaries would undermine the strict social classification that defined the samurais as the ruling class and expose the nation to military conquest by European powers. This underlying ambivalence toward foreigners continued after the Edo era, with the exception of limited policy-driven migration between Imperial Japan and its colonies, Taiwan and Korea, during the early twentieth century.

The 1951 Immigration Control and Refugee Act established the general legal framework for immigration control in postwar Japan, which "sought to prevent foreign workers from staying in the country for long periods of time."⁵² Under the act, all foreigners must qualify for one of the defined residency categories, and types of work not permitted under such residential status were, in the absence of a special exemption, prohibited. The categories of residency status have been generally limited to high-skilled labor, thus designed to prevent the influx of "unskilled foreign workers." In light of the Potsdam Declaration in 1945, Korean and Taiwanese people lost their Japanese nationality and were expected to either return to their countries of origin or get naturalized and become Japanese citizens by accepting a Japanese name.

Despite rapid economic growth throughout the following decades, Japan, as a rare exception among industrial democracies during this period, managed to avoid heavy reliance on foreign workers. According to Morita and Iyotani, during the rapid economic growth in the 1960s, the nation successfully overcame labor shortage, mainly through a vast supply of returning soldiers and seasonal migration from rural areas within Japan.⁵³ While in West Germany and France, primary sector employment rates had already dropped to around the 10 percent mark by the early 1960s, Japan still had an abundance of primary sector workers in its villages to supply more than 10 million workers to the manufacturing and service sectors in urban areas.

As the reservoir of seasonal workers available for industrial labor had mostly been exhausted by the end of the 1960s, the challenges of labor shortage once again became apparent. Sociologist Yoko Sellek points to a combination of factors that allowed the government to maintain rapid economic growth without resorting to the introduction of foreign migrant workers into the unskilled industrial sector during the late 1960s to mid-1970s: (1) increased productivity through optimization and mechanization within the manufacturing industry; (2) maintaining long working hours; (3) encouraging elderly workers to stay longer in the workplace through the extension of the mandatory retirement age to sixty; (4) increased supply of middle-aged housewives to low-wage labor (10.7 million in 1970), caused by the expansion of the service sector and the government's human resource policy, (5) relatively weak labor unions enabling flexible hiring policies; and (6) gradual shift to offshore production in the late 1970s.⁵⁴

The 1980s and 1990s saw a steady influx of foreign workers and residents in Japan, led by white-collar workers attracted by the reputation of Tokyo and other major Japanese cities as a new global financial and business hub. The number of registered foreigners more than doubled during these decades from approximately 780,000 in 1980 to 1.7 million in 2000—although that is still very limited, by international comparison. During this period, the Japanese government solidified its two-tier approach toward migrant workers, whereby it would (1) actively recruit highly skilled foreign workers due to their potential to contribute to Japan's internationalization and economic growth but (2) remain cautious about admitting unskilled foreign workers. Although subject to a few amendments, this practice continues to the present day.

However, since the 1990s, as the serious consequences of labor shortage caused by the decreasing birth rate and a rapidly aging society became widely recognized, the LDP has quietly implemented measures to allow unskilled workers to enter the country without upsetting the party's conservative support base. Despite the official policy to not accept unskilled foreign workers, two major loopholes were established. First, due to an amendment in the Immigration Control Act in 1990, *nikkeijin* (people of Japanese descent) up to the third generation, mainly from Latin American countries such as Brazil and Peru, were granted the status of "long-term resident" and allowed to enter the labor market with unrestricted access to work. This amendment was a result of strong lobbying from industry sector seeking to supplement shortages in the labor force, especially for manufacturing. Second, Japan's *gino jisshu seido* (technical internship program) was established in 1993 to allow trainees and technical interns, mainly from China and other Asian countries, to enter into an employment contract with their employers after the completion of their training for a period up to one year (later extended to a maximum of three years). The program was originally designed to transfer "practical technology, skills, and/or knowledge to developing countries" and to cultivate "human resources to lead their economic advancement."[55] However, this trainee program and its successors have come under severe criticism not only as a back door for inviting unskilled foreign labor but as a breeding ground for exploitation of foreign workers for wages below the minimum and other human rights violations.

More recently, the Japanese government appears to have introduced a bilateral approach to relax entrance from specific countries for specific industries in desperate need of labor, while maintaining control against an overflow of unskilled foreign workers. In 2008, the Economic Partnership Agreement between Japan and Indonesia came into effect. This treaty granted entry and temporary stay of ninety days (which may be extended) to short-term business visitors. In addition, the treaty included provisions for temporary stay of one to three years for intra-corporate transferees, investors, those who engage in professional services (such as lawyers qualified as *bengoshi* under Japanese law; patent attorneys qualified as *benrishi* under Japanese law, and so on), and those who engage in business activities with public/private organizations in Japan with advanced knowledge or skills such as engineers or "specialist in humanities/international services."[56] It also granted entry and temporary stay for a period of one year (which may be extended for an additional year, but not more than twice) to nurses or careworkers qualified in Indonesia, who would undertake training and pass the national examination to become qualified under Japanese law. Once they become qualified in Japan, they are granted entry and temporary stay for a period of up to three years, which may be extended.[57] Similar treaties were signed with the Philippines in 2008 and Vietnam in 2012.

When the DPJ became the ruling party in 2009, sweeping the LDP from power in a landslide election victory, the party put forward a progressive policy initiative to grant permanent foreign residents the right to vote in local elections. "Japan is increasingly depopulated, and it is important to get foreign residents to join together in the process of developing local communities. But to encourage their sense of being an interested group themselves, it is necessary to give them their rights and duties," said Shinkun Haku, an Upper House lawmaker, emphasizing the need to improve Japan's legal infrastructure to better integrate foreigners.[58] However, as discussions regarding the bill progressed, the DPJ administration faced strong opposition both publicly and from within the coalition, and eventually gave up. "There was always strong opposition against the bill," recalls Katsuya Okada, a key proponent of the bill who served as the minister of foreign affairs under Prime Minister Hatoyama. "We were already struggling with the Futenma base transfer issues, and then the North Koreans launched missiles, and those even within the ruling party became increasingly reluctant to push forward with the bill. It was politically impossible to submit the bill."[59] Not surprisingly, Japan's conservative approach toward accepting foreign workers continued throughout the ruling days of the DPJ from 2009 to 2012, despite the regime change.

RECENT DEPARTURE FROM TRADITIONAL RESTRICTIVE IMMIGRATION POLICIES

In recent years, Japan's traditional reluctance toward relying on foreign workers has been put under tremendous pressure in the face of the unprecedented pace of the nation's population decline. By 2053, Japan's population, currently above 120 million, is projected to drop below 100 million, and by the same time, the percentage of senior citizens (over sixty-five) is projected to increase to 38 percent of the overall population.[60] More shocking, the nation's working age population (fifteen to sixty-four) is estimated to shrink by more than 30 percent, to 52 million. The dramatic shift in demographics is considered "the biggest challenge in Japanese history," seriously jeopardizing the nation's economic strength, cultural identity, self-confidence, and social sustainability.[61]

Despite these challenges, Shinzo Abe, who won back the prime minister's office in late 2012, has maintained until recently the government's traditional restrictive approach toward immigration. In his UN speech in 2015, Abe stated, "I would say that before accepting immigrants or refugees, we need to have more activities by women, elderly people, and we must raise our birth rate."[62] However, while carefully managing its political rhetoric and avoiding public attention, the Abe administration has been quietly undertaking a dramatic policy shift to introduce unskilled foreign workers into Japan.

Tackling labor shortage was always central to Abe's economic policies since he assumed office in 2012. With the recovery of the economy under his policy package of "Abenomics," the nation's unemployment rate dropped rapidly and Japanese corporations quickly found themselves facing serious labor shortage problems. While the government launched powerful campaigns to encourage women and elderly population to return to work, which were relatively successful, in the face of an unprecedented shrinkage of the working age population, the gap is simply too large to resolve domestically. In light of these circumstances, the Abe administration has nearly doubled the number of foreign workers from 0.69 million in 2012 to 1.28 million in 2017.[63]

A large source of the above expansion of foreign workers derives not from an influx of skilled workers but from doubling the size of the *gino jisshu* (technical intern training program) and scaling up admission of foreign "students." However, while the government boasts the increase in the number of "students" entering Japan, in reality, the number of foreign students at advanced educational institutions such as universities and graduate programs has remained relatively constant, and the increase largely derives from students studying at Japanese language schools or specialized training schools. Since "students" are allowed to work up to twenty-eight hours per week, many of them spend less time studying in the library and more time working in convenience stores or restaurants, supplying much-wanted sources of low-skilled labor.

In June 2018, the government surprised many by announcing a bold new initiative to introduce a new breed of low-skilled foreign workers into Japan. In its *Honebuto* (basic policy on economic and fiscal management and reform), which summarizes the main policy initiatives of the government each year, the Abe administration proposed to create a new five-year residency status applicable to certain industries suffering labor shortage, such as construction, agriculture, elderly care, shipbuilding, and hospitality, significantly relaxing the requirements for professional and technical skills.[64] The report highlights the serious negative impact of the nation's labor shortage and advocates that Japan must not limit itself to only foreign workers who meet the traditional strict professional and technical standards, but should establish a system to broadly welcome "foreign human resources" who are equipped with a certain level of professional knowledge and skills to contribute immediately.[65] Although the report attempts to balance concerns from the conservative camp by noting that the new policy is "not an immigration policy," the new residence status is clearly designed to substantially relax the knowledge and skill requirements under the current system to invite foreign workers who were traditionally rejected as low-skilled labor.[66] Abe stressed that inviting foreigners who can contribute immediately is of urgent importance and announced an aggressive policy target of inviting an additional 500,000 foreign workers by 2025 under this newly created residence status.[67]

While the rapid increase in numbers of foreign workers under the Abe administration has benefited Japan's economic growth, it has also brought attention to early signs of rising social tensions related to their integration into society. According to a recent study announced by the Ministry of Justice, 39.3 percent of foreigners living in Japan experienced denial of housing for not being Japanese[68] and 30 percent suffered defamation or some kind of discriminatory language for being a foreigner.[69] Such tensions become particularly visible in certain cities and areas that attract a high concentration of foreign workers. For example, in Kawaguchi, a medium-size city approximately half an hour away from central Tokyo, the ratio of foreign residents has dramatically increased over the past five years from 3.7 percent to 5.5 percent,[70] transforming certain areas of town into a "new Chinatown" dominated by Chinese signboards and restaurants.[71] This rapid demographic change has given rise to serious tensions between the Japanese locals and the new Chinese residents over differences in lifestyle and culture, such as a significant number of complaints over garbage disposal and noise issues. The city government introduced various measures to ease such tensions, for example, by putting up sign boards on garbage disposal rules in six different languages. Local volunteers and nonprofits have also supported these efforts by offering free Japanese language classes for foreign workers and their family members and planning cross-cultural social events. Mayor Nobuo Okunoki of Kawaguchi recalls receiving frequent complaints from local residents living in the public housing complex that was accepting many of the incoming foreign workers four years ago, when he first assumed office. He states that such complaints have largely diminished, due to continuous efforts by the landowner and the apartment community association, such as providing Chinese translations to all sign boards and notifications within the housing complex. However, he also recognizes that these integration challenges will not be resolved easily, and admits: "It will take time for these common rules to be accepted."[72]

It is clear that, if implemented, the series of policy initiatives proposed by Abe will mark an important departure from the nation's long-standing reluctance to invite unskilled foreign workers and will help Japan tackle the serious challenges of labor shortage. However, Katsuya Okada criticizes such rapid policy shift by the Abe administration as "extremely indecisive," pointing out that Abe intends to dramatically expand the number of low-skilled foreign workers while denying them long-term residency and officially maintaining the government's conservative approach toward immigration.[73] He warns that such political maneuvering will circumvent important and difficult political discussions and decisions on the obvious integration challenges awaiting Japan and could make the nation more vulnerable in the future to hostile attitudes against foreign workers and the globalized economy.

The Relevance of the Japanese Model and Japan's Role

The Japanese model provides a number of interesting insights into policy options, which could ease the mounting antielitist and antiglobalization fury among global citizens.

Japan was fortunate, but also creative, in being able to successfully navigate a narrow path to overcome labor shortage during the postwar decades without reliance on unskilled foreign labor. In addition to increased productivity from technological innovation, self-sacrifice and cooperation by the workers likely contributed to stretching the capacity of the Japanese economy. Basically turning its back on refugee and asylum requests from the international community allowed Japan to limit the inflow of unskilled foreign residents, but at the expense of strong ethical criticism from overseas. Once the need for foreign labor became inevitable, politicians explored back-channel policy methods in the form of "trainees" or "students" to disguise the reality of a gradual relaxation of inviting unskilled foreign labor.

Japan was also quick to introduce effective social welfare systems that served to mitigate the pain of increasing economic inequality. Effective redistribution policies in the form of universal pension coverage, medical insurance, and long-term care have controlled the disposable income disparity between urban and rural areas, diffusing frustration against the elites and globalization. However, while the government was busy fixing intergenerational inequality concerns, intra-generational inequality issues, especially those among the working generation, were left behind, putting, for example, many single-parent households in poverty and despair. The egalitarian welfare state also came with a high price tag, which is now starting to haunt the nation's fiscal wellbeing and exhausting the financial foundations of the nation's future generations.

As can be seen, the Japanese model is not a recipe for all, nor an easy policy mix to emulate. However, it provides a unique case study of policy alternatives—distinct from what other industrialized countries are doing—to explore what aspects may or may not be useful in combating the weakening foundations of liberal democracies. On the other hand, Japan should be mindful of the upcoming challenges from the forces opposed to it upholding the liberal international order, challenges that could gain increasing momentum as the safeguards that have shielded the nation in the past become increasingly difficult to sustain.

NOTES

1. Ronald F. Inglehart and Pippa Norris, "Trump, Brexit, and the Rise of Populism: Economic Have-Nots and Cultural Backlash," HKS Working Paper RWP16-026 (Cambridge, Mass.: John F. Kennedy School of Government, August 2016), 2.

2. See Philip E. Auerswald, "The Origin of Populist Surges Everywhere," https://medium.com/the-code-economy/the-origin-of-populist-surges-everywhere-1146f89e04bb.

3. Adam Gabbatt, "Former Occupy Wall Street Protesters Rally around Bernie Sanders Campaign," *Guardian*, September 17, 2015.

4. Quoted in Michelle Ye Hee Lee, "Bernie Sanders's Claim that 99 Percent of New Income Is Going to Top 1 Percent of Americans," *Washington Post*, February 17, 2015.

5. Ginger Hervey and Mark Scott, "Inequality and Brexit," *Politico*, December 19, 2017.

6. See Danny Dorling, "Brexit: The Result of Rising Inequality, Not Rising Immigration," http://www.dannydorling.org/?p=6373.

7. See Oxfam, "How to Close Great Britain's Great Divide," https://oxfamilibrary.openrepository.com/bitstream/10546/620059/1/mb-great-britains-great-divide-130916-en.pdf, 1.

8. Ben Kamisar, "Trump: Suspend Immigration from Areas with 'Proven History of Terrorism,'" *Hill*, June 13, 2016.

9. See Chicago Council on Global Affairs, "2017 Chicago Council Survey of American Public Opinion and U.S. Foreign Policy: What Americans Think about America First," https://digital.thechicagocouncil.org/what-americans-think-about-america-first, 25.

10. See Pew Research Center, "2016 Campaign: Strong Interest, Widespread Dissatisfaction," http://www.pewglobal.org/2017/02/01/what-it-takes-to-truly-be-one-of-us/, 31.

11. See Ipsos Mori, "June 2016 Economist/Ipsos MORI Issues Index," https://www.ipsos.com/sites/default/files/migrations/en-uk/files/Assets/Docs/Polls/issues-index-june-2016-charts.pdf, 2.

12. Sir Andrew Green, "So What do the French and Germans Know that We Don't?" *Daily Mail*, May 2, 2016.

13. Matthew Whitaker, "Dis-United Kingdom? Inequality, Growth, and the Brexit Divide," https://www.resolutionfoundation.org/media/blog/dis-united-kingdom-inequality-growth-and-the-brexit-divide/.

14. Stephen Clarke and Dan Tomlinson, "In the Swing of Things: What Does Donald Trump's Victory Tell Us about America?" https://www.resolutionfoundation.org/app/uploads/2016/11/In-the-swing-of-things-FINAL.pdf.

15. John Burn-Murdoch, "Personal Values Trump Education as Driving Factor in Populist Successes," *Financial Times,* November 22, 2016.

16. Billy Ehrenberg-Shannon and Aleksandra Wisniewska, "How Education Level Is the Biggest Predictor of Support for Geert Wilders," *Financial Times*, March 2, 2017; John Burn-Murdoch and others, "French Election Results: Macron's Victory in Charts," *Financial Times*, May 9, 2017.

17. National Police Agency, "Keibi jōsei o kaerimite: Tokushū 'kongo no daikibo saigai ni sonaete'" [Looking at the Security Situation: Featured Report "Preparing for Future Large-Scale Disasters"], https://www.npa.go.jp/bureau/security/publications/syouten/syouten286/pdf/00.pdf.

18. Public Relations Office of the Cabinet Office, "Zu 18-1 Seikatsu no teido: Kokumin seikatsu ni kan suru seron chosa" [Figure 18-1, Standard of Life: Public Opinion Survey on the Life of the People], https://survey.gov-online.go.jp/h29/h29-life/zh/z18-1.html.

19. Public Relations Office of the Cabinet Office, "Zu 18-2 Seikatsu no teido (jikeiretsu): Kokumin seikatsu ni kan suru seron chosa" [Figure 18-2, Standard of Life (time series): Public Opinion Survey on the Life of the People], https://survey.gov-online.go.jp/h29/h29-life/zh/z18-2.html.

20. Ministry of Health, Labor, and Welfare in Japan, "Heisei 26 nen: Shotoku sai bunpai chōsa hōkoku-sho" [2014: Income Redistribution Research Report], https://www.mhlw.go.jp/file/04-Houdouhappyou-12605000-Seisakutoukatsukan-Seisakuhyoukakanshitsu/h26hou.pdf, 6.

21. Defined as "the proportion of people below 50 percent of median income."

22. Ministry of Health, Labor, and Welfare in Japan, "Heisei 28-nen kokumin seikatsu kiso chōsa no gaikyō [Overview of the Comprehensive Survey of Living Conditions in 2016]," https://www.mhlw.go.jp/toukei/saikin/hw/k-tyosa/k-tyosa16/dl/16.pdf, 15.

23. Ministry of Health, Labor, and Welfare in Japan, "Heisei 29 nenban: Kousei roudou hakusho: shakai hoshou to keizai seicho" [2017 Version, white paper: Social Security and Economic Growth], https://www.mhlw.go.jp/wp/hakusyo/kousei/17/dl/all.pdf, 39.

24. Ministry of Health, Labor, and Welfare in Japan, "Heisei 29 nen: Shotoku sai bunpai chōsa hōkoku-sho" [2017: Income Redistribution Research Report], https://www.mhlw.go.jp/toukei/list/dl/96-1/h29hou.pdf, 10.

25. See World Inequality Database, "Top 1% National Income Share," https://wid.world/world/#sptinc_p99p100_z/US;FR;DE;CN;WO;JP;GB/last/eu/k/p/yearly/s/false/5.497/30/curve/false/country.

26. Masato Shikata, "Nihon no shisan kakusa—JHPS to Rukusenburuku shisan

chōsa ni yoru kokusai hikaku" [Wealth Inequality in Japan: International Comparison by JHPS and Luxembourg Assets Survey], Joint Research Center for Panel Studies Discussion Paper Series (Tokyo: Joint Research Center for Panel Studies, Keio University, 2011), 6.

27. Mizuho Research Institute, *Dētabukku kakusa de yomu nipponkeizai* [Data Book: Economic Disparity in Japan's Economy] (Tokyo: Iwanami Shoten, 2017), 120.

28. Mari Miura, *Welfare through Work: Conservative Ideas, Partisan Dynamics, and Social Protection in Japan* (Cornell University Press, 2012), 48–51.

29. Interview with Shiro Yamasaki, Tokyo, August 20, 2018.

30. Taro Miyamoto, *Fukushi Seiji* [Politics of Social Welfare] (Tokyo: Yuhikaku, 2008).

31. Organization for Economic Cooperation and Development, "Social spending," https://data.oecd.org/socialexp/social-spending.htm.

32. Ministry of Finance, "Kokumin futan-ritsu no kokusai hikaku (OECD kamei 35-kakoku)" [International Comparison of the People's Burden Rate (35 OECD Members)], https://www.mof.go.jp/budget/topics/futanritsu/sy3002c.pdf.

33. Ministry of Health, Labor, and Welfare, "Annual Health, Labor, and Welfare Report, 2017," https://www.mhlw.go.jp/wp/hakusyo/kousei/17/index.html, 19.

34. Cabinet Secretariat, Cabinet Office, Ministry of Finance, and Ministry of Health, Labor, and Welfare, "2040-Nen wo misueta shakai hoshō no shōrai mitōshi (giron no sozai)—gaiyō" [Prediction of Social Welfare toward 2040 (Theme for Discussion): Outline], https://www5.cao.go.jp/keizai-shimon/kaigi/minutes/2018/0521/shiryo_04-1.pdf.

35. Ibid.

36. Cabinet Office, "Heisei 29-nenban kōrei shakai hakusho (zentai ban)" [Annual Report on the Aging Society (Complete Version)], https://www8.cao.go.jp/kourei/whitepaper/w-2017/html/zenbun/s1_1_1.html.

37. Cabinet Secretariat and others, "2040-Nen wo misueta shakai hoshō no shōrai mitōshi (giron no sozai)—gaiyō," 13.

38. Ministry of Economy, Trade, and Industry, "Fuan'na kojin, tachisukumu kokka: Moderu naki jidai o dō maemukini ikinuku ka" [Anxious Individual, Confused State: How to Go Forward in an Age with No Model], Jikan/Wakate Purojecto [Project of the Vice-Minister and Young Bureaucrats of METI] May 2017, 28; Ministry of Health, Labor, and Welfare in Japan, "Heisei 29 nen: Shotoku sai bunpai chōsa hōkoku-sho" [2017: Income Redistribution Research Report], https://www.mhlw.go.jp/toukei/list/dl/96-1/h29hou.pdf.

39. Organization for Economic Cooperation and Development, "CO2.1: Income Inequality and the Income Position of Different Household Types," http://www.oecd.org/els/soc/CO_2_1_Income_inequality_by_household_type.pdf, 3; Mizuho Research Institute, *Dētabukku kakusa de yomu nipponkeizai*, 139.

40. Ministry of Economy, Trade, and Industry, "Fuan'na kojin, tachisukumu kokka," 25.

41. Ministry of Internal Affairs and Communications, "Kokusei senkyo ni okeru nendai betsu tōhyō-ritsu ni tsuite" [Voter Turnout by Age Group in National Elections], http://www.soumu.go.jp/senkyo/senkyo_s/news/sonota/nendaibetu/.

42. Mutsumi Nishida, "Minshu ha 'Itami' wo Katareruka" [Can the Democratic

Party of Japan Talk about "Pain"], *Nikkei*, May 4, 2008.

43. NHK World—Japan, "Missing Workers," https://www3.nhk.or.jp/nhkworld/en/tv/documentary/20180729/4001301/.

44. Ibid.

45. Interview with Shiro Yamasaki.

46. Prime Minister of Japan and His Cabinet, "Dai hyaku-kyujyu-nana kai ni okeru Abe naikaku sori daijin shoshin hyomei enzetsu" [Speech by Prime Minister Abe in the 197th Diet], https://www.kantei.go.jp/jp/98_abe/statement2/20181024shoshinhyomei.html.

47. Ipsos MORI, "Global Views on Immigration and the Refugee Crisis," https://www.ipsos.com/sites/default/files/ct/news/documents/2016-09/Global_Advisor_Immigration.pdf, 4.

48. See Organization for Economic Cooperation and Development, "OECD Data: Foreign Population," https://data.oecd.org/migration/foreign-population.htm#indicator-chart.

49. Ministry of Internal Affairs and Communications, "Jūmin kihon daichō ni motozuku jinkō, jinkō dōtai oyobi setai-sū" [Population, Demography, and the Number of Households Based on Basic Resident Registration], http://www.soumu.go.jp/main_sosiki/jichi_gyousei/daityo/jinkou_jinkoudoutai-setaisuu.html; Nicola White, "Population of the UK by Country of Birth and Nationality: 2017," *Statistical Bulletin*, Office for National Statistics, May 24, 2018.

50. United Nations High Commissioner for Refugees, "Global Trends: Forced Displacement in 2017," June 25, 2018, 45.

51. Rei Shiba, "Nintei-ritsu wa 0. 2-Pāsento 'nanmin ni tsumetai Nihon'—senmonka, NPO, tōjisha-ra ga kataru kadai to tenbō" [Accepts Only 2 Percent, "Japan's Coldness Toward Refugees"—Experts, NPOs, and Concerned People Speak of the Task and Prospects], https://news.yahoo.co.jp/byline/shivarei/20180509-00084621/.

52. Jennifer Lind, "Nationalist in a Liberal Order: Why Populism Missed Japan," *Asia-Pacific Review*, vol. 25, no. 1 (2018), 67.

53. K. Morita and T. Iyotani, "Japan and the Problem of Foreign Workers," in W. Gooneratne, P. Martin, and H. Sazanami (eds.), *Regional Development Impacts of Labour Migration in Asia* (Nagoya: UNRCD Research Report Series No. 2, 1994).

54. Yoko Sellek, *Migrant Labor in Japan* (New York: Palgrave Macmillan, 2001), 21–25.

55. Japan International Training Cooperation Organization, "Technical Internship Program (TIP)," https://www.jitco.or.jp/english/overview/tip/tip.html.

56. Ministry of Foreign Affairs of Japan, "Annex 10 Referred to in Chapter 7: Specific Commitments for the Movement of Natural Persons," https://www.mofa.go.jp/region/asia-paci/indonesia/epa0708/annex10.pdf.

57. Ibid.

58. Setsuko Kamiya, "DPJ Weighs Voting Rights for All Permanent Residents," *Japan Times*, May 3, 2008.

59. Interview with Katsuya Okada, Tokyo, September 13, 2018.

60. Statistics Bureau, Ministry of Internal Affairs and Communications, "Japan Statistical Yearbook 2018: Chapter 2. Population and Households: Future Population," https://www.stat.go.jp/data/nenkan/67nenkan/zuhyou/y670202000.xls.

61. Rebuild Japan Initiative Foundation, *Japan's Population Implosion*, edited by

Yoichi Funabashi (Tokyo: Shinchosha Publishing, 2015; New York: Palgrave Macmillan, 2018).

62. Quoted in Justin McCurry, "Japan Says It Must Look After Its Own Before Allowing in Syrian Refugees," *Guardian*, September 30, 2015.

63. Cabinet Office, "Gaikoku jin rōdō-ryoku ni tsuite [About Foreign Workers]," http://www5.cao.go.jp/keizai-shimon/kaigi/minutes/2018/0220/shiryo_04.pdf.

64. Cabinet Office, "Basic Policy on Economic and Fiscal Management and Reform 2018," https://www5.cao.go.jp/keizai-shimon/kaigi/cabinet/2018/2018_basicpolicies_en.pdf.

65. Ibid.

66. Ibid., 34.

67. "Japan to Welcome 500,000 Foreign Workers to Help Plug Labor Shortage," *Kyodo News*, May 30, 2018.

68. Center for Human Rights Education and Training, "Gaikoku jin jūmin chōsa hōkoku-sho: Teisei ban" [Report on Foreigners Living in Japan (Revised Edition)], http://www.moj.go.jp/content/001226182.pdf, 23.

69. Ibid., 37.

70. "Zōka suru gaikoku jin jūmin, dō taiō kyōsei e, rūru rikai sokushin gengo bunka, kanmin de torikumi" [Increasing Number of Foreign Residents: How to Cope with Living, Language, and Culture, Promoting Rule Understanding, Public and Private Initiatives], *Nikkei Shimbun*, September 22, 2018.

71. "Chūgokugo dake de kuraseru shin Chaina taun Nishikawaguchi e ittemita" [Went to Nishikawaguchi, the "New Chinatown"], *News Post Seven*, July 16, 2018.

72. "Zōka suru gaikoku jin jūmin."

73. Interview with Katsuya Okada.

7

Winds, Fevers, and Floating Voters

POPULISM IN JAPAN

KEN VICTOR LEONARD HIJINO

For decades, observers of Japan's democracy have worried about its apparent deficiencies. The foremost concern has been the predominance of the Liberal Democratic Party and a chronically feeble opposition. As of this publication, the conservatives have held power for sixty-one out of sixty-five years since 1955. This lack of government alternation has been accompanied by, according to critics, an unaccountable and excessively autonomous bureaucracy, constrained pluralism, a weak civic culture, and lack of female representatives, among other ills. The country has been described in the past as being a *keizai ichiryu, seiji sanryu* (first-rate economy, third-rate politics) and more recently as a "democracy without competition" marred by "an inability to decide" crucial policy.[1]

Yet recent years have seen a curious inversion of this critique.

Japan has neatly sidestepped the kind of populist politics that, in Western democracies, have undermined the liberal international order from its foundations. The country is a place "where populism fails" and a "rage-free zone" not caught "in the grip of anti-establishment" politics.[2] Ironically, it appears as if the dominance of the LDP is the very source of its enviable political stability and social cohesion. The current Abe administration—despite fears that this traditionally flexible and moderate ruling party had, in recent years, become dominated by ideologue nationalists—has continued to steer a moderate course. We find few parties in Japan espousing radical Right xenophobia, economic nativism, and disengagement from international institutions. No new force has emerged to denounce capitalism and globalization as a system "rigged" in the interests of the wealthy against the ordinary. Japan's political discourse is relatively free of antipluralist attacks delegitimizing the media, courts, and legislatures as "enemies of the people."

As chapter 6 by Akihisa Shiozaki and chapter 10 by Kaori Hayashi demonstrate, "demand-side" socioeconomic conditions—such as relatively low levels of immigration, unemployment, and inequality—make Japan a poor breeding ground for populist movements seen in the West. In addition, the ruling conservatives' long-standing illiberal positions on free trade and immigration have minimized backlashes against globalization. On the "supply-side," Japan's majoritarian electoral system and campaign rules make it difficult for populist leaders and new parties to make substantial inroads in the national political arena.

Though free from the convulsions of Western-style populism, the stability of Japan's current politics is not built on strong foundations of civic engagement and support for democratic ideals. The health of Japanese democracy is, by many indicators, as poor as—or even worse than—that of many populist-prone states. Political participation, trust and confidence in the political elite, and commitment to democratic institutions have long been comparatively weak in Japan and continue to atrophy. This has resulted in ever-higher levels of partisan dealignment and disengagement. What emerges is a substantial tier of capricious unaffiliated voters. These voters are usually disengaged but sometimes prone to "fevers" over new, charismatic politicians and easily blown about by winds generated by contingent events and media cycles.

As we show in this chapter, such overall political anomie has been punctured by short bouts of antiestablishment insurgencies described as "populist" within Japan. These include high-profile maverick leaders, such as former prime minister Junichiro Koizumi (2001–06), who vowed to *bukkowasu* (bust up) his own party. They are also represented by influential local politicians, such as Toru Hashimoto, former mayor (2008–11) and governor of Osaka (2011–15), and Yuriko Koike, the current governor of Tokyo. These local insurgents founded new parties locally and nationally to capture, as Hashimoto described it, the *fuwatto shita minni* (floaty will of the people) and "reset" the status quo. Though differing in dynamic, we also examine the rise of identity politics initiated by the late governor of Okinawa, Takeshi Onaga (2014–18), who promised to fight for the "pride of Okinawa" against the central government. In what way were these movements populist? And how, if at all, did their promises and actions threaten the internal foundations of the liberal international order?

This chapter examines the nature and limits of these cases of Japanese "populism." Koizumi, Hashimoto, and Koike stirred up underlying resentment among voters against what they defined as the people's enemy: unaccountable vested interest groups. They targeted urban unaffiliated voters directly with media-savvy techniques, generating excitement through divisive and combative rhetoric. Ideologically, they were neoliberal, promoting greater economic globalization and deregulation, and leaning toward liberal cultural values. Once in office, they did not pursue antipluralist or nationalistic policies, but they acted pragmatically in their pursuit of their economic reform agenda. In Okinawa, Onaga exploited an underlying sense among islanders that they were forced to shoulder an unfair share of the national security burden. It was not antiliberal or antielite but rather an anti-Tokyo appeal. It resulted in a breaking down of traditional Left-Right partisan divisions and the birth of an identity-based coalition opposing national security policy.

We show how these local populists and their movements, however brilliant their initial rise, were unable to translate local successes onto the national level. Institutional and organizational barriers prevented these newcomers from achieving sustained nationwide support. That the failure was ideational was equally important. These populists failed to present a program and vision that could attract voters beyond their own localities.

An exclusive focus on the potential threat of populists, however, risks overlooking how mainstream parties themselves have been behaving in response to these insurgencies. We therefore also turn our attention to whether the second Abe administration has acted in ways that may potentially threaten the liberal international order. Has there been a "shift to the Right" in Japanese politics, which some observers claim is embodied by the Abe administration? Have the mainstream parties pursued illiberal and nativist positions that may be incompatible with multilateralism, free trade, liberal values, and liberal democratic institutions?

Finally, we engage with the idea that populists are not merely a negative pathology threatening liberal democracy. Populists gain support by responding to grievances and frustrations among voters that had been heretofore ignored or muffled by the political elite. In that sense, bouts of antiestablishment revolts in Japan illuminate issues that need addressing. These include long-standing disengagement with the political and bureaucratic establishment and different kinds of socioeconomic injustices felt by both urban and rural voters. We conclude by examining how these threats could be exacerbated or contained.

Populism in Japan

Though Japan has been seen as being immune to the kind of populist politics shaping democracies elsewhere, closer observation reveals episodes of antiestablishment politics in recent years, particularly at local levels, which reflect a range of voter dissatisfactions.

PERCEPTIONS OF POPULISM IN JAPAN

Public interest in populism in Japan peaked before the emergence of Donald Trump as a U.S. presidential candidate or the U.K. Brexit referendum in 2016, two key events that triggered global concerns about populist trends. Google Trends data shows that the term "populism" in Japanese was most frequently searched in September 2012, followed by October 2016 to February 2017 (figure 7-1). Newspaper article databases show that articles about populism surged in three waves: 2003–04, 2012, and 2016–17 (figure 7-2).

Looking through these articles from *Asahi* and *Yomiuri*, the term "populism" has been primarily used in reference to the following: Prime Minister Koizumi and his snap election in 2005; the Democratic Party of Japan and its manifesto in 2009; the victory of the regional parties led

FIGURE 7-1. Google Search Trends for "Populism" in Japanese, 2004–18

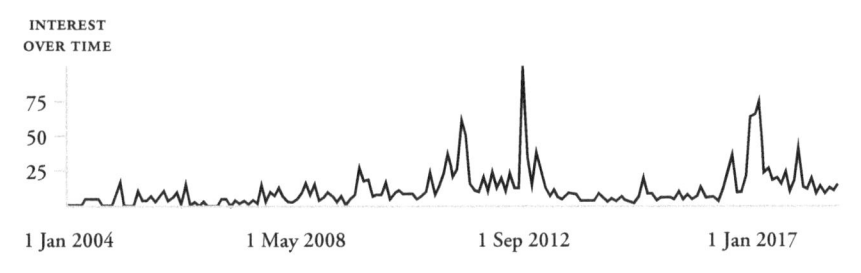

INTEREST OVER TIME

Source: Compiled by the authors from Google Trends, searching *popyurizumu* in Japan.

FIGURE 7-2. Number of Newspaper Articles Including the Term "Populism," 1990–2018

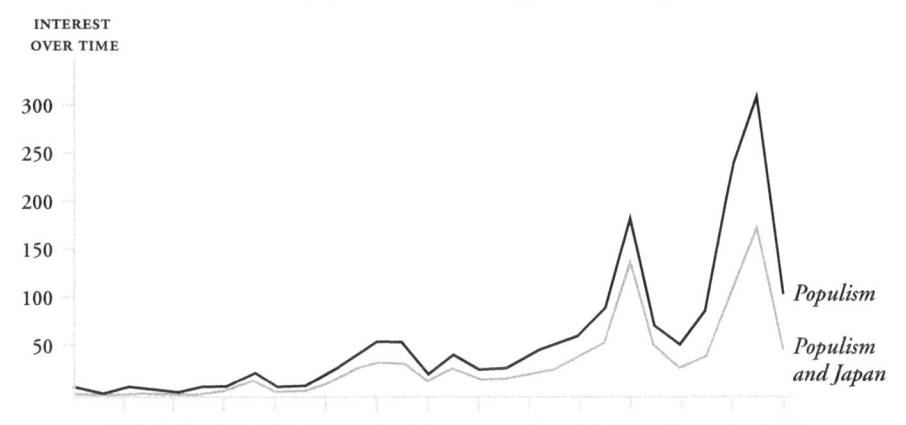

INTEREST OVER TIME

Source: Compiled by the authors from *Asahi* and *Yomiuri* article databases.

by Osaka governor Hashimoto in local elections in 2011; the launching of a national party by Hashimoto in 2012; Brexit and Trump from 2016 to 2017; and the launching of Tokyo Governor Koike's national party in 2017. There was a total of nearly 1,700 articles with the term "populism" in both newspapers between 1990 and 2018. Among these articles, the Japanese politicians most commonly mentioned, by order of frequency, were Toru Hashimoto (119 articles), Junichiro Koizumi (60), Shintaro Ishihara (48), and Yuriko Koike (44).

It is notable that a large number of high-profile governors and mayors in Japan have been frequently described as "populists." They include not only Governors Koike, Ishihara, and Hashimoto, as previously mentioned, but also figures such as Nagano governor Yasuo Tanaka (2000–06), Shiga governor Yukiko Kada (2006–14), Nagoya mayor Takashi Kawamura (current), and Miyazaki governor Hideo Higashikokubaru (2007–11). These local politicians share features of being outsiders to the political establishment, having had careers as writers, celebrities, lawyers, or academics before becoming high-profile politicians. Most important, in campaigning, these governors and mayors were, or at least presented themselves as, independent of mainstream parties and unconnected to various interest groups.

The rise of such independent governors since the mid-1990s primarily reflects two factors. First, it reflects the growth of unaffiliated voters dissatisfied with the establishment parties at the national and local levels, seeking to take a chance with antiestablishment figures. Second, it reflects government decentralization reforms in this period, which elevated the stake of local elections and has led to a greater decoupling of local politics from national parties.[3] An additional structural reason for the frequency of the success of such challengers against establishment party candidates is the nature of gubernatorial and mayoral elections. These are single-shot electoral contests, unlike parliamentary elections, and thus do not require sustained or nationwide organizations to win.

A number of books have been published, including several on Koizumi and Hashimoto, analyzing these trends of populism in Japan and claiming the existence of a "Japanese-type populism."[4] Otake observes that Japanese-style populists, such as Koizumi and his ministers, who defined the people's "enemy" as bureaucrats, have affinity with neoliberal reforms and effectively used mass media to directly appeal to voters.[5] Ikeda claims Japanese-type populism is irresponsible pandering that avoids making difficult political decisions.[6] These observations are illuminating in understanding norms of democratic representation but not very helpful in putting Japanese populism in a comparative context.

FEATURES OF JAPANESE POPULISM

Cas Mudde has famously defined populism as a binary worldview that frames politics as a struggle between two homogeneous groups: a righteous people against a corrupt elite[7] (see the introductory chapter for more detailed definitions of populism). By this measure, these so-called Japanese populists were indeed populist in their rhetoric and strategy. They appealed to the average voter against differing establishment groups, exploiting resentment and a sense of injustice about these unaccountable elites. But the targeted enemies and policy prescriptions of this binary worldview were very different from the kind offered by the Western populist movements and parties, characterized by the radical Right, Trump, or Brexit. Rather than hostility to minorities, open borders, and economic globalization, these Japanese populists were primarily focused on framing and attacking an unaccountable and wasteful public sector.

With the exception of an identity politics driven by Okinawan regionalism, Japanese populism was primarily neoliberal. The worldview it offered was that of the average law-abiding (usually urban) taxpayer being hurt by groups that benefited unjustly from government subsidies and protection. Through combative rhetoric, they attacked what they deemed as "vested interests" comprised of bureaucrats, public employees, interest groups, and their affiliated politicians. In Okinawa, the populist worldview framed the elite as the indifferent and unresponsive central government and mainstream parties in Tokyo who discriminated against proud, peace-loving islanders.

Another vital feature, but arguably not a necessary component of populism in general, is its antiliberalism. As Jan-Werner Müller argues, in the struggle against the elite, the "will of the people," as defined and represented by the populists, is the only political voice that is legitimate.[8] All other political actors and voices are treated as illegitimate and to be disregarded in democratic decisionmaking. Using this measure of populism as antiliberalism, however, the Japanese populists, both in campaigning and in office, appear not to be very populist. In their worldview, the status quo did not represent the average citizen and the collective good. Instead, the political elite were seen to be focused on rigging markets and funneling public monies to themselves and their supporters. The solution, according to the populists, was to generate greater competition and accountability through radical structural and administrative reform. More responsiveness and accountability by improving the democratic processes is not an antipluralist or antiliberal position.

We now turn to four key examples—one at the national level and three at the local level—and demonstrate that Japanese populism is characterized by an antielitism that is not necessarily antiliberal.

KOIZUMI

At the national level, Prime Minister Junichiro Koizumi has been analyzed frequently as a populist in rhetoric, campaigning style, and strategy. Otake argues that Koizumi implemented a strategy of "dramatized politics," in which he "depicted himself as a 'hero' representing the average citizen against professional politicians and bureaucrats depicted as self-interested 'villains' in a drama of good against evil."[9] These villains were labeled *teikou seiryoku* (reactionary forces) and included the bureaucracy, affiliated public sector companies, and politicians representing special interest groups that resisted deregulation and privatization.[10]

Koizumi, though a third-generation politician, was adept at casting himself as a political outsider and champion of the ordinary voter. Through an extremely popular email newsletter, which had over 2 million subscribers,[11] and unorthodox speaking style combining forceful and blunt rhetoric, he personalized the office of the prime minister. Koizumi became a master of the short, informal interview in which he delivered quotable sound bites to the media to shape public opinion, in what became described as "one-phrase politics." Many of the major policy decisions during his administration, including postal and highway privatization and responses to the first Iraq War and the North Korean abductee issue, were orchestrated as a "political drama" to generate broader support.[12]

Koizumi's main policy agenda was characterized by neoliberal principles of transforming Japan *kan kara min he* (from the public to the private sector) on the domestic front and economic liberalism and multilateralism on the international front. Structural reforms of government finances, including fiscal decentralization, reducing public works spending, disposing of bad loans, revitalizing the financial sector, and reforming pension and medical systems, as well as privatization and deregulation, took up the five years of his administration. In terms of trade, Koizumi promoted FDI and greater liberalization, signing Japan's first economic partnership agreement with Singapore in 2002 and with Mexico in 2005.

In terms of diplomacy, while actively supporting Japan's alliance with the United States through contributions to the war against terrorism, Koizumi strengthened multilateral links with Asia, Africa, and the EU through frequent attendance of summits, international organization meetings, and fostering personal links with world leaders. Although Koizumi's visits to the Yasukuni Shrine severely damaged relations with China and South Korea, the visits were seen as primarily driven by electoral considerations rather than historical revisionist ideology. As Nakakita notes, "While pursuing neoliberal reforms through populist strategy, Koizumi showed very little interest in the traditional right-wing nationalism of the LDP, including the party goal of establishing Japan's own constitution."[13]

Koizumi's populist strategy generated an unprecedentedly high level of support in polls throughout his five-year administration, with much of it coming from unaffiliated voters.[14] These voters, many of them in urban areas, tended to be hostile toward "wasteful" public works spending and resentful of the preferential treatment of rural interests. This dynamic is a notable inversion to the kind of populists in the West supported by "left-behind" rural heartlands of a country reacting against a cosmopolitan elite.

Koizumi's top-down push toward privatization, deregulation, and decentralization generated a backlash from within the party, particularly among politicians and local branches of the LDP in rural areas. In 2005, veteran LDP politicians from rural districts left the ruling party in opposition to privatizing the postal office. Led by Shizuka Kamei and Tamisuke Watanuki, these politicians formed the People's New Party, a name with clearly populist leanings. Though opposing neoliberalism and globalization, they did not define and attack a particular group such as big business, banks, or a cosmopolitan elite as "enemies," unlike populists in the West. Nor did they call for economic nativism, but rather tempering of free trade. Their electoral success was minimal, and the party won only a handful of parliamentary seats before being disbanded in 2013.

HASHIMOTO

Toru Hashimoto, governor (2008–11) and later mayor (2011–15) of Osaka, was renowned for his combative style of politics and mastery of the media. Hashimoto's modus operandi was to set up "enemies," which he would attack in the name of the average voter, and generate controversy and "battles" that would fuel media exposure. This constant cycle of controversy mobilized unaffiliated voters and allowed him and his party to win successive elections against local incumbents, who, in contrast, relied primarily on organized votes. As Hashimoto himself states, this was a conscious strategy: "In order to get the Osaka people interested, it has to be entertaining. The easiest way is to have a combative approach. Everybody watches a battle."[15] Lacking organized support from parties, interest groups, or unions, as a political outsider, Hashimoto was keenly aware of the need to maintain media exposure: "I am a politician that cannot survive without the media. Once the media starts ignoring me or stops reporting on me, I am finished."[16]

The groups or issues framed as "enemies" varied and shifted. Hashimoto railed against the central government and ministries in Tokyo, which prevented greater regional autonomy and decentralization. Hashimoto lambasted local public servants—particularly the public sector unions, local teachers, and educational authorities—for lack of professionalism and resisting decisions made by their political masters. He also constantly battled with the media and academic commentators, criticizing them as being ignorant and irresponsible in reportage or commentary.[17]

Hashimoto often resorted to colorful invectives to define enemies—such as calling the education committee members *kuso kyoiku iinkai* (shit), journalists *baka* (idiots), and central ministries *bottakuri bar* (rip-offs). Hashimoto primarily did this through Twitter, where he compulsively tweeted throughout his terms in office and has the most widely followed account among Japanese politicians. As of 2018, Hashimoto has over 2 million followers, even after retiring from office, almost double that of the Prime Minister Shinzo Abe.[18] Hidehiko Koguchi, a media analyst and former adviser to the LDP, points out that "Hashimoto was, even before Trump, a master of serial tweeting. It makes one almost imagine that Trump had studied the art of tweeting from him."[19]

Hashimoto's administration was not just about tweets. As governor and mayor of Osaka, Hashimoto focused and succeeded in balancing local government finances through various cost-cutting measures, improving accountability and transparency of the public sector. Another key issue was the goal to turn the Osaka prefectural and city administration into one *tokoso* (metropolitan area) to improve administrative efficiency and decisionmaking in Osaka. These local policy goals were primarily neoliberal in that they focused on economic efficiency, competition, and downsizing the public sector. The Japan Innovation Party (JIP), which was initially launched by Hashimoto in 2012 as the Japan Restoration Party, was based on the same principles. Its goal is to create "self-reliant individuals, regions, and nation" by "smashing vested interests" and "reforming the governance system." Its manifesto emphasizes decentralization, deregulation, and changing the administrative system to encourage greater competition and accountability, while espousing diversity of social values.[20]

Hitoshi Asada, policy chairman for the JIP, describes the party as "a team of pragmatists—not based on any particular ideology. We are neither of the old Left seeking to liberate workers nor the nationalist Right doing everything for the state."[21] The party shows signs of such ideological flexibility by combining costcutting with expanding government services elsewhere, such as education and childcare services. The party, Asada says, is one of the few parties pushing for "intra-generational redistribution of wealth from richer elderly to poorer elderly," to reduce the burden on younger generations to support pensioners.

The party is also in "complete agreement" with the values of the liberal international order, including the rule of law, democracy, and liberalism.[22] The national party has been in favor of free trade, including various free trade agreements and expanding FDI; using skilled foreign labor; solidarity with other liberal democracies; and engagement with international organizations, including the use of the International Court of Justice. However, according to Asada, the party's 2012 merger with the far-Right Sunrise Party (later, Next Generation Party), led by Shintaro Ishihara, created a false impression of Hashimoto and his party as right-wing ideologues. In other areas, Hashimoto also denounced the anti-Korean and anti-Chinese hate speech activities of the *Zaitokukai* (Association of Citizens against the Special Privileges of the Zainichi). Osaka has one of the highest concentrations of Korean residents in Japan, but this has not led the Osaka-based party, or any of the other locally represented parties, to embrace anti-immigration or antiforeigner positions.

However, Hashimoto has also been accused of "fascism" (spelled *hashizumu*, as a pun on his name) by critics on the Left, following his claim that "What Japanese politics needs now is dictatorship. What will keep it in check is the assembly, elections, and the media."[23] Similarly, he has claimed that Japan's governance system is a "democracy in which no one makes decisions and hence a democracy in which no one takes responsibility."[24] But the emphasis on majoritarian, winner-takes-all electoral democracy does not make Hashimoto or his party antipluralist or antidemocratic. The party espouses diversity in society. It has also squarely accepted electoral defeat as a failure to persuade the public of the rightness of the party's proposals, following the 2014 general election and 2015 defeat of a referendum on merging Osaka city and prefecture. An antipluralist populist would have denounced the legitimacy of these electoral results as not reflecting the "people's true voice."

In his latest book, Hashimoto himself acknowledges how the media frequently referred to him as a "populist," and he seems to have embraced the label:

> There are many people who criticize populism as an "evil." So-called intellectuals, scholars and commentators assume that populism is evil . . . But I do not believe populism to be an evil at all. To be more accurate, there is good populism and faulty populism. If, for example, citizens are idiots or democracy is immature in a country, then populism is not good. But if citizens are wise, a politics that follows the majority will is, of course, good. In that regard, the level of the Japanese voter is high, compared to other countries across a whole range of things, including education standards and maturity of democracy . . . Of course, a populism that does not disclose information or tries to take majorities by deceiving citizens with false information is a bad populism. Then there is a risk of destroying the political order.[25]

However, Hashimoto's and his party's dramatic victories in local mayoral, gubernatorial, and assembly elections within Osaka did not translate into similar successes at the national level. Between 2012 and 2018, most of the single-member district constituencies the JIP won nationally came from in and around Osaka prefecture. After various mergers and splits, the party's peak seat share in the Lower House has fallen from a high of 54 out of 479 seats in 2012 to 11 out of 465 seats in 2018.

One key source of weakness has been the JIP's failure to establish party organizations and support infrastructure in regions beyond Osaka, particularly in rural areas still dominated by the LDP.[26] According to Ichiro Matsui, governor of Osaka and leader of both the local and national manifestations of the JIP, the long-term strategy for his party is to build from the bottom up. To achieve national success, he says, the party is seeking to capture as many local executive positions as possible, increase the number of local assembly members, and build up a track record of delivering visible change in local administration. Another strategy is to realize as many of their policy goals nationally through their parliamentary presence. Examples of this include pushing the Abe administration to legalize integrated resorts and casinos and triggering debate about free public education.

Another reason for the limitations of the JIP at the national level has been ideational. Its policy agenda and framing of enemies—targeting wasteful spending, decrying intergenerational inequalities, and redesigning political institutions—have been limited in appeal to more urban, younger, and intellectual voters. Reflecting this narrow appeal, the JIP's national support ratings have been in the low single digits after its first general election campaign in 2012, and by October 2018, JIP support ratings had slipped to under 1 percent. This is compared to 28 percent support for the LDP, a combined 7.7 percent support for the other six opposition parties, and a whopping 59 percent of voters who do not support any party.[27]

"Political and fiscal reform, as well as decentralization, have been the two central agendas we have been pushing," says Governor Matsui. "But there is no magic wand to make committed supporters of our party out of the majority of non-partisan Japanese voters."[28]

More substantially, the strategy of exploiting divisions between the average taxpayer and those seen as benefiting unjustly from the public sector may not work nationwide. In other large cities with a dynamic of unaffiliated voters and protected public-sector employees and companies, similar populist appeals have emerged with some success. For example, Nagoya mayor Takashi Kawamura and, as we examine below, Tokyo governor Yuriko Koike. But for most smaller cities and rural areas, where residents depend on government subsidies or are employed by the public sector, directly or indirectly, such appeals have limits. A successful populist party, let alone a new party, from these regions with less dynamic economies has yet to emerge in Japan.

KOIKE

Yuriko Koike, a veteran parliamentarian and former minister of environment and minister of defense, left the LDP to run and win as a candidate for Tokyo governor in 2016. The following year, she launched her own local party—the Tokyoites First—and later a national party—the Party of Hope. Her brief but meteoric rise in local politics and failed bid for national-level expansion was marked by populist rhetoric attacking the political elite and generalized appeals to the common sense and wisdom of average voters.

In her gubernatorial campaign, Koike attacked the incumbent parties—particularly the local LDP—for deciding things behind closed doors. Voters were receptive to this kind of criticism, as the Tokyo metropolitan government had suffered a series of high-profile scandals, including two of its earlier governors, Naoki Inose and Yoichi Masuzoe, resigning over political financing and improper use of public funds, respectively. In her turn, Koike promised politics in which *tomin ga kimeru* (Tokyo residents will decide).[29] Once elected, she framed veteran members of the assembly as sabotaging reforms. She denounced former governors, including Shintaro Ishihara, and the Olympic committee led by former prime minister Yoshiro Mori (2000–01) for nontransparent decisionmaking and wasteful spending over construction and preparation for the games. She launched a local party—Tokyoites First—aimed at combating what she described as the opaque politics of a self-serving elite.[30] In a similar vein, her national party called for the "eradication of vested interest groups, opaque interests, and fetters of the past in order to achieve a politics of the 'voters first.'"[31]

Masaru Wakasa, former member of parliament and cofounder of the Party of Hope, has said of the party that "Our strategy was not antiestablishment or antielitism per se, but rather to combat what we called *shigarami seiji* (vested interest politics)—the opaque and unaccountable system of decisionmaking in Japan."[32]

In place of corrupt, closed-door politics, Koike proposed more pluralistic, transparent, and accountable governance. Her policy proposals centered around a neoliberal growth strategy of deregulation and interregional competition, remaking Tokyo into a global financial center and accepting skilled immigrants. These measures were combined with pluralist appeals of increasing social diversity by promoting women in the workplace and opposing discrimination, including against sexual minorities.[33]

Koike initially benefited from a strong distrust of the local political elite, following scandals of previous governors as well as strong media criticism over the local assembly in its planning for the Tokyo Olympics and the transfer of the Tsukiji fish market. In both her gubernatorial race (2016) and the lead-up to her local parties' landslide victory in the Tokyo metropolitan elections (2017), polls show Koike securing broad support from unaffiliated voters as well as voters who supported the national ruling parties (LDP and Komeito). In addition, women voters were also more prone to support Tokyo's first female governor.[34]

But just like Hashimoto, Koike failed to parlay this local enthusiasm into success nationally. In its first and only national election in 2017, her party lost more seats than it had started out with, shrinking from fifty-seven to fifty seats in the Lower House. The few who retained their district-level seats were veteran parliamentarians with strong personal organizations. Even in its home ground of Tokyo, the Party of Hope did poorly, winning only one of the twenty-four Tokyo districts that it had contested. Within a month of the national elections, Koike stepped down as party leader, and the party itself was soon merged into another opposition party.

The electoral defeat primarily reflected the collapse of popularity for Koike herself and lack of preparation for the new party. Following controversial remarks by Koike that she would "exclude" more liberal and Left-leaning members in merger negotiations with other opposition parties, hopes for a united centrist opposition to the LDP were dashed. After the "exclusion" statement, Koike's personal support ratings also collapsed from as high as 66 percent in September 2017 to around 32 percent in October 2017.[35] Wakasa believes Koike was the victim of a "jet-coaster ride of support" generated by media coverage. "I do not think Koike herself was a populist to start out with—but rather it was the media that built her up to increase audience ratings. They also brought her down to gain ratings."[36]

Besides the inability to cooperate with other opposition parties, the party did not have time to prepare for a national campaign, with less than a month from launching the party to when votes were cast in October 2017.[37] The Party of Hope also failed to sufficiently differentiate itself from the LDP ideologically and programmatically. Aside from opposition to nuclear power and raising the consumption tax, the governor's policy positions on economic growth, redistribution, security policy, and constitutional reform were largely indistinguishable from those of the ruling conservatives.[38]

Summing up the short, brilliant flash of support for Koike, Wakasa explains: "There were two groups dreaming different dreams and supporting Koike. There were those that opposed the LDP administration in principle and dreamed of a non-Abe government. And then there were those who were simply looking for something different. These voters were seeking spectacle, almost like wanting to enter a ghost house—an unreal but exciting world that could break the mundane sense of being hemmed in."[39]

The collapse of Koike's support from local to national elections within the short span of a year suggests that most of her supporters were the latter type—seeking something different, but not in a determined manner. That is, the majority of her supporters were not driven by strong ideological commitment to her program, which did not change substantially from gubernatorial to metropolitan to national elections. Although Koike emphasized the Abe administration's lack of transparency in a series of recent scandals (Moritomo, Kake, and Self-Defense Forces movements in Iraq), these attacks were not enough to generate national momentum. A lack of policy differentiation, organizational preparation, and collapse in personal backing led to evaporating support for the populist's bid for national power.

ONAGA

An exception to Japanese "populists" driven primarily by an agenda of neoliberal reform is the regionalist identity politics of Takeshi Onaga, the late governor of Okinawa Prefecture. Though few have described the Okinawan governor as populist, the combination of identity politics and resentment mobilized by Onaga through his us-versus-them ideology demonstrates strongly populist features.

Onaga mobilized Okinawan voters by appealing to Okinawan identity, pride, and history to oppose the central government over U.S. base issues. Using Ryukyuan phrases throughout his speeches, Onaga emphasized the distinctiveness of Okinawan identity to "unite the Okinawan people's heart" against the rest of the country, which he claimed was acting in concert to maintain unpopular U.S. military bases stationed in the prefecture.[40] In November 2014, Onaga won the Okinawan gubernatorial election by calling for voters "to overcome divisions between the Left and the Right." He promised "growth with dignity" and to "protect Okinawan pride" by opposing the construction of a new U.S. military base in Henoko.[41] Appealing to "identity, not ideology," a catch phrase of his campaign, Onaga successfully built a coalition bridging conservatives and progressive forces.

Driving this regionalist populism is strong disillusionment with the central government and the mainstream parties on the Left and Right, along with the sense that mainland Japan does not understand the Okinawan islanders. The perception of a divide between Okinawa and the mainland attitudes increased between 2002 and 2012, before reaching peak levels in 2017, when a survey found that 71 percent of respondents believe the mainland Japanese do not *rikai* (understand) Okinawa, compared to 19 percent who believe they do.[42] A similar trend can be seen in partisan support among Okinawan voters for national parties, which shows a surge of those supporting no party in the same period.[43]

Onaga exploited this growing sense of estrangement of Okinawa voters from the mainland. In 2012, two years before his gubernatorial campaign and at the end of the DPJ administration, he argued:

> Even if a hundred thousand Okinawans protest against the deployment of U.S. Osprey helicopters in the prefecture, the mainland does not pay the slightest attention. The U.S. bases are fine so long as they are placed far from where any mainlander can see, while nobody in the mainland wants these bases near them. Nor do any of them want to say anything to the Americans. . . I have become disillusioned to the point of feeling that mainlanders are all the same.[44]

Similar language was employed when Onaga addressed the UN Human Rights Council (UNHRC) on September 21, 2015, in Geneva. The emphasis is on discrimination against the rights of the Okinawan people, and he sought international support based on appeals to the core values of the liberal international order:

> I would like the world to pay attention to Henoko, where Okinawans' right to self-determination is being neglected. After World War II, the United States military took our land by force, and constructed military bases in Okinawa. We have never provided our land willingly. Okinawa covers only 0.6 percent of Japan. However, 73.8 percent of U.S. exclusive bases in Japan are in Okinawa. Over the past seventy years, U.S. bases have caused many incidents, accidents, and environmental problems in Okinawa. Our right to self-determination and human rights have been neglected. Can a country share values such as freedom, equality, human rights, and democracy with other nations when that country cannot guarantee those values for its own people?[45]

Onaga's regionalist populism is not xenophobic or exclusionary, as perhaps some regionalist movements such as the Italian Lega Nord or the Belgian Vlaams Belang have been characterized. Onaga envisioned Okinawa to become an island of tourism and trade open to the world—serving as a "bridge" to connect conflicting regions of Asia.[46] In contrast, some of Onaga's opponents have responded with xenophobic anti-Okinawan rhetoric. In 2016, an Osaka riot police officer sent to guard the base construction in Henoko was filmed shouting the word *dojin* (aborigines)—a racist slur of Okinawans—at anti-base protestors.[47] Those writing into right-wing chat sites and blogs have attacked the governor and his supporters variously as *hannichi* (anti-Japanese), *baikokudo* or *hikokumin* (traitors), or *shinajin, Chugoku no tesaki* (Chinese, or Chinese spy).[48] With such racist language from the mainland gaining attention, an angry regionalist populism in Okinawa driven by a sense of discrimination may become harder to defuse.

The pan-partisan, anti–center coalition under Onaga was successful electorally and embraced confrontational tactics against Tokyo over base policy. Faced with a determined central government, however, the governor was only able to slow down rather than prevent new base construction. In later periods, electoral losses to pro-base candidates backed by the LDP, including key elections such as the mayorship of Nago (in which the new Henoko base is being constructed), also hurt the coalition. The movement has been very much centered around Onaga as an individual and has not coalesced into a clear organization or party.

Onaga's successor, however, has inherited the strategy of identity politics. Before his death, Onaga designated Denny Tamaki, a former radio personality and Diet member of the Liberal Party, as his successor candidate for the 2018 gubernatorial elections. Tamaki campaigned on an image of "a rich and proud Okinawa," with similar tropes of regional identity and pride. Tamaki opposed base construction and promised to continue Onaga's legacy.[49] In a surprise outcome, and against a rival candidate who had received unprecedented backing from the LDP headquarters, Tamaki triumphed. This has revitalized the progressive camp, with further conflict over base construction likely between the center and Okinawa, including a planned prefectural referendum on the issue in 2019.

Explaining these trends, Mikio Shimoji, member of parliament for Okinawa, formerly of the People's New Party and currently of the JIP, sees voters in Okinawa becoming less ideological in recent elections.

"The center in Okinawa has become stronger, and those committed ideologically on either the Left or the Right are weakening. And this center is also very conscious of what the central government is doing," says Shimoji. "When Tokyo takes a hard line, these voters are persuaded by those who say Okinawa is being discriminated against. And when Tokyo does something dynamic and interesting for voters, they swing toward those linked to the center."[50]

These swings to the Left and Right in the past twenty years of Okinawan elections are less about strong Left-Right ideological positions, structural changes, or partisan polarization, says Shimoji. These are voters being carried by *kaze* (winds) shaped by contingencies on the ground and being swayed by *jyo ni uttaeru* (emotional appeals) such as those used by Onaga and his successor, Tamaki, over Okinawan identity and pride.

Pragmatism, Nationalism, Inequality, and Disengagement

Despite surges of antiestablishment politics, Japanese conservatives have been able to rebuff these challenges from below. What has been the source of their resilience to such backlashes until now, and what future developments might strengthen populism or lead to unwelcome political instability?

PRAGMATIC RESPONSES TO BACKLASHES

In sum, Japanese "populists" share antielitist features of presenting themselves as political outsiders who champion ordinary people against a clearly defined enemy—be they interest groups and bureaucrats, old-boy networks of politicians, or an unresponsive central government. But these populists are not antipluralist. They support the core principles of the liberal international order: free trade, globalization, internationalism, and the limits that the rule of law and liberalism places on state power.

Another commonality is that these populists are not supported, in the main, by voters with strong ideological convictions or deep-rooted hostility to particular elites. Fickle, undecided voters have carried them into office locally, attracted by the charismatic spectacle provided by the leaders and reacting to recent scandals or missteps of the establishment. Attempts to scale-up local revolts failed due to the barriers of creating nationally institutionalized bases of support. This meant they could not compete when contingent tailwinds died down and turnout dropped, with the ruling conservatives' significant base of support from organized voters and strong network of local politicians.

The ruling conservatives have also repeatedly shown a pragmatic capacity to adjust and co-opt policies in the face of emergent challengers, whether populist or not. This tendency to change tack after electoral upsets by the LDP—what Kent Calder famously called the "crisis and compensation" dynamic—has been a common feature of the postwar period.[51] Widespread political protest over security issues was defused by promises of "doubling income" in the early 1960s. The rise of progressive governors backed by socialists and communists in the 1970s caused the LDP to adopt and co-opt more stringent pollution regulations and expand welfare programs. As the rural population declined, and urban voters became more important following electoral reforms since the mid-1990s, the LDP shifted its policy focus and campaign strategy to the urban floating voter. Koizumi's structural reforms and direct populist appeals were a drastic break from past LDP clientelism, but also a spectacularly successful, albeit short-lived, electoral adaptation to changing circumstances.

More recently, the LDP has again changed tack following electoral defeats in 2007 and 2009. The LDP recognized these defeats as a "revolt of the regions" and the weakening of support from client groups due to pro-market structural reforms. This prompted the party, under Prime Minister Taro Aso (2008–09), to promise to "distance itself from excessive market fundamentalism" prior to the 2009 elections.[52]

The second Abe administration has also sought to modify unadulterated market liberalism with measures to shore up support from its traditional bases. Abenomics combines both the structural reforms of deregulating sectors, such as agriculture and healthcare, with expansion of traditional public works spending. It is, according to Nakakita, an "attempt to sublate (that is, assimilate) the contradiction between neoliberal reforms that have troubled the LDP and its traditional clientelistic practices."[53] The delayed but ultimately responsive reaction of the conservatives to both urban and rural pressures has blocked a full-scale revolt from either disgruntled urban voters or rural areas that have lost out in structural reforms over the past two decades.

Can the electoral pragmatism, which has allowed the ruling conservatism in Japan to reinvent itself and survive over the past three-quarters of a century, be upended? There is a number of potential scenarios that could upset this current stability of Japanese politics.

THREAT OF NATIONALISM?

The first threat may be a shift to more uncompromising, xenophobic nationalism among the political elite and/or electorate. Observers have argued that ideological diversity has declined within the LDP. Moderate conservative leadership has been replaced with strident nationalists, who have come to dominate discourse in the party.[54] The membership of many cabinet members, Abe included, in the Nippon Kaigi—a Far Right nationalist organization championing revisionist historical views and conservative values —is seen as symptomatic of this shift. The conservatives' illiberal 2012 constitutional reform proposal that seemed to imply the preeminence of the state and family over individual rights is another.

There are various explanations for why the Japanese political elite has embraced nationalist themes in recent years. These include weakening traditional, materially driven client groups being supplanted by more ideologically driven interest groups, such as the Association of Shinto Shrines.

Electoral dynamics under more majoritarian rules introduced in the mid-1990s have pushed parties to differentiate themselves from the opposition.[55] It has also elevated the importance of programmatic promises, including those on foreign policy, leading to an emphasis of nationalist positions in elections.[56] The centralization of the party under the party leader and policy program in the new electoral system has reduced the broad range of ideological positions within the party.[57] At the same time, heightened tensions and potential security threats from Asian neighbors (China and North Korea) have triggered nationalist responses.

But it is far from clear that nationalist appeals alone can win elections. Or that the majority of voters can stomach the kind of right-wing agenda held by Nippon Kaigi and harbored by some in the conservative leadership of the LDP. Challengers with a nationalist platform farther Right of the LDP, such as Makoto Sakurai and Toshio Tamogami, have failed dismally in local and national elections. The support ratings of nationalist Right parties such as Next Generation Party (in 2014 and 2015), which included arch-nationalists Shintaro Ishihara and Takeo Hiranuma as party executives, peaked at about 0.5 percent of the electorate. In recent years, the Zaitokukai—an extremist group founded in 2006, which campaigns against resident Koreans and opposes welfare and suffrage to foreign residents—has attracted attention with their virulent hate speech and street demonstrations. But their political impact has been limited. The former leader of the Zaitokukai, Makoto Sakurai founded his own Japan First Party (Nippon Dai Itto) in 2017 and stood candidates for local elections[58] without success after failing his bid for Tokyo governorship. In response to Zaitokukai, local governments and courts have also restricted hate speech demonstrations and activities, with the Japanese Diet legislating anti-hate speech laws in 2016.

Equally significant, the ruling conservatives have generally been "tough" on immigrants: opposing foreigners' voting rights and using strong rhetoric against illegal immigrants and "law-breaking foreigners."[59] This has made it difficult for new parties to gain traction by criticizing the mainstream as "soft" on foreigners. The existence, and dominance, of a staunchly conservative party, not only in terms of immigration but also of cultural and family values, has arguably deflated radical Right insurgencies in Japan. It is important to note that during LDP's time in opposition more ideologically driven nationalist appeals emerged from the party, including the 2012 constitutional reform proposal. This was an attempt by the LDP to differentiate itself from the liberal DPJ administration and also preempt support of non-LDP right-wing parties—such as Tachiagare Nippon, later referred to as Taiyo no To—that had emerged at the time. The LDP's electoral dominance has thus functioned in moderating and restraining the emergence of a viable force further to its Right.

At the level of the electorate, nationalist pride and sentiment have only moderately increased in the past two decades. The proportion of Japanese saying they feel strong or moderate love for their country has only increased by a few percentage points from 50 percent to around 55 percent between 1998 and 2018.[60] Comparatively, those "proud" or "very proud" of their own nation among Japanese respondents of the World Values Survey in 2014, though increasing along with electorates elsewhere, is the lowest among sampled countries.[61]

In an NHK survey, around 15 percent of Japanese voters felt that their jobs were being taken or their culture was being damaged by immigrants, a level far lower than the United States or many European countries. Fifty-six percent of respondents agreed that immigrants should have the same rights as Japanese citizens, one of the highest levels among other countries.[62] A majority (56 percent) of those polled in the same survey also felt that the level of immigrants, which is one of the lowest in the world, was currently at optimum levels. Only 20 percent agreed that Japan should increase the number.

If there is one worrying trend, the Japanese have acquired a particularly strong strain of Sinophobia, as opposed to general xenophobia, in the past decade. Following anti-Japanese riots in Chinese coastal cities in 2005 and territorial disputes in 2012, Japanese voters have been highly distrustful of China, with around 90 percent "holding negative impressions of China" since 2012 (such attitude was only at 38 percent in 2005).[63] Yet anti-China sentiment is not necessarily equivalent to exclusive and myopic nationalism. In fact, the need to counteract the strong threat of China is pushing Japan further into an embrace with international organizations and the liberal international order rather than with go-it-alone nationalism.

Moreover, anti-China sentiment appears distinct from denying Japan's imperialist and colonialist past. Historical revisionist views—that is, denying that Japan waged a war of aggression and imperialism in Asia—are limited in the Japanese electorate. In a 2015 *Asahi* poll, 74 percent of respondents said they would continue to support the Murayama and Koizumi statements in which the Japanese governments "apologized for Japan's invasion" of neighboring countries in the past. Only 13 percent opposed the two statements.[64]

In this context, Abe's nationalist agenda during his first round as prime minister (2006–07) backfired, contributing in part to collapsing support ratings and his early resignation. During his second and current round as prime minister, Abe has learned to temper this nationalist agenda. In rhetoric and action, his administration has pursued active internationalism and been committed to defending the liberal international order; strengthening ties with the United States and other partner countries seeking free trade agreements and economic partnership agreements; upholding multilateral institutions internationally and opening Japan to both capital and greater immigration. Constitutional revision has been put on hold as well, despite the LDP having had one of the best opportunities in its history to revise the constitution. Together with coalition partners and potential pro-revisionist sympathizers, the LDP controlled two-thirds of the seats in both houses, which was enough to propose a revision bill. But over six years into Abe's commitment to "putting an end to the postwar regime," electoral pragmatism has appeared to win out and constitutional reform, once again, has been postponed.

THREAT OF INEQUALITY?

The second threat may come from embracing further immigration and free trade to secure economic growth without maintaining the necessary safeguards to minimize socioeconomic disruption. Japan has avoided xenophobic populism by containing fallout from globalization: economic insecurity and cultural anxiety caused by mass immigration, excessive socioeconomic inequality, and creation of less-educated "left behind" groups of voters.

The assessment of how significant a role economic inequality plays in national politics appears mixed among Japanese politicians themselves, reflecting their ideological commitments and constituencies.

The JIP leader and Osaka governor Ichiro Matsui argues that inequality is too limited and will never become so severe as to trigger a populist backlash in Japan:

> There is no country like Japan in terms of a lack of inequality. Nobody starves to death in Japan, and with a little work you can have a roof over your head and some food to eat. Those in most need have access to medical care and minimum protections, while there are no parties saying we should slash benefits for those at the bottom. That lack of life-threatening inequality, compared to the rest of the world, means many Japanese voters—though they might be frustrated—are resigned to the status quo.[65]

Such a view is countered by Member of Parliament Mikio Shimoji, who represents a district in Okinawa, the poorest prefecture in Japan with an average per capita income less than half that of Tokyo:

> There is a magma of frustration building up over inequality and poverty in rural areas. Some Okinawan voters may wrongly interpret this as a result of discrimination from the center. In fact, it is the result of faulty policy choices by successive local governments. . . . But the reality is, Tokyo is the universe containing everything, whereas rural areas are the ends of the earth.[66]

Masaru Wakasa, cofounder of the Party of Hope, suggests that the steady hand of the current administration on the economy is central to their stability:

> Whatever you say, for example that the benefits of Abenomics only work for the major cities and do not reach the peripheries, the economy is on the upswing. It is certainly better than under the DPJ. The business world is completely behind the LDP, because it is too risky to change the current administration economy-wise. In the last judgment, voters who have the failure of the DPJ administration burned into their memories are likely to avoid risk. Perhaps a generation of voters must emerge that have forgotten the ineptness of the DPJ.[67]

Based on past trends, it seems unlikely that Japan's political elite would embrace sudden and disruptive immigration or trade liberalization, or permit economic inequalities to expand out of hand. The public is largely cautious of greater economic liberalization and satisfied with current levels of immigration, while also intolerant of excessive inequality. The repositioning of the conservatives and other parties following the backlash to Koizumi's structural reforms suggests underlying responsiveness of the political system. So long as the political elite remembers that the ideological excesses of neoliberalism under Koizumi or naked nationalism under Abe hurt it electorally in 2007 and 2009, it will likely stay on a moderate and deliberate course.

THREAT OF DISENGAGEMENT?

The third, and most serious, threat is further disengagement of Japanese voters from the political process.

For many comparative indicators, the Japanese public is less enthusiastic and confident in their democracy than many populist-prone OECD states. A World Values Survey in 2010–14 found that Japanese respondents who have confidence in the national government (24 percent) and political parties (15 percent) is lower than an average of a sample of nine OECD countries (respectively 36.9 percent and 20 percent). In the same survey, the mean level of importance attached to living in a democracy by Japanese voters (between 1 = not at all important and 10 = absolutely important) was 8.27, the lowest among the above sample of nine OECD countries.[68] More worryingly, a substantial number of Japanese voters are willing to consider nondemocratic options such as rule by experts, strong leaders, or military rule, at higher proportions than the public in many other OECD states, according to a Pew Research report on global democracy in 2017.[69]

Reflecting a weak civic culture, a large majority of Japanese voters are unwilling to engage in politics beyond voting and feel political actions to be ineffective (see chapter 10 by Kaori Hayashi). A 2014 survey found that a majority of respondents said they had never and do not plan in the future to participate in political meetings (69 percent), contact politicians and bureaucrats (73 percent) or media (76 percent) to voice political opinions, or participate in a demonstration (75 percent).[70] Nearly 70 percent also said they would not act against a law under deliberation that they opposed, with 80 percent of respondents believing that even if they were to act, the national Diet would be unlikely to heed their demands. All of these indicators of political disengagement have worsened, compared to a similar survey conducted a decade ago.

Such widespread political anomie is reflected in the electoral process. Recent election turnout for national elections—under 50 percent—put Japan near the bottom of OECD rankings.[71] Alongside the increase in abstentions, a majority of Japanese voters do not support any party: voter dealignment has stood over 60 percent in some polls. This type of floating voter is now common among both older and younger voters, and they remain uncommitted to any party even days before casting their vote.[72] Furthermore, party membership for all parties has also been in overall decline, with per capita party membership rates for the Japanese electorate at 1.75 percent,[73] significantly lower than the 4.5 percent average in Western European countries in 2008–09.[74] When these uncommitted voters—what Koguchi calls the "capricious tier"—decide to participate, they may do so only moments before an election, based on whatever has become topical in the news.[75]

The apathy of these Japanese voters has been occasionally punctured by "fevers" of media and voter hysteria over political outsiders with a penchant for combative, populist rhetoric. Koizumi, Hashimoto, and Koike triggered some of the largest and longest "fevers" or "spectacles" of politics, but there have been others. Yet the support for such individual figures is fleeting. Once the leader resigns or loses popularity, the populist insurgency itself quickly evaporates.

The policies that these populists promote—postal privatization, merging of Osaka city and prefecture administrations, increasing transparency in local governance—are primarily administrative and technical, rather than deeply held ideological issues. These Japanese populists' key issues are also very distinct from the long-standing and polarizing questions such as on the EU, immigration, trade, or taxes, which animate populist insurgencies in the West. Japanese populists lack a substantial core of loyal and ideologically driven supporters characterizing the core of Trump supporters or radical Right and Left populist parties in Europe.

Support for the ruling conservatives has also been passive rather than enthusiastic. The snap election under Koizumi in 2005, the 2009 election in which the DPJ won in a landslide, and local elections for Hashimoto and Koike temporarily reversed declines in turnout. Yet overall, the trend has been toward less turnout and less mass media reporting on hard political news. In its place, media analyses show greater interest in celebrity news or political scandal, such as that which led to the resignation of the Tokyo governor in 2016 and generated unceasing reportage (see chapter 10 for more detail).[76]

Faced with such capricious voters, parties may be tempted to turn to more reliable core voters. Though unable to ignore unaffiliated voters, they will prefer to manage their image with them, primarily during election time, rather than engage in sustained fashion or to make them more committed supporters. It is worth noting that the LDP has repeatedly benefited from low turnout in the past, reducing incentives to revive participation and reengagement. In this context, there is a risk that the policy preferences of nonrepresentative interest groups and lobbyists—particularly ideologically driven ones—may be increasingly prioritized over the nonvoting majority. The larger the gap between the government's policy agenda and the nonvoting majority, the more room there will be for populist entrepreneurs to emerge. And if a charismatic populist packages an illiberal and antipluralist message effectively to inflame dormant public frustrations at a national level, all bets are off.

Conclusion

In the concluding section of his book *How Democracy Ends*, which challenges any lazy thinking on the subject, David Runciman turns to Japan and Greece as perhaps "the best guides to how democracy might end up."[77] Runciman continues:

> Francis Fukuyama cited Japan (along with the EU) as the likeliest illustration of what we could expect from the end of history: the triumph of democracy would turn out to be stable, prosperous, efficient, and just a little bit boring. Then the Japanese bubble burst—

along with the Japanese stock market—and the future belonged to someone else. Japan became instead a fable of the dangers of hubris . . . Today Japan and Greece are rarely invoked by politicians in other democracies as exemplars of the possible fate that awaits us all. They do not work as morality plays, because their message has grown too ambiguous. Japan remains stuck in a political and economic rut, yet it continues to function perfectly well as a stable, affluent society that looks after its citizens . . . Instead of the drama reaching a climax, democracy persists in a kind of frozen crouch, holding on, waiting it out, even if it is far from clear what anyone is waiting for. After a while, the waiting becomes the point of the exercise. Something will turn up eventually. It always does.[78]

The moral of Japanese democracy is indeed ambiguous. As this chapter has shown, it has avoided angry and divisive populism, in part through restrictive policies on immigration and trade that have contained fallout from economic globalization. The predominance of one party over more than a half-century has brought stability. But it has equally contributed to widespread voter disengagement and indifference. An affluent and educated population has averted outbursts of political anger but stymied political dynamism. Yet there are forces and choices that could upset the current stability. Rather than just "wait" in a "frozen crouch" for the next thing, there is much to be learned and acted upon.

Populism provides hints. For populism not only threatens but also provides a chance to correct democracy by bringing ignored public frustrations to the political surface. The limited bouts of populism in Japan make clear that there are underlying resentments that must be addressed. Improving the quality of media reporting, and the media literacy of the public, matters in ensuring voters are not misled by the kind of populists who deceive with faulty information and appeals to unreflecting emotion. Nurturing liberal values and democratic processes along with open-minded national confidence (civic, not ethnic, nationalism) will make the public less prone to populist xenophobia or authoritarianism. The most vital challenge for Japan, or any mature democracy, is how to combat disengagement: not only to engage voters but to do so without resorting to emotionally charged and polarizing appeals. Too much politics could be equally as dangerous as too little politics. These challenges are obviously many and complex, so the prescriptions should not be narrowed down to any one improbable silver bullet.

NOTES

1. See, for example: Ethan Scheiner, *Democracy without Competition in Japan: Opposition Failure in a One-Party Dominant State* (Cambridge University Press, 2006); "Kimerarenai Seiji no Minamoto" [The Origins of Indecisive Politics], *Nikkei Shimbun*, September 23, 2012; Kevin K. Maher, *Ketsudan Dekinai Nihon* [The Japan that Can't Decide] (Tokyo: Bungei Shunjusha, 2011), 31.

2. Yoichi Funabashi, "Japan, Where Populism Fails," *New York Times*, February 8, 2017; John Plender, "How Japan Resists the Populist Tide," *Financial Times*, December 31, 2016.

3. See Sunahara (2017) and Hijino (2017) about the impact of decentralization on local electoral processes and party organizations. Yosuke Sunahara, *Bunretsu to Togo no Nihon Seiji* [Japan's Politics of Division and Integration] (Tokyo: Chikura Shobo, 2017); Ken VL Hijino, *Local Politics and National Policy: Multilevel Conflicts in Japan and Beyond* (New York: Routledge, 2017).

4. Hideo Otake, *Koizumi Junichiro Popyurizumu no Kenkyu: Sono Senryaku to Syuho* [A Study of Populism of Junichiro Koizumi: Its Strategy and Method] (Tokyo: Toyo Keizai Shinposha, 2006); Masahiro Zenkyo and Haruya Sakamoto, "Ishin no Kai Shiji Taido no Bunseki" [An Analysis of Favorable Attitudes toward Ishin no Kai], *Senkyo Kenkyu*, vol. 29, no. 2 (2013); Mitsuru Matsutani, "Popurizumu: Ishihara—Hashimoto Chiji wo Shiji suru Hitobito no Tokucho towa nani ka?" [What Are the Characteristics of Supporters of Governor Ishihara and Hashimoto?] in *Gaikokujin eno Manazashi to Seiji Ishiki: Shakai Chosa de Yomitoku Nihon no Nashonarizumu* [Opinions on Foreigners and Political Awareness: An Analysis of Japanese Nationalism Based on Social Research] (Tokyo: Keiso Shobo, 2011); Shinsaku Arima, *Gekijōgata Popyurizumu no Tanjō* [The Birth of Theatrical Populism] (Kyoto: Minerva Shobō, 2017).

5. Hideo Otake, "Nihongata Popyurizumu: Seiji heno Kitai to Genmetsu" [Japanese-Style Populism: Hopes and Disillusion toward Politics] (Tokyo: Chuko Shinsho, 2003), 122–31.

6. Ikeda Nobuo, "Tsuyosugiru Jiminto no Byori: Rojin Shihai to Ninhongata Popyurizumu" [The Pathology of a Too Strong LDP: Domination by the Elderly and Japanese-Style Populism] (Tokyo: PHP Shinsho, 2016).

7. Cas Mudde, "The Populist Zeitgeist," *Government and Opposition*, vol. 39, no. 4, 543.

8. Jan-Werner Müller, *What Is Populism?* (London: Penguin UK, 2017), 3.

9. Otake, *Koizumi Junichiro Popyurizumu no Kenkyu*, 2.

10. Ibid., 5.

11. Internet Watch, "Koizumi Souri ga toujyo Sakaiya-shi wa 'Brodobando Fukyu ni Gekiteki na Kouka' to Zessan," [Prime Minister Koizumi Agrees with Mr. Sakaiya

on "Dramatic Effect of the Internet"], https://internet.watch.impress.co.jp/www/article/2001/1219/impaku.htm.

12. Otake, *Koizumi Junichiro Popyurizumu no Kenkyu*, 5–8.

13. Rebuild Japan Initiative Foundation (RJIF), *Minshuto Seiken Shippai no Kensho: Nihon Seiji ha Nani wo Ikasu ka* [The Democratic Party of Japan in Power: Challenges and Failures (title from English version)] (Tokyo: Chuo Koron Shinsha, 2013), 102.

14. "*Mutohaso no Hyo, Tairyo ni Jimin e: Jiko Kyoryoku wa Isso Shinten*" [Many Independent Voters Voted for LDP: Cooperation between LDP and Komeito Progresses Further], *Yomiuri Shimbun*, September 12, 2005.

15. *Yomiuri Shimbun* Osaka Honsha Shakai bu [City Desk, *Yomiuri Shimbun* Osaka Head Office], *Hashimoto Gekijo* [Hashimoto Theater] (Tokyo: Chuo Koron Shinsha), 204.

16. Ibid., 191.

17. *Sankei Shimbun* Osaka Shakai bu [City Desk, *Sankei Shimbun* Osaka], *Hashimoto Goroku: Dokusaisha ka Kaikakusha ka* [The Sayings of Hashimoto: Dictator or Reformer?] (Tokyo: *Sankei Shimbun* Shuppan), 2012, 159.

18. "Twitter Japan 'Politicians and Members of the Diet': Ranking by Number of Followers from 1st to 50th," https://meyou.jp/ranking/follower_politician.

19. Interview with Hidehiko Koguchi, August 1, 2018.

20. See home page of Nihon Ishin no Kai (https://o-ishin.jp/about/) and policy explanation of Nihon Ishin no Kai (https://o-ishin.jp/policy/).

21. Interview with Hitoshi Asada, July 17, 2018.

22. Ibid.

23. *Sankei Shimbun* Osaka Shakai bu, *Hashimoto Goroku*, 50.

24. *Yomiuri Shimbun* Osaka Honsha Shakai bu, *Hashimoto Gekijo*, 88.

25. Tōru Hashimoto, *Seiken Dasshu Ron: Tsuyoi Yato no Tsukurikata* [Theory of Seizing Political Power: How to Establish a Strong Opposition Party] (Tokyo: Asahi Shinsho, 2018), 56–57.

26. Ken VL Hijino, "Bamboo Shoots and Weak Roots: Organizational Expansion of New Parties in Japan," *Japanese Journal of Political Science*, vol. 16, no. 3 (2015).

27. "Seito Shiji ritsu no Suii" [Shifts in the Approval Ratings of Political Parties], https://www.jiji.com/jc/graphics?p=ve_pol_politics-support-politicalparty.

28. Interview with Ichiro Matsui, October 15, 2018.

29. Yuriko Koike, *Senkyo Koho* [Tokyo Gubernatorial Election 2016 Official Campaign Pamphlet], 2016.

30. Tokyoites First, *Metropolitan Assembly Election Manifesto* (Tokyo: Tokyoite First, 2017).

31. Party of Hope, 2017 General Election Manifesto (Tokyo: Party of Hope, 2017).

32. Interview with Masaru Wakasa, August 29, 2018.

33. See Tokyoites First, "Kibo no To, Kihon Seisaku" [Fundamental Policy of Party of Hope], https://kibounotou.jp/policy; Tokyoites First, "Koyaku no Shinchoku" [Our Policy], https://tomin1st.jp/policy/.

34. See, for example, "Tochiji Sen, Omo na Shiji Seito betsu no Tohyo doko, 2016nen 7gatsu" [Tokyo Gubernatorial Election, Voting Trend Based on Each Major Parties' Supporters, July 2016], https://www.jiji.com/jc/graphics?p=ve_pol_election-local20160731j-07-w450; *Asahi* 24–25/06/2017 (survey date), "Koike Yuriko Tochiji no Shijiritsu

Geraku mo, 7 wari cho" [The Approval Rate for Tokyo Governor Yuriko Koike Is over 70 Percent Even though It Has Decreased], *Sankei Shimbun*, April 17, 2017.

35. "Koike Yuriko Tochiji no Shijiritsu ga Kako Saitei, 11 pointo gen no 29%, Kibo no To Kanbu 'Mou To to Kankei nai' " [The Approval Rate of Tokyo Governor Yuriko Koike Hits a Low of 29 Percent Due to 11 Percent Decrease, an Executive of the Party of Hope: "Ms. Koike Has Nothing to Do with This Party"], *Sankei Shimbun*, December 18, 2017.

36. Interview with Masaru Wakasa, August 29, 2018.

37. "Tokyo's Governor Gets a Crash Course in the Perils of Populism: Slipshod Platform Left Japan Opposition Candidates with Little to Run On," *Nikkei* Shimbun, November 23, 2017.

38. Jeff Kingston, "Koike Tests Possibilities and Perils of Populism in Japan," *Japan Times*, August 26, 2017.

39. Interview with Masaru Wakasa, August 29, 2018.

40. Ken VL Hijino and Gabriele Vogt, "Identity Politics in Okinawan Elections: The Emergence of Regional Populism," IPSA/AISP 25th World Congress of Political Science, July 21–25, 2018, at Brisbane, Australia (unpublished paper), https://wc2018.ipsa.org/events/congress/wc2018/paper/identity-politics-okinawan-elections-emergence-regional-populism.

41. Takeshi Onaga, Gubernatorial election campaign manifesto, 2014.

42. Kei Kono, "Okinawa Beigun Kichi wo Meguru Ishiki, Okinawa to Zenkoku: 2017nen 4gatu Hukki 45nen no Okinawa Chousa" [Awareness over U.S. Bases in Okinawa, Okinawa and Japan: Survey of "45 Years Have Passed since the Reversion of Okinawa to Japan"], *Houso Kenkyu to Chosa*, August 2017, 27.

43. Kei Kono, Okinawa Beigun Kichi wo Meguru Ishiki, 31; Kei Kono, "Hondo Hukki go 40 nenkan no Okinawa Kenmin Ishiki" [Okinawans' Consciousness during 40 Years after the Reversion of Okinawa to Japan], *NHK Hoso Bunka Kenkyu Jo Nenpo*, 2013, 140.

44. "Intabyū: Okinawa no hoshu ga tsukitsukeru. Naha-shicho Onaga Takeshi-san" [Interview: Demand from an Okinawan Conservative (Takeshi Onaga, mayor of Naha)], *Asahi Shimbun*, November 14, 2012.

45. Takeshi Onaga, "Oral Statement at the United Nations Human Rights Council by the Governor of Okinawa," http://dc-office.org/post/574.

46. See, for example: Kota Hatachi, "Hihan koe, sekaiteki na kankochi ni shinka shiteiku Okinawa, Onaga chiji ga kataru" [Okinawa, the Evolving Worldwide Famous Tourist Place: Onaga's Dream], https://www.buzzfeed.com/jp/kotahatachi/onaga-5; Takeshi Onaga, "Heiwa Sengen Zenbun, 2018nen Irei no hi" [Declaration of Peace, at the Memorial Day of Okinawa], *Ryukyu Shimpo*, July 23, 2018.

47. "'Dojin' hatsugen kara 1 kagetsu, hamon hirogaru Okinawa" [One Month Has Passed since the Problematic Term of "Dojin"], *Okinawa Times Plus*, November 18, 2016.

48. Kei Kono, "Okinawa Beigun Kichi wo Meguru Ishiki: Shasetsu: 'Kidōtai "dojin" hatsugen', kenmin wo gurōsuru mono da" [Opinion: Problematic Term of "Dojin" Used by a Police Officer Insulted Okinawan People], *Okinawa Times*, October 20, 2016.

49. Denny Tamaki, "Hokori aru Yutaka na Okinawa, Shin Jidai Okinawa" [Proud and Wealthy Okinawa, The New Era of Okinawa], gubernatorial candidate election pamphlet (Okinawa: Hiyamikachiumanchu no Kai, September 2018).

50. Interview with Mikio Shimoji, October 18, 2018.

51. Kent E. Calder, *Crisis and Compensation: Public Policy and Political Stability in Japan, 1949–1986* (Princeton University Press, 1988).

52. Koji Nakakita, *Jiminto: "Ikkyo" no Jitsuzo* [Liberal Democratic Party: The Real State of Unopposed Party] (Tokyo: Chuo Koron Shinsha, 2017), 198.

53. Ibid., 202.

54. Rebuild Japan Initiative Foundation (RJIF), *Sengo Hoshu wa Owatta no ka* [The Decline of Postwar Moderate Conservatism in Japan] (Tokyo: Kadokawa, 2015), 38; for a summary of the reasons for this shift, 309–11.

55. Nakakita, *Jiminto: "Ikkyo" no Jitsuzo*, 282–86.

56. See, for example, Frances McCall Rosenbluth & Michael F. Thies, *Japan Transformed: Political Change and Economic Restructuring* (Princeton University Press, 2010), 160–61; Amy Catalinac, *Electoral Reform and National Security in Japan: From Pork to Foreign Policy* (Cambridge University Press, 2016), 22–23.

57. RJIF, *Sengo Hoshu wa Owatta no ka*, 75–76.

58. Japan First (Nippon Daiitto) candidates in Tokyo metropolitan elections, July 2017, http://www.asahi.com/senkyo/togisen/2017/kaihyo/E24.html, and in Naka city elections, December 2018, https://japan-first.net/news/2018-09-09-nakashigisenkyo/.

59. Chris Winkler, "Populism in Japan between Sub-national Success and National Level Failure" in *Populism in Asia: Contours, Causes, Consequences*, Monash University, Malaysia (November 2017), unpublished.

60. "Kuni wo Aisuru Kimochi no Teido" [The Extent of Patriotism], https://survey.gov-online.go.jp/h29/h29-shakai/zh/z01-2.html.

61. Robert Stefan Foa, "It's the Globalization, Stupid: Don't Blame Low Working-Class Wages or the Financial Crisis for the Populist Wave that Produced Trump and Brexit. The Data Show the Tide Started Decades Ago," *Foreign Policy*, December 6, 2018.

62. Hiroko Murata, "Kuni e no aichaku to tai gaikokujin isiki no kankei: ISSP koksuai hikaku chosa 'Kuni eno kizoku isiki' kara" [The Correlations between Patriotism and Consciousness toward Foreigners: Based on an ISSP International Comparative Survey about a Sense of Belonging to the Nation], *Hoso Kenkyu to Chosa*, March 2017.

63. "Dai 13 kai Nicchu Kyodo Yoron Chosa" [The 13th Japan-China joint opinion poll survey], Genron NPO, 2017.

64. "Murayama Koizumi Danwa 'Dato' 74%" [74 Percent Said that the Statement by Murayama-Koizumi Is "Appropriate"], *Asahi Shimbun*, April 4, 2015.

65. Interview with Ichiro Matsui, October 15, 2018.

66. Interview with Mikio Shimoji, October 18, 2018.

67. Interview with Masaru Wakasa, August 29, 2018.

68. "Online Data Analysis (2010–14)," World Values Survey. Sampled countries: United States, Germany, Spain, Sweden, Netherlands, Poland, South Korea, Taiwan, and Japan.

69. Richard Wike and others, "Globally, Broad Support for Representative and Direct Democracy: But Many Also Endorse Nondemocratic Alternatives," Pew Research Center, October 16, 2017.

70. Toshiyuki Kobayashi, "Teika suru Nihon jin no seiji teki shakai teki katsudo iyoku to sono haikei: ISSP kokusai hikaku chosa 'Shimin ishiki,' Nihon no Kekka kara" [The Decline of Willingness to Participate in Political and Social Activity among Japa-

nese People and Its Reasons: Based on the Results for Japan in the ISSP International Comparison Survey about "Citizenship Counsciousness"], *Hoso Kenkyu to Chosa*, January 2015, 34, 37.

71. OECD, *How's Life? 2017 Measuring Well-Being* (Paris: OECD Publishing, 2017), figure A.33.

72. Masao Matsumoto, "'Sonotsudo Shiji' no seiji teki myakuryaku: Tanki teki sentaku to senkyo banare" [The Political Context of "Giving Instructions Each Time": Short-Term Choices and Declining Political Turnout], *Japanese Journal of Electoral Studies*, vol. 29, no. 2, 2013.

73. LDP membership 1.07 million in 2018, https://www.sankei.com/politics/news/180305/plt1803050017-n1.html; JCP membership 300,000 in 2018, https://www.sankei.com/politics/news/170115/plt1701150012-n1.html; Komeito membership 420,000 in 2018, https://www.komei.or.jp/komei/about/outline.html; Kokumin Minshuto membership 70,000 in 2018, https://www.nikkei.com/article/DGXMZO33622330R30 C18A7PP8000/; other smaller parties with less than 10,000 members have been disregarded in calculations. Japanese electorate in 2017 is 106.1 million, http://www.soumu.go.jp/senkyo/senkyo_s/data/shugiin48/index.html; 1.86 divided by 106.1 is 1.75 percent.

74. Ingrid Van Biezen, Peter Mair, and Thomas Poguntke, "Going, Going, . . . Gone? The Decline of Party Membership in Contemporary Europe," *European Journal of Political Research*, vol. 51, 2012.

75. Interview with Hidehiko Koguchi, August 1, 2018.

76. Ibid.

77. David Runciman, *How Democracy Ends* (London: Profile Books, 2018), 208.

78. Ibid., 207–08, 210.

8

Japan's Incomplete Liberalism

JAPAN AND THE HISTORICAL JUSTICE REGIME

THOMAS BERGER

In many respects, Japan is the ideal candidate in East Asia to lead the fight to preserve the international liberal order. Like Germany in Europe, Japan has been unstinting in its support for both global and regional institution-building. Also like Germany, Japan has eschewed the development of offensive military power, though it is well within its capacity to develop the full panoply of great power military instruments, including nuclear weapons. It remains a leading source of foreign aid and investment for developing countries. Unlike China, which has surpassed it to become the leading economic power in Asia, Japan is a democratic society in which civil liberties, including freedom of speech and freedom of association, are well protected. In recent years, Japan's overall international image has regularly ranked among the top ten countries in the world in terms of favorability,[1] and it has been lauded for its cultural achievements (both traditional and contemporary), to the point where some analysts have called it a "soft power superpower."[2]

Japan's ability to actually play a leadership role, however, is commonly believed to be undermined by its stance on historical issues. In particular, Japan's relative unwillingness to address its record of aggression and atrocity in the pre-1945 period, and to offer apologies and compensation to its victims, has been the source of constant friction with its closest neighbors—China and South Korea—and at times has caused trouble in its relationship with the United States. Critics claim that Japan's stance on the historical issue deprives it of the moral legitimacy needed to play a leading role in international affairs.[3] Often, Japan is compared unfavorably to Germany in this regard. Germany, it is argued, has openly repented for its history of aggression and the crimes of the Nazi regime. As a result, it has been able to build closer relations with its neighbors than Japan has and lay the foundation for the creation of the EU—a set of institutions that come as close to approximating a liberal vision of international relations as any in the world today.

To be sure, the history issue has weakened Japan's ability to take on a leadership role in Asia. This is particularly true in the context of South Korea, which in many respects should be a natural partner for Japan and which shares many of its liberal instincts in terms of foreign policy. However, the received wisdom on Japan's history problem is flawed on three levels. First, a closer examination of what Japan has done with respect to the history issue shows that, in fact, Japan is not as much of an outlier in terms of its approach to the history issue as it is commonly made out to be. Many countries are reluctant to deal with the darker episodes in their history, and most countries have had a difficult time getting to the point where they are ready to pursue reconciliation with their neighbors on historical issues. This is true also of the exemplar of forthright apologizers, Germany. Second, Japan has apologized and sought to make amends for past misdeeds. While Japanese conservatives have indeed tried to whitewash Japanese modern history, one of the main reasons further progress has not been made on historical issues is the fact that the broader constellation of political interests that are at work in Japan's two closest and most important neighbors, China and South Korea, do not favor reconciliation. Even if Japan were to apologize completely and forthrightly, with no reservations on the part of its leaders and with the full support of the Japanese population and political elites, there is no guarantee that its apologies would be accepted. Other countries who arguably have suffered at Japan's hands, including the United States and the nations of Southeast Asia, do not experience the same complex of domestic political factors that make history such a source of tension with Japan. Third and finally, despite the tensions that arise over historical issues, Japan has actually been able to manage its relations with China and South Korea, cooperating with them when it was clearly in their mutual interest to do so.

This does not mean, however, that Japan can safely ignore the history issue, as some Japanese conservatives and foreign analysts suggest.[4] The history issue is a major problem for Japan, one that—quite aside from whatever moral issues are at stake—it is in Japan's interest to address. Moreover, it is a problem that in certain respects has become more grave over time, spilling over into and exacerbating other contentious domains—most important, the territorial disputes over the Senkaku/Diaoyu and Dokdo/Takeshima islands. If Japan is to continue to enjoy the support of other members of the community of nations that share its commitment to maintaining the liberal international order, it needs to prevent these disputes from metastasizing further, while demonstrating its adherence to liberal international norms concerning historical injustices.

Japan in the Context of the Development of the Historical Justice Regime

Battles over history and demands for justice for past misdeeds have long been a central issue in the politics of many countries. Only recently, however, have historical issues become an important factor in international relations.[5] In the past, more concrete national interests, such as military security and economic benefit, have trumped questions of historical justice.[6] Today, however, we see historical issues becoming of central concern in the relations between many countries—see, for example, the impact of the Armenian genocide on Turkey's relations with Europe, the memory of the Stalin era in Russia's relations with former Soviet states, or the profusion of apologies offered by various leaders, from Barack Obama to the pope, for a wide range of past misdeeds. While still vague and diffuse, there has emerged a set of norms and institutions regarding how countries should deal with past transgressions that are coming together to form what could be termed an International Historical Justice Regime, just as there are international regimes that help govern trade, the use of the oceans, and the management of the global environment.[7]

A variety of forces drive this trend. The spread of democracy and more pluralist political systems has allowed victim groups to more effectively voice their grievances. Increased international interdependence has created more avenues through which pressure can be exerted on governments, while the spread of human rights norms provides a language and way of legitimizing such demands for historical justice.[8]

These forces are outgrowths of the liberal international order, and today are as much an integral part of that order as freedom of trade or the open exchange of ideas and knowledge across borders. The impact of these forces varies widely, according to local and regional factors, and the forces pushing for historical justice are far from inexorable. Nonetheless, if Japan is to exercise leadership effectively in support of the liberal international order, it is important that it is perceived as complying with norms and principles that undergird that order, including the standards that govern historical justice issues.

In this regard, although Japan is often portrayed as being unrepentant regarding its history of pre-1945 wartime aggression and colonial oppression, it does not compare poorly to other advanced industrial societies that have come under pressure to address historical injustices. As shown in table 8-1, there are eleven OECD countries that have been the targets of campaigns urging them to address their history of colonial oppression.[9] Of these, Japan is, in fact, the first to have offered even a partial apology—made in 1985 by Prime Minister Yasuhiro Nakasone to South Korea, when he referred to Japanese rule over Korea as *Shokuminchi no Shihai* (colonial oppression). And with the Murayama statement of 1995, Japan is the only country (with the possible exception of Prime Minister Silvio Berlusconi's 2008 apology for Italy's brutal colonization of Libya) to have offered an extensive apology to one of its former colonial subjects. Belgium, France, Germany, the Netherlands, and the United Kingdom have offered only partial apologies for their colonial pasts. Portugal, Spain, Turkey, and the United States have remained steadfastly unrepentant—militantly so, in the case of Turkey.

Japan is also one of the few countries to have offered even limited compensation, in the form of the 1995 Asian Women's Fund, for the harm inflicted by its colonial rule upon the so-called comfort women, the estimated 200,000 women who had been lured or coerced into sexual service to the Japanese army. Only three other countries have offered compensation, all at much later dates: Belgium, for the murder of Patrice Lumumba in the Congo; and the Netherlands and the United Kingdom, for massacres that occurred during the Indonesian and Kenyan wars of independence, respectively. Only Italy may have outdone Japan in 2008, when it gave US$5 billion to Libya as part of an apology for its colonial past.[10] France, Portugal, Spain, Turkey, the United States, and even that paragon of repentance, the Federal Republic of Germany, have, as of 2018, offered no compensation to their former colonial possessions.

With respect to having sided with the Axis powers during World War II, Japan again does not come off as being particularly impenitent. Of the five OECD countries that sided with the Axis powers during World War II (Finland, Hungary, Italy, Germany, and Japan), only Germany can be said to have done more than Japan by the way of apologies for waging a war of aggression. In the case of Japan, its first partial apology came in 1985, and a full apology came in 1995, with Prime Minister Tomiichi Murayama's statement on the fiftieth anniversary of the end of the war. Japan has offered no official compensation for the damages it inflicted in the war, with the exception of some limited aid to Western prisoners of war. If one expands the list to include the seventeen OECD countries, many of whose citizens collaborated with the Nazis during occupation in World War II,[11] eleven have offered extensive apologies, while five others have offered at least partial apologies and admissions of guilt. Four have also offered extensive reparations for the victims of Nazi persecution, and seven have offered at least partial compensation.

In sum, despite its poor reputation, Japan is by no means an outlier in terms of its compliance with international norms regarding historical justice. While it is often compared unfavorably with Germany for its lack of contrition,[12] Germany is exceptional, because of the gravity of the Nazi atrocities and because of the intense international pressure that it came under to face up to that past. Moreover, even in the case of Germany, in the early postwar period, there was a strong tendency to hedge its apologies and to avoid offering redress to certain categories of victims, especially those living in Communist Eastern Europe, where the greatest Nazi atrocities had occurred.[13] Japan's stance on the past should not by itself rule out Japan's ability to play a leading role in shoring up the liberal international order.

TABLE 8-1. OECD countries and apologies to external groups[a]

Country	Issues	Date of First Extensive Apology	Partial Apology	Date of Commencement of Extensive Compensation	Date of Commencement of Partial Compensation
Australia					
Austria	Holocaust collaboration	1991 Chancellor Franz Vranitzky		1992	
Belgium	Colonialism (Congo)		2002 for murder of Patrice Lumumba	2003 compensation for orphans of deported parents	
	Holocaust collaboration	2007 Prime Minister Guy Verhofstadt		2008 Belgian banks and government offer jointly US$170 million compensation fund	2002 US$3.25 million fund
Canada					
Chile					
Czech Republic	Holocaust collaboration				1998 lump sum payment for labor camp and other survivors
	Expulsion of ethnic Germans	1990 President Vaclav Havel			
Denmark	Holocaust collaboration	2005 Prime Minister Fogh Rasmussen			
Estonia	Holocaust collaboration	2005 Prime Minister Andrus Ansip			
Finland	Holocaust collaboration Axis Minor ally		2000 Prime Minister Paavo Lipponen for turning over 3,000 Soviet prisoners		

France	Colonialism (Algeria)		2012 President Francois Hollande for Algeria	
	Holocaust collaboration	2005 President Jacques Chirac		
Germany	Colonialism (Namibia)		2004 Minister Heidemarie Wiezorek-Zeul	
	Holocaust	1985 President Richard von Weizsaecker	1948 Chancellor Konrad Adenauer	1952 Luxembourg Agreement
Greece	Holocaust collaboration			
Hungary	Holocaust collaboration			1998 Limited payment to Shoah victims
Iceland				
Ireland				
Israel	Expulsion of Palestinians			
Italy	Colonialism (Libya)		2008 Prime Minister Silvio Berlusconi to Libya	US$5 billion to Libya
	Holocaust collaboration		2000 Chamber of Deputies established Day of Remembrance	
Japan	Colonialism	1995 Murayama Tomiichi	1985 Prime Minister Nakasone Yasuhiro	
	War of aggression	As above	As above	1995 Asian Women's Fund
Korea				
Latvia	Holocaust collaboration	2002 President Vaira Vike Freiberge recognizes role of Latvians	1990 Institution of Day of Remembrance	1995 Compensation regardless of citizenship

TABLE 8-1 CONTINUED

Country	Issues	Date of First Extensive Apology	Partial Apology	Date of Commencement of Extensive Compensation	Date of Commencement of Partial Compensation
Lithuania	Holocaust collaboration	1995 President Brauzaskas	1990 Lithuanian Supreme Court issues statement		1991 Restitution of most of property of Lithuanian citizens
Luxembourg	Holocaust collaboration	2015 Chamber of Deputies and prime minister apologize			1974 Social Security allows some claims
Mexico	Colonialism		2011 Apology for Independence War massacres		2011 Compensation for massacre victims
Netherlands	Holocaust collaboration		2005 – Prime Minister Jan Peter Balkende: "black day in the history of the Netherlands"		1974 Compensation for victims of WWII persecution
New Zealand					
Norway	Holocaust collaboration	2012 Prime Minister Jens Stoltenberg apologizes	1998 recognition of Norwegian role in the Holocaust	1999 restitution for Jewish persons persecuted in Norway	1998 US$60 million to Norwegian Jews and Jewish organizations
Poland	Holocaust collaboration	2001 President Andre Kawniewski acknowledgment of Polish role in Jewish persecution			
Portugal	Expulsion of ethnic Germans Colonialism/ role in the slave trade				
Slovak Republic	Holocaust collaboration		1990 Slovak Parliament expresses sympathy for Jewish citizens and offers apology		1999 compensation for deported Slovak citizens and heirs
Slovenia	Holocaust collaboration				1995 special protection and compensation for Slovenian citizens
	Expulsion of ethnic Italians				

Spain	Colonialism		
	Use of poison gas in Morocco		
Sweden	Indirect support for Nazi Germany		
Switzerland	Nonreturn of Jewish property	1997 Ambassador Bnai Defago apologizes	1998 US$1.25 billion in claims settled
	Turning away of Jewish refugees	1999 President Ruth Dreifuss apologizes	
Turkey	Imperialism	Active denial	
	Armenian genocide		
United Kingdom	Imperialism and colonialism	1997 Prime Minister Tony Blair apologizes for the Potato Famine, first of a series of apologies	2013 Prime Minister David Cameron sets up a fund of 19.9 million pounds to compensate massacres in Kenya
United States	Colonialism (Philippines)	2016 President Obama visits Hiroshima	
	Atomic bombings		

a. This chart is only a partial overview of government policies pertaining to historical memory. It covers only members of the OECD, which, because of its status as a "rich countries' club," may represent the leaders of the International Liberal Order. It excludes, however, very powerful countries that may have an impact on the normative order on both the global (China and Russia) and regional levels (India and Singapore).

The chart only refers to policies made in response to demands or pressures emanating from outside groups or governments. It does not reflect demands for historical justice coming from groups within the country. The chart covers only a limited range of the types of policies that governments take with respect to historical justice issues. It focuses only on policies covering injustices involving the citizens of other countries. Since it does not note retractions or qualifications of earlier policies, it may inadvertently create the appearance of a teleological progression toward apology.

As a rough gauge of the scale of government action, it distinguishes between extensive apologies and compensation policies and partial ones. Extensive apologies refer to authoritative statements by a head of state or the government that offer a blanket apology for past events and the nation's role in those events. Partial apologies are ones that cover only limited instances of the historical injustice in question—for example, British or Dutch massacres of insurgent groups during the wars of independence, as opposed to apologizing for colonial domination of Kenya or Indonesia more generally.

Compensation does not include compensation and restitution that was negotiated as a condition for the ending of a state of war or occupation. It thus does not include Japan's relinquishment of very substantial properties that were held in parts of the former Japanese empire, nor the very large indemnities that were forced on Austria, Germany, and various Axis Minor allies as part of the end of World War II. Extensive compensation refers to large sums (hundreds of millions and billions) paid for general historical injustices. Partial compensation is smaller sums covering limited categories of victims of injustice.

Nonetheless, the fact remains that Japanese diplomacy, at least in East Asia, faces considerable obstacles because of intense acrimony over historical issues. While the actuality is that Japan is not particularly unapologetic, it is perceived as being such.[14] To understand why and evaluate the prospects for Japan to overcome these obstacles, we need to move beyond a general analysis of Japanese compliance and explore the evolution of the history issue in the regional context.

The Evolution of the History Problem and Its Legacies

The history problem in Asia has evolved over time, shaped and reshaped by the interaction between the historical narratives that exist in each country and changing domestic and geopolitical exigencies. In each country, there have emerged different historical narratives based on the varying historical experiences. These narratives are grounded at least in part in the lived experiences of the populations and the stories based on those experiences that have been passed on to subsequent generations. At the same time, political leaders and other elites often try to use or manipulate historical narratives to pursue economic and political agendas. Doing so, however, requires the expenditure of political capital and incurs risks—especially in more pluralistic or democratic political systems. Part of what has made the history issue so intractable in the Asian context is the way in which the politics of history in the three countries of East Asia have led to a dangerous deadlock in the early twenty-first century. Historical narratives have come into place and been married to political agendas in ways that make the history issue a chronic source of tension between China, South Korea, and Japan.

To understand how this situation developed, it is necessary to briefly trace the genealogy of the historical narratives in the region. Essentially, the history issue in East Asia has gone through three phases: an early phase, in which the basic parameters regarding history were put in place; a second period, in which Japan came under intensified regional pressure to seek reconciliation with its neighbors; and the third period—which we are still in—in which history has become a chronic and increasingly dangerous source of tension between Japan and its two closest neighbors, China and South Korea.

THE FORMATIVE PERIOD, 1945–82

The history issue first emerged in Asia in the immediate aftermath of World War II. The immense suffering and devastation that the war left in its wake created a wave of anger and a burning desire to punish those responsible. In Japan, the anger focused on the military and wartime leadership in what came to be known as the debate on *sensō sekinin* (war responsibility). Outside of Japan, there was a more generalized attitude of anger and a desire for revenge on Japan as a whole. This was particularly true in those countries that had been invaded and occupied by Japan, but there were similar sentiments in the United States and other Western allied countries.

These sentiments, however, were very much tempered by the geopolitics and domestic politics of the time. Inside of Japan, the Left, freed of their pre-1945 restraints and concentrated in the Japan Socialist Party (JSP), sought to tap popular anger over the defeat to attack Japanese conservative elites. Their goal was to transform Japan into a very different society, one that was completely demilitarized and organized along socialist principles. In turn, Japanese conservatives and many centrists, including many who were quite critical of the pre-1945 militarists, were compelled to try to contain or deflect the Left's attacks. The Japanese debate on history split along deeply polarized Left-Right lines. As a result, the historical issue became intertwined with the broader cleavages that dominated Japanese domestic politics, including, most important, defense and national security issues. A pattern emerged that whenever there was at least partial consensus on the need for new initiatives in the area of defense and national security, conservative leaders pushing nationalistic messages—including on history—would take charge. When the conservatives were perceived as going too far on historical and other ideological issues, however, opposition would intensify and many centrists would quietly begin to withdraw their support.

The paradigmatic example of this pattern was the 1960 battle over revising the U.S.-Japan Security Treaty. Clearly, the treaty needed to be revised, and there was a general consensus among Japanese leaders in favor of doing so. However, the arch-conservative character and strongly nationalistic rhetoric and policies of Prime Minister Nobusuke Kishi provoked a wave of protest that led to many politicians—including many in his own party—and business leaders to call for his ousting. While in the end the treaty was revised, Kishi was forced to resign, and constitutional revision as well as revival of a more traditional form of Japanese nationalism was put on hold.

Outside of Japan, the situation was just as complicated. American policy was guided by a complex set of impulses and calculations. First and foremost, there was the desire to punish Japan and ensure that Japan would never again become a threat to international peace. These sentiments were tempered, however, by the fear that an overly draconian peace settlement could backfire. A humiliated Japan might one day seek to strike back at what it would view as an unjust peace, just as the Treaty of Versailles that ended World War I in Europe had created resentments in post-1919 Germany, which ultimately fueled the rise of Hitler. Re-educating Japan and reintegrating it as a peaceful member of the international community would far better serve the interests of the United States while appealing to the liberal sentiments of the American people.[15]

For the Americans, rebuilding Japan soon took priority over extracting reparations from Japan or purging figures who had been associated with the old militarist regime. With the onset of the Cold War in 1947, the pressure to rehabilitate Japan's prewar elites as a counterweight to the Japanese Left grew even stronger. Under the terms of the Treaty of San Francisco, which ended the U.S. occupation, Japan was forced to give up substantial property claims in its former empire and to accept the verdict of the Allied War Crimes tribunals. However, Japan had to pay only relatively limited compensation to Western prisoners of war and offer limited amounts of foreign aid to formerly colonized and occupied areas. Both Japan and the Western Allied nations agreed to abandon all claims—both on the part of their governments and of their citizens—to further compensation.[16]

Asian countries were not party to the Treaty of San Francisco. Many, in particular Taiwan and South Korea, would have favored a harsher settlement, including the payment of extensive reparations. At the time, however, Asian countries had only limited leverage over Japan. In the end, they all normalized relations with Japan, including South Korea in 1965 and the People's Republic of China in 1978, on terms broadly similar to the San Francisco Treaty. From the perspective of Japan in the late 1970s and early 1980s, in many ways it seemed that the issue had been resolved.

GROPING FOR RECONCILIATION, 1982–2002

In the 1980s, however, that equilibrium began to break down when another conservative leader, Yasuhiro Nakasone, followed in Kishi's footsteps in combining a significant upgrading of Japan's Self-Defense Forces and the U.S.-Japan alliance with a campaign to revive a healthy sense of Japanese patriotism. An important component of that campaign was propagating a more positive appraisal of modern Japanese history. While domestically the tensions proved manageable—unlike in Kishi's era—the international backlash forced a recalibration of Japanese policy. The opening salvo came in 1982, when controversy erupted over Japanese textbooks that appeared to downplay Japan's responsibility for the war. An even greater controversy developed in 1985, when Nakasone made an official visit to the controversial Yasukuni shrine in Tokyo, dedicated to Japan's fallen soldiers and sailors, including over one thousand convicted as war criminals.

Behind these developments were broader regional and international changes. First, on the international level, new global norms had emerged regarding how countries approached historical injustices. In particular, the issue of how European nations dealt with the Nazi past set new standards for repentance. Second, Japan had become economically and politically far more tightly integrated with the rest of Asia than it had been during the early Cold War period. As a result, it had become far more vulnerable to pressure on historical issues. Finally, the 1980s saw a pluralization of the political discourse in both South Korea and, to a more limited extent, in China. In South Korea, democratization allowed victims groups to air their grievances. The previous authoritarian governments' willingness to trample human rights in the name of national interest was bitterly criticized as a continuation of the mind-set of the Japanese-era colonial administration. The ultimate symbol of this became the cause of the comfort women, who for decades had lived in shamed silence. Standing up for the comfort women became a matter of national pride in the new democratic South Korea, and no Korean politician could afford to completely neglect the issue lest they be branded as unpatriotic, authoritarian, and misogynistic.

In China under Deng Xiaoping, the trend toward liberalization was far less profound but nonetheless significant. First, by adopting market mechanisms, the Chinese government had critically undermined Maoism as the unifying ideology for a country undergoing wrenching social and economic changes. To create a new, ideological glue for the country, the party turned to a more traditional form of Chinese nationalism, one that both extolled the glories of Chinese civilization in the past and bemoaned the tragedies that had befallen it. The humiliation of China after the Opium Wars became part of a new historical narrative, the so-called Century of Humiliation, and the Chinese Communist Party's role in helping end China's travails became the central legitimizing ideology of the Communist regime.[17] In addition, as part of the new atmosphere of reform, ordinary Chinese citizens were given considerable space to express their views on a wide variety of topics. As in South Korea, it became possible for ordinary Chinese to discuss Japanese atrocities.[18] Chinese leaders began to make frequent use of the history issue to attack their opponents in the party. For instance, Chen Yun used Nakasone's visit to Yasukuni to criticize Hu Yaobang, who was accused of being too close to Japan.[19]

The intensity of the resulting debate over history caught Japan by surprise. Egged on by domestic liberal sentiment as well as pragmatic concerns regarding a potential loss in Japan's regional influence, Japanese leaders scrambled to adjust. Over the next twenty years, a string of apologies resulted, beginning with Prime Minister Nakasone's 1984 acknowledgment of the invasion of China as a war of aggression and Japanese rule of Korea as colonial oppression. The culmination of this trend came with the 1995 Murayama statement on the fiftieth anniversary of the end of World War II.

Japan's campaign to pursue reconciliation with its neighbors on historical issues had some success. In 1998, Prime Minister Keizo Obuchi met with South Korean president Kim Dae Jung at a summit meeting in Tokyo. Not only did Obuchi reiterate Japan's earlier apologies for its past transgressions but, more important, Kim Dae Jung accepted them, ushering in a period of markedly improved Korean-Japanese relations. Less progress was made between Tokyo and Beijing. Nonetheless, the relatively muted Chinese response to Ryutaro Hashimoto's 1996 visit to Yasukuni, as well as the limited fallout from a clash over historical issues between Obuchi and Chinese leader Jiang Zemin in 1998, led many to conclude, erroneously, that history would prove a mere irritant, not a major obstacle to smooth regional relations. After all, there were many compelling reasons for the countries of the region to work together in areas of mutual interest, especially in the economic sphere.

Apology Fatigue and Growing Tensions over History and Territory, 2002–19

Unfortunately, the underlying forces that shaped the discourse on historical issues in the region's major countries, and the structural forces that had led to the emergence of the history issue in the 1980s, remained in place. At the same time, the geopolitics of the region created powerful pressures that reopened the fissures between Japan and its closest neighbors. As in the previous two periods, the stimulus for a new round of acrimony came from the security sphere. Even as the Asian region continued to grow increasingly prosperous and more integrated economically, the security environment began to deteriorate dramatically, as detailed in chapters 1 and 5 of this volume, first with the emergence of a nuclear armed North Korea, which periodically threatened to turn its neighbors—including Japan—into a "sea of fire," and second with rapid expansion of the Chinese military. Further complicating matters was a sharp intensification all across Asia of maritime disputes, triggered by growing resource competition and a rush to stake out claims to special rights in exclusive economic zones (EEZ) under the terms of the UN Convention on the Law of the Seas (UNCLOS), which had come into effect in 1982.

The need to respond to this increasingly complex and perilous security environment led to the reemergence of the old pattern of new conservative political leaders simultaneously pushing national security policy reforms and a nationalist political agenda, including the promotion of revisionist views of Japanese history. Ironically, the key figure here, Prime Minister Junichiro Koizumi, was not particularly conservative, ideologically. However, Koizumi was forced to appeal to ideological conservatives inside his Liberal Democratic Party of Japan (LDP) in order to broaden his otherwise shallow support base within the LDP. In 2001, during the election to become the head of the LDP, Koizumi promised to officially visit the Yasukuni shrine, a promise he made good on every year he was in office as prime minister.

Koizumi's repeated visits to Yasukuni enraged Kim Dae Jung's successor, Roh Moo-Hyun. Roh had come into office intending to continue his predecessor and mentor's policy of pursuing improved relations with Japan. Faced with Koizumi's repeated visits to Yasukuni, however, Roh suddenly and dramatically changed tack. In 2005, Roh declared a new policy of waging diplomatic war on Japan, cutting off senior-level meetings with Japan and launching a campaign to vigorously press Japan for more sincere apologies to the comfort women while underlining South Korea's claim to Dokdo/Takeshima. In China, as well, the response to Koizumi's policies was furious, reinforced by a groundswell of popular nationalism.[20]

As a result, historical issues exploded on the domestic and international political stages, leading to eruptions of passion on the issue in 2005–06, 2010, and especially 2012. As in the 1980s, mass demonstrations and protests were a central feature of the new wave of tension. What was new, however, was the explicit linkage of the history issues to territorial disputes. In his 2005 television address, President Roh stated that Japan's claim to Dokdo/Takeshima was a direct assault on the sovereignty of the Korean nation, reminding his listeners that Japan had annexed the islands in 1905, before it went on to annex all of Korea in 1910. Likewise, in 2012, Chinese foreign minister Wang Yi said in an address to the UN General Assembly that Japan had "stolen" the islands from China and that Japan's claims on the island were an attempt to reverse the results of the "great anti-fascist war" of seventy years before.[21] While this linkage between the territorial disputes and historical issues had always existed beneath the surface, Roh's and Wang's speeches now formally linked the two factors, reducing their governments' room to maneuver on the issue, as making any concessions would involve a considerable loss of face, and increasing the risk of inadvertent escalation—possibly to the military level.

To make matters worse, in many ways, China and South Korea seemed to be egging each other on. When Roh Moo-Hyun announced diplomatic war on Japan in 2005, China soon joined it, and the two countries began to work together to try to isolate Japan diplomatically. Roh's successor, Lee Myung-Bak, a former Hyundai executive, initially was intent on restabilizing relations with Tokyo and focusing on economic and security cooperation between the two U.S. allies. However, Lee came under pressure from South Korean civil society—and, just as important, the Korean judiciary—to push Japan to address the comfort women issue. When a carefully negotiated deal to restart the Asian Women's Fund fell through in 2012, Lee was infuriated, and he made a point of flying to the disputed Dokdo/Takeshima island, demanding an apology from Japan precisely at the moment when Sino-Japanese tensions with China over the Senkaku/Diaoyu islands were hitting a new high.

In response to these pressures, Japan tried to assuage its neighbors. Koizumi, for his part, sought to find ways to make his trips to Yasukuni less provocative. His successor Shinzo Abe—in his first term as prime minister—stopped making formal trips altogether. When the Democratic Party of Japan (DPJ) government came into office in 2009, the new Yukio Hatoyama government promised to make Asia the center of its foreign policy. These efforts had only limited effect, however, as new tensions over history and territory reemerged with depressing regularity. Increasingly, the dominant mood in Japan became one of "apology fatigue." One of the unfortunate legacies of Japan's repeated efforts to try to find a settlement on the history issue was the perception that no matter how much Japan appeared to try, its efforts seemed doomed to failure.

It was against this background that the second administration of Shinzo Abe began in 2012. It was a particularly sensitive year in terms of historical issues because it was a period of nearly simultaneous political transitions in not only Japan but China and South Korea as well. In all three cases, the leaders who emerged were strongly nationalistic, to the extent of being almost uniquely bound up with their countries' long battles over history.

In Japan that summer, the intensely nationalistic governor of Tokyo, Shintaro Ishihara, led a public campaign to raise funds to buy the Senkaku/Diaoyu islands from their private owner. Fearing what Ishihara might do with those islands if he were able to purchase them, the liberal DPJ government under Prime Minister Yoshihiko Noda tried to forestall Ishihara by having the national government purchase the islands instead. The Japanese government anticipated that this move would provoke a Chinese response, since it could be interpreted as strengthening Japan's legal claim to the islands. It hoped, however, that it would be able to placate the Chinese by promising through back channels to continue to observe a policy of not developing, not stationing personnel, and not even conducting scientific research on the islands. Unfortunately, in China, the new leadership of Xi

Jinping was trying to consolidate its control after a notably nasty and contentious leadership fight, in which one of Xi's rivals, Bo Xilai, was arrested and imprisoned along with his wife. Xi felt it was impossible for him to appear weak on territorial issues. Moreover, some speculate that creating a crisis over the territorial dispute with Japan made it possible for Xi to further tighten his control over the defense and national security apparatus. As a result, China responded furiously to Noda's policy of nationalizing the islands, sending in dozens of Chinese paramilitary ships and planes—backed by the Chinese navy—to assert China's claims to the islands.[22]

China's provocations in the Senkaku/Diaoyu islands dealt a fatal blow to the credibility of Noda and the DPJ and, along with other policy failures, opened the door for the return of the conservative LDP to power. It also helped revive the fortunes of Shinzo Abe, who had resigned in 2007 after a disastrous Upper House election and because of health issues. Abe was known as a strong, pro-defense conservative, precisely the kind of strong, nationalist leader that the LDP tended to elect when there was a perceived need to strengthen the Japanese armed forces and the U.S.-Japan alliance. He beat out more moderate figures in the race to become the leader of the LDP, in part precisely because of his conservative credentials. Like Xi, Abe was inclined to take a tough stance on territorial issues. He was also well known for holding revisionist views on history and other ideological issues, particularly with respect to the Yasukuni Shrine and the comfort women.

Once again, the disputes over territory and history paralyzed regional diplomacy. China and South Korea joined together in trying to diplomatically isolate Japan in Asia. China even used the history issue to strengthen its ties with South Korea while driving a wedge between the two U.S. allies, opening up in the Chinese city of Harbin an exhibition dedicated to An Jung-Geun, the Korean activist who had assassinated the first Japanese governor general of Korea, Hirobumi Ito.[23] To make matters worse, there was now also a greatly heightened risk of a real military clash between China and Japan in the East China Sea, as the two sides scrambled ships and planes to assert dominance over the disputed territory.

The U.S. government under president Barack Obama began to be alarmed by the deepening crisis in the Asian region. For decades, the United States avoided becoming involved in the history issue. American diplomats and policymakers had tended to see history as a peripheral issue, despite the evidently strong emotions that it evoked, secondary to concrete economic and security issues. In addition, many Americans believed that no matter what the United States did, if it tried to mediate on historical issues, it would be perceived by one or possibly all the parties as taking sides, and any agreements that were reached with the help of American mediation would be seen, or portrayed, as having been forced on the region by Washington. To have any lasting effect, therefore, the parties would have to reach an agreement through their own volition and take ownership of it. Now, however, as Chinese and Japanese forces began to play what looked like a game of brinksmanship around the disputed islands, and as fissures between Tokyo and Seoul continued to widen, Washington felt it had no choice but to take a more active stance to prevent the situation from escalating further.[24]

The first visible sign of this new stance came when the United States took the highly unusual position of chiding the Abe government after Abe visited the Yasukuni Shrine in December 2013. Behind the scenes as well, the United States exerted pressure on Abe to restrain his revisionist instincts. During the LDP election campaign, it was rumored that Abe would seek to reverse the 1993 Kono statement, an important expression of official Japanese responsibility for the wartime comfort women system. There was also talk that Abe might abolish the Miyazawa doctrine on textbooks, set in 1982 to ensure educational textbooks would bear in mind the considerations of neighboring countries. Partly, however, as a result of American pressure, neither of these two policy shifts came to pass. In August, and while in office, Prime Minister Abe chose to take a more moderate stance on the history issue. While many members of his cabinet would visit Yasukuni, Abe himself chose to make no further official visits, sending gifts and emissaries instead. In 2015, Abe issued a carefully worded statement on the occasion of the seventieth anniversary of the end of World War II. While the statement was rather lengthy and convoluted, leaving room for interpretation as a considerable watering down of Japanese responsibility for war and a denial of guilt, it also contained certain key phrases—including an apology and expression of deep remorse to the victims of the war, as well as the use of the words "invasion" and "colonial oppression" to describe Japanese invasion of China and domination of Korea—which allowed the statement to be read as an expansion of previous apologies as well.[25]

The sharp escalation of the Sino-Japanese territorial dispute put new pressures on the Mutual Security System. For the first time in the relationship, U.S. policymakers were concerned that Japan might drag the United States into a conflict in which it had no interest, described as "reverse entrapment" by Adam Liff in chapter 1. Japanese reassurance that it would not needlessly provoke China over historical and territorial issues played a critical role in encouraging the United States to support Tokyo.[26] Most crucially, first Secretary of State Hillary Clinton in 2013, and then President Barack Obama in 2014, made it clear that the United States was committed to helping Japan repel a Chinese attack on the Senkaku/Diaoyu islands. The United States also went out of its way to praise Japan for its efforts to pursue reconciliation, and in 2015, the United States helped broker a deal between Tokyo and Seoul on the comfort women, with Japan offering financial support for the comfort women without offering a new apology.[27] Unfortunately, Abe insisted that this should be the final settlement of the issue—a guarantee that, it should have been clear, no Korean leader could make in good faith, given the convoluted and emotional politics of the issue in South Korea. Yet President Park Geun-Hye, eager to please the United States at a time when tensions with North Korea were increasing and her poll numbers falling, agreed.

Finally, shortly before he left office in 2016, President Barack Obama made a historical visit to Hiroshima, highly successful on the symbolic level, laying a wreath at the Hiroshima Peace Memorial Park and meeting some of the surviving victims of the atomic bombings. Obama did not offer a direct apology for U.S. actions. All the evidence suggests that Obama probably was motivated not so much by considerations of strengthening the U.S.-Japan alliance as by a desire to tap the symbolic capital of the memorial site to make a final appeal for one of the cornerstones of his foreign policy—the one for which he was awarded a Nobel Peace Prize in 2009—the call for nuclear disarmament. Nonetheless, the gesture was much appreciated in Japan and widely seen there as a symbol of the deepening of U.S.-Japan reconciliation. A few months later, Prime Minister Abe became the first Japanese head of government to visit the memorial to the USS *Arizona* sunk in the Japanese attack on Pearl Harbor.

U.S. efforts and the willingness of South Korea and Japan under President Park Geun-Hye and Prime Minister Shinzo Abe to follow the U.S.

lead on the issue helped prevent a further, potentially dangerous escalation of tensions on historical issues. However, the underlying causes of the history problem in Asia, which have grown over many decades and are reinforced by growing geostrategic cleavages as well as domestic political factors, remain firmly in place. For South Korean political leaders, especially on the progressive side of the political spectrum, challenging Japan to do more for the comfort women and fiercely rejecting Japan's claims to Dokdo/Takeshima remains the litmus test of a leader's patriotic credentials and commitment to human rights. For China, Japan continues to be a convenient villain, unrepentant for its role in China's century of humiliation and scheming, together with the United States, to thwart China's rise to its rightful place as the leading power in Asia and beyond. In both countries, unscrupulous politicians are ready to tap into these sentiments, which are real and rooted in their political cultures, to boost their own legitimacy or to attack their political rivals.

The limits of U.S. diplomatic brokering were soon revealed after President Park Geun-Hye was replaced by the more progressive President Moon Jae-In. Almost as soon as he came into office, Moon announced he would reexamine the 2015 comfort women agreement, and South Korean nonprofits, with government support, erected statues and plaques dedicated to the comfort women across the country, including outside of the Japanese consulate in Busan. Even worse, the South Korean courts have taken long-threatened steps that may throw Japanese-Korean relations into chaos. On October 30, 2018, the Korean Supreme Court upheld Lower Court rulings and ordered Japan's Nippon Steel and Sumitomo Metal to pay 100 million won (approximately US$80,000) in compensation to four elderly former forced laborers, potentially opening the floodgates for more cases, as evidenced by a similar ruling against Mitsubishi Heavy Industries a month later.[28] The court found that—contrary to the claims of the Japanese government that the issue of compensation for forced laborers had been settled by the 1965 Normalization Treaty between Japan and Korea, a position that in 2005 the South Korean government had appeared to accept—the laborers had, in fact, retained the right to demand compensation for their suffering.

Meanwhile, the PRC has tried to mend its ties with Japan, partly to help prop up its flagging economy, partly in hope of enlisting an ally in its economic battles against President Donald Trump. Yet in China, as well, the underlying forces that have led to explosions of acrimony over historical issues remain firmly rooted in Chinese society and its political culture. There is every reason to believe that China, as well as the region as a whole, is only experiencing a lull before the next storm.

Conclusion—What Is to be done?

As the foregoing analysis has shown, with respect to historical justice issues, Japan is far from an illiberal outlier. Japan is just as penitent—or impenitent—as most other advanced industrial democracies. While it is not as penitent for its participation in World War II and waging a war of aggression as Germany or Austria, it is not entirely alone in this regard. With respect to apologizing for its historical role as a colonial power, Japan is arguably somewhat more penitent than any of the other colonial countries, including not only Britain, France, or the United States but also Germany. It is worth emphasizing here that this is not a normative judgment—certainly, a strong case can be made on moral grounds that Japan, as well as other former colonial powers, should be considerably more apologetic about the things that they have done and ought to offer greater compensation for the harm inflicted.

A further upshot of the argument presented here is that countries and political leaders tend to respond to demands on pragmatic grounds. Regardless of their personal views on historical issues, leaders have a responsibility to pursue the national interest. When it comes to historical issues, they tend to make efforts to make amends for past wrongs only when they perceive there is a strong practical need for them to do so. One of the main reasons why Germany chose to offer the extensive apologies and pay the extensive compensation that it did (by some estimates, the Federal Republic paid close to US$100 billion in restitution by the end of the Cold War, and many billions more since) was because it felt it had to. Put simply, apologizing and paying reparations were the price of readmission to the club of West European democracies after 1945 and for stabilizing relations with the East after 1991. When pressures mounted in the 1990s on Austria, Switzerland, and other countries to address their role in the Holocaust, they did so as well. In Eastern European countries such as Hungary or Poland, where public sentiment was much more impenitent and a strong sense of victimization at the hands of the Soviet Union tempered popular feelings of guilt over the complicity of some Eastern Europeans in the persecution of the Jews, contrition tended to be much shallower, and once the pressure of needing to win acceptance into the EU passed, professions of guilt evaporated.

Again, some caveats are in order. To say that Germany and other European countries became penitent out of necessity is not to say that the sentiments that many Germans and others expressed over the horrors of the past are not genuine. While in at least some, and perhaps most, cases the apologies offered may have been disingenuous, once the psychological barriers to acknowledging guilt were removed, powerful emotions could be engaged with, which led to profound and very real changes in how people—both on the elite and mass level—think about their histories.

In the case of Japan, it is possible to discern a similar pattern. In the initial Cold War period, there were powerful forces that encouraged Japan, like most other societies emerging out of a deeply traumatic period, to put the issue of historical justice aside and concentrate on the urgent task of reconstructing a ruined nation and reintegrating a deeply wounded and divided society. At the same time, views on responsibility for the war became one of the key ideological dividing lines in post-1945 Japanese politics. The dominant Japanese conservative elites did not see pursuit of the issue to be in their interests. They were helped along by an international environment where the United States, Japan's key external partner, became convinced that pursuing the issue was also not in its own strategic interests. Other countries, including the two Chinas and South Korea, were simply not in a position to effectively pressure Japan on the issue. As a result, Japan was able to dispense with the issue with a minimal level of contrition, offering no or very limited apologies (for example, Foreign Minister Shiina Etsusaburo's personal apology to South Korea in 1965, or Prime Minister Kakuei Tanaka's expression of regret in Beijing in 1972) while offering economic aid and trade in place of reparations.

In the 1980s and 1990s, when pressure from Asian countries over historical issues began to intensify, Japanese leaders, like counterparts in other parts of the world, began to respond on a pragmatic basis, with some success. Geostrategic pressures, however, intervened in ways that have undermined Japan's ability to achieve a stable equilibrium on historical justice with its two closest, and by far most powerful and important neighbors, China and South Korea. The strong tendency of the Japanese political system to push a nationalistic message at the same time as it seeks extensive security reforms undermined Japan's efforts to pursue reconciliation with its neighbors, especially during the Koizumi era and again during the second Abe administration. At the same time, the South Korean government's vulnerability to societal pressures on historical issues, and the recourse of the PRC government to a traditional form of popular nationalism, created powerful domestic political currents that tended to disrupt the two countries' relations with Japan. By the early twenty-first century, trends in all three countries and in the region led to an increasing spillover of acrimony over historical issues into long-standing territorial disputes in ways that are both potentially very dangerous and difficult to reverse.

Worse yet, with the advent of the Trump administration in the United States and the rise of populist antisystem parties on both the political Left and Right, such as the 5 Star movement in Italy or the Alternative für Deutschland (AfD) in Germany, there is a real danger that the fundamental consensus favoring the liberal international order could come undone. A collapse of that order could have a devastating spillover effect in Northeast Asia, further fanning the flames of an unreasoning form of nationalism and encouraging the rise to power of revisionist leaders who could take the region in dangerous and destructive directions.

Japan has an important role in this context: to help prevent the further erosion of the liberal international order in Asia. As we have seen, Japan's stance on history does not disqualify it from taking a leadership role in trying to preserve the liberal international order. Nor has its position seriously damaged its overall standing on the global stage. With the exception of its relations with China and South Korea, Japan's overall international image, including in Southeast Asia, is excellent, as reflected in opinion polls, the spread of Japanese popular culture, and general interest in Japan.[29] What it does have to do, however, is to address the history issue. As we have seen, historically rooted distrust and acrimony have proven a major obstacle to Japan's ability to convert Japanese soft power into diplomatic influence in the Asian region and heighten the risk that territorial disputes may escalate to the level of an actual military conflict. Moreover, recent developments suggest that if Japan needlessly provokes South Korea and China over historical issues, or overreacts to South Korean or Chinese provocations, its chief security partner, the United States, will be disinclined to help it. While U.S. policymakers are unlikely to abandon Japan over history issues alone, what is unique about the current situation is that for the first time it is the United States—rather than Japan—that fears it could become entangled in a conflict in which it has no interest. It is crucial, from a strategic standpoint, that Japan reassure not only its neighbors but also the United States that it will act in accordance with international norms regarding historical justice issues.

In practice, this means first and foremost damage control: not acting in ways that can be guaranteed to trigger a strong emotional response in neighboring countries. Making official visits to Yasukuni should be avoided. Ideally, other ways of commemorating the war dead should be found, such as possibly returning to the options explored in the Yasuo Fukuda Commission on the issue in 2001, or alternatively working with the *Izokukai* (Association of the War Bereaved) and the Yasukuni authorities to make visits to the shrine less controversial. Likewise, Japan should not revoke the Kono statement or the Miyazawa policy on textbooks, and Japanese leaders should continue to use the language of the Murayama statement when discussing Japan's pre-1945 history. Similarly, while Japan cannot and should not be expected to abandon its territorial claims in the East China Sea or to Dokdo/Takeshima, it would be well advised to continue to not press them more aggressively than is necessary. In the case of the Senkaku/Diaoyu, Japan is fortunately in possession of the islands. In the case of Dokdo/Takeshima, there is no need to launch noisy publicity campaigns asserting Japan's claims to the islands. Under international law, the occasional diplomatic demarche is sufficient to sustain Japan's legal claim.

Beyond not needlessly aggravating the situation, it is equally important that Japan not overreact to what it perceives as being Chinese or South Korean provocations. This is particularly important in the case of South Korea, where powerful public pressures are driving the government to pursue policies with respect to the comfort women and forced laborers issues, which almost seem designed to embarrass Japan as much as to pressure it to do more to help the surviving victims of Imperial Japanese policies. In this respect, Japanese diplomatic efforts to counter the South Korean campaign to erect plaques and memorials dedicated to the comfort women throughout the United States is a particularly good example of the Japanese reacting to South Korean policies in a counterproductive way. For most Americans, the comfort women issue is perceived primarily as a symbolic gesture to underline the international communities' determination to condemn gender-based violence. The issue is not seen so much as anti-Japanese per se as reflecting a commitment to broader international norms. Even Japanese-American politicians are unwilling to support Japanese diplomatic efforts in this regard. Japanese efforts to prevent the erection of these monuments, therefore, seem almost incomprehensible. They reinforce the perception that Japan is out of step with the rest of the world on a critically important human rights issue.

For similar reasons, Japan should not overreact to the erection of the comfort women statues in front of the Japanese embassy in Seoul or the consulate in Busan, much less in other parts of South Korea. While the statues may make Japanese diplomats uncomfortable and even impede the day-to-day operations of Japanese diplomatic outposts, opposing the statues is both futile and counterproductive.

Japan needs to display similar equanimity in response to Seoul's cancellation of the 2015 comfort women deal. That deal suffered from at least two critical flaws. First, it claimed that the agreement would be a final resolution of the issue. This was probably an unrealistic expectation from the beginning, and the Japanese government should not be surprised that the South Korean side proved incapable of keeping the bargain. Second, the deal was worked out on a largely government-to-government basis. The crucial task of rallying civil society support for the agreement—a task that should have been initiated by the South Korean government but supported by the Japanese side as well—was neglected.

In response to the current crisis in Japanese–South Korean relations, the Japanese government should first signal a willingness to return to the bargaining table and negotiate a new deal, based purely on humanitarian considerations and out of a commitment to the goal of promoting reconciliation between the Korean and Japanese peoples. At the same time, Japan should strongly protest South Korea's breaking of the terms of the 1965 Normalization Treaty. Japan could point out that, in principle, the

Japanese government and individual Japanese people could press claims against South Korea for the loss of property from the colonial period, and that, moreover, the South Korean move undermines the spirit of the entire 1952 San Francisco Treaty system, which is the lynchpin of the post-1945 international order in Asia. While the South Korean government is bound to respect the rulings of its courts, it could set up its own compensation fund to meet the humanitarian needs of the former forced laborers. Japan could, without assuming legal liability, support such an effort, both financially and politically, in the name of promoting Japanese–South Korean friendship and reconciliation. The United States and other Western countries would be likely to be sympathetic to a Japanese stance that is both conciliatory on historical issues and firm on respecting diplomatic principles and the rule of law. While South Korea might get diplomatic support from some quarters—notably, China—it would find itself largely isolated in the broader international community.

Eventually, South Korea is likely to want to come back to the bargaining table, and it will be in Japan's interest to respond. It is, therefore, important that any future new agreement include greater buy-in from South Korean, and possibly Japanese, civil society actors. Difficult as it may be, it is vital that the South Korean government identifies and works with South Korean nonprofits that support the comfort women, so they can participate in negotiating the outlines of a new deal with Japan and be involved in delivering services aimed at helping the few surviving comfort women who have come forward. Japanese women's groups that have worked with their South Korean counterparts on this issue in the past may prove itself to be a people-to-people mechanism to build a bridge between the two sides. A separate agreement on Korean forced laborers may also prove not only necessary but desirable, and it as well should be based on similar principles. While the financial costs might be significant, several billion dollars, they pale in comparison to what they would have been in an earlier era, when more survivors were still alive, or with the diplomatic costs of continued South Korean–Japanese acrimony.

The steps outlined above could be described as an effort at damage control. However, if such agreements can be implemented and are successful in dealing with the current crisis, Japan and the South Korean government should explore the possibility of pursuing a more ambitious program aimed at promoting a reshaping of societal attitudes and the achievement of something greater than the superficial reconciliation of the past. Such a program would require a strong bipartisan consensus in both countries and would have to be implemented across a range of policy dimensions. These include meetings between senior leaders designed to underline the two nations' commitment to improving relations. Japan should continue to acknowledge its history of wrongdoing; South Korea, in turn, should accept Japan's apologies and emphasize that Japan today is very different from Japan in the past and that the two countries should work together for a better common future. The sponsorship of joint exhibitions and historical research exploring the more positive as well as negative sides of the two countries' histories would be another vital dimension. Third and finally, similar ideas regarding the two countries' histories should be promoted through the Korean and Japanese school systems. If such a program could be successfully implemented, it could revive the thaw in Japanese–South Korean relations that began with the 1998 Kim Dae Jung–Keizo Obuchi summit and lead to a genuine intersocietal reconciliation that would help stabilize relations between the two countries in much the same way that the history issue has been tamed between the Western European countries.

The question then emerges, how should Japan respond if similar demands come from neighboring countries? Here Japan will need to respond pragmatically and on a case-by-case basis. Japan cannot and need not respond to every demand for compensation. It may be useful for it to issue general guidelines regarding the preconditions for entering into negotiations aimed at resolving historical legacy issues. First and foremost, there should be a shared commitment to the ideals of peaceful coexistence, as reflected by a respect for the peaceful resolution of territorial issues and the maintenance of military forces that are strictly geared for self-defense. Only once fundamental geopolitical interests are in line with one another is it possible to pursue intersocietal reconciliation. Neither China nor North Korea would qualify under such a definition, certainly not under current conditions, although various Southeast Asian nations, as well as South Korea, would. Such a precondition could be legitimized with reference to the principles of the UN Charter as well as the ASEAN Treaty on Amity and Cooperation. Second, as for South Korea, the immediate goal would be damage control, but ideally it would open the door to intersocietal reconciliation along the lines of the Japanese–South Korean program described above. Third and finally, claims for reparations or compensation could require strict documentary support, thus allowing Japan to avoid potential abuse of the system and to moderate potential Japanese liability, if necessary.

In the current climate of escalating regional geostrategic tensions, a growing mood of "apology fatigue" in Japan, and rising nationalism in China and Korea, it may seem difficult to imagine that Japan can make much progress on historical issues. Nonetheless, it is of vital importance that despite its frustrations, Japan at least manages the tensions over history. If allowed to escalate too far, they are likely to undermine any efforts on Tokyo's part to maintain a liberal international order, damage its strategic partnership with the United States, and contribute to the erosion of liberal values within Japan itself. Japan needs to maintain a calm, patient approach to the question of accepting responsibility for the darker sides of modern Japanese history while holding open the door for a more earnest and realistic program to promote genuine reconciliation. There are trends in the region—such as increased societal interaction and intergenerational changes—that may eventually create the conditions for a more stable relationship between Japan and its neighbors.

NOTES

1. Japan's international image consistently shows that it is among the top ten countries in the world in terms of its favorable international image, and according to one well-regarded index, in 2018 it was the fifth overall in the world, behind the United States but ahead of Canada and Switzerland. See USC Center on Public Diplomacy, *The Soft Power 30: A Global Ranking of Soft Power 2018* (Los Angeles: USC Center on Public Diplomacy, 2018). For a comprehensive look at the different ways in which Japan exercises leadership, see *Reinventing Japan: New Direction in Global Leadership*, edited by Martin Fackler and Yoichi Funabashi (Santa Barbara, Calif.: Praeger, 2018).

2. See *Soft Power Superpowers: Cultural and National Assets of Japan and the United States*, edited by Yasushi Watanabe and David L. McConnel (Armonk, N.Y.: M. E. Sharpe, 2008). For a particularly enthusiastic Japanese version of this argument, see Uemura Kazuhide, *Nihon no Sofuto Pawaa: Honmono no Fukko ga Sekai wo Ugokasu* (Tokyo: Sougensha, 2012). For a more negative assessment, see Thomas Berger, "The Triumph of Hope over Experience: The False Promise of Japanese Soft Power in East Asia," in James D. J. Brown and Jeff Kingston, *Japan's Foreign Relations in Asia* (New York and London: Routledge, 2018).

3. See, for instance, Keiichi Tsunekawa, "Why So Many Maps There? Japan and Regional Cooperation," in *Remapping East Asia: The Construction of a Region*, edited

by T. J. Pempel (Cornell University Press, 2005), 106, 142; Gilbert Rozman, "East Asian Historical Issues in a Contemporary Light," in *East Asia's Haunted Present: Historical Memories and the Resurgence of Nationalism*, edited by Tsuyoshi Hasegawa and Kazuhiko Togo (Westport, Conn.: Praeger, 2008), 55–56.

4. See, for instance, Shinzo Abe and Hisahiko Okazaki, "Chūgoku no yokoguruma wo yurushite naru mono ka," *Shokun* (August 2005), 37–44. Along somewhat different lines, see Jennifer Lind, "The Perils of Apology: What Japan Should Not Learn from Germany," *Foreign Affairs*, vol. 88, no. 3 (May/June 2009), 132–46.

5. Henry Kissinger goes so far as to argue that the introduction of the historical justice regime, and of the International Criminal Court in particular, counts as perhaps the only genuinely new element in international relations in recent decades. See Henry Kissinger, *Does America Need a Foreign Policy? Toward a Diplomacy for the 21st Century* (New York: Simon and Schuster, 2001), chapter 7.

6. For an excellent recounting of this process with respect to international tribunals, see David Bass, *To Stay the Hand of Vengeance: International War Crimes Tribunals* (Princeton University Press, 2000).

7. See *International Regimes*, edited by Stephen D. Krasner (Cornell University Press, 1983). For a recent overview, see Raymond Hopkins and Benjamin Meiches, "Regime Theory," *International Studies*, November 2012. On the international justice regime, see Elazar Barkan, *The Guilt of Nations: Restitution and Negotiating Historical Injustices* (Johns Hopkins University Press, 2001); *The Politics and the Past: Repairing Historical Injustice*, edited by John Torpey (Lanham, M.D.: Rowman & Littlefield, 2003); *The Age of Apology: Facing Up to the Past*, edited by Marc Gibney and others (University of Pennsylvania Press, 2009).

8. I develop this argument at greater length in Thomas U. Berger, *War, Guilt, and World Politics After World War II* (Cambridge University Press, 2012).

9. Belgium, France, Germany, Italy, Japan, the Netherlands, Portugal, Spain, Turkey, the United Kingdom, and the United States. Some would make the case that Israel should be added to that list.

10. "Italy to Pay Libya US$5 Billion," *New York Times*, August 31, 2008. Self-interest, including a chance at billions' worth of infrastructure projects; Libyan help with migration; and securing oil and gas supplies are said to be behind Italy's generosity. See Patrick Fitzgerald, "Italy's Colonial Apology Smacks of Self-Interest," *Foreign Policy*, September 2, 2008.

11. Directly: Austria, Belgium, the Czech Republic, Denmark, Estonia, France, Greece, Latvia, Lithuania, Luxembourg, the Netherlands, Norway, Poland, Slovakia, and Slovenia. Indirectly: Sweden and Switzerland.

12. See, for instance, Ian Buruma, *The Wages of Guilt: Memories of War in Germany and Japan* (New York: Farrar, Straus, and Giroux, 1994); Iris Chang, *The Rape of Nanking: The Forgotten Holocaust of World War II* (New York: Basic Books, 1997).

13. See Norbert Frei, *Vergangenheitspolitik: die Anfänge der Bundesrepublik und die NS Vergangenheit* [Adenaur's Germany and the Nazi Past: The Politics of Amnesty and Integration] (Munich: Beck, 1996).

14. Public opinion surveys conducted by the ASAN institute in South Korea reveal that despite repeated apologies on the part of Japanese leaders, the Korean public is remarkably unaware that such apologies have been offered. See Youngshik Bong, "In

Search of a Perfect Apology: Korea's Response to the Murayama Apology," in *Japan and Reconciliation in Postwar Asia: The Murayama Statement and Its Implications*, edited by Kazuhiko Togo (New York: Palgrave Macmillan, 2013), 46–67.

15. Meirion Harries and Susie Harries, *Sheathing the Sword: The Demilitarization of Japan* (New York: Macmillan, 1987). For a brilliant analysis focusing on Germany, see Jeffrey K. Olick, *In the House of the Hangman: Agonies of German Defeat 1943–1949* (University of Chicago Press, 2005).

16. For the text in English, see "Treaty of Peace with Japan," http://www.taiwandocuments.org/sanfrancisco01.htm. In Japanese, see "San Fransisuko Heiwa Jhoyaku [Nihonkoku tono Heiwa Jhoyaku]" (Treaty of San Francisco [Treaty of Peace with Japan]), http://worldjpn.grips.ac.jp/documents/texts/docs/19510908.T1J.html.

17. Zheng Wang, *Never Forget National Humiliation: Historical Memory in Chinese Politics and Foreign Relations* (Columbia University Press, 2012).

18. See James Reilley, "China's History Activists and the War of Resistance against Japan," *Asian Survey*, vol. 44, no. 2 (March/April 2004), 276–94.

19. Christopher R. Hughes, "Japan in the Politics of Chinese Leadership Legitimacy: Recent Developments in Historical Perspective," *Japan Forum*, vol. 20, no. 2 (2008), 245–66.

20. See Jessica Chen Weiss, *Powerful Patriots: Nationalist Protest in China's Foreign Relations* (Oxford University Press, 2014).

21. "Japan 'Stole' Diaoyu Islands, China Tells UN," *South China Morning Post*, September 28, 2012.

22. Tsuyoshi Sunohara, *Antō Senkaku Koku Yūka* [Secret Feud: Nationalization of the Senkakus] (Tokyo: Shinchosha, 2013), 180–86.

23. Jane Perlez, "China Exhibit, Part of an Anti-Japan Campaign, Reflects an Escalating Feud," *New York Times*, February 8, 2014.

24. Based on numerous off-the-record conversations with various former and active officials from the State Department and the National Security Council, Washington, D.C., Spring 2016.

25. Shin Kawamura, "How to Read the Abe Statement," *Diplomat*, August 20, 2015.

26. Joseph A. Bosco, "Entrapment and Abandonment in Asia," *National Interest*, July 8, 2013.

27. Mikyoung Kim, "The U.S. the Big Winner in 'Comfort Women' Agreement," *East Asia Forum*, January 7, 2016.

28. Ock Hyun-Ju, "Court Orders Japan Firm to Compensate Wartime Forced Laborers," *Korea Herald*, October 30, 2018; Choe Sang-Hue, "South Korean Court Orders Mitsubishi of Japan to Pay for Forced Wartime Labor," *New York Times*, November 29, 2018. For more background on the long-running debate, see Hideki Okuzono, "South Korean Judiciary Shakes Japan–South Korea Relations," https://www2.jiia.or.jp/en/pdf/digital_library/korean_peninsula/160331_Hideki_Okuzono.pdf. For a Korean perspective, see "Fifty Years after Korea-Japan Pact Some Issues Won't Go Away," *Korea Joong Ang Dailey*, June 23, 2015.

29. See "Sharp Drop in World Views of U.S., U.K.: Global Poll for BBC World Service," BBC, July 3, 2017.

9

The Perils and Virtues of Constitutional Flexibility

JAPAN'S CONSTITUTION AND THE LIBERAL INTERNATIONAL ORDER

KENNETH MORI McELWAIN

The Constitution of Japan (COJ)—ratified in 1946 and implemented in 1947—is very much a product of its drafters. The General Headquarters of the Allied Occupation, which wrote the COJ in nine days, placed strong emphasis on demilitarizing Japan and replacing imperial sovereignty with popular democracy. In addition, many of the staffers were New Deal Democrats with a progressive commitment to the primacy of individual and social rights. As a result, the COJ enumerates a large number of fundamental human rights—in fact, more than virtually any other preceding constitution.[1]

The COJ is also a product of its time. Much attention has been paid to Article 9's pacifist vision and restrictions on war potential, but it is also less internationalist than most constitutions today, saying very little about obligations to international organizations or national commitments to free markets and trade. However, this silence is typical for its era. While newer constitutions can be quite detailed in specifying their nation's positions in the international arena, the COJ predated the establishment of critical international institutions and laws in the postwar period.

The structure of the COJ continues to shape constitutional debates in Japan today, more than seventy years after its ratification. It is the oldest unamended constitution in the world, but it has been the frequent target of criticism from conservative politicians, media, and scholars. In particular, it is denounced for unnecessarily constraining the "normal" foreign and security policy autonomy of the nation, of elevating individual rights above civic duties, and more generally of being too antiquated to deal with emerging international problems.

This chapter examines the viability of the Japanese constitution in the coming decades through the use of comparative constitutional data and a careful examination of Japanese elite and public opinion. First, does the COJ limit Japan's role in the liberal international order? On Article 9, the answer is messy but illustrative. While there are clear limits on having an unfettered military, the government has reinterpreted the constitution and passed special laws to permit limited international engagements. The COJ's ability to bend without breaking exemplifies its central feature: flexibility. It is the fifth shortest constitution in the world, leaving many details about political institutions and government powers to be settled by law. As a result, even where the COJ does not explicitly demand that the government participate in the liberal international order, it also does not forbid it. Put differently, elected representatives—and through them, Japanese citizens—have considerable discretion to settle contentious issues through normal legislative processes.

This, then, makes it crucial to understand how Japan's elected elites and general public think about the need for COJ amendment. While the ruling Liberal Democratic Party (LDP) has made constitutional revision part of its historical mission, there is significant disagreement among legislators on *which parts* to amend first. In addition, voters appear to prioritize the protection—and, if possible, expansion—of human rights, such as the right to privacy and greater government transparency, to which the LDP has given less attention. For the constitution to change, this discrepancy among and between elites and the mass public needs to be resolved.

This project's survey experiment on "Japan and the Liberal International Order" points to how public opinion can be swayed (more details on the survey experiment can be found in chapter 11). Voters' attitudes toward constitutional amendment are indelibly linked to their views on the American-led liberal international order. Support for amending Article 9 is greater among those who believe that U.S. leadership has been crucial to peace in the Asia-Pacific region and who worry about America's weakening military commitment to East Asian security. Looking forward, demands from the United States government for a more equal alliance and its threats to withdraw troops from Asia have the potential to transform how the Japanese public conceives of the merits and limits of the current constitution.

The COJ and the Liberal International Order

There is a clear historical dimension to the content of national constitutions. Newer constitutions that were established after World War I, when universal suffrage expanded globally, include more "socioeconomic rights," such as the right to education or healthcare, which only came into vogue with the extension of political participation to poorer citizens. Likewise, they are more likely to include explicit protections for traditionally disadvantaged groups, such as ethnic minorities, women, and immigrants, reflecting gradual changes in human rights norms. Newer constitutions also specify political institutions in greater detail, as the expansion of government powers in the twentieth century engendered concerns about leaving the machinery of politics to customary practice. In sum, newer constitutions tend to be longer and more comprehensive than older documents.[2]

The Constitution of Japan is, in that sense, an outlier. Research I conducted with Christian G. Winkler, an expert on Japanese political philosophy, notes that the COJ is one of the shortest constitutions in the world: its English translation is just under 5,000 words, compared to the current global median of 13,630 words.[3] The Allied Occupation's constitutional drafters were focused on transforming Japan into a stable, demilitarized democracy, built on three constitutional pillars: popular sovereignty with a symbolic emperor (Article 1), pacifism (Article 9), and fundamental human rights (Article 11).[4] As a result, the COJ enumerates more rights than other contemporary constitutions, but it also tends to be quite vague on political institutions, leaving most details about the architecture of government to be determined by law. The occupation's drafters, working on an abbreviated schedule, believed that upending the political system would sow confusion and derail a swift, orderly transition to democracy.[5] As such, quite substantial matters, such as the electoral system for the Diet (Article 47) or the organization and powers of local governments (Article 92–95), can be changed by a simple parliamentary majority.[6]

The COJ is similarly quiet about Japan's role in the world, except for the prescription of nonaggression in Article 9, described in greater detail in chapter 1 by Adam Liff. We can place this in a comparative and historical context using data from the Comparative Constitutions Project, which codes the content of approximately nine hundred national constitutions since the eighteenth century.[7] Table 9-1 lists whether certain principles related to the liberal international order are enumerated in the constitution. Meiji and "COJ" refer to whether these topics are specified in the Meiji Constitution, which was in force in 1889–1946, or the current COJ. The numbers "1946" and "2010" show the proportion of constitutions that make reference to the relevant topics in those years.

The Meiji and postwar constitutions are fairly similar in their content related to the liberal international order, except for the latter's silence on military matters. In fact, all but nine constitutions in the world today mention the word "military."[8] Both Japanese constitutions mention international law and treaties, with the COJ writing in Article 98, "The treaties concluded by Japan and established laws of nations shall be faithfully observed." However, neither discusses membership in international organizations, which is quite commonplace (65 percent) today. That said, it would be fair to describe the COJ as a product of its era. The topics it excludes—except for military matters—were not prevalent among world constitutions in 1946, when the COJ was ratified.

While constitutions have become more "global" or "internationally oriented" over the postwar period, the virtues of enumerating concepts related to the liberal international order are not straightforward. On the one hand, they reflect the symbolic importance and practical necessities of operating in an internationalized world, where countries—particularly small ones—are dependent on foreign trade and international security al-

TABLE 9-1. International comparison of constitutions

Category	Specification	Meiji	COJ	1946	2010
Trade	Int'l Trade			42%	22%
	Foreign Invest			30%	15%
Int'l Law	Int'l Law	O	O	89%	93%
	Treaties	O	O	100%	93%
	Int'l Orgs			11%	65%
Military	Military	O		94%	92%
	C in Chief	O		75%	74%

Source: Data calculated from the Comparative Constitutions Project (Zachary Elkins, Tom Ginsburg, and James Melton, The Endurance of National Constitutions (Cambridge University Press, 2009). Comparative Constitutions Project data can be downloaded from http://comparativeconstitutionsproject.org/).

Note: Shaded cells note principles that were included in a majority of constitutions in that year. Coding guidelines are as follows:

Int'l Trade: mentions foreign or international trade
Foreign Invest: mentions foreign investment or foreign capital
Int'l Law: provisions concerning relationship between constitution and international law
Treaties: mentions international treaties
Int'l Orgs: provisions concerning international organizations
Military: mentions military or armed forces
C in Chief: mentions head of state or of government as commander in chief

liances. On the other hand, the *absence* of constitutional specification does not preclude countries from passing legislation that achieves similar goals or courts from compelling governments to act on those matters. After all, the fact that the COJ does not mention foreign trade or capital hardly means that the Japanese economy is hermetically sealed.

The biggest peril with constitutional vagueness is the difficulty in resolving competing interpretations of permissible government actions. For example:

> Article 9.1. Aspiring sincerely to an international peace based on justice and order, the Japanese people forever renounce war as a sov-

ereign right of the nation and the threat or use of force as means of settling international disputes.

Article 9.2. In order to accomplish the aim of the preceding paragraph, land, sea, and air forces, as well as other war potential, will never be maintained. The right of belligerency of the state will not be recognized.

This can be read as a blanket prohibition on any military power, but the Self-Defense Forces have existed since the 1950s. The Cabinet Legislation Bureau, which acts as legal counsel to the cabinet and issues opinions on the legality of bills and regulations, has historically argued that capabilities for self-defense are permissible even under the confines of Article 9.[9] However, its interpretation of what constitutes "self-defense" has evolved over time. In 1991, the SDF was dispatched overseas for the first time on a naval minesweeping mission after the Gulf War and again for the UN-sanctioned peacekeeping operations in Cambodia starting in 1992. In 2014, it approved the Abe cabinet's declaration that Article 9 allowed for the right to engage not only in individual defense but also the "limited" exercise of collective self-defense.

The post–Cold War expansion of SDF missions has been strongly contested by left-wing opposition parties and activists, but the only actor with the formal authority to rule on this matter definitively is the supreme court, defined in Article 81 as being the final arbiter of the constitutionality of laws. However, Japanese courts have largely been passive, with only ten laws being judged unconstitutional in the entire postwar period. The supreme court has never ruled on the constitutionality of the SDF or its missions, due to two factors. First, it is hard to demonstrate concrete harm from the SDF's existence. Second, the supreme court has abided by the *tōchikōi-ron* (political question doctrine), wherein certain topics are deemed to be a political, not legal, question, and hence outside of the purview of the courts. While not applied frequently, this doctrine allows the courts to defer making a final judgment on politically controversial cases.

This interpretive vacuum has given room for various actors to step in and sway public opinion. Politicians from the government and the opposition have long posited the merits of looser versus tighter constraints under

Article 9, but public reaction to their arguments is inevitably colored by partisanship. A third party that has played an unusually large role in public debates is academic experts. A critical spark was the unanimous Diet testimony of three constitutional scholars, including one called by the LDP, that collective self-defense was unconstitutional under Article 9.[10] In June 2015, the *Asahi Shimbun* conducted a survey of 122 constitutional scholars, of whom 119 said that collective self-defense was clearly or possibly unconstitutional.[11] A further 77 stated that the Self-Defense Forces themselves were possibly unconstitutional, and 99 deemed that amendments to Article 9 were unnecessary. Given that most of these constitutional scholars do not specialize in Article 9, we should not see their opinions as being definitive. That said, their impact on public discourse should not be underestimated, either: even Prime Minister Shinzo Abe has argued that Article 9 should be amended to clarify the constitutionality of the SDF, citing the doubts of constitutional experts.[12]

Of course, constitutional amendment is not solely about Article 9, as both political elites and the public at large have complex views about whether to amend different portions of the COJ. A key focus of this chapter is how people's beliefs about the historical merits and future challenges to the liberal international order influence these preferences. I turn to this issue next.

COJ Amendment: The Elites

The COJ is the oldest unamended constitution in the world today, remaining word-for-word the same document since its enactment. While no concrete amendment proposal has even been submitted to the Diet, its contents have been contested repeatedly, notably by the long-governing Liberal Democratic Party (LDP). Winkler argues that most conservatives accept the current three constitutional pillars of popular sovereignty, pacifism, and respect for fundamental human rights but also see revision as a critical element of a "post-postwar Japan"—that is, unshackled from the memories and guilt of World War II, explored in greater depth in chapter 8 by Thomas Berger.[13] The conservative LDP has tried to chart a delicate course between criticism of postwar politics, which it has charted since its formation in 1955, and a blueprint for the future, which it hopes to shape. Few mainstream figures have called for a return to the authoritarian, traditionalist Meiji Constitution, but many more are supportive of rebalancing the primacy of "individual rights" over "public welfare" and of altering Article 9 to permit collective self-defense explicitly.

The procedure for constitutional amendment is outlined in Article 96, which requires the assent of an absolute two-thirds in both houses of the Diet, followed by a simple majority in a national voter referendum. This process is fairly "standard": the two-thirds hurdle is required by around 75 percent of contemporary constitutions, and of those, approximately half provide for additional confirmation via a national referendum.[14] Nevertheless, the parliamentary hurdle has remained an obstacle for the LDP, as it has never unilaterally held the requisite two-thirds in the Diet. Of course, constitutional amendment processes are designed to prevent divisive changes to foundational rules, so Article 96 is arguably doing exactly what it is supposed to. In most countries, surmounting the parliamentary hurdle requires the assent of multiple political parties, as has been the case in Germany, whose Basic Law has been amended more than sixty times despite having the same two-thirds requirement as the COJ. The historical problem for the LDP has been its inability to gain support from other political parties.

Initiatives to revise the COJ picked up steam in 2012, which marked the sixtieth anniversary of the San Francisco Peace Treaty and the return of sovereignty to Japan after the Allied Occupation. A variety of conservative parties, including the LDP, published comprehensive revision drafts that year. When the LDP-Komeito coalition returned to power in December 2012 after a three-year break, Prime Minister Abe declared constitutional amendment to be one of his top priorities. After parties favoring constitutional revision—the LDP and Komeito, along with Nippon Ishin no Kai (Japan Innovation Party) and Party for Japanese Kokoro—combined to win the requisite two-thirds in the Lower House (2014) and Upper House (2016), the political timing finally seemed ripe.

However, one central obstacle is the remarkable lack of agreement on *how* to amend the constitution. The LDP has long prioritized Article 9 revision, but its coalition partner Komeito has expressed greater enthusiasm for adding new environmental rights. Japan Innovation Party, an urban party, has pushed for greater decentralization to lessen the fiscal redistribution from metropolitan to rural areas. The newly formed Constitutional Democratic Party (CDP) is firmly against Article 9 revision, but it is open to constraining the parliamentary dissolution powers of the cabinet and mandating government transparency, both of which it believes the Abe administration has transgressed. Two progressive parties, the Social Democrats and the Communists, vehemently oppose any changes to the COJ at all.

Constitutional disagreements exist also within the LDP itself. The LDP had published an earlier constitutional revision proposal in 2005, the fiftieth anniversary of the party's founding and the sixtieth anniversary of the end of World War II, but its contents differ in illuminating ways from the more recent 2012 version. The 2005 draft, written when the LDP was in government, focused more on rationalizing the political process, such as by allowing for greater fiscal decentralization. In contrast, the 2012 draft, crafted by the LDP when it was out of power, was designed to spotlight how its ideological vision of Japan's future differed from that of the then-governing Democratic Party of Japan. It barely mentioned the institutional reforms of the 2005 draft and instead focused on conservative red-meat issues, such as establishing a *Kokubōgun* (National Defense Army) in Article 9, formally granting the emperor the title of "head of state," and mandating that the exercise of individual rights be balanced against collective public welfare.[15]

Intra-LDP disputes extend into the preferred political tactics for constitutional revision. Hajime Funada, an LDP Diet member and former head of and current adviser to the party's Constitutional Reform Promotion Headquarters, stated that many pro-revision voices in the party prefer the *first* amendment to be on a relatively uncontroversial topic, such as environmental rights or a government commitment to fiscal discipline, rather than a contentious issue like Article 9.[16] However, this approach was upended by Prime Minister Abe's statement on May 3, 2017, that his priority was to formally enshrine the Self-Defense Forces, add the right to free tertiary education, and establish procedures for national emergencies.[17]

Intra- and inter-party differences can be measured using the UTokyo-Asahi Survey, conducted jointly by Masaki Taniguchi of the University of Tokyo and the *Asahi Shimbun*, which polls all election candidates on their positions on a variety of policies, ideologies, and constitutional matters.[18] In the 2017 House of Representatives (Lower House) election, each political party took clear stances on constitutional revision in its manifesto and campaign speeches. Figure 9-1 tabulates the proportion of election *winners* who supported COJ revisions to Article 9, state of emergency procedures, political decentralization, the addition of environmental rights, limits on the prime minister's parliamentary dissolution powers, and government transparency.

Of all winners, 82 percent expressed support for amendment generally, including 97 percent of those from the LDP and 85 percent from Komeito. However, backing for any specific revision fails to win a majority, much less the requisite two-thirds. For example, only 42 percent supported changes to Article 9: while 62 percent of LDP winners saw it as a priority, only 10 percent of the Komeito winners felt the same. The most popular topic is to establish state of emergency provisions (47 percent of total) in the constitution, but it is not considered a priority by Japan Innovation Party (0 percent), which strongly prefers greater fiscal decentralization (21 percent of total). The addition of environmental rights, government trans-

FIGURE 9-1. Support for Constitutional Revision among Election Winners

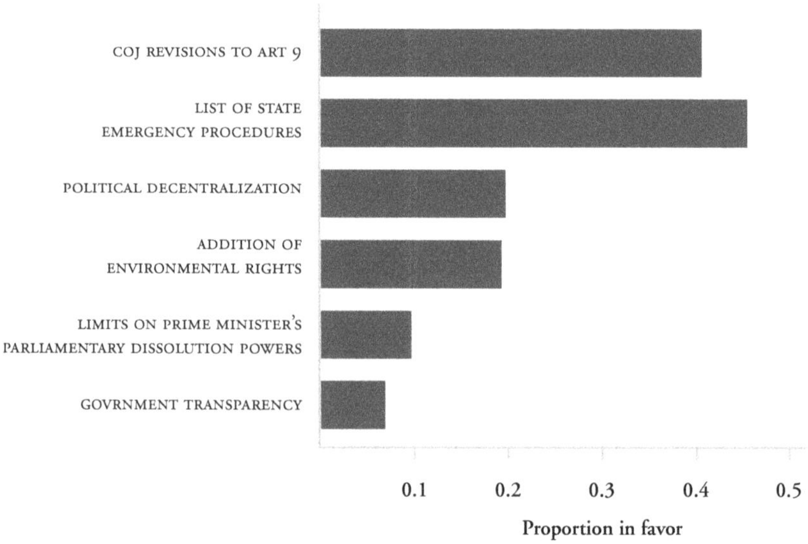

Source: Data on candidate positions from UTAS2017.

parency, or restrictions on snap elections, backed by opposition parties, all poll below 20 percent.

COJ Amendment: The Public

While political elites may have their own private preferences, their discourse is inevitably shaped by public opinion. Since any amendment requires popular assent in a national referendum, its contents must be crafted delicately to ensure majority support among voters. However, public sentiment over constitutional amendment is fairly volatile, shaped by debates over the merits and faults of the constitution that date back to its ratification.

There are few reliable opinion polls from the immediate postwar period, but Shiro Sakaiya finds that much of the public favored the new COJ because it would preserve the imperial system, not because of the merits of Article 9.[19] While some conservatives viewed the shift from a sovereign emperor to a symbolic one as an assault on the Japanese polity, Article 1 was broadly seen as an acceptable compromise by the public, especially given the reality of wartime defeat.

Few surveys on the constitution were conducted in the 1960s and 1970s, as Japan enjoyed the fruits of the "economic miracle" and the security of the American nuclear umbrella. The end of the Cold War and Japan's hesitance toward sending the SDF overseas during the Gulf War galvanized concerns, particularly among elites, that Japan needed to rethink its place in the world. Constitutional amendment became one facet of this debate, with Article 9 firmly in the crosshairs. That said, the public has remained divided over amending the COJ. Figure 9-2 shows the net support rate (support minus opposition) for constitutional revision, taken from the *Yomiuri Shimbun*'s annual surveys since 1991.[20] Net support rose steadily through the 1990s and 2000s, hitting a peak of +42 percent in 2004, but it has declined quite dramatically since then. The two dashed vertical lines in 2005 and 2012 correspond to years that the LDP published comprehensive constitutional revision drafts. It appears that even when the public seems amenable to amendment in the abstract, they balk when confronted with concrete LDP, conservative proposals.

Public apprehension about the conservative turn of the LDP's 2012

FIGURE 9-2. Public Support for Constitutional Revision

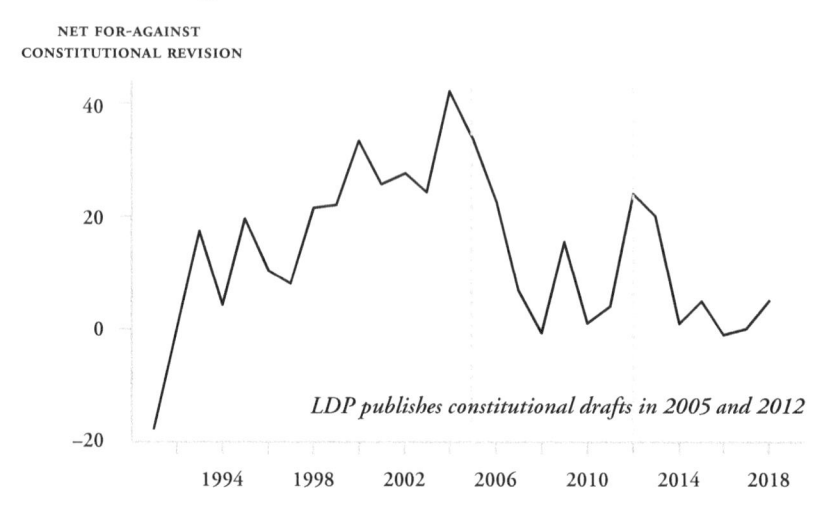

NET FOR-AGAINST
CONSTITUTIONAL REVISION

LDP publishes constitutional drafts in 2005 and 2012

Source: Annual *Yomiuri* Surveys on Constitutional Revision.

draft can be seen in the *Yomiuri* surveys' questions on *why* people are in favor of or against amendment. The proportion that are for amendment because of the illegitimacy of the COJ's occupation-era origins has fallen since the mid-2000s, from a peak of 21 percent in 2004 to 11 percent in 2018. Instead, double the number focus on the fruits of the COJ than its provenance. In 2018, 25 percent were against amendment because they were proud of the "peace constitution," compared to 12 percent in 2004.[21] Similarly, those who see amendment as a necessary means of enhancing national defense poll at about 22 percent, compared to 25 percent who are more worried about creeping militarism. It is important to note that "oppose" sentiments have risen during the Abe administration, suggesting that many voters mistrust the current government's intentions in pursuing constitutional amendment.

How Threats to the Liberal International Order Shape Public Opinion

While these surveys provide valuable insight into shifting trends in public opinion, they are less useful in understanding *why* the public holds those views. What types of people favor different amendment topics, and how might their views be swayed by changes in Japan's domestic or international environment? These are crucial dimensions for understanding how threats to the liberal international order or America's commitment to the Asia-Pacific region may transform public opinion in the future.

The survey experiment commissioned for this project provides a useful solution to these challenges. As discussed in chapter 11 to this volume, the survey is divided into two parts, separated by an "information treatment" that exposes the Japanese respondents to different information about the liberal international order. The first half, or the pretreatment component, asks for respondents' baseline views about foreign nations, government performance, and the importance of the liberal international order. They are then randomly assigned to one of four treatment groups, each of which includes different statements about new challenges posed by weakening U.S. commitment to the region and by the rise of China. In the second, posttreatment half, respondents answer future-oriented questions about preferred policy responses to the changing international environment. Questions about constitutional revision are embedded in both sections of the survey. In the first half, respondents are asked about the necessity of amending the constitution on six discrete topics, corresponding to priorities raised by government and opposition parties in the 2017 House of Representatives election. In the posttreatment section, respondents are asked about their reasons for or against amending Article 9.

The discussion that follows is based on a statistical analysis of these survey responses. First, given that constitutional scholars—who generally oppose amendments to Article 9—are often relied upon by the government and media to provide legal commentary, we test whether respondents who trust "specialists and academics," as opposed to politicians, are more likely to oppose amendments. Second, we examine whether views on the importance of U.S. leadership and/or the liberal international order to peace in the Asia-Pacific region make people more supportive of amendments to Article 9. Finally, we test whether concerns about the long-term viability of the liberal order, induced through the information treatment, change people's views about constitutional revision.

According to our survey, the only amendment topics that received majority support were the addition of new rights to "enjoy a clean environment" (56 percent support) and to "privacy" (55 percent).[22] This was followed by the addition of "state of emergency" provisions (47 percent) and amending Article 9 to formally recognize the SDF (42 percent). Guaranteeing free higher education (37 percent) and outlining the conditions for dissolving the House of Representatives (37 percent) came in last. While this suggests substantial disagreement on amendment priorities, it should be noted that 70 percent of respondents listed at least one topic on which they favored constitutional change.

Table 9-2 summarizes the statistical results for the six amendment topics in the pretreatment section.[23] The numbers given show the change in probability of supporting that amendment (of answering 4 or 5 on a five-point scale) based on that respondent's background characteristics and views on related topics, known as marginal effects.[24] Our first finding is that greater trust in specialists and academic experts reduces support for amending Article 9 by 8.5 percentage points, while increasing support for all other amendment topics. By contrast, trust in politicians increases support for Article 9 (+26.7 points) and state of emergency provisions (+53.6), which are favored by the LDP, but reduces support for adding environmental or privacy rights, which are advocated by opposition parties. To some extent, respondents' answers capture partisanship: supporters of the government are more likely to trust politicians, while opponents prefer experts. However, the estimated effects are independent of partisanship per se. For example, LDP supporters are more likely to support most amendment topics, regardless of their views of experts or politicians, while those of the Constitutional Democratic Party are generally opposed.

Our second finding is that beliefs about the underpinnings of post–Cold War peace in the Asia-Pacific region affect amendment attitudes. Those who believe that U.S. leadership was crucial are more likely to support Article 9 amendment (+31.2 percentage points). Positive sentiments extend to enumerating provisions for a state of emergency and conditions for the dissolution of the Lower House. Beliefs about the importance of the liberal international order for peace in the Asia-Pacific did not influence LDP-backed amendments, but they improve support for expanding environmental rights and privacy rights, suggesting there is a broader progressive ideology associated with these factors.

The pretreatment questions discussed above should be considered baseline attitudes of the Japanese public, or how respondents think about the constitution today. The experimental treatment, described more fully in chapter 11, is designed to test how responses change when people are prompted to worry about the United States's commitment to the liberal international order. Respondents were randomly assigned to four groups. The "control" group only read a brief statement describing the current status of Japan's reliance on the liberal international order. "Treatment 1" includes additional descriptions of the U.S. weakening *military* commitment to the liberal international order, while "treatment 2" adds text about America's declining commitment in the *economic* sphere. "Treatment 3" includes both the *military* and *economic* texts. They are then asked a battery

TABLE 9-2. Japanese public opinion on constitutional amendments

Q: Do you think it is necessary to amend the constitution to add or change the following provisions?

Marginal Effects[a]	Article 9 (recognize SDF)	State of emergency	HoR dissolution	Free higher education	Guarantee environment	Guarantee privacy
Trust politicians[b]	+26.7%	+53.6%	–	–	–18.0%	–22.6%
Trust experts[b]	–8.5%	+12.2%	+17.0%	+24.4%	+31.1%	+28.5%
LIO = peace[b]	–	–	–	–	+18.6%	+17.1%
U.S. leadership = peace[b]	+31.2%	+28.6%	+18.5%	–	–	+10.5%
LDP[c]	+27.3%	+24.5%	+4.6%	–	+7.3%	+7.8%
CDP[c]	–13.0%	–14.5%	–10.5%	–	–	–

a. Marginal effects are the change in probability of answering either 4 or 5 on amendment necessity. Variables that are not statistically significant are not listed in the table.
b. Marginal difference between answering 5 (strongly agree) and 1 (strongly disagree)
c. Marginal difference between supporting that party and being an independent

of questions about what they believe Japan's future policy trajectory should be, including one question about Article 9 specifically:

> Article 9 of the current constitution mandates the renunciations of war (Article 9.1) and the possession of war potential (Article 9.2). The interpretation of Article 9 has changed a number of times. Do you think it is better to amend Article 9 or to not amend Article 9?

Overall, 35 percent of respondents favor amending Article 9, while 36 percent are opposed. However, this needs to be interpreted with care, since the answers are colored by the type of information treatment they received in the experimental portion. Table 9-3 shows the results from the statistical analysis of Article 9 amendment preferences. The model is identical to that in the preceding analysis, with one notable difference: we estimate the causal effect of being assigned to each treatment group.

The main result confirms our intuition: when respondents are worried about the future of the liberal international order, their support for amending Article 9 increases while their opposition decreases. Concerns about the U.S. military commitment to the Asia-Pacific (treatment 1) raises support for amending by 6.4 percentage points (and reduces opposition by 6.4 points), while that for economic commitments increases support by 4.4 points (reduces opposition by 4.4 points). Put differently, the *net* swing from the treatments are 12.8 points and 8.8 points respectively, a sizable change in public opinion that would likely be enough to change the result of a national referendum.

It is worthwhile to explore *why* people support or oppose changes to Article 9. The experimental treatment does not have a strong effect on the reasons given for amendment, but we find interesting patterns nonetheless.[25] For example, the most common answer given for supporting Article 9 is "to officially recognize the Self-Defense Forces" (64 percent), but that answer falls by 15 points for those who trust "experts." By contrast, those who believe the liberal international order was instrumental for peace in the Asia-Pacific region are 26 points more likely to say that Article 9 should be changed, so that Japan can "better contribute to international peace." On the flip side, opponents of amendment who also believe in the importance of the liberal international order are more likely to say that chang-

TABLE 9-3. Reasons given by the public for supporting or opposing Article 9 revision

Q: Article 9 of the current constitution mandates the renunciations of war (Article 9.1) and the possession of war potential (Article 9.2). The interpretation of Article 9 has changed a number of times. Do you think it is better to amend Article 9 or to not amend Article 9?

	Support	Oppose
Marginal Effects[a]		
Treat 1 (military)	6.4%	−6.4%
Treat 2 (economy)	4.4%	−4.4%
Treat 3 (military + economy)	–	–

Overall Averages

Reasons for support [35% favored]		*Reasons for opposition [36% opposed]*	
Officially recognize SDF	64%	Proud of peace constitution	66%
Stabilize Asia-Pacific	39%	Contributes to peace and stability	44%
Contribute to international peace	35%	Prevents militarism	39%
Make U.S.-JPN Alliance equal	34%	Will destabilize Asia-Pacific	24%
To possess military potential	32%	Adjust through reinterpretation	20%

a. Marginal effects are the change in probability of answering 4 or 5, that is, to support amendment. Variables that are not statistically significant are not listed in the table. The analysis is conducted using a censored sample of respondents who spent at least 450 seconds (7.5 minutes) in answering the survey, to ensure that they gave sufficient attention to the treatment statements.

ing Article 9 will destabilize the region (+23 percentage points) and that amendment is unnecessary because the constitution already contributes to peace and stability (+37 points).

Overall, we observe important differences in the relationship between attitudes toward the liberal international order and constitutional revision. Those who believe in the importance of the liberal international order to peace and security in the Asia-Pacific are not necessarily committed to changing Article 9, as many also worry about the possibility of disrupting the status quo. By contrast, those who believe strongly in the importance of U.S. leadership in the region are more willing to back constitutional amendment. My interpretation is that this reflects an awareness—and, frankly, the reality—that the U.S. security umbrella is crucial to regional peace, at least in the short run. However, there is no agreement about whether this is better long-term, as evinced by some doubts about the disruptive effect of changing Article 9, as well as the weight placed by many respondents on the dissenting opinion of constitutional scholars.

Constitutional Politics and Japan's Role in the Liberal International Order

One of the core principles of constitutions—and of statutes generally—is to "do no harm." Writing rights or rules into the constitution hamstrings the policy flexibility of the executive and legislative branches, while giving greater interpretative discretion to the judiciary. It also risks "locking in" policy priorities or proscriptions, since amending the constitution requires more onerous steps than passing a new law. The key question regarding the COJ and the liberal international order, then, is whether the constitution's structure hinders the government's ability to respond to disruptions in the liberal international order. The answer, it seems, is no.

First, the COJ's vagueness on political institutions and international commitments allows the government to adjust public policy priorities by statute or regulation. During the 1990s, the electoral system was fundamentally changed and various decentralization initiatives were undertaken, all by simple majorities in the Diet. In many countries, some, if not all, such revisions would require a constitutional amendment. The same "looseness" applies to Article 9. While the Peace Clause has historically been interpreted—albeit contentiously—to only permit "defensive defense," the term's exact meaning has evolved over time (see chapter 1 by Adam Liff). Special legislation sanctioned the SDF's deployment on overseas peacekeeping (noncombat) missions in the 1990s. The cabinet reinterpreted Article 9 to permit collective self-defense in July 2014, and the ratification of two new laws, together called *Heiwa Anzen Hōsei* (Legislation for Peace and Security), formalized this interpretation. At the same time, the supreme court's deference to the elected branches has meant that the courts have not inhibited Japan's role in the liberal international order in any meaningful, constitutional way.

That said, the fact that the COJ is not a hindrance does not mean that it cannot be improved upon. Japan *can* expand its commitment to the liberal international order, should its citizens—through their elected representatives—desire it. As discussed above, a supermajority of elites seems to support constitutional amendment, but not in a way that fundamentally changes Japan's relationship with the world. While a concrete amendment proposal has yet to be issued, the LDP's plans for Article 9 revision seem aimed at locking in the status quo rather than changing the nature of the SDF. This reflects the political reality that the LDP needs to get the more pacifist Komeito on board, even as voters seem more interested in competing priorities, such as the expansion of environmental and privacy rights.

The survey experiment suggests further that popular sentiment itself adapts to changing geopolitical conditions. The Trump administration's rhetoric and actions clearly cast doubt on America's long-term commitment to the liberal international order. When our Japanese survey respondents think that American commitment to the Asia-Pacific is imperiled, they are more likely to back changes to Article 9 in order to keep their primary ally happy.

Adapting constitutional content to changing geopolitical needs is not a bad thing, since the ability of citizens to enjoy their rights is contingent on the very existence of the polity. In fact, amendments can be crucial to preserving constitutional legitimacy. However, if Article 9 can be interpreted so broadly as to allow for collective as well as individual self-defense, as is the status quo in Japan today, then it can breed public cynicism that the COJ is endlessly elastic. If the constitution is not seen as fulfilling its function in constraining the government, then its utility as the supreme law of the nation is diminished, independent of the policy merits of expanding the SDF's missions or improving relations with the United States. Put simply, it may, in fact, be better to amend Article 9 so that the constitution and reality are better aligned, or at least put it to a national referendum so that voters can settle the issue directly, rather than continue the current state of confusion and acrimony over its exact bounds.

NOTES

1. Kenneth Mori McElwain and Christian G. Winkler, "What's Unique about Japan's Constitution? A Comparative and Historical Analysis," *Journal of Japanese Studies*, vol. 41, no. 2 (2015), 249–380.

2. *The Politics of Constitutional Change in Industrial Nations: Redesigning the State*, edited by Keith G. Banting and Richard Simeon (London: The MacMillan Press Ltd., 1985), 8.

3. McElwain and Winkler, "What's Unique about Japan's Constitution?" 260.

4. These principles drew on two sources: the Potsdam Declaration, which defined the terms of Japan's surrender in World War II, and the "MacArthur Notes," which listed General Douglas MacArthur's priorities for constitutional revision. A more detailed discussion of the historical background of constitutional adoption, as well as the text of these two sources, can be found on the National Diet Library's website, http://www.ndl.go.jp/constitution/e/outline/00outline.html.

5. Dale M. Hellegers, *We the People: World War II and the Origins of the Japanese Constitution, vol. 2* (Stanford University Press, 2001), 616.

6. The preceding Constitution of the Empire Japan, known more commonly as the Meiji Constitution, was also quite short at 3,381 words. As the Meiji government was originally designed as a monarchic oligopoly, it enumerated few details about political institutions and substantially less about fundamental human rights.

7. Zachary Elkins, Tom Ginsburg, and James Melton, *The Endurance of National Constitutions* (Cambridge University Press, 2009). Comparative Constitutions Project data can be downloaded from http://comparativeconstitutionsproject.org/.

8. Other constitutions that do not mention military matters are those of Monaco, Liechtenstein, Andorra, Iceland, Samoa, Nauru, Tuvalu, St. Kitts and Nevis, and Barbados. The average population of these countries is less than 120,000.

9. In 1954, Shuzo Hayashi, then the head of the Cabinet Legislation Bureau, explained that Article 9 does not proscribe the possession of limited self-defense powers for defending Japanese territory from foreign infringement. Kunio Yamada, "Jieiken no Ronten" [Issues on the Right of Self-Defense], National Diet Library Series *Kenpō no Ronten 12* (2006), 13.

10. "Shudanteki Jieiken Kosi, Zensankonin ga 'Iken,' Shuin Kenposhin" [All Expert Witnesses Assessed the Exercise of the Right to Collective Self-Defense as "Unconstitutional" at the Commission on the Constitution of the House of Representatives], *Nihon Keizai Shimbun*, June 4, 2015.

11. "Anpo Hoan, Gakusya Anketo" [Questionnaire on Japan's Legislation for Peace and Security to Scholars of Constitutional Law], *Asahi Shimbun*, July 11, 2015.

12. "[Jimintō Taikai] Abe Shinzō Shushō, Kenpō Kyujō heno Jietai Meiki wo Uttae; Jimintō Taikai de 'Iken-ronsō ni Shūshifu wo Utsu'" [LDP Conference: Prime Minister Abe Shinzō Calls for the Enumeration of the Self-Defense Forces in Article 9; "putting an end to debates about unconstitutionality"], *Sankei Shimbun*, March 25, 2018.

13. Christian G. Winkler, *The Quest for Japan's New Constitution: An Analysis of Visions and Constitutional Reform Proposals (1980–2009)* (New York: Routledge, 2010), 23.

14. Based on the author's analysis of data from the Comparative Constitutions Project in Elkins and others, *The Endurance of National Constitutions*.

15. An English summary of the proposed amendments in the 2012 draft can be found on Liberal Democratic Party of Japan, "LDP Announces a New Draft Constitution for Japan," https://www.jimin.jp/english/news/117099.html.

16. Author's interview with Hajime Funada, July 31, 2018.

17. Tomohiro Osaki and Daisuke Kikuchi, "Abe Declares 2020 as Goal for New Constitution," *The Japan Times*, May 3, 2017.

18. The full UTAS data, which received responses from 97 percent of all candidates (1,142 out of 1,180), can be found online at the *Asahi Shimbun* (only in Japanese), http://www.asahi.com/senkyo/asahitodai/. The survey is conducted before Election Day, and the results are made public.

19. Shiro Sakaiya, *Kenpō to Yoron: Sengo Nihonjin wa Kenpō to Dō Mukiatte Kitanoka* [The Constitution and Public Opinion: How the Japanese Have Come to Face Up to Its Constitution in the Postwar Period] (Tokyo: Chikuma Shobou, 2017), 68.

20. The *Yomiuri Shimbun* is a center-right daily newspaper with the largest circulation in Japan. It has run the longest time-series survey on the constitution, which makes it a valuable source of public opinion. However, its estimates of support for amendment tends to be higher than that of the center-left *Asahi Shimbun*, largely due to differences in the phrasing of questions. While we should take the point estimates for support or opposition with a grain of salt, the trends over time likely reflect actual fluctuations in public sentiment.

21. "Kenpō Yoron Chōsa: Omona Shitsumon to Kaitō" [Constitution Public Survey: Main Questions and Answers], *Yomiuri Shimbun*, April 30, 2018, Tokyo morning edition, 13.

22. In both the pre- and posttreatment sections, respondents were asked to rate their support for constitutional amendment on a five-point scale, where 1 = strong opposition, 2 = weak opposition, 3 = neutrality, 4 = weak support, and 5 = strong support. For ease of interpretation, I discuss them here as the percentage of respondents who say they are in favor of amendment, that is, gave scores of 4 or 5.

23. The analysis is based on a logistic regression model. In addition to the independent variables identified in the table, the model also controls for gender, age deciles, occupation, region of residence, income, and education attainment (greater than high school or not).

24. Variables that are not statistically significant are not listed in the table.

25. Marginal effects for each covariate, including those not listed in table 9-3, are available from the author upon request.

10

The Silent Public in a Liberal State

CHALLENGES FOR JAPAN'S JOURNALISM IN THE AGE OF THE INTERNET

KAORI HAYASHI

Public-Politics-Media Triads

Open social communication and adequately informed citizenry are the lifeblood of liberal democracy. However, in advanced Western democracies, these two premises are in crisis. Political polarization, populism, and the distrust in media are said to be growing hand in hand. The 2017 Reuters Digital News Report, for example, concluded that distrust in media is driven not so much by fake news spread by internet users as by "deep-rooted political polarization and perceived mainstream media bias."[1]

In 2016, the degree and extent of polarization became particularly conspicuous in two of the world's most advanced liberal democracies, the United Kingdom and the United States, through the Brexit decision in a referendum on whether to leave the EU and the victory of Donald J. Trump in the presidential election of the United States. These events had a profound impact on the Japanese people, who, for more than a century, have looked up to the United States and the United Kingdom for achievements in and attainment of liberalism and democracy. These two nations had introduced many Japanese to new science and industry as well as social and political institutions, including media and journalism, and inspired them to become part of the West and build a nation that would be regarded as equally civilized and enlightened. But now it seems the model that Japan has followed is in trouble. Through the political choices of their voters, it looks as if they are discarding many of their ideals and rejecting the modern achievements they used to take pride in, such as free trade and freedom of speech.

In light of this background, this chapter investigates whether or not, or to what extent, the triad of polarization, populism, and media applies to contemporary Japanese society, the oldest and one of the most well-established liberal democracies in Asia, and what can be expected of Japan in this present situation. Is the triad of populism, media distrust, and divisive society a universal phenomenon common to all liberal democracies, or is it culturally conditioned? Can there be another President Trump condemning a liberal equivalent of CNN in Japan? Will Japan follow a similar path to become a polarized, divisive society, like other advanced industrial nations in the world?

So far, it seems that the American version of polarization is a result of contentious identity politics. Hahn and others contend that current polarization in the United States does not only mean party-based division over policies and political views. Rather, it can be better understood as "affective polarization" that permeates not only people's judgments about political parties but also personal beliefs and views that affect interpersonal relationships.[2] Such spillover effects of partisan identity is believed to be a byproduct of secularized and globalized modernity, which acts "to fill the void left when their other attachments wither away—religious, ethnic, communal, and familial."[3]

Because polarization has more to do with affection and emotion, it can easily turn into populistic discourse and movements, often fanned by media's sound-bite clichés and fake news that appeal to people's hearts. This digression from factual reporting by the media, in turn, becomes the reason to distrust it. So this turns into a vicious cycle, which can be seen in many Western countries. Polarization, populism, and media distrust are a triadic phenomenon understood as "a byproduct of the liberal world order's success" and a result of "a liberal democratic malaise"[4] (This will be referred to as "the Western triad" in this essay, although it is not meant to imply that this phenomenon applies uniformly across all Western nations.)

How does Japan fare? Simply put, Japan in its current state does not exhibit a similar level in the polarization of political opinions, contrasting starkly to the growing populistic protests or high level of distrust in the media seen in other nations. Media distrust seems to be not as strong as in other parts of the world. Malicious attempts to circulate "fake news" via social media to manipulate voters either for fun or political ambition are also rarities when compared with other advanced industrial nations. Rather, the Japanese variation of the triad can be summarized as political disinterest, public apathy (silence), and indifference to the media. My argument is that this is a circumstance every bit as alarming as the triad found in major Western nations, since it can deprive Japanese society of the cohesion and civic power necessary to run a democratic nation. More important, what we see in common in both the Western and Japanese triads is that it is deeply rooted in the nation's history, political culture, and contemporary social climate, and therefore it is hard to separate the three interrelated ties.

To investigate the situation in Japan, I first see to what extent the present Japanese public is alienated from politics. Second, I point out some of the structural and organizational characteristics of the Japanese media, which, in my opinion, have at least partly caused the public to become disengaged from journalism and politics. Finally, I analyze the significance of the impact of the internet. In Japan, like elsewhere, more and more people are turning their back on conventional media and are getting accustomed to using the internet and social media for their news gathering and communication activities. I discuss whether these new media outlets, which promote more horizontal and interactive communication, have the potential to change Japan's political culture that is traditionally based on more authoritative and vertical social relationships.

FIGURE 10-1. West and Japan: Political challenges in the twenty-first century

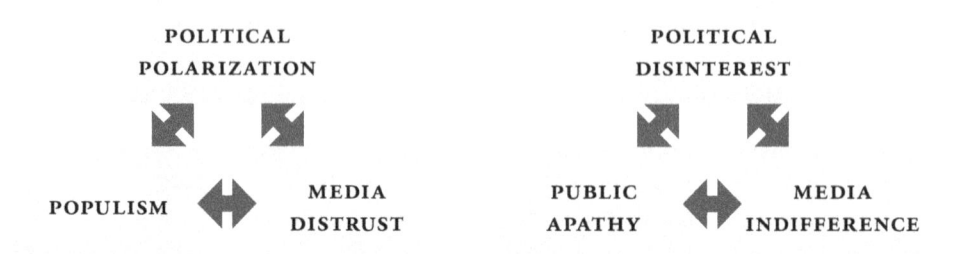

POLITICAL POLARIZATION

POPULISM ⟷ MEDIA DISTRUST

United states and other western societies

POLITICAL DISINTEREST

PUBLIC APATHY ⟷ MEDIA INDIFFERENCE

Japanese society

Public-Politics

To investigate the relationship between the public and politics, the first question is whether present Japanese politics is suffering from a "liberal malaise" as with other Western societies. Have the Japanese also gone too far in carrying out the project of liberalism and modernization in their society?

A SILENT PUBLIC

Japan takes pride in being the first adopter of Western liberal democracy among Asian countries,[5] embracing basic human rights and democratic governance. Among the most important basic rights in Japan, freedom of speech is critical. This is particularly so since the nation experienced a totalitarian regime that manipulated the media and silenced the public during the Pacific War. The English translation of Article 21 of the present Constitution of Japan, promulgated after the war, reads as follows:

> Article 21. Freedom of assembly and association as well as speech, press, and all other forms of expression are guaranteed.
>
> No censorship shall be maintained, nor shall the secrecy of any means of communication be violated.[6]

Constitutional scholars in postwar Japan have generally held the view that this right takes precedence over all other basic rights guaranteed in the constitution (such as the right to choose one's occupation and the right to engage freely in economic activities). Masami Itō, one of the most renowned liberal scholars in Japanese constitutional law, as well as a former Supreme Court judge, has stated:

> The principle of democracy is that the government should be led by the majority opinion, which is formed by citizens who freely choose their opinion from a range of ideas. For that, every conceivable political discourse should be presented to the citizens with no restrictions, including those that may only be supported by few or even abhorred by many. . . . Freedom of speech, accordingly, is directly connected with the essence of democracy and can be judged to have a value that deserves greater constitutional protection than economic rights, which are not directly related to the basic principle of governance.[7]

As seen in this statement, it has been understood, at least in legal and political academic circles, that the right to free speech is eminently fundamental to the proper functioning of democratic polity in Japanese society. Legal scholars and lawyers have concerned themselves with what exceptional circumstances, if any, could possibly justify putting restrictions on free speech and expression. So, from the viewpoint of Japan's formal system, society incorporates the basic constitutional framework that facilitates free speech and the free press.

However, how truly democratic a society is cannot be measured only by the legal structure and interpretations of legal precedents. Here we should turn to the words of John Dewey, the great American scholar of democracy in the twentieth century. In his *The Public and Its Problems*, published in 1927, he argued that democracy is more than just an attribute of a political system or institution. He argued that democracy should not remain as a technical term for politicians and experts. Instead, democracy requires an active public willing to communicate with each other and participate in communal governance. Democracy is, according to Dewey, "a way of life."[8]

Dewey's radical understanding of democracy inspired many of his contemporaries in the United States and the world. Japan was no exception. After the Constitution of Japan was drafted and implemented by the progressive U.S. New Deal Democrats (see chapter 9 by Kenneth Mori McElwain), who were Dewey's contemporaries, the notion of democracy was promoted by a number of philosophers and activists in Japan, such as Shunsuke Tsurumi, a Harvard graduate who introduced Dewey's pragmatism to Japan, and Masao Maruyama, a University of Tokyo professor and political scientist, among others. In Japan, the kind of democracy built upon this new postwar constitution was named *sengo minshushugi* (postwar democracy).

Nowadays, however, this phrase, "postwar democracy," once a symbol of peace and freedom, is increasingly used with derogatory and cynical nuance by conservatives. It has even become the target of attack by many on the Right, who argue that the constitution was imposed by the United States in the first place.[9] In this context of revisionist movements, the ruling Liberal Democratic Party, which has drafted a revision of the constitution in 2012, wishes to add a clause to the present Article 21. The revised version says: "Notwithstanding the provisions of the preceding paragraph, engaging in activities with the purpose of harming the public interest and public order and forming associations to attain such objectives shall not be approved."[10]

It suffices to note that, despite efforts of many postwar liberal legal scholars and experts, the right to free speech and expression, originally understood as the fundamental element of Japan's postwar democracy, has not been sufficiently appreciated as a core norm of the nation among its citizens, or even among politicians. This is exemplified in social practice of people's routine in Japan. In everyday lives, people are repeatedly reminded of the need to "read the atmosphere" (or, more literally, "air"), which essentially means they should adjust their thoughts to what others might be thinking and feeling, so as to avoid rocking the boat. Stating the truth is often regarded as "going too far" and "crossing the line."[11] Among ordinary citizens, "good" and "mature" members of society are those who can control what they really want to say, especially in public, in order to conform to social expectations. A handful of courageous people who are willing to raise their voice end up being ostracized from their communities. For example, Toshiro Semba, a former police officer, recalled how he was banished from his workplace when he blew a whistle on a slush fund amassing inside the police department. His everyday life was literally shattered after he held a press conference. In another case, mothers in Fukushima, who publicly criticized the Tokyo Electric Power Company for the radiation leakage caused by the Great East Japan Earthquake in March 2011, were harshly censured for their "egoistic behavior" because they prioritized their individual interests over communal consensus.[12] The notion of "liberal order" arrived in Japan after the war, but its most important element was appreciated and enjoyed only by liberal scholars, politicians, and journalists, namely the elite tier of the society.

JAPAN'S "WORD OF THE YEAR"

At the end of 2016, we learned that Oxford Dictionary chose "post-truth" as its Word of the Year. It is an adjective defined as "relating to or denoting circumstances in which objective facts are less influential in shaping public opinion than appeals to emotion and personal belief."[13] The word was chosen as the public opinion was led by media's populistic discourse and politicians' capricious and demagogic speeches in two of the world's most significant political events of the year: the referendum on whether the United Kingdom should stay in the EU and the U.S. presidential election. The choice of the word symbolized the critical state of the Western world, in which politics became increasingly irrelevant to facts and the reality. The choice implied a critique of those populistic politicians who would use irresponsible, anything-goes rhetoric in order to gain votes.

In 2017, the Japanese version of the Word of the Year was the word *sontaku* (to surmise the group sentiment to avoid conflicts and complications).[14] This word gained wide circulation after it was used by Yasunori Kagoike, who allegedly scored a notoriously cheap deal (90 percent discount) for acquiring public land because of his close ties with Prime Minister Shinzo Abe and his wife. Kagoike said in a press conference that the deal was made possible only because of *sontaku*—that is, the government officials claimed to have surmised the prime minister's implicit wish to do a favor for his friend.[15] Since then, this somewhat bookish word began to be heard in everyday conversations because it aptly describes and symbolizes the Japanese mind-set. The word connotes cynicism toward those who think only about the needs of their inner circle and lose sight of what should actually be considered as just and appropriate.

The words *sontaku* and "post-truth" both symbolize the present climate of the respective societies. Whereas the "post-truth" mood was born in cultures where politicians and the press have tried to aggressively manipulate voters with explicit language, the *sontaku* mood was born in a world where people would quietly determine in advance what to say and how to act based upon carefully surmising the predominant sentiment and context of their inner circle. A *sontaku* culture is only possible where people's expectations are more or less predictable. In the case of Japan, society is being run primarily by Japanese males.[16]

Critics in the West lament and criticize the abuse of free speech/free press in the post-truth era, whereas experts and scholars in Japan criticize the daunting climate of self-censorship and overdose of deference at the expense of individual freedom and will. In both cases, what is at stake is the premise of modernity that every citizen has the power to think, distinguish what is true from what is false, and determine and act in the best interest of society. A democratic system and governance can only work based upon this premise. To state it in contrasting terms, on the one hand, we have Western culture, which emphasizes individual freedom, and on the other, we have Japanese culture, which emphasizes reserve and consideration. Both are theoretically possible in a liberal democratic society, and seem good if they exercise their values to an appropriate degree, but it seems both are now going too far with their own logics and have lost sight of the original end.

In short, the present Japanese public sphere, theoretically embracing the full-fledged freedom of speech, has been restrained and limited, but not in the classic sense that the government explicitly censors media and people. On the surface, the Japanese public looks free, peaceful, and highly integrated. They are enjoying a wide range of journalistic writings and entertainment. Journalism in Japan has also reported on corruption and government's secrets, pulling down prime ministers and other high-ranked government officials through investigative reporting.[17] Nevertheless, the majority of the people are silent, not because they are forced to be so by a dictator but because they subscribe to their own tacit sense of social consensus. The image of a "good citizen" is somebody who is following and working hard for the nation, and not criticizing or protesting against it. This is opposite of the theory of Western liberalism, which encourages people to think and act independently and, if necessary, argue with those who have different views and opinions in order to change the world.

DISINTEREST AND DISPASSION ABOUT POLITICS

Growing political alienation has become a political issue in many media-saturated liberal democracies. Japan is not an exception, and its declining voting rate is one good indicator for this phenomenon. For example, the voting rate for the Lower House Election in 2017 was as low as 53.7 percent,[18] the second lowest among all elections in the post–World War II period. The highest was 76.99 percent, marked more than half a century ago, in 1958.[19] The rates had hovered around 70 percent until the 1980s, but since then it has been declining. What is most alarming is the low voting rates among the younger generation. Government statistics show that only 33.85 percent of voters in their twenties voted in the abovementioned election in 2017 (figure 10-2). The figure was reported to be the lowest level among OECD nations.[20]

The floundering voting rate is one indicator of people's indifference to current affairs in society. True, it should be noted that countries such as

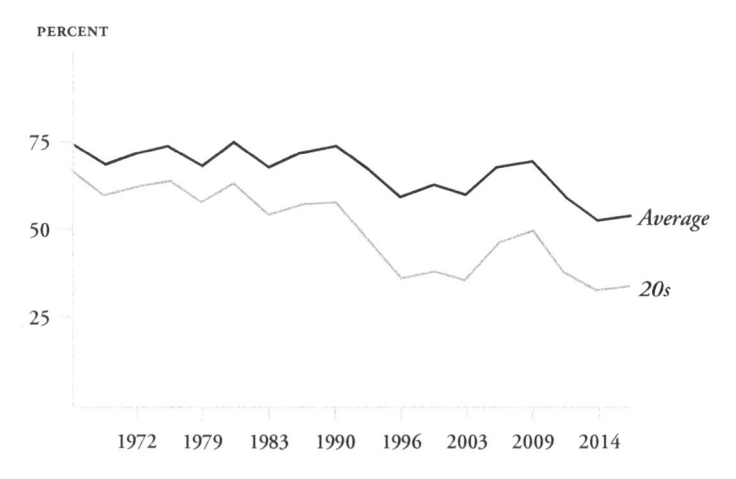

FIGURE 10-2. Voting rates for the Lower House elections

Source: Ministry of Internal Affairs and Communications, "*Kokusei Senkyo no Touhyoritsu no Suii ni tsuite*" (Trends in the Voting Rate in Political Elections), http://www.soumu.go.jp/senkyo/senkyo_s/news/sonota/ritu/.

Luxembourg, Belgium, and Australia enforce compulsory voting, and thus the voter turnouts alone do not necessarily show the true degree of the political interest, but ranking fifth from the bottom among OECD countries makes it quite obvious that the level of political interest in Japan is very low compared to other nations.[21]

The lack of engagement in politics can also be seen from a cross-national comparison of the self-declared degree of interest in international and domestic news. Figure 10-3 shows that the level of political interest in Japan, regardless of whether the news concerns domestic or international matters, is the second lowest after Colombia.

In contrast to the weak interest in political news, Japanese interest in soft news, such as entertainment, celebrity, arts, sports, and lifestyle news, is conspicuously strong relative to other nations. Reuters Institute's 2016 Digital Report shows that 34 percent of the respondents answered they

FIGURE 10-3. Public interest in international and domestic news coverage

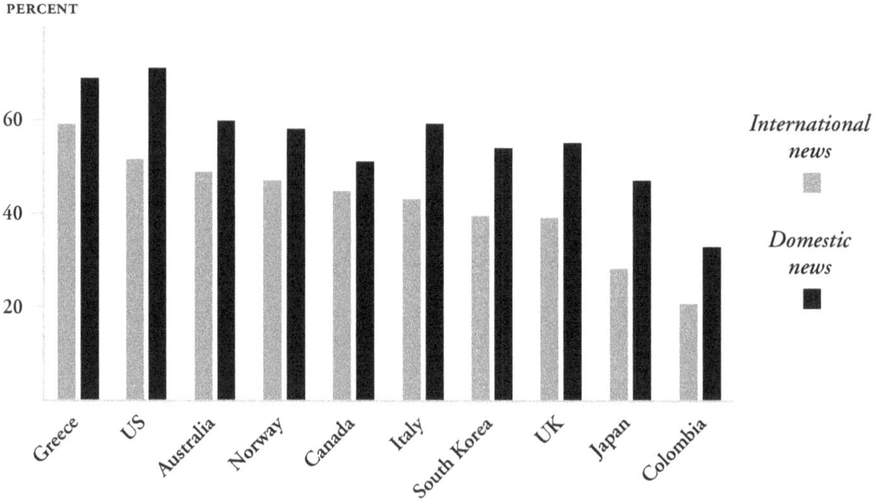

Source: Toril Aalberg and others, "International TV News, Foreign Affairs Interest, and Public Knowledge: A Comparative Study of Foreign News Coverage and Public Opinion in 11 Countries," *Journalism Studies*, vol. 14, no. 3 (2013), 387–406, 13. "Generally speaking, how interested are you in national events and issues?" and "Generally speaking, how interested are you in international events and issues?" The answer categories ranged on a five-point scale where 1 corresponded to "not at all interested" and 5 corresponded to "extremely interested." Respondents who chose 4 and 5 on this scale have been classified as interested in domestic and international news.

are more interested in soft news, the highest among twenty-six countries (figure 10-4).[22] This strong preference for soft news indicates at least two things: first, people in Japan are really not interested in political news; second, and more important, the figures imply that Japanese society at large does not expect its people to be interested in political news because these figures are based on self-declaration and thus likely to show what the respondents think society expects of them rather than what they really think. For a liberal democratic nation, the first issue—that people are not interested in politics—is bad enough. But the second one—that people do not feel they *should* be interested in politics—is actually worse because it potentially undermines the foundation of democracy in the future.

Other evidence shows public's distance and alienation from politics. In 2014, NHK Broadcasting Culture Research Institute surveyed the public's willingness to participate in political activities. According to its data, the majority of citizens are not motivated to take part in political activities such as demonstrations, political gatherings, or writing letters to politicians or editors of media outlets. In 2014, as many as 70 percent of respondents replied that they have never taken part in any such political activities or events, and do not plan to do so in the future, either.[23]

To further investigate this apathetic state of the public, I interviewed Hidehiko Koguchi, who has served as an adviser to the LDP for its elec-

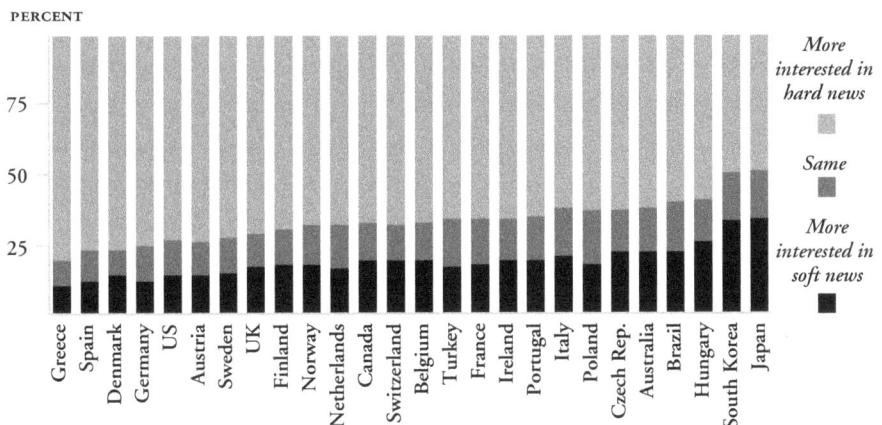

FIGURE 10-4. Proportion of respondents more interested in hard news or more interested in soft news

tion campaigns during the time it was an opposition party between 2009 and 2013 and then brought it to victory in the 2013 Upper House election. Koguchi estimates about 40 to 50 percent of voters in Japan are so-called *mutōhasō* (nonparty affiliates). "Before each election, 10 to 15 percent start to support one of the parties they happen to like at the time because of whatever news items they have just seen on TV," he said. "These people are inconsistent," Koguchi explains, "but they hold the casting vote in Japan." Political scientist Aiji Tanaka also contends that it is these nonparty affiliates that decide the direction of Japanese politics.[24] Tanaka wrote in his 2012 essay that they were educated and not necessarily uninterested in politics, but Koguchi explains that trends are moving in a different direction today. "The poor management and governance of the Democratic Party of Japan government [the ruling party 2010–13] is deeply embedded in people's minds, so the LDP could leverage their failure to get the voters to turn back to support the LDP."[25] But he said it has become very hard nowadays to keep track of what the floating voters want, think, read, and watch. To every politician, reaching the heart of the independents, who account for almost half of the Japanese electorate, is the crucial challenge of any election campaign. "We are now in 2018, in which we have little idea what works best to attract the independents."[26]

As noted, many Japanese people do not vote today. They admit they are not interested in politics and are more interested in soft news. But the above interview shows that if they do vote, a substantial number do so rather whimsically for a party they happen to prefer at the time. The media may play a role in this decision, but it is not possible to know exactly which media was most influential and at what point, particularly in this age of the internet. What seems to be lacking in Japan is a sense of persistence and continuity in politics and commitment of the people, including politicians, to any beliefs or convictions in one way or another along political lines. Between 2000 and 2018, in a country that prides itself on stability and coordination, there have been nine prime ministers—in contrast to four in the United Kingdom and two chancellors in Germany. It is likely that media may be supporting or conditioning the framework of such political culture. Therefore, it is necessary to look at how Japanese media is structured and organized.

Media-Politics

Our next concern is the relationship between media and politics in Japan. Political apathy or disinterest may be ascribed to many social factors, but here I examine how Japanese media reflects this political disaffection and whether it strengthens that kind of social sentiment. After all, critics have argued that populistic media seems to enhance populist politics in most of today's world. It is worth considering whether the same is true of Japan.

CORPORATE MEDIA AS A PUBLIC UTILITY

It is interesting to note: the majority of the Japanese audience do not seek out media that confirm their own ideas and views. This may come from the fact that, as stated in the previous section, people do not have firm political viewpoints and interests. Asked whether they think "I can trust most of the news I consume most of the time," 44 percent of the Japanese responded in the affirmative. This was almost the same number as the 43 percent who said they trusted the news in general.[27] This means that people perceive no difference among coverages of various media institutions. This contrasts with the United States, where there is a wide gap between the trust of the media people consume and that of the media overall. The former stands at 53 percent and the latter at 38 percent.[28]

In Japan, the market for mass nonideological newspapers is highly developed.[29] It has been spearheaded by two giant national dailies—the *Yomiuri Shimbun*, with a daily circulation of 9 million copies, and the *Asahi Shimbun*, with 6 million. The total circulation of the "Big Five" national dailies (*Yomiuri, Asahi, Mainichi, Nikkei*, and *Sankei*) amounts to more than 50 percent of all newspapers sold in Japan.[30]

The best known battle over the market share is between the *Yomiuri* versus the *Asahi*, particularly in the 1960s and 1970s. They fought hard to gain the market share all over Japan.[31] This competition was somewhat reminiscent of Hearst and Pulitzer during the 1920s, but in Japan, it was nationwide and did not really lead to yellow-press sensationalism, or "dumbing down" of the content. Instead, the competition accelerated depoliticization and homogenization of the content. As a result, people began to perceive newspaper subscription as a utility. For example, if one moved to a new home, the first thing to do was to call the water and power companies—*and* a local newspaper sales office to get a newspaper subscription. Newspaper sales shops in the area were also always looking out for moving trucks coming to their distribution district. They competed to be the first to visit the household in order to sell a subscription. As a result, according to the survey by the Japan Newspapers Publishers and Editors Association, virtually every household in Japan was subscribing to at least one newspaper until the early 2000s.[32]

The secret of Japan's exceptionally large numbers of newspaper circulation is that papers have come to be more or less accepted by society as a nonideological commodity, something like a product of Fordism, with highly formatted and balanced contents delivered to homes every morning and evening.[33] This is somewhat in contrast with the understanding of journalism in the West, where the idea of journalism "aligns itself with post-Enlightenment notions that one can observe and know the world; with an association to politics."[34]

In addition to these utility-like mass newspapers, Japan has a large and powerful public broadcaster, NHK, as well as five commercial networks overseen by Tokyo-based stations that are closely affiliated with five national dailies. NHK is run solely by license fees collected from residents in Japan, and its annual budget, amounting to approximately US$6 billion (700 billion yen), needs approval from the national Diet.[35] Time and again, scholars and experts have observed that this budgetary system allows indirect censorship on the part of the government, particularly in the interest of the ruling party.

There is another piece of evidence that illustrates the lack of liberalism, or less openness in the market structure of the Japanese media industry. Compared with the American media market, where newspaper companies and TV stations are as much a target of buyouts and mergers by media moguls or billionaires as any other company, the Japanese media industry is largely protected from the vagaries of the free market. The industry has so far rarely experienced mergers or buyouts, not to mention the kind of bankruptcies that a number of media institutions in the United States and Europe have experienced.

One of the most telling events for this stable landscape is the failure of the attempt by Rupert Murdoch to buy out TV Asahi. In 1996, Murdoch purchased 21 percent of TV Asahi's shares, one of the five most influential Tokyo-based key broadcasters in Japan, but the attempt failed after the station's affiliated newspaper, *Asahi Shimbun*, bought back the shares and ousted the global media tycoon. A similar incident happened in 2005. Livedoor, a novice internet company led by a young entrepreneur, Takafumi Horie, attempted to buy shares of Nippon Hoso, an affiliate radio station of Fuji TV, another key TV station in Tokyo. The ultimate aim of the shareholding acquisition was to take over Fuji TV. This attempt failed as well after Fuji TV fought to buy back their shares. Later, in a separate case, Horie was convicted and imprisoned on charges of having circulated false information about his company, Livedoor, to manipulate its stock prices. These occurrences were a lesson to even the most ambitious global market players or cocky young internet entrepreneurs that the market of the established Japanese media companies is off-limits because it is a closed territory, and no one should approach it without careful behind-the-scenes negotiations.

THE COLLUSIVE KISHA-KURABU SYSTEM

The stable media landscape has served, on the one hand, as an instrument to integrate postwar Japanese society. But on the other hand, it has obstructed the formation of a marketplace of ideas where contentious opinions and minority views are represented. Under such circumstances, the unchanged membership of Japanese corporate journalism has nurtured closed institutional arrangements, including the *kisha-kurabu* (press club) system that structurally discriminates against outsiders such as foreign reporters, freelancers, and rising internet companies. The *kisha-kurabu* system, in a nutshell, is an arrangement by which news-gathering activities are administered by the editorial offices of the member companies of the Nippon Shimbun Kyokai (Japan Newspaper Editors and Publishers Association). At the moment, there is a total of about eight hundred *kisha-kurabu* in Japan.

The *kisha-kurabu* system has long been the target of criticism, particularly by overseas media and freelancers, due to its role in establishing and upholding the closed industrial structure. Inside Japan, media institutions contend that the press club system is something that exists in other parts of the world as well, and it is simply a group representing the media sector. Outside Japan, however, Japan's *kisha-kurabu* system is regarded as "the last obstacle to a mature press."[36] It is interesting to note that the club system, which virtually controls major news conferences and other information channels within Japan, has not succeeded in attaining the status of a professional association that can be seen in the Western world. The perennial debates over this institution suggest that it is not so much the institution itself that matters as the way journalism should be understood in a given social and cultural system, particularly in terms of the social relations and positionalities between news reporters and news sources. In Japan, most public officials and politicians do not feel obliged to hand over information to those with whom they do not have established personal contacts and do not share emotions and trust, even though Japanese law requires administrative institutions to disclose as much information as possible to further transparency for democratic governance.[37] Therefore, the more important the news becomes the more leaks news sources will provide to reporters with whom they have close relationships, established via the *kisha-kurabu* networks. Inevitably, this whole system favors the established institutions and strengthens the conventional working culture, the members of which are people more or less of the same cultural, social, and educational background—namely, salaried journalists who are male Japanese graduates of elite universities.

COLD INTERNATIONAL EYES

To the dismay and disappointment of Japanese media executives and journalists, the freedom of press in Japan turned out to be ranked 67th among 180 nations in the 2018 World Press Freedom index issued by Reporters Without Borders.[38] Although freedom of speech is constitutionally guaranteed in Japan and legal scholars clearly acknowledge its importance, and despite investigative reporting making the national headlines in Japan and setting the national political agenda,[39] the international monitoring organization has given a severely negative appraisal of Japanese journalism. The reasons behind this poor assessment are the lack of transparency and the various restrictions long nurtured by the classic old-boys' network of the media, government officials, and other industry executives,[40] as I stated above.

Other experts have faulted Japanese journalism, too. One recent example is the report written by David Kaye, the UN Special Rapporteur on freedom of expression. Kaye visited Japan in April 2017 in order to "assess compliance with international standards on the right to freedom of opinion and expression." In the report, he concluded that "despite this very solid base (of the constitution), including, importantly, the lack of governmental censorship," there are "significant worrying signals" regarding the freedom of speech and expression in Japan.[41] Kaye, moreover, pointed out that the "lack of basic elements of confidence and unity" on the part of Japanese journalists is due to the fact that most of them are "employed by large media empires." He sees that "the very structure of media employment in Japan can affect efforts to withstand pressure from government or to develop cross-outlet solidarity among journalists." Indeed, despite several efforts in the past, there are no professional associations for journalists in Japan.[42]

Kaye's report was another verdict by a Western expert on the deficiencies of liberal spirit in Japanese journalism. As Kaye rightly assessed, the poor evaluation from the outside comes from the *industry structure* that prevents an outsider from ever seeing through the many local rules and rituals. Within media companies, reporters are expected to learn and abide by the unique company culture if they are to go up the career ladder. This tacit knowledge can only be acquired by committing to lifelong employment with minimally paid in-house training.[43] As such, there are very few cross-outlets, external institutions that provide journalism education in Japan. All this makes Japanese journalism less open and free, which are core liberal values.

CURTAILED INTERNATIONAL COVERAGE

A liberal state must have media that provide the domestic public with news from the world. In this section, I will briefly describe how Japanese media covers foreign news and examine whether they are committed to reporting global issues. According to a 2013 research investigation into international news reporting, Japanese media coverage, especially that by TV and Web, does not place an emphasis on international and foreign affairs (as shown previously in figure 10-3).[44] The amount of international coverage can be regarded as one strong indicator of the degree of media organizations' commitment to journalism, since it incurs costs but seldom contributes to increasing viewership/readership.

In order to check whether the relative scarcity of global news coverage comes from the explicit managerial decision to cut costs and shift toward commercialism, a number of overseas offices of the Japanese media have been researched since 1980. According to the industry surveys and websites of each company, the Nikkei currently has thirty-seven offices abroad, the largest number of overseas operations among five national dailies and public broadcaster NHK. Next comes Asahi with thirty-one offices, followed by NHK's thirty. These figures are comparable to the BBC's thirty-eight and CNN's twenty-seven and show Japanese media do invest in foreign operations.[45] All five national newspapers (*Asahi*, *Mainichi*, *Nikkei*, *Sankei*, and *Yomiuri*), as well as public broadcaster NHK, have branch offices in Washington, D.C., New York, London, Paris, Berlin, Cairo, Moscow, Beijing, Shanghai, Taipei, and Seoul. In particular, the two rival national dailies, *Yomiuri* and *Asahi*, have a wide range of world operations and keep their offices in cities such as Havana, Rome, Jerusalem, Johannesburg, Teheran, Bangkok, Jakarta, New Delhi, Hanoi, Shenyang, Guangzhou, Hong Kong, and others. This means that they have adequate organizational structure and professional staff to cover overseas affairs.

Liberal aspirations, and even individual motivations, can be found in many instances in Japan. For example, editorials of all five national dailies unanimously criticized President Trump's abrupt decision to pull the United States out of the Trans-Pacific Partnership Agreement (TPP). This is one example that demonstrates the support of the Japanese media for a nonisolationist position with regard to trade liberalization, a key component of the liberal international order, as discussed by Mireya Solís in chapter 2. However, Japanese media outlets do not seem to make full use of their resources to increase coverage on other international issues, particularly humanitarian issues, to energize the public to take a less isolationist stance.

Media-Public

Finally, I now turn to examining the relationship between the media and the public in Japan to close the triangle, which is considered to be one of the most important relationships for liberal democracy.

THE DECLINE OF TRADITIONAL MEDIA

Japanese people count on TV as their main news source far more than social media and the internet. According to the 2017 survey by the Reuters Institute of Journalism, 44 percent of respondents in Japan said that their main news source was TV, while the internet was 29 percent and social media 7 percent.[46] Since the content of Japanese TV is strictly regulated by broadcast law that requires objectivity and neutrality, the majority of people in Japan are not directly exposed to polarized news coverage or outright sensational contents.

A number of people subscribe to newspapers as well, though not as many as before. Forty million printed copies are still being sold every day and delivered directly to each subscriber household, thanks to meticulous delivery networks developed in the postwar era.[47] These papers also more or less comply with the principles of "neutrality and objectivity," as their professional guidelines and ethics stipulate.[48]

However, the crisis taking over Japanese traditional media companies is more serious than one might glean from these figures. In the year 2009, the advertising revenues of the internet caught up with those of the newspapers. In 2010, respondents who chose the internet as the most indispensable medium were tied with those who chose newspapers as the most indispensable, at 14 percent. But in 2015, the number of those who chose the internet as the most indispensable rose to 23 percent, while that number for newspapers dropped to 11 percent.[49] Additionally, an NHK survey shows that the total hours of watching television decreased in 2015 for the first time since 1985. Those who responded "seldom or never watch TV" doubled in the age group between twenty and twenty-nine.[50]

Moreover, newspaper readers in Japan are aging. According to an NHK survey, an average teenager spends as little as one minute of a weekday reading newspapers.[51] This contrasts with those who are seventy or older, who, on average, spend forty-five minutes on daily newspaper reading. TV is also becoming unpopular among younger generations. The average daily viewing time of teenagers stands less than a hundred minutes, whereas those aged seventy and older spend well over five hours in front of TV. The tendency is reversed for viewing hours of the internet [figure 10-5]. Given these figures, we can assume that the dominance of traditional media will not last long even in Japan, where traditional media has enjoyed a preeminent status both economically and socially for a long time. Some industry experts say that the present-day newspaper delivery network, which has sustained the newspaper business in Japan, will collapse when the number of newspaper circulations is halved from the current 40 million. If so, the media landscape is destined to change radically.

NO CHANGE TO THE TRIAD?

Traditional media are losing their power, not only economically but also in terms of weakening ties with their audience. People simply do not regard them as an intermediary to politics anymore. Seventy-six percent of people replied to an NHK survey that they have never sent their opinion to the media and they do not intend to do so in the future, either. Growing indif-

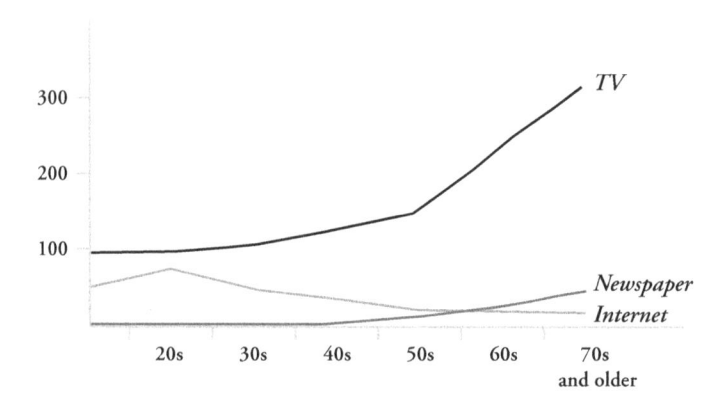

FIGURE 10-5. Average minutes spent on the consumption of each media on a weekday (male)

Source: "Kokumin Seikatsu Jikan Chousa Hokokusho" [Survey of Use of Time of Japanese People], NHK Hoso Bunka Kenkyujo (2016), 9, 21, 24.

ference to allying and interacting with media is particularly pronounced among younger generations in the past decade.[52]

Newspapers and television are perhaps not the ideal medium to represent civic voices. But the internet seems not to be the ultimate solution to make Japanese people feel more relevant to politics, either. Japanese people are equally reluctant to share news or participate in any forms of interactions over the internet. As many as 62 percent of respondents replied that they never share news or participate in online activities. This compares with Germany's 48 percent, the United Kingdom's 43 percent, South Korea's 38 percent, and the United States's 26 percent.[53]

This goes back to my original point of the triad. Japanese people are generally dispassionate about politics. Political news coverage remains unappealing to the public, and because media know that the public interest does not lie in politics, their coverage becomes increasingly depoliticized. Therefore, media outlets lose the power to shape a critical public that monitors the power of authorities and effectively performs its watchdog function. This cycle is becoming remarkably prominent in contemporary Japanese society.

Signs of Change? Popularity of the Internet and the Rise of Polarized Discourse

Will this triad last forever? Unless there is an effective external force, the relationship between politics, journalism, and the public in Japan seems unlikely to change anytime soon. Selling scoops, scandals, gossips, and polarized positions to stimulate, if not manipulate, the public opinion has not been the signature business among Japan's established corporate media. Japanese politics do not launch media-savvy, extravagant campaigns as seen in the presidential election in the United States. Japan's media coverage is restrained, aloof, often boringly balanced, factual, detailed, and distant. It strictly and cautiously tends to "impartiality" so as to do no harm and to appeal to the largest possible audience. This has been its way of profit maximization since the 1950s.

However, exceptions have begun to appear in the industry recently. The best example is *Sankei Shimbun*, known for its right-wing tendency, hostile discourse toward leftists and liberals, and its close ties with conservative groups. *Sankei* brands itself *mono wo iu shimbun* ("a paper that speaks up"). On their website, they explain their journalism as follows:

> *Sankei Shimbun* protects freedom and democracy. We are known as taking the line of *seiron* ("just argument"), which thinks of national interest first. We were very quick to divulge the truth of China's Cultural Revolution. We have discovered and investigated the abduction cases by North Korea. We have criticized history textbooks that proliferated self-tormenting views of our nation's history, which deprived our children of a sense of pride and confidence in our nation. We do not play up to the majoritarian trend of the time and we take a firm stand on our arguments, which we believe are correct from an independent point of view. Our brand has been appreciated as "a paper that speaks up."[54]

Sankei has been known as the weakest among the five national newspapers. It also has the smallest circulation and the smallest number of overseas operations among the five. It gave up publishing their evening edition for the Tokyo and Kanto region in 2001.[55] Because the paper does not sell well, they went online as early as in the 1990s, to look for new chances to develop on the internet, while other papers remained reluctant to do so, weighed down by the legacy costs of their distribution system. This transition is said to have made the paper more polarized, as it began targeting and securing certain segments of the online audience that had more extreme political views.[56]

Critical opinions of *Sankei* are particularly directed toward *riberaru* (liberals). *Sankei* columnist Kumiko Takeuchi created the phrase *Nippon-gata riberaru* (Japanese-style liberals), by which she means "those who still stick to communism and socialism, even if these proved to be a failure and fiction." This, according to her, is a uniquely Japanese phenomenon.[57]

An example of *Sankei*'s hostile attitude toward *riberaru* is its coverage of the long-debated "comfort women" issue. The paper has shown no hesitation in choosing provocative and belligerent language against those who hold liberal views on this issue. In particular, it continues to accuse *Asahi Shimbun*, once the opinion leader of the liberal league on the issue, of its "lies" and its "betrayal of our own country."[58] In the 1990s, *Asahi* demanded that the Japanese government admit the Imperial Government of

Japan had systematically coerced women in their colonies to provide sexual services to Japanese soldiers during World War II.[59]

In recent years, *Sankei* has taken up more than 70 percent of the entire coverage on "comfort women" in Japan (figure 10-6), whereas *Asahi* has become more cautious and ceased to cover the topic actively after 2000. In 2014, *Asahi* featured the theme thoroughly for two consecutive days, reflecting on its own past coverage. The feature admitted that some articles contained factual errors, which were the reason *Sankei* and other conservative media have persisted in criticizing *Asahi* as unpatriotic. Thus, the paper decided to carry the feature for the purposes of "correcting its past mistakes to move forward." But instead of going "forward," the feature was criticized nationally because it did not include words of apology by the company, and its circulation dropped dramatically. The criticisms toward *Asahi* also turned personal, as one of the retired reporters, Takashi Uemura, who covered the comfort women issue in the 1980s and 1990s, and his family members were exposed to ugly harassment and bullying, and even threatened with direct violence. However, despite such illiberal attacks on journalists, Prime Minister Abe merely expressed concerns for the reporting of *Asahi* and urged the newspaper to make further efforts "to restore Japan's damaged reputation."[60] In fact, prior to this incident, Prime Minister Abe had repeatedly pointed out that *Asahi*'s coverage of comfort women was biased and damaged Japan's international image.

Political scientist Koichi Nakano contends that the current public sphere in Japan is leaning to the Right, along with the conservative prime minister Shinzo Abe, who has been long known for his active accusations of liberals, including the *Asahi*, and has close ties with conservatives and nationalists, some of whom are journalists of the *Yomiuri* and *Sankei*.[61] In the face of the weakened liberal *Asahi*, *riberaru* in Japan, in other words, are faring poorly, with no strong support from politicians of opposition parties and a relatively inactive civil society.

So now we face another question: is such polarization happening only to the print sector in Japan? As I have stated, Japanese broadcasting stations are all licensed and strictly regulated by the Broadcast Act. Experts say, however, a change will take place in the broadcasting sector as well, even if not in the very near future. Recently the Abe administration was reported to have prepared a draft proposal to scrap Article 4 of the Japanese

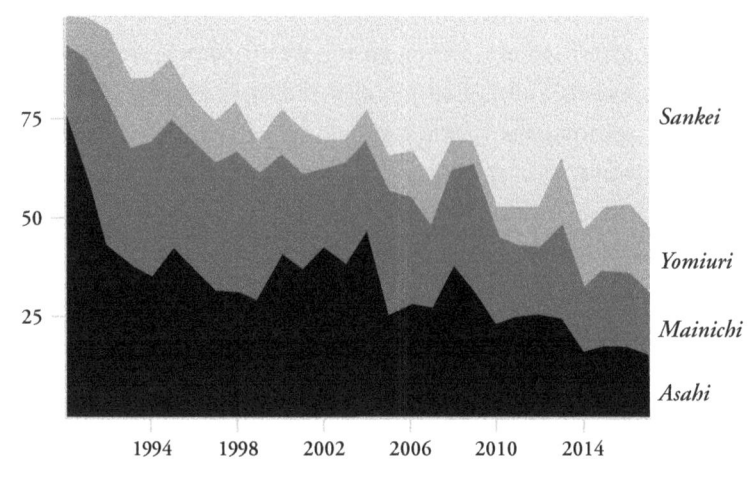

FIGURE 10-6. Proportion of the coverage of "comfort women" among four national newspapers

Source: Figure created by the author. The results are based on a keyword search for "ianfu" (comfort women) using the newspaper search engine Nikkei Telecom.

Broadcast Law, which requires broadcasters to be impartial and balanced in their contents. This mandate by Article 4 is comparable to the Fairness Doctrine in the United States, which was repealed in the deregulatory moves under the Reagan administration. The repeal of the Fairness Doctrine is widely believed to have given rise to politically active right-wing talk radios and cable channels, working to the effect of accelerating polarization in broadcast contents in the United States.[62, 63] In the case of Japan, after having been met with protests from a wide range of experts, scholars, and media companies, the proposal has been shelved for now. However, Masaaki Taira, the head of digital strategies at the Public Relations Department of the LDP headquarters and a member of the Lower House, sees this movement as tentative and believes regulation will be loosened in the long run: "Of course, we can keep the broadcast law if we want, but I believe the television companies will decline anyway, and in the end, they will all be bought out by internet companies, and the telecommunication and broadcasting sectors will merge inevitably."[64]

Another public relations expert, who asked to stay anonymous, agrees: "As the demographics are changing in Japan, do you think we really need five commercial broadcasters in Tokyo? I do not think so. It may not be so apparent now, but in reality they must be having a hard time securing enough advertising revenues."

Meanwhile, in the world of the internet, so-called internet TV channels are on the rise, including the right-wing Nippon Bunka Channel Sakura, which "broadcasts" ultraconservative, nationalistic content. Moreover, internet TV is considered the Wild West for Japanese TV producers who think anything goes. One of the emerging companies is the Abema TV, a venture by TV Asahi and CyberAgent, an internet advertising company. Producers of Abema TV "experiment" with content they would not be allowed to make for ordinary TV programs. These include vulgar language, violence, and nudity, often abusing aspiring actresses and female idol stars.

Until now, Japan has been known for having highly regulated broadcasting and relatively well-behaved newspaper journalists. They distinguished themselves from publications such as gossip-based popular weekly tabloids or sport papers and established themselves as elite institutions that led the society. Newspaper and television companies have enjoyed high social esteem and did not have to live for scoops and scandals. But with high market pressure from the internet, they may have to change. In these times, they will have to think seriously about how they can better appeal to their audience through their content.

Japanese Variation of Liberalism

Before digitization, conventional Japanese media were the only channels that provided citizens with necessary information on politics and society. Like water and electricity, mass media was regarded as the public utility that catered to the good, civilized lives of Japanese people. This understanding had much to do with Japan's historical condition at the end of the nineteenth century, when the government actively promoted newspapers to make Japan into a modernized society while controlling the media and successfully ousting rebellious journalism. While major U.S. or European newspapers such as the *New York Times* or the *Guardian* enjoy the exclusive readerships of, more or less, the well-educated middle to upper socioeconomic class,[65] Japanese mainstream newspapers, particularly national dailies, target the entire Japanese population regardless of sociodemographic attributes and create nationwide discourse to support the advancement of modern Japan. In short, subscribing to a newspaper has been taken as evidence of citizenship in Japan.

The Japanese public has been reluctant to take part in politics, and it seems the degree of reluctance has been reinforced in recent years. The Japanese also seem to lack enthusiasm for engaging in open social communication. Thus, Japan may seem to be doing well at the formal level in the attainment of liberal democracy, but in actual practice, this democracy has failed to permeate people's everyday lives or workplaces. In this sense, the argument that opinion polarization, populism, and media distrust are inevitable byproducts of liberal democracy does not apply to the situation in Japan.

Liberalism and the liberal international order is a grandiose project that looks universal at first glance, but it has its diverse cultural faces and facets. Originally, it was brewed, grown, and propagated in the United Kingdom and the United States during the era of British and then American hegemony. It is also embedded in its own cultural assumptions. Accordingly, it is not surprising that Japan has followed a Japanese path and faced Japanese challenges, as it developed its own version of liberalism. However, at the same time, this path has had several overlaps with the American or British paths.

First, to a large extent, liberalism in the United States (and in most European countries) has benefited and protected the already privileged and established tiers—namely, white, male, educated intellectuals, industrialists, and politicians. This applies to the Japanese version of liberalism as well. Liberalism in postwar Japan has worked more to the advantage of powerful LDP politics; large corporations, including media; and elite educational institutions, all of which consist predominantly of Japanese men. The case of Japanese media may be also taken as evidence that liberal idealism has given support to a social structure that strengthens elite homogenous reporter circles.

Second, because liberalism is, as a matter of course, liberal, it can also attract the wrong friends, and work even in their favor, often at the expense of its real friends. For example, hate speech or vulgar content are not only tolerated but might be encouraged in the name of liberalism.

Verbal slander, often combined with physical attacks, are directed at social, cultural, and ethnic minorities, the population groups for whom the right to free speech was originally established. As a result, there are too many people in Japanese society who cannot really perceive and experience its goodness in their everyday lives. The problem with liberalism seems to me, therefore, that it is always good in theory, but never enough in reality, and thus does harm to the weak and underprivileged while somehow enriching those in the establishment. Against such a background, we need more thoroughly detailed, pragmatic, and, above all, contextualized remedies and reflections to revise the liberalism we have known in the past, rather than taking another sweeping assessment or theoretical model from the West and imposing it on other cultures. As we have seen in the case of Japan, the nation has indeed profited significantly from liberalism and the liberal international order, but to what extent it is accepted and enjoyed by the population should be carefully examined. Very often, the degree of acceptance hinges largely on the existing social structure, cultural habits, and history of each country.

The above analysis shows that Japan, like its Western counterparts, also suffers from "liberal malaise." While the country formally maintains liberal democracy and believes in liberal creed and its achievements, it struggles to make liberalism work effectively because of broad idealism and unfounded optimism. The challenge Japan faces, however, is different from that of the Western countries. The public in Western countries seems to have lost the consensual common ground, as it continues to pursue its model of liberalism and democracy amid increasing globalization and diversification of society. Meanwhile, the public in Japan seems to have lost the common goal to become a global power now that it has achieved its "economic miracle." The media industry is no exception. It profited very much from the rapid economic growth of the postwar period and is now losing sight of the goal of being the nation's "mass media." Mass media companies in Japan are being forced to redefine their role in a society where they are increasingly faced with a significant loss of their audience.

Outlook for the Japanese Media Industry in an Age of the Internet

In the case of the media in Japan, there is some hope that it will not become completely like the present U.S. media landscape. In Japan, there remains an idea of *kōkyōsei* (publicness) about media, meaning that media should cater to everyone's needs and interests. Even if people interpret this "publicness" as a notion that is only comparable to public utility, there is still a tacit agreement among them that they should keep and share the media as a public good for their common ground.

Another advantage today's Japan seems to have, relative to the United Kingdom and the United States, is that neoliberalism—a subspecies of liberalism born in the course of postwar capitalism—has not thoroughly penetrated the media sector, as we have seen in this chapter. As far as the media industry is concerned, the solution is not necessarily "the more liberal the better," as can be confirmed by referring to the cases of the British tabloid market or American television landscape. The majority of local newspapers in Japan, for example, are independent and make tireless efforts of serving local communities in their own ways, such as providing firsthand information for young mothers or the local elderly population.

Despite such advantages, there are causes for concerns. Rodney Benson and others calculated that public media spending per capita in the United States is now as low as US$3.32. This compares with Norway's US$176.60, Germany's US$134.70, and the United Kingdom's US$99.96. According to their calculations, Japan stands at US$42.59, which is higher than the United States but not as high as European countries.[66] The U.S. style of eradicating the role of the state or any other regulatory body in the media sector has already proven to be a failure.

We have to think of a "third way"—namely, neither the traditional Japanese cartel-like, highly regulated and ossified media nor a totally deregulated media industry seen in the United States—that will bring about a better media landscape that matches the cultural needs and economic demands of the society. Here again, we have to contextualize liberalism in the culture to which it was transplanted and think of appropriate solutions.

In order to maintain such publicness, media in Japan should become more vigilant of and relevant to people's pain and suffering and reconsider the definition of "politics" to create a desirable synergy to make Japanese society more open to new ideas and innovation. The media should address more diverse themes with more firsthand voices of citizens of different nationalities, gender, ethnicities, ages, and so on. As Aarlberg and others state, "the prominent reporting of democratic voices in television news is associated with the view that ordinary citizens matter."[67] At the moment, Japanese TV news, for example, decidedly lacks democratic voices, namely, "those of the political opposition, civil society (narrowly understood as public interest groups, trade unions, and religious/ethnic/professional associations), and individual citizens."[68] The ultimate weakness of Japanese media lies not in the amount of freedom but the amount of diversity.

With the rise of the internet, anybody can directly visit websites of official sources and obtain firsthand information. People can also be instant reporters and upload their photos and essays at any time from anywhere. The definition of journalism has been broadened. Taking this as an advantage of the digital era, Japanese media companies should open themselves up and cooperate with a variety of specialized nonprofits, higher education institutions, and think tanks that can provide in-depth information. These organizations are sometimes in a better position to report on complex issues of modern society more comprehensively and can eventually fill the gaps between the public and the media.

Finally, for a more open and liberal media that truly respects diversity and freedom, I propose that Japanese media reform its close-knit society. As stated, first and foremost, they have to introduce more diversity in the newsroom. This will not only make them more relevant to society, it will also reduce the risk of making errors and producing fake news. Given that Japanese society will be further globalized in the near future, news value, as well as the range of perspectives for coverage, should be reconsidered. As such, they will have to change their conventional working style that requires all reporters to work long hours day-in and day-out. In addition, the conventional composition at the management level, overwhelmingly male and Japanese, should be altered. All these specific changes are related to the core of the organizational structure that Japanese media companies have long depended upon. Without such step-by-step small but *structural* innovations, it will be difficult to attain a substantially higher ranking in the World Press Freedom index, and they will not gain the due recognition they expect from the allegedly "liberal" postwar framework.

With the transition from print to digital, or with mergers of the communication and broadcast industries, some major newspaper companies or television stations will very likely experience an existential crisis, a phenomenon Japan has never experienced before. But as a truly liberal democratic society, Japan should regard the present crisis as a chance to rejuvenate its dated journalism culture. A new style of architecture for the media industry in Japan will require careful planning, but if successful, it will bring a new type of democracy that stimulates the aspirations and ambitions of younger generations and resonates more with truly liberal orders of society.

NOTES

I thank Yoichi Funabashi and G. John Ikenberry for their insightful comments and suggestions in finishing this essay. My sincere thanks also go to Yujin Yaguchi for his valuable comments and checking and correcting my English. Last but not least, I thank Harry Dempsey and Takato Nakamura and all other API members for helping me with this research and proofreading.

1. Nic Newman and others, *Reuters Institute Digital News Report 2017* (Oxford: Reuters Institute for the Study of Journalism, 2017), 9.

2. Kyu S. Hahn and others, "Red Media, Blue Media: Evidence of Ideological Selectivity in Media Use," *Journal of Communication*, vol. 59 (March 2009), 19–39; Shanto Iyengar, Gaurav Sood, and Yphtach Lelkes, "Affect, Not Ideology: A Social Identity Perspective on Polarization," *Public Opinion Quarterly*, vol. 76, no. 3 (September 2012), 405–31; Shanto Iyengar and others, "Fear and Loathing across Party Lines: New Evidence on Group Polarization," *American Journal of Political Science*, vol. 59, no. 3 (July 2015), 690–707.

3. David Brooks, "When Politics Becomes Your Idol," *New York Times*, October 30, 2017.

4. Daniel Deudney and G. John Ikenberry, "Liberal World: The Resilient Order," *Foreign Affairs*, vol. 97, no. 4 (July/August 2018), 16–24.

5. Céline Pajon, "Democracy in Asia: Models, Trends, and Geopolitical Implications," https://www.ifri.org/en/publications/editoriaux-de-lifri/lettre-centre-asie/democracy-asia-models-trends-and-geopolitical.

6. The Constitution of Japan, https://japan.kantei.go.jp/constitution_and_government_of_japan/constitution_e.html.

7. Masami Ito, *Gendai Shakai to Genron no Jiyu* [Contemporary Society and Freedom of Speech] (Tokyo: Yushindo, 1974), 22; See chapter 4, by Maiko Ichihara, for explanation of Japan's ODA policy in which economic rights are seen as the most fundamental element for democratic governance.

8. John Dewey, "Democracy and Educational Administration," *School and Society*, vol. 45 (April 3, 1937), 457.

9. Shinichi Fujiwara, "(Oshiete Kenpo) GHQ ni Oshitsukerareta," [Constitution Imposed by GHQ], *Asahi Shimbun*, February 16, 2018.

10. Liberal Democratic Party, Nihonkoku Kempo Kaisei Soan [Proposal for the Revision of the Constitution of Japan], https://jimin.ncss.nifty.com/pdf/news/policy/130250_1.pdf.

11. There is a popular saying in Japanese, *Sore wo icchaa oshimaiyo* (You have crossed the line). It is used by Tora-san, a national hero in the movie series *Futen no Tora-san*. This phrase became a familiar warning to people who talk too much. It means that telling the truth would disrupt conversation and start a fight. A member of the parliament I interviewed cited this phrase in explaining why he would not be able to fully exercise his right to the freedom of expression. He said, truth obstructs dialogue. In this regard, he said, "Despite having Mr. Trump as president, the United States continues to have more freedom."

12. Asahi Journalism School, *Journalism*: "Ehimekenkei no Uraganekokuhatsusha ga kataru Media ga hatasubeki Shimei" [The Responsibility of Media. An Interview with the Whistleblower about the Off-the-Book Money at the Ehime Prefectural Police], February 2010, no. 237, 4–10; Kaori Hayashi, "A Journalism of Care," in *Rethinking Journalism Again: Societal Role and Public Relevance in a Digital Age*, edited by Chris Peters and Marcel Broersma (Abingdon, U.K.: Routledge, 2016), 146–60.

13. "Word of the Year 2016 is . . ." https://en.oxforddictionaries.com/word-of-the-year/word-of-the-year-2016.

14. Linda Sieg, "Japan's 'Sontaku' Clouds Where the Buck Stops in School Scandal," Reuters, March 15, 2018.

15. Ibid.

16. Japan placed 114th among 144 countries in the World Economic Forum's global gender equality rankings for 2017. "Japan Drops by Three to 114th in Gender Equality Rankings by World Economic Forum," *Japan Times*, November 2, 2017.

17. The abovementioned dubious land sale to Mr. Kagoike was first uncovered by *Asahi Shimbun*. Because of this scoop, the head of the National Tax Agency, Nobuhisa Sagawa, resigned in March 2018. There have been countless achievements by Japanese journalism that revealed government secrets and scandals of high-ranking officials.

18. Ministry of International Affairs and Communications, "Kokuseisenkyo no Nendaibetsu Touhyoritu no Suii ni Tsuite" [The Changes in Voter Turnout of National Elections by Age Group], http://www.soumu.go.jp/senkyo/senkyo_s/news/sonota/nendaibetu/.

19. Ministry of International Affairs and Communications, "Kokuseisenkyo ni okeru Tohyoritsu no Suii" [The Changes in Voter Turnout of National Elections], http://www.soumu.go.jp/senkyo/senkyo_s/news/sonota/ritu/index.html.

20. "(2017 Shuinsen) Senkyo ni Ikanu Nihon no Wakamono Touhyouritsu 32.6% OECD Saikai" [2017 Lower House Election: Japanese Young People Do Not Vote. The Turnout Rate Is 32.6 Percent, the Lowest Number in OECD Countries], *Nihon Nogyo Shimbun*, October 13, 2017.

21. Voter turnout database for parliamentary elections of OECD countries. Data is for the most recent elections, https://www.idea.int/data-tools/regional-entity-view/OECD/40.

22. "Hard news is typically used to refer to topics that are usually timely, important, and consequential, such as politics, international affairs, and business news. Conversely, soft news topics include entertainment, celebrity, and lifestyle news." Cited from David

Levy and others, *Reuters Institute Digital News Report 2016* (Oxford: Reuters Institute for the Study of Journalism, 2016), 97.

23. Toshiyuki Kobayashi, "Teikasuru Nipponnjin no Seijiteki, Shakaiteki Katsudou iyoku to sono Haikei. ISSP Kokusai Hikaku Chousa 'Shimin Ishiki' Nippon no Kekka kara. Hoso Kenkyu to Chousa" [Background behind Declining Willingness for Political and Social Action: From the Results of ISSP International Comparative Research on Civilian Attitudes], *Hoso Kenkyu to Chosa*, vol. 65, no. 1 (January 2015), 25.

24. Aiji Tanaka, "Japan's Independent Voters, Yesterday and Today," Nippon.com, August 16, 2012, https://www.nippon.com/en/in-depth/a01104/.

25. Interview with Hidehiko Koguchi, Tokyo, August 1, 2018.

26. Ibid.

27. Newman and others, *Reuters Institute Digital News Report 2017*, 48.

28. Ibid., 103.

29. This structure was established already before World War II. To prepare the nation for the war, the government forced newspaper companies to merge and slashed the number drastically in order to better manipulate the press. Since then and to this day, the market structure has remained almost unchanged and is called "one paper per prefecture." Therefore, the competition takes place only among a handful of the existing members of the industry in each region.

30. Mikko Villi and Kaori Hayashi, "The Mission Is to Keep This Industry Intact," *Journalism Studies*, vol. 18, no. 8 (November 2015), 960–77; doi: doi.org/10.1080/1461670X.2015.1110499.

31. Eiji Oshita, Shimbun *no Onitachi. Shosetsu Mutai Mituso* [Newspaper Monsters: The Novel of Mitsuo Mutai] (Tokyo: Kobunsha, 1999).

32. "Newspapers," Japan-Guide.com, https://www.japan-guide.com/topic/0108.html.

33. Villi and Hayashi, "The Mission Is to Keep This Industry Intact."

34. Barbie Zelizer and Stuart Allan, *Keywords in News and Journalism Studies* (Open University Press, 2010), 63.

35. "NHK Corporate Profile 2018–19," https://www.nhk.or.jp/corporateinfo/english/publication/pdf/corporate_profile.pdf, 6.

36. William de Lange, *A History of Japanese Journalism: Japan's Press Club as the Last Obstacle to a Mature Press* (London: Psychology Press, 1998).

37. Kaori Hayashi and Gerd G. Kopper, "Multi-Layer Research Design for Analyses of Journalism and Media Systems in the Global Age: Test Case Japan," *Media, Culture & Society*, vol. 36, no. 8 (August 2014), 1144.

38. Reporters without Borders, "2018 World Press Freedom Index," https://rsf.org/en/ranking.

39. There have been a number of extraordinary, even globally influential achievements in the postwar history of Japanese journalism. One of the early examples is a report by a journalist at a small regional office of the Yomiuri. He reported on the severe accident by radiation exposure of twenty-three crew members of a small Japanese fishing boat, *Daigo Fukuryumaru*. The report elucidated that the crew suffered because they encountered a U.S. hydrogen bomb test in the South Pacific Bikini Atolls in 1954. It triggered a global debate over the offshore nuclear experiments by the United States.

40. The world of Japanese media is dominated by men and is exclusively Japanese. In the survey conducted in 2009 by the International Women's Media Foundation, women

held only 1.4 percent of the positions of the top-rank management and 4.8 percent of the senior-level positions in the entire media industry. In 2017, the women's division of the national union of the commercial broadcasters reported that the women's ratio of board members at five Tokyo-based commercial broadcasters and the NHK remained 1.4 percent.

41. The report also criticized the government of Japan for interfering in history teaching and reporting, as well as passing the Specially Designated Secrets Act. The report was strongly refuted by the government of Japan, which argued the criticisms are based on hearsay and inaccurate understandings of Japan. The Japanese government decried this report as "degrading the authority of the UN Human Rights Council." Justin McCurry, "Japan Accused of Eroding Press Freedom by UN Special Rapporteur," *Guardian*, June 13, 2017; Jeff Kingston, "Arrogant Abe Disrespects UN and the Press," *Japan Times*, June 10, 2017.

42. It has been argued that the current Abe administration is stepping up its control over the media behind the scenes. But Japanese media companies have not united themselves to withstand such government pressures. This is in contrast to how U.S. media have reacted against President Donald Trump. In August 2018, more than two hundred U.S. newspapers published an editorial on the dangers of the administration's assault on the press. Jaclyn Peiser, "The *New York Times* Joins Effort to Combat Trump's Anti-Press Rhetoric," *New York Times*, August 14, 2018.

43. Kaori Hayashi and Rika Tanioka, *Terebi Hodo Shoku no Wa-ku Raifu 'Anbaransu': 13 Kyoku Danjo 30 Nin no Kikitori Chosa kara* [Work-Life "Unbalance" of TV Reporters: Based on Interviews with Thirty Men and Women from Thirteen TV Companies] (Tokyo: Otsuki Shoten, 2013).

44. Data obtained from the survey the author and her international team undertook for Aarlberg and others, 2013.

45. Data obtained from *Nihon Shimbun Nenkan 1980–2017* [Japan Newspaper Annual].

46. Newman and others, *Reuters Institute Digital News Report 2017*, 48.

47. Ibid., 120.

48. "Shimbun Rinri Koryo" [Ethical Principles of Newspapers], *Nihon Shimbun Kyokai*, June 21, 2000.

49. Noriko Kimura and others, "Television Viewing and Media Use Today: From 'The Japanese and Television 2015' Survey" (NHK Broadcasting Culture Research Institute, 2016).

50. Ibid., 5.

51. "Kokumin Seikatsu Jikan Chousa Hokokusho" [Survey of Use of Time of Japanese People] (NHK Broadcasting Culture Research Institute, 2016), 21.

52. Kobayashi, "Teikasuru Nipponnjin no Seijiteki," 25.

53. Newman and others, *Reuters Institute Digital News Report 2017*, and Kobayashi, "Teikasuru Nipponnjin no Seijiteki." The survey asked: "During an average week, in which, if any, of the following ways do you share or participate in news coverage?" The options presented ranged from social media (Facebook, Twitter, and such) to communicating online or face-to-face with friends and colleagues.

54. "Mono wo Iu Shimbun Sankei Shimbun" [A Newspaper that Speaks Up: *Sankei Shimbun*], *Sankei Shimbun*.

55. "Sankei Shimbun, Yu-ka Haishi he/ Rainen 4-gatsu kara" [*Sankei Shimbun* to Give Up Publishing of Evening Edition Starting Next April], *Sankei Shimbun*, November 7, 2001.

56. Yoichi Jomaru, *Shokun Seiron no Kenkyu. Hoshu Genron wa dou Henyoshitekitaka* [The Research of *Shokun* and *Seiron*: How the Conservative Opinion Has Changed] (Tokyo: Iwanami Shoten, 2011).

57. Kumiko Takeuchi, "Seiron: Nihongata Riberaru no Shinso ha Nani ka Doubutsu Kodo Kenkyuka Esseisuto Takeuchi Kumiko" [Sound Argument: What Is the Essence of Japanese-Style Liberals? Kumiko Takeuchi, an animal behavior researcher and essayist], *Sankei Shimbun,* March 28, 2018.

58. "Tashi no Houdou ha" [How Other Newspapers Are Reporting], https://www.asahi.com/articles/ASG7L7GGWG7LUTIL05Y.html.

59. "Kiji wo Teisei, Owabishi Gosetsumei Shimasu, Asahi Shimbun Sha" [Article Revised, Apology and Explanation by the *Asahi Shimbun* Company], *Asahi Shimbun*, December 23, 2014, morning edition, 37.

60. Mizuho Aoki, "Abe Tells *Asahi Shimbun* to Help in 'Recovering Japan's Honor,' " *Japan Times*, October 6, 2014. Also from "Report of the Special Rapporteur on the Promotion and Protection of the Right to Freedom of Opinion and Expression on His Mission to Japan," 9.

61. Koichi Nakano, *Ukeika suru Nippon Seiji* [Japanese Politics that Drifts to the Right] (Tokyo: Iwanami Shoten, 2015).

62. Yoshiyasu Shida and Ristuko Ando, "Japan's Abe Seeks to Remove 'Balance' Requirements in Broadcast News," Reuters, March 26, 2018.

63. Victor Pickard, "Media and Politics in the Age of Trump," *Origins: Current Events in Historical Perspective*, vol. 10, no. 2 (November 2016).

64. Interview with Masaaki Taira on August 3, 2018.

65. For example, for the sociodemographic analysis of the readership in the United Kingdom, please see http://www.nrs.co.uk/latest-results/nrs-print-results/newspapers-nrsprintresults/. There are clear differences of sociodemographic attributes among newspaper brands.

66. Rodney Benson, Matthew Powers, and Timothy Neff, "Public Media Autonomy and Accountability: Best and Worst Policy Practices in Twelve Leading Democracies," *International Journal of Communication*, vol. 11 (January 2017), 5.

67. James Curran and others, "Reconsidering 'Virtuous Circle' and 'Media Malaise' Theories of the Media: An Eleven-Nation Study," *Journalism*, vol. 15, no. 7 (September 2014), 14.

68. Ibid., 12.

11

Japan and the Liberal International Order

A SURVEY EXPERIMENT

ADAM P. LIFF | KENNETH MORI McELWAIN

As noted in the introduction and other chapters throughout this volume, there is a widely and increasingly held view among many policymakers and international relations scholars that the liberal international order faces a major crisis. Permeating this discourse are two widespread assertions: first, in light of recent domestic political developments, the United States is increasingly ambivalent about championing the liberal order it built. And second, that it is, therefore, incumbent upon Japan and other advanced liberal democracies to "step up" to do more to support it.

Yet much of this discourse occurs at a very "elite" level. To assess the feasibility of democratic Japan playing a significantly more proactive role in international affairs, it is important to gauge where the Japanese public stands on related policy questions. How realistic is it to expect Japan's political leaders—who must, at the end of the day, answer to voters at the polls—to pursue a more proactive role championing international liberalism? Do they risk popular backlash if they do? These are particularly salient questions in the case of Japan, which has long been reluctant to adopt certain aspects of the more assertive posture in foreign affairs that many appear to now be asking it to—especially in the security domain.

This chapter contributes to the discussion by summarizing the results of an original survey experiment we put into the field across Japan in September 2018. The goal of this survey experiment is to assess the public's openness to Japan adopting a greater leadership role in the regional and global order particularly in domains that commentators have identified as being under threat—such as security affairs and free trade—but also with regard to international institutions and promotion of democracy. This survey experiment achieved this through two components. First, we assessed the static views of respondents through a straightforward opinion survey, analogous to those regularly deployed by Japanese newspapers. Second, we tested how preferences *change* when respondents are exposed to information highlighting threats to the sustainability of the liberal international order, particularly deepening ambivalence in the White House vis-à-vis U.S. security alliances, free trade, international institutions, and other key features of what many refer to as the "rules-based liberal international order."

Taken collectively, the results suggest that Japanese citizens believe the liberal international order has been crucial to postwar national prosperity and peace and stability in the Asia-Pacific region. There is also robust support for Japan adopting a relatively more proactive posture in international trade and security affairs—within limits. In the economic domain, survey respondents strongly support the idea that Japan has benefited greatly from international free trade and should play a leadership role in that domain *regardless of what the United States does*. This comports with Solís's argument that Japan is no longer a follower on free trade, as reflected in its effort to champion the Comprehensive and Progressive Agreement for Trans-Pacific Partnership (CPTPP, also known as TPP-11) after the Trump administration's withdrawal from the twelve-member Trans-Pacific Partnership in January 2017. With regard to security affairs, the survey reveals strong support for strengthening ties with the United States, for Japan deepening ties with other countries in the region as a counterweight to China, and for pursuing more robust defense capabilities to bolster deterrence, such as increased defense spending. These goals all appear congruent with U.S. policies. The survey also supports the notion that Japan is generally not falling victim to the sort of narrow, inward-looking populism that has affected many other developed democracies.

This chapter is organized as follows: We first explain our rationale for conducting a survey experiment and briefly describe our survey design. We then summarize key findings from the survey experiment's constituent parts: pretreatment questions, the control group responses to posttreatment questions, and an analysis of treatment effects for the three treatment groups. After noting a few important caveats, a final section concludes and discusses how our approach could be replicated (and improved upon) in future studies of Japan or other countries.

Why Conduct a Survey Experiment?

Though public opinion does not predetermine the foreign and domestic policy decisions of political leaders, it can certainly empower or constrain them. For example, concerns about the expected social costs of immigration can make leaders leery of opening national borders, while popular fears about perceived threats from a neighboring country can create political space for leaders to significantly increase defense spending or change force structure. Accordingly, any discussion of Japan's ability—to say nothing of its willingness—to sustain or actively champion the liberal international order would be incomplete without analyzing public opinion on related issues. While some prominent surveys—including from Japan's Cabinet Office, the Pew Research Center, or domestic media organizations—periodically poll the Japanese public about foreign policy, there are important questions directly applicable to this volume that are rarely or never asked. Furthermore, most of these widely read surveys provide *static* snapshots of public opinion: they typically do not attempt to measure how public opinion *changes* when respondents are presented with new information about Japan's external environment.

This chapter addresses these gaps with a customized survey experiment tailored to deepen our understanding of what factors shape Japanese perceptions of global affairs. In particular, to what extent does the Japanese public believe it is important to sustain and strengthen the liberal order (and its constituent parts) and for Japan to play a leadership role in doing so? Do they share the concerns of many of the scholars and other observers noted throughout this volume? Are Japanese citizens more concerned about threats to the economic or security aspects of the order? Are they more willing to commit to the liberal order when an ally appears increasingly unreliable or uncommitted, or when political or opinion leaders shape the narrative about real world events in particular ways?

To begin answering these questions, we need to know how public opinion can be shaped by political leaders or by new geopolitical developments. In addition to gathering valuable information on static opinions relevant to Japan's role in the liberal order, the survey experiment's "treatment" section tests whether different informational cues change respondents' willingness to support policies directly related to the liberal rules-based order. Specifically, our experiment presents respondents with three real-world scenarios designed to stimulate concerns about Japan's external environment, ranging from direct threats to national security to vaguer concerns about global insecurity and free trade. Consistent with the premise of this volume, these treatments focus on what many observers perceive to be declining U.S. commitment to security and/or economic dimensions of the order. They are based on real-world developments or specific statements made by political leaders (for example, U.S. president Donald Trump). Comparing the responses of those "treatment groups" to the "control group" allows us to measure the causal effect of the associated cues. Simply put, our approach is designed to measure each scenario's relative impact on the Japanese public's preferences concerning Japan adopting a more (or less) active role in global affairs, which, in turn, helps us draw broader conclusions about Japanese citizens' support for measures aimed at sustaining and championing the liberal international order.

Survey Design

Our survey experiment was conducted across Japan from September 3 to September 6, 2018, with 3,380 respondents sampled nationally by NTTCom Online Market Solutions.[1] The survey was divided into three blocks. Block 1 (pretreatment) posed questions relating to general attitudes about foreign countries, the Japanese government and political parties, and the historical importance of the liberal international order.[2] Block 2 provided the experimental component, namely the information treatment, which is described in greater detail below. Block 3 (the posttreatment block) inquired about respondents' opinions concerning various liberal international order-relevant policy options that Japanese leaders may consider.

The most innovative component of this study is the "information treatment." Respondents were randomly assigned to four experimental groups, each of which was exposed to different information about the position of Japan and emerging threats to the liberal order.[3] In aggregate, these treatments, which were developed based on real-world rhetoric and events, were designed to measure the Japanese public's reaction when presented with the same sort of information that has in recent years caused many foreign policy elites to express concern about a "crisis" of liberal internationalism. After exposure to their randomly assigned treatment, all respondents answered common questions in block 3. Since treatment assignment was completely randomized, any differences in the answers given between groups can be understood as the causal effect of the information treatment.

The complete text of the information treatments is available at the end of this chapter. To summarize: The control group (C; n=811) was shown a short factual statement containing information about a few key features of Japan's status quo most relevant to this study. They were told that the U.S.-Japan security treaty was asymmetric, with the United States committed to defending Japan but Japan not offering a commensurate commitment to the security of the United States; that Japan's defense budget as a percentage of GDP was lower than that of other major U.S. treaty allies, such as South Korea and most major NATO members, as well as China's; that international trade accounted for a significant fraction of Japan's GDP, and that China was Japan's largest trading partner.[4]

The three "treatment" groups were shown the above "control" statement, followed by other additional information of the sort that has contributed to deepening concerns among foreign policy elites about the liberal order's sustainability. The basic goal was to see whether and how such information might cause respondents to become more or less supportive of Japan adopting a more proactive leadership role in foreign affairs. U.S. policies and rhetoric were a major component of the treatments. However, the U.S. president was never referred to by name, in order to keep the focus on specific trends, rhetoric, institutions, and policies rather than on any particular leader that might evoke stronger or weaker reactions for reasons unrelated to the liberal order itself. All information provided was factually accurate and focused on real-world developments between January 2017 and August 2018.

The first treatment group was given the "security treatment," which was designed to elevate concerns about U.S. security commitments to treaty allies. It noted that the U.S. president had effectively agreed to North Korean and Chinese requests to halt a bilateral military exercise with its South Korean ally, due to—in the president's words—its alleged high costs and "provocative" nature. In addition, it stated that Washington has been demanding more equitable burden-sharing from U.S. allies, noting that the U.S. president had recently referred to the U.S. security commitments as "unfair," even demanding that NATO members increase their defense budget targets from the current 2 to 4 percent of GDP. (By comparison, Japan has for decades spent less than 1 percent of GDP on defense.)

The second treatment group received the "economic treatment," also based on actual events but focused on highlighting concerns about U.S. commitments to free trade, its willingness to impose tariffs on allies to reduce the U.S. trade deficit, and its criticism of global organizations responsible for supporting free trade. Specifically, it noted the U.S. administration's unilateral withdrawal from the Trans-Pacific Partnership (TPP) of twelve nations, among which the United States and Japan had been far and away the largest economies, as well as threats from the U.S. president to impose tariffs on steel and aluminum and his criticism of the alleged unfairness of the WTO dispute settlement mechanism.

The third and final treatment group was exposed to *both* of the aforementioned prompts. We introduced this combined treatment with an expectation that it would exert the strongest influence on respondents' opinions, due to its focus on stimulating concerns about security *and* economic aspects of the liberal international order simultaneously.

Summary of Results

In this section, we turn to the results of our survey experiment, broken down by question category. Some care must be taken when analyzing responses to the survey. The "pretreatment" questions can be analyzed directly, that is, we can calculate average responses or categorical breakdowns, such as by gender or age, across the full 3,380-person sample. However, answers to the "posttreatment" questions must be analyzed separately by treatment group, since respondents in each respective group are answering the same questions after having been exposed to different informational cues.

Accordingly, we divide the analysis into three parts: a pretreatment section (A), which examines responses of all respondents before they were randomly assigned to one of four treatment groups; a posttreatment control-group-only section (B), in order to assess baseline attitudes about the posttreatment questions; a posttreatment experimental section (C), which examines the differential effects of the three treatments (T1 security only; T2 economics only; T3 security and economics combined). Because space constraints prevent a full assessment of responses to dozens of questions, we highlight only the results we judge to be most relevant to the core objective of this volume: assessing the likelihood that Japan's leaders will be able and willing to proactively champion the liberal international order.

ANALYSIS OF ALL RESPONSES TO PRETREATMENT QUESTIONS (N=3,380)

One of the most noteworthy recent shifts in Japan's approach to regional politics and security affairs is more active outreach to perceived "likeminded" countries beyond the United States, due in significant part to deepening threat perceptions vis-à-vis China and North Korea. Expanding security links with U.S. allies and partners across the Asia-Pacific and in Europe is a major feature of Japan's 2013 National Security Strategy (see chapter 1 by Adam Liff). The survey results are striking for the consistency with which Japanese survey respondents rate these security partners of the United States (and, increasingly, also of Japan) positively. Respondents expressed the strongest affinity toward the United States (51 favorable, 14 percent unfavorable), despite the unpopularity of President Donald Trump (13 percent favorable, 59 percent unfavorable). While affinity scores between leaders and their countries generally correlate, our finding is consistent with other surveys of Japanese and many other foreign publics revealing that the United States is far more popular (and trusted) than its current president.

Positive sentiment toward other long-standing democratic allies follows closely behind, with +40 percentage points net favorability (positive minus negative affinity) for Australia, +37 for United Kingdom, +36 toward Germany, and +32 toward France. India (+13) and the Philippines (+15) also fare relatively well, as does Vietnam (+20). Perhaps not coincidentally, these countries are widely seen in U.S. and Japanese foreign policy circles as key security partners in the region and their leaders have also publicly expressed concerns about China's military development and certain controversial policies, including in the South China Sea. The glaring exception among U.S. democratic allies is South Korea (–40). This low affinity probably reflects persistent political frictions between Seoul and Tokyo over the legacy of the colonial period and how contemporary political leaders in both countries approach it, as discussed in chapter 8 by Thomas Berger. It is also worth noting that Russia (–43), China (–57), and North Korea (–78)—three countries regularly identified in Japanese and U.S. foreign policy circles as threats to the liberal order—score quite poorly.

Other results suggest that respondents identify connections between the security and economic components of the liberal international order, with key constitutive elements generally viewed positively. In the security domain, the average respondent believes that free trade (+32 percentage points), the UN (+25), the liberal international order (+31), and U.S. leadership (+22) all contributed to post–Cold War peace and stability in the Asia-Pacific. The exception is nuclear deterrence, which is viewed negatively (–3). This is not particularly surprising, given widespread antinuclear sentiment in Japan—the only country to have ever suffered a nuclear attack. Respondents also generally identify the postwar system supporting international trade and free economic competition as having contributed positively to the spread of democracy around the world (+38), Japan's economy (+48), their daily life (+23), and international peace (+28).

That said, the pretreatment responses also reveal clear concerns about major issues relevant to the regional order's sustainability in the Asia-Pacific. In particular, respondents say that they worry regularly about the North Korean nuclear threat (70 percent of respondents) and economic inequality (63 percent). Though not a trend directly linkable to the liberal order itself, it is also worth noting that China's economic development also elicits concern (54 percent). Perhaps most significantly, only 12 percent of respondents stated they were not worried about U.S. "withdrawal from Asia," with 51 percent expressing concern.

ANALYSIS OF CONTROL GROUP RESPONSES TO POSTTREATMENT QUESTIONS (N=811)

After reading a brief, neutral factual statement describing Japan's current military and economic status within the liberal international order, the control group respondents shared their views on various issues relevant to the order affecting Japan.

As it concerns decades-old international institutions seen as core components of the liberal order (for example, UN, G7, World Bank, IMF, WTO, Asian Development Bank (ADB), Asia-Pacific Economic Cooperation (APEC), and NATO), it appears that the baseline ("untreated") feeling among the Japanese public is positive, with net favorability ranging between +24 and +31 percentage points. In contrast, international initiatives generally seen as China-led initiatives—the Asian Infrastructure and Investment Bank (AIIB; –2) and the Belt and Road Initiative (BRI; –24)—are viewed negatively.

Control group responses also demonstrate relatively strong support for two other ideational features of the liberal international order: that free economic competition and international trade have been good for Asia-Pacific peace and stability (+38 percentage points) and world peace (+32). Asked about the most appropriate means for dealing with trade frictions and threats of tariffs from countries violating WTO regulations and rules, the respondents show strong support for working in a manner consistent with existing liberal international principles. The most favored responses are pursuing free trade agreements with other countries (+50) and relying on WTO dispute mechanisms (+46). The least favored response is retaliatory tariffs (+16). Significantly, when asked whether Japan should play a role as a leader of the liberal trading system and actively promote TPP and other free trade agreements, the response is unambiguous, with net support of +57.

As for whether Japan should proactively address major global challenges, respondents openly support tackling climate change (+74 percentage points favor action over inaction), nuclear nonproliferation (+68), terrorism (+66), economic inequality (+58), and promoting democracy (+57). The one area (of the six offered) where respondents express greater ambivalence is whether Japan should accept refugees (–1).

In response to questions about Japan's security, China's military power (+74 percentage points) and activities in the South China Sea (+75) and East China Sea (including the Senkaku Islands; +75) were all identified as *more severe* threats than even North Korea's nuclear weapons and ballistic missiles (+69)—though all are clearly identified as major concerns. Fears of Chinese economic influence (+66), tightening relations between China and Russia (+61), and American withdrawal from multilateral trade agreements (+52) and international organizations (+56) were significant as well. It is also clear why many security experts highlight severe abandonment concerns: there is remarkable ambivalence among respondents about the credibility of U.S. commitments to come to Japan's aid in a military crisis affecting Japanese territory (+4 believe the U.S. commitment is more credible than not), other Asian countries (+3), or the peace and stability of the Asia-Pacific region more generally (+10).

As it applies to measures to strengthen deterrence, 36 percent of respondents expressed a view that Japan should pursue a more "equal alliance" by committing more fully to defending U.S. forces even if Japan itself is not threatened directly; 20 percent back the status quo. Support also appears strong (+41 percentage points) for Japan's policy of developing deeper SDF and coast guard ties with Southeast Asian countries involved in territorial disputes with China. There was net-positive support for deploying the SDF to participate in freedom of navigation operations in opposition to China's claims in the South China Sea (+22) and in UN-led counter-proliferation operations (+25).

Finally, we asked respondents about their views concerning whether Japan should revise the so-called peace clause (Article 9) of its constitution, which renounces the threat of force to settle international disputes and the development of war potential. Views are quite evenly matched: 35 percent of respondents are in favor of amendment, while 38 percent are opposed. Among the subset of respondents who are pro-amendment, the most popular rationale (65 percent) was the importance of stipulating the constitutionality of the Self-Defense Forces—basically identical to a proposal Abe put forward in 2017. By contrast, among the subset of respondents who oppose amendment, 67 percent stated it was because they were proud of the pacifist constitution (for further details, see chapter 9 by Kenneth Mori McElwain).

TREATMENT EFFECTS

Given these baseline attitudes among the control group, how do respondents' positions change when they are exposed to new informational cues designed to prompt concerns about America's weakening commitment to the liberal international order? Under such circumstances, does the Japanese public believe it is important for Japan to provide more proactive leadership in efforts to sustain and strengthen the liberal order?

To answer these questions in the context of the larger project, we randomly sorted our full sample of 3,380 respondents into one control group (discussed above) and three treatment groups.[5] Each treatment group was presented with different informational cues that raise doubts about America's commitment to the security and economic dimensions of the liberal order. All groups were then asked the same "posttreatment" questions to gauge their beliefs about the appropriate policy response. This framework allows us to compare each treatment scenario's impact on public preferences to participate in or withdraw from global affairs.[6]

Space constraints prevent a full discussion of every post-treatment question, so below we focus on results which we found to be particularly noteworthy/counterintuitive, in relation to Japan's ability and willingness to contribute to sustaining the liberal international order. Our first finding is that inducing concerns about the liberal international order makes respondents less trustful of international, multilateral institutions. For example, respondents generally have a fairly neutral view of international institutions, with the UN, G7, WTO, and NATO receiving positive ratings from 44 percent to 62 percent of respondents. However, when presented with the combined treatment—that is, cues to prime both security and economic threats to the liberal international order (T3)—support fell significantly for the UN (–5 percentage points), the G7 (–5), and the IMF (–4), as well as for the ADB (–5).

That said, this negative turn does not necessarily produce a desire to go it alone, at least in the economic sphere (T2). When asked how Japan should respond to a country that violates WTO rules, the treatment does not reveal any statistically significant effects on preferences about enacting retaliatory tariffs, and support for negotiating a bilateral free trade agreement with a third country declines (–5 percentage points). Instead, we observe an increase in support for forging stronger diplomatic relations with Japan's partners in South and Southeast Asia. Exposure to the security treatment (T1) increases the probability of backing improved ties with Australia (+4), the Philippines (+5), and Singapore (+4), while economic threats (T3) do so for India (+5).

On the security front more generally, however, we observe some significant effects of the treatments as it concerns attitudes about Japan's security vulnerabilities and desirable policy responses. On the one hand, the combined military and economic treatment (T3) increases the perception that the liberal international order has been critical to Asian peace and stability after the Cold War (+6). On the other hand, the treatment increases threat perceptions vis-à-vis the economic rise of China (+4), although there is no notable difference in concerns about North Korea's nuclear and ballistic missile capabilities or declining U.S. commitment to the liberal international order.

Uncertainty about the future of the liberal order also increased enthusiasm for deepening Japan's defense cooperation with existing partners. The economic threat treatment causes a +5 percentage point increase in support for Japan changing its defense policy to lean closer to the United States rather than China. Treatments also produced stronger support for improving cooperation with other American allies (+6; T2); with Southeast Asian countries involved in territorial issues with China in the South China Sea (+5; T3); and participation in Freedom of Navigation Operations–type (FONOPS) exercises to counter China's controversial claims in the South China Sea (+6; T3). Support for international cooperation is even stronger when the potential partner is a democracy (+7; T3).

Exposure to different threats to the liberal international order also increased net support for amending Article 9 by +12 (T1) and +9 (T2) percentage points, a remarkable shift given that most contemporary surveys show a public that is evenly divided on its merits (see chapter 9 by Kenneth Mori McElwain).

Overall, the combined security + economic threat treatment (T3) had a stronger effect on preferences than the pure security (T1) or economic (T2) threat. This is consistent with the simple expectation that anxiety or worry in *more* policy domains should stimulate greater changes in people's preferences. However, it is equally important to note which attitudes were not affected by the information treatments. This lack of a statistically significant effect suggests relatively stable beliefs. For example, the treatments had no statistically significant effect on respondents' views about defense spending, whether Japan should pursue a "more equal" alliance with the United States, the credibility of U.S. security commitments to Japan or the wider region, or the advisability of new policies to enhance Japan's defense posture and deterrence against external threats.

Our summary of the qualitative significance of these effects is as follows. When respondents are concerned about the U.S. commitment to the liberal international order, they tend to evaluate international institutions more negatively, be more worried about North Korean military threats, and decrease affinity toward China. They are more likely to support bilateral or multilateral military exercises with other countries, particularly when those countries are democracies. In other words, perceived declining U.S. commitment to the liberal international order does not seem to make Japanese people turn more toward existing multilateral institutions. Rather, it appears they wish for Japan to seek greater autonomy and, on specific topics of concern, conditional partnerships with other democracies.

Caveats

While our survey experiment sheds light on Japanese preferences concerning the liberal international order, there are some important caveats we should also highlight. First, because this survey experiment has only been conducted once (in September 2018), we do not have a baseline against which to compare our conclusions. As a result, we cannot ascertain changes in attitudes over time, such as the effect of the Trump administration on Japanese views, relative to the Obama administration. As several chapters in this volume point out, foreign policy experts' concerns about "international order" significantly predate January 2017.

Second, we did not require respondents to confront the inevitable tradeoffs and make the kinds of "tough" choices that a (responsible) political leader would factor into decisions about foreign policy. For example, though it was remarkable that so many respondents supported increasing Japan's defense spending by 50 percent—an amount equivalent to ~2.5 trillion yen (US$22.5 billion) per year—or more, they answered this question without any prompting to consider the opportunity costs for Japan's public deficit or other policy priorities. These are, obviously, factors that political leaders—and especially the Ministry of Finance—regularly take into account, and which almost inevitably will present practical headwinds to funding a more ambitious international role.

Conclusions

Taken in aggregate, the results of our survey experiment of over three thousand Japanese respondents in September 2018 suggest that Japanese citizens seem to believe the liberal international order has been crucial to postwar national prosperity and peace and stability in the Asia-Pacific region. There also appears to be strong support for Japan continuing to tie its future to the advanced democracies of the world, as well as adopting a relatively more proactive posture in international trade and security affairs. Survey respondents generally agree with the idea that Japan has benefited significantly from free trade and should champion it *regardless of what the United States does*. In the security domain, there is robust support for Japan bolstering ties with the United States and other countries in the region to balance China and deter North Korea—both overwhelmingly seen as threats to Japan's security—as it invests more in its own defense capabilities, such as increased defense spending. In both cases, these goals appear congruent with U.S. policies.

In addition, the results strongly suggest openness to Japan adopting a relatively more proactive leadership role in regional economic and security affairs, as well as contributing to solving global problems such as climate change, global economic inequality, and international terrorism. This helps explain why over the past seven years the Abe administration's ambitious, forward-leaning posture in regional and global economic and security issues—from championing CPTPP to deepening security ties with various U.S. allies and partners—has not resulted in a major popular backlash in terms of cabinet support rates or at the polls—at least so far. It also comports with the idea that, unlike some other democracies, Japan's domestic politics do not appear to be shifting in the direction of a sharply more narrow, inward-looking populism.

This survey experiment was designed to establish an empirical baseline and replicable framework for future studies—both of Japan and other countries. For example, Japanese citizens' concerns about threats to the liberal international order may vary in response to the vicissitudes of Sino-Japanese or U.S.-Japan relations, especially changes in government leadership or foreign policy strategy. Our results can serve as a reference point against which future Japanese survey experiments can be measured, allowing for a deeper understanding of Japanese beliefs about the importance of the postwar liberal order, as well as how these change over time in response to new external (or domestic) circumstances. Relatedly, our approach may also be of interest to scholars exploring similar questions with regard to other major democratic powers, such as Australia, the United Kingdom, France, and Germany—countries that have also been called upon to adopt (and, in some cases, whose own leaders have themselves called for adopting) a more proactive role in sustaining the liberal international order. With some changes in the text of the information treatments and in the wording of policy responses to adapt to the circumstances of the specific country, this study's framework can yield new cross-national insights about how publics view the costs and benefits of the liberal international order in other countries. This, in turn, can help policymakers and scholars better assess the feasibility of other advanced democracies playing a more proactive role championing the liberal order in an era of more questionable U.S. leadership and gauge where their publics stand on related issues.

Information Treatment (*translation of original Japanese-language survey)

Information
[treated groups]

Instruction: Please read the following passage about Japan and international society.
(Fix the screen for 30 seconds)

CONTROL

[all respondents]

Japan has a defense alliance only with the United States, but the United States also has alliances with South Korea and NATO (the North Atlantic Treaty Organization). Moreover, the United States promises to defend Japan, yet Japan makes no promise to intervene in response to the use of military force against the United States.

Japan's defense budget is 0.9 percent to 1 percent of its GDP, but the corresponding figure is 3 percent to 5 percent for the United States and 2.6 percent for South Korea. The average defense budget of the 29 members of NATO is currently 1 percent to 2 percent (of GDP), but all of them have promised to increase it to 2 percent by 2024. China's defense spending is over three times the amount of Japan's, and it has increased over the past 20 years at an average annual rate of over 10 percent.

Furthermore, it is said that the U.S.-led liberal (literally, free and open) international trading system has been indispensable to Japan's postwar recovery and economic development, and the total value of Japan's trade accounts for 30 percent to 40 percent of its GDP. Until recently, the United States was Japan's largest trading partner, but China has held that position since 2007.

SECURITY TREATMENT [treatment groups 1 and 3]	Recently, it has been said that the United States is in the process of withdrawing its engagement in and commitment to peace and order in East Asia. In June 2018, the United States announced the suspension of U.S.–South Korean bilateral military exercises in exchange for North Korea stopping its missile tests—a proposal suggested by North Korea and China. At the time of the announcement, the U.S. president claimed that U.S.–South Korean bilateral military exercises were "expensive" and "provocative." Moreover, the U.S. president has criticized U.S. allies for taking advantage of the United States, insisting that the American people are demanding more equal burden-sharing. For example, the U.S. president has claimed that the U.S. military burden in NATO is "unfair" and has pressed NATO members to raise their defense budgets to 4 percent of their GDP, up from the 2 percent target mutually agreed upon in 2014.
ECONOMIC TREATMENT [treatment groups 2 and 3]	Recently, it has been said that the United States is in the process of withdrawing its economic participation in and commitment to East Asia. In January 2017, the United States withdrew from the Trans-Pacific Partnership (TPP), the largest free trade agreement in history signed by 12 Asia-Pacific countries (representing 40 percent of global GDP). Moreover, along with criticizing trading partners for taking advantage of it, the United States has also demanded that they reduce trade deficits. For example, the U.S. president has claimed that tariffs imposed on American products are "ridiculous and unacceptable," and notified EU members that the United States would raise tariffs on steel and aluminum imports. Additionally, the U.S. president has criticized the dispute settlement process of the World Trade Organization (WTO) as unfair toward the United States.

NOTES

1. Respondents were sampled nationally by gender, age (deciles, restricted to 20–79), and geography (8 regions) to match census distributions. Respondents who answered too quickly or gave identical responses to all questions were excluded and resampled. The survey instrument was approved by the Research Ethics Committee of the Institute of Social Science, University of Tokyo.

2. Prior to the main survey, respondents were first asked questions about their demographic profile, for sampling purposes. The question ordering was randomized within section 1, but not for section 3, the latter in order to preserve thematic consistency and reduce the cognitive burden for respondents.

3. The treatment page was frozen for thirty seconds to better ensure that respondents read the provided information carefully.

4. It should be noted that there is no "null" category, wherein respondents are shown no information about the liberal international order. This was a conscious design choice by the authors to ensure that all respondents had a minimal baseline knowledge of the liberal international order, so that their responses would reflect how they might respond to real events that may emerge in the future.

5. C: N=811; T1 (security): N=843; T2 (economy): N=869; T3 (security + economy): N=856. In the regression analyses, we exclude don't know / no answer (DKNA) responses.

6. We use a regression framework to estimate the causal effect of treatment assignment to one of the four groups on responses to the posttreatment questions. More specifically, we use a logistic regression with robust standard errors. Responses to the posttreatment questions were rescaled to a binary measure, where 1 = scores larger than the middle option and 0 = middle scores or smaller. Recall that the treatments are designed to induce concerns about American commitment to the security (T1), economic (T2), and security + economic (T3) dimensions of the liberal international order. The coefficients for the treatment groups, which we discuss below, denote the *average treatment effect* (ATE), or the causal effect of being exposed to each information treatment relative to the control group. We have rerun the regressions using ordinary least squares (OLS), but differences in results were minimal in terms of substantive or statistical significance. Control variables in our regression include: party identification (strong or weak identifiers); gender; marriage status; age (deciles); income (deciles); educational attainment (more than high school or not); occupation; region of residence (8-part) and its urban-rural score (3-part).

Contributors

NOBUMASA AKIYAMA is professor at the Graduate School of Law and School of International and Public Policy in Hitotsubashi University. He specializes in nonproliferation, Japan's national security, and nuclear energy, publishing extensively and presenting papers on these topics at various conferences. He is an adjunct research fellow at the Japan Institute of International Affairs. He is a member of various governmental consultative groups and study groups at the ministries of foreign affairs and defense, the Japan Atomic Energy Commission, and the Nuclear Regulatory Commission of Japan and adviser to the Japanese delegation to the Nonproliferation Treaty Review Conferences. He also was a leader of the working group for the Independent Commission on the Investigation of the Fukushima Nuclear Accident.

THOMAS BERGER is director of the Center for the Study of Asia and professor of international relations at Pardee School of Global Studies at Boston University. He specializes in German and Japanese politics, international relations, comparative government in East Asia, and political culture. He joined Boston University in 2001, after having taught for seven years at the Johns Hopkins University. In 2018, he was appointed director of the Center for the Study of Asia (BUCSA). He is the author of *War, Guilt and World Politics After World War II* (Cambridge University Press, 2012), *Cultures of Antimilitarism: National Security in Germany and Japan* (Johns

Hopkins University Press, 1988), and is coeditor of *Japan in International Politics: The Foreign Policies of an Adaptive State* (Lynne Rienner, 2007). His articles and essays have appeared in numerous edited volumes and journals, including *International Security*, *Review of International Studies*, *German Politics*, and *World Affairs Quarterly*.

YOICHI FUNABASHI is cofounder and chairman of Tokyo-based think tank Asia Pacific Initiative (formerly Rebuild Japan Initiative Foundation) and the former editor-in-chief of the *Asahi Shimbun* (2007–10). He is an award-winning Japanese journalist, columnist, and author. He has written extensively on foreign affairs, the U.S.-Japan Alliance, geopolitics and geoeconomics in Northeast Asia, and historical issues in the Asia-Pacific. He served as correspondent for the *Asahi* in Beijing (1980–81) and Washington, D.C. (1984–87), and as American general bureau chief (1993–97). His books in English include *Meltdown* (Brookings, forthcoming), *The Peninsula Question* (Brookings, 2007), *Reconciliation in the Asia-Pacific*, ed. (USIP, 2003), *Alliance Adrift* (Council on Foreign Relations Press, 1998), and *Managing the Dollar: From the Plaza to the Louvre* (Peterson Institute for International Economics, 1988), among others.

KAORI HAYASHI is professor of media and journalism studies in the Graduate School of Interdisciplinary Studies at the University of Tokyo. She is an expert in mass media, journalism studies, and comparative media studies. She worked as an economic correspondent at Reuters Japan from 1988 to 1991. After completing her PhD at the University of Tokyo in 2001, she was a postdoctoral researcher in the Sociology Department at the University of Bamberg. She is a member of the Broadcasting Ethics and Program Improvement Organization, guest researcher at the *Asahi Shimbun*, and board member of the German Institute for Japanese Studies and Japan Society for Mass Communication and Journalism Studies. For the list of her publications, please see www.hayashik.iii.u-tokyo.ac.jp/.

KEN VICTOR LEONARD HIJINO is associate professor of law at Kyoto University. He specializes in party politics and local democracy in Japan. After graduating from Wesleyan University, he worked as a journalist at the *Financial Times* Tokyo bureau. He earned his PhD at the Cambridge University Faculty of Oriental Studies. He was an associate professor in Keiō University's Graduate School of System Design and Management until taking up his present post in 2014. His most recent work is *Local Politics and National Policy: Multilevel Policy Conflicts in Japan and Beyond* (Routledge, 2017).

MAIKO ICHIHARA is associate professor at the Graduate School of Law and School of International and Public Policy in Hitotsubashi University, and a visiting scholar at the Center on Democracy, Development and the Rule of Law at Stanford University. She also serves on the steering committees of the World Movement for Democracy, East Asia Democracy Forum, and Partnership for Democratic Governance (Japan), and is a co-chair of Democracy for the Future project at the Japan Center for International Exchange. She focuses on international relations, Japanese foreign policy, and democracy support. She earned her PhD in political science from the George Washington University. Her recent publications include *Japan's International Democracy Assistance as Soft Power: Neoclassical Realist Analysis* (Routledge, 2018).

G. JOHN IKENBERRY is the Albert G. Milbank Professor of Politics and International Affairs in the Department of Politics and Woodrow Wilson School of Public and International Affairs at Princeton University. He is one of the world's foremost experts on the liberal international order. He is the author of seven books, including *Liberal Leviathan: The Origins, Crisis, and Transformation of the American System* (Princeton, 2011). His book *After Victory: Institutions, Strategic Restraint, and the Rebuilding of Order after Major Wars* (Princeton, 2001) won the 2002 Schroeder-Jervis Award presented by the American Political Science Association for the best book in international history and politics. Ikenberry has also been the editor or coeditor of fourteen books and has authored 130 journal articles, essays, and book chapters.

ADAM P. LIFF is assistant professor of East Asian International Relations at the Hamilton Lugar School of Global and International Studies (HLS) at Indiana University, where he also serves as founding director of its 21st Century Japan Politics & Society Initiative. His research focuses on international security and the Asia-Pacific, with particular emphasis on the foreign relations of Japan and China; U.S. Asia-Pacific strategy; the U.S.-Japan alliance; and the rise of China and its regional and global impact. He is also a Non-resident Senior Fellow at the Brookings Institution and associate-in-research at Harvard University's Reischauer Institute of Japanese Studies and Fairbank Center for Chinese Studies. Liff holds a PhD and an MA in Politics from Princeton University and a BA from Stanford University.

PHILLIP Y. LIPSCY is associate professor of political science, Chair in Japanese Politics & Global Affairs, and director of the Centre for the Study of Global Japan at the University of Toronto. His fields of research include international and comparative political economy, international organizations, and the politics of East Asia, particularly Japan. Lipscy's book *Renegotiating the World Order: Institutional Change in International Relations* (Cambridge University Press, 2017) examines the ways countries seek greater international influence by reforming or creating international organizations. His research is published in outlets such as the *American Journal of Political Science, International Organization, Annual Review of Political Science, Journal of East Asian Studies, Japanese Journal of Political Science*, and *Foreign Affairs*.

KENNETH MORI MCELWAIN is associate professor of political science at the Institute of Social Science at the University of Tokyo. He specializes in constitutional design, political institutions and parties, and public opinion. Born in Ireland but raised in Japan, he graduated from Princeton University before earning his PhD in political science at Stanford. He was a postdoctoral fellow at Harvard University's Weatherhead Center for International Affairs and an assistant professor at the University of Michigan before taking his present post in 2015. He has edited and contributed to numerous books on Japanese politics.

AKIHISA SHIOZAKI is an attorney and partner at Nagashima Ohno and Tsunematsu. He worked in the prime minister's office as a senior policy adviser from 2006 to 2007. He served as a core working group member in the Independent Investigation Commission on the Fukushima Nuclear Accident. He graduated from the University of Tokyo in 1999, earned an

MA in international policy studies from Stanford University in 2000, and holds an MBA from the Wharton School of the University of Pennsylvania. He was named Asia Legal Awards' Compliance/Investigations Lawyer of the Year 2017. He has contributed chapters to the books *Japan's Worst-Case Scenario—Nine Blind Spots* (CLSA, 2014) and *The Democratic Party of Japan in Power* (Routledge, 2016).

MIREYA SOLÍS is co-director and senior fellow of the Center for East Asia Policy Studies and the Philip Knight Chair in Japan Studies at the Brookings Institution. She is an expert in Japan's foreign economic policies, domestic politics, and East Asian multilateralism. Her main research interests include Japanese politics, political economy, and foreign policy; international and comparative political economy; international relations; and government-business relations. Solís earned a PhD in government (1998) and an MA in East Asian studies (1991) from Harvard University, and a BA in international relations from El Colegio de México (1989). Previously, Solís was an assistant professor (2003–08) and a tenured associate professor (2008–14) at American University's School of International Service, an assistant professor in the Department of Politics at Brandeis University (1999–03), an adviser to Mexico's Ministry of Economy on the Japan-Mexico FTA (1999), and a visiting professor at El Colegio de México's Center for International Relations (1997–99). She joined the Center for East Asia Policy Studies at Brookings Institution in 2012. Her most recent publication is *Dilemmas of a Trading Nation* (Brookings, 2017), which was awarded the 2018 Masayoshi Ohira Memorial Prize.

Index

Note: Page numbers followed by "f" indicate figures or tables.

Aarlberg, Toril, 353
Abe, Shintaro, 122–123
Abe, Shinzo: on *Asahi*'s coverage of comfort women, 347; COJ amendment priorities of, 309, 310, 369; on FOIP and Japan-China relations, 152; on immigration, 228; and Kagoike, 331; length of term, 203–204; and nationalism, 21–22, 260, 288; on regional security cooperation, 63; relationship with Trump, 124. *See also* Abe administration
Abe administration: Abenomics (economic policy), 22, 228, 257, 261; Article 9 interpretations, 308; CDP opinions on, 311; and climate change, 126–127; and COJ, 19, 64–65, 314; foreign policy of, 16–19, 308; and historical issues, 287; and immigration, 228–231; and liberal international order, 204, 260; moderation of, 238; and populism, 20–22; shift to the Right, 239–240; and TPP free trade agreement, 99, 204; and U.S., 289; and values diplomacy, 146; and welfare system, 217–218. *See also* Liberal Democratic Party (LDP)
Abema TV, 349
age demographics, 23; elderly population, 14, 211, 216–217, 218, 228; and generational inequality, 14, 24, 216–219; and news media preferences, 343–344f, 345; and survey experiment responses, 365; and voter turnout, 333
agricultural sector, 90, 94, 98, 99, 100
Akashi, Yasushi, 113
Allison, Graham, 172
Amari, Akira, 17, 99
Anti-Ballistic Missile (ABM) Treaty, 167, 172
antinuclearism. *See* nuclear disarmament
apologies. *See* historical justice
Arab Spring (2011), 150, 157
Arc of Freedom and Prosperity, 145, 152
Argentina, public opinion on immigration in, 220f, 221f, 222f
Article 9 (COJ): and Japan's role in Asia-Pacific security order, 59; pacifist spirit of, 303; restricts international

383

Article 9 (COJ) (*cont.*)
engagement, 303, 304; revision of, 19, 64–65; self-defense interpretations, 62, 308, 309, 320, 321

Article 9 (COJ), opinions on amending: of CDP, 311; of constitutional experts, 309, 317, 320; of elected officials, 311–313, 321; on formal recognition of SDF, 19, 316, 317–320, 321; of LDP, 310–311, 321; of public, 19, 305, 309, 313, 315, 317–320, 321; rationale, 318–320, 321; to reflect status quo, 321; survey experiment questions, 315, 317–320; U.S. military commitment to Asia-Pacific region affects, 305, 318–320, 321

Asada, Hitoshi, 247

Asahi Shimbun (newspaper): coverage of comfort women, 348f; and Murdoch attempt to buy out TV Asahi, 339; poll on support for Murayama and Koizumi statements, 260; "populism" term used in, 240–241f; *Sankei* criticizes, 346–347; survey of constitutional scholars on Article 9, 309; UTokyo-Asahi Survey, 311–312; *Yomiuri* rivalry, 337, 342

ASEAN (Association of Southeast Asia Nations), 8, 14–15, 16

ASEAN Defense Ministers Meeting-Plus, 45, 70

ASEAN Regional Forum, 45, 52, 70

Asia-Africa Growth Corridor, 97

Asian Development Bank (ADB), 114, 115, 367, 369

Asian financial crisis (1997), 25, 111, 140–141

Asian Infrastructure Investment Bank (AIIB), 80, 85, 114, 367

Asian Monetary Fund, 115

Asian Women's Fund, 274, 287

Asia-Pacific Economic Cooperation (APEC), 6, 114, 115, 367

Aso, Taro, 145

asylum seekers. *See* refugee policy

"atoms for alliance" incentive program, 171, 176–178

Australia, 6; and nuclear nonproliferation regime, 195; public interest in news coverage, 334f; public opinion on immigration in, 220f, 221f, 222f; and regional infrastructure cooperation, 97; security cooperation with, 63–64, 67, 145, 146; survey experiment responses about, 365, 370

Austria, 276f, 335f

Bangladesh, 150

Belgium: and historical justice, 274, 275, 276f; public opinion on immigration in, 220f, 221f, 222f

Belt and Road Initiative (BRI), 8; and China-Japan diplomatic relations, 17, 152; concerns about, 80, 85; favorability ratings for, 114, 367; FOIP as alternative to, 18; Japan's response to, 97; and liberal international order, 143; used for coercion, 7

Benson, Rodney, 352

Blaker, Michael, 155

Bolton, John, 3

Brazil, public opinion on immigration in, 220f, 221f, 222f

Brexit decision (2016): and economic inequality, 206; and education levels, 208; and immigration, 207; and liberal trading order, 80; and polarization, 325; and "post-truth" populism, 331

Brzezinski, Zbigniew, 4

Bush, Laura, 123

Bush administration, 50, 123, 142

Cabinet Legislation Bureau (Japan), 308

Calder, Kent, 137, 155, 256

Cambodia, 156, 308

Campbell, Kurt, 85

Canada: foreigners residing in, 223f; public interest in news coverage, 334f; public opinion on immigration in, 220f, 221f, 222f

Carter administration, 191
Chen Yun, 284
Chiang Mai Initiative Multilateralization (CMIM), 115
China: assistance/spread of governance model, 159–160; as beneficiary of liberal international order, 1; and democratization, 138; and economic order, 7; and FOIP, 151–152; gray zone operations, 48, 50–52, 66–67, 70; and great power diplomacy, 143; and historical justice, 272, 282, 283–284, 288, 291, 294; income disparity in, 213f; and international organizations, 110, 117, 143; Japan's diplomatic relations with, 17, 138, 142, 286; liberalization in, 283–284; and liberal trading order, 8, 80, 83–87, 91, 95–97, 98–99, 100; loans from, 144; military buildup of, 6, 47–48; nationalism in, 284; and North Korea, 181–182; and nuclear nonproliferation regime, 167–168, 174, 179, 181–182, 186, 188, 189; PCA ruling (2016), 52–53, 56, 57; "Peaceful Rise" era, 49–50; policies on regional issues, 7; and postwar Asia-Pacific security order, 40, 45, 46, 47–54, 61; public opinion on/Sinophobia in Japan, 259; and regional infrastructure cooperation, 97; relations with, 98–99, 152–153; and security cooperation, 147; and shifting global balance of power, 6–8; in survey experiment, 363, 364, 365, 366, 368, 370, 374; and technology, 8, 11–12, 84, 133; threat to liberal international order, 7; and values diplomacy, 143–144, 145–146. *See also* Belt and Road Initiative (BRI); Senkaku/Diaoyu Islands
China Coast Guard (CCG), 50–52, 66, 70
China Foreign Ministry, 52, 286
Chinese Communist Party, 86, 284
climate change, 117, 125, 126–127, 367

Clinton, Hillary, 55, 205, 290
COJ. *See* Constitution of Japan (COJ)
Colombia, 334
colonial oppression: apologies for, 260, 274, 276f–279f, 284, 289, 292; compensation for, 274–275, 276f–279f, 282
"comfort women" of WWII: compensation for, 274, 290; news coverage, 346–348f; and South Korean nonprofits, 297; and South Korean political discourse, 283, 287, 291, 295–296
Committee on Foreign Investment in the United States (CFIUS), 96
Comparative Constitutions Project, 306
compensation: for colonial oppression, 274–275, 276f–279f, 282; for comfort women, 274, 290; for forced laborers, 291
Comprehensive Progressive Trans-Pacific Partnership (CPTPP, also known as TPP-11), 16, 71, 93, 153, 204, 360
conservative-liberal divide: and historical issues, 281, 293; and Japanese media, 345–347, 349
Constitutional Democratic Party (CDP), 311, 316, 317
constitutional experts, 309, 317, 320, 328–329
Constitution of Japan (COJ), 303–321; amendment procedure, 306, 309, 310; Article 21, 328, 330; Article 81, 308; Article 96, 310; Article 98, 306; criticism of, 304; drafters of, 303, 305, 306, 330; flexibility of, 304, 320; and freedom of speech, 328–329, 340, 341; historical context of creation, 303–304, 309; human rights pillar, 303, 304, 305–306, 309; legal rulings on, 304, 308; length of, 304, 305; Meiji Constitution proceeds, 306, 307, 310; militarism and, 303, 305, 307–308, 314, 319; pacifism pillar, 303, 309, 314, 319; popular

Constitution of Japan (COJ) (*cont.*) sovereignty pillar, 309; structure of, 304, 310; vagueness on international engagement, 303–304, 306–309, 310, 320. *See also* Article 9 (COJ)

Constitution of Japan (COJ), opinions on amending, 19, 28, 304–305; Article 21, 330; of CDP, 311, 316, 317; on education rights, 316, 317; on environmental rights, 310, 311, 312, 316, 317, 321; on House of Representatives dissolution conditions, 316, 317; issue prioritization, disagreements on, 310–311, 312, 316–317, 321; of LDP and elites, 260, 304, 309–313, 313–314, 316–317, 321, 330; opposition to, 311, 314, 315, 316, 318–319f; privacy rights, 304, 316, 317, 321; put on hold by Abe administration, 260; rationale, 314, 315–320, 321; state of emergency provisions, 311, 312, 316, 317; support for, 305, 312f, 313–314f, 315–317, 318–319f, 321; survey experiment questions, 315–320, 321, 368–369, 370. *See also* Article 9 (COJ), opinions on amending; public opinion on amending COJ

constitutions: "do no harm" principles, 320; Germany, 310; international comparisons, 307f, 310; militarism in, 306, 307–308; newer *vs.* older, 305. *See also* Constitution of Japan (COJ)

corporate media, as public utility, 337–339. *See also* media, Japanese

CPTPP. *See* Comprehensive Progressive Trans-Pacific Partnership (CPTPP, also known as TPP-11)

"Creating Conditions for Nuclear Disarmament (CCND)" (working paper), 183

Crimea, Russia's annexation of, 56, 110

CyberAgent, 349

cybersecurity, 67, 127

Cybersecurity Law (2017) (China), 84

cyberspace, surveillance in, 8, 144

Czech Republic, 276f, 335f

Daily Mail, 207
debt, public, 14, 23
debt diplomacy, 144
decentralization initiatives, 311, 320
defense budgets, 6, 66; China's, 47; in survey experiment, 68, 363, 364, 372, 374, 375
defense forces. *See* Self-Defense Forces (SDF)
defense technology cooperation, 64, 146
deindustrialization, 87–88
democracy: China's interpretation of, 143–144; defined, 329; and values diplomacy, 136, 138–139, 148, 150–151, 157
democracy, Japanese, 264–265; health of, 237–238; postwar democracy (*sengo minshushugi*), 330; voters' engagement with, 262–263
Democratic Party of Japan (DPJ): vs Abe's pragmatic nationalism, 22; and foreign residents, 227–228; LDP compared with, 261, 311; and Senkaku/Diaoyu islands, 287
democratization, 148, 150–151, 157
demographics: as challenge to liberal international order, 12–14; forgotten demographic, 23–24; and income inequality, 211, 212f, 216–218; shift in, 228, 230; and welfare budget, 216. *See also* age demographics
Denmark, 276f
Deudney, Daniel, 172
Development Cooperation Charter (2015), 147
Dewey, John, 329–330
Diaoyu Islands. *See* Senkaku/Diaoyu Islands
Diet: and anti-hate speech laws, 258; and COJ amendments, 19, 309, 310; and electoral system changes, 320; NHK budget approval by, 338
digital economy agreement, 94
digital Leninism, 8, 144

digital trade and technology, 16–17
diplomacy: China-Japan diplomatic relations, 17, 138, 142, 286; as a member in Asia, 136–137. *See also* foreign policy; U.S.-Japan alliance; values diplomacy
disaster relief and disaster risk reduction, 158
Dokdo/Takeshima islands, 286, 287, 295
domestic politics, 19–25; as constraint on Japan's leadership in regional security order, 67–68; and liberal trading order, 97–100; and populism, 19–22. *See also* Japanese triad; politics, in Japan; populism, Japanese; welfare state
Dorling, Danny, 206
Dulles, John Foster, 44

East Asian Economic Caucus (EAEC), 6
East China Sea. *See* South and East China Seas
economic inequality, 212f, 213f; and elderly population, 14, 211, 216–217, 218; increase in, 210–211, 231; and populism, 205–206, 209, 260–262; and redistribution, 210f, 231; and values diplomacy, 158; and welfare state, 209–213
economic order, 2, 57–58. *See also* liberal trading order
economic partnership agreements (EPAs): with EU, 16, 153; with Indonesia, 227; with Mexico, 244; with Singapore, 244
economic policy, survey experiment questions on, 360, 362, 364, 365–371, 372, 375
economic sanctions, 139
education, 207–208, 316, 317
elderly population: economic inclusivity for, 13, 228; and income inequality, 14, 211, 216–217, 218; increase in, 228; and welfare budget, 216
elections, 311–312; of LDP, 336; and party affiliations, 336; of Trump, 325, 331; and voter turnouts, 333f–334, 336. *See also* politics, in Japan
electoral system changes, 320
elites: and COJ, 304, 309–313, 321; and freedom of speech, 331; and international organizations, 111, 114; and nationalism, 257; perception of, 24–25, 210; and populism, 20, 209, 243, 250. *See also* economic inequality
Environmental Democracy Index, 158
environmental protection: and COJ, 310, 311, 312f, 316, 317, 321; and values diplomacy, 158
Estonia, 276f
European Union (EU): and international organizations, 111, 117; populism's effects on liberal trading order in, 80–81; Strategic Partnership Agreement with, 16, 153, 155; trade deals with, 16, 92, 153; trilateral cooperation with, 95, 96; and WTO reform, 96. *See also* Brexit decision
expert opinions, and COJ, 309, 317, 320

Fairness Doctrine (United States), 348
fake news, 143, 325, 327. *See also* Western triad (polarization, populism, and distrust in media)
Fifth Strategic Energy Plan, 193
financial crisis of 2008, 25
financial instability: international system's inability to deal with, 126
Finland, and historical justice, 276f
floating voters. *See* unaffiliated voters
foreign aid, 144, 147–151. *See also* Official Development Assistance (ODA)
foreign investment, constitutions on, 306, 307f
Foreign Investment Risk Review Modernization Act (2018) (United States), 96
foreign policy, 14–19; of Abe administration, 16–19, 308; change in approach to, 116; international organizations in, 113; and Japan as "rule-shaper," 14–15. *See also* Article 9 (COJ); liberal

foreign policy (*cont.*)
    trading order; postwar Asia-Pacific security order; values diplomacy
foreign workers, 23; exclusion of, 224–228; increase in, 228–231
Forum on China-Africa Cooperation, 159
France: defense technology cooperation with, 64, 146; employment rates in, 225; foreigners residing in, 223f; and historical justice, 274, 275, 277f; income disparity in, 213f; and nuclear nonproliferation regime, 174, 179; plutonium stockpile in, 193; populism in, 205, 208; public interest in news coverage, 335f; public opinion on immigration in, 220f, 221f, 222f; survey experiment responses about, 366
Frankel, Benjamin, 175
Free and Open Indo-Pacific (FOIP) strategy, 18, 71, 97; Japan's influence on Trump administration's adoption of, 124; Japan's promotion of, 63; and relations with China, 151–152; and values diplomacy, 151–152, 157
freedom of speech, 328–329, 330–331, 332, 340–341
free trade. *See* trade liberalization; Trans-Pacific Partnership (TPP)
Fuji TV (television station), 339
Fukagawa, Yukiko, 98–99
Fukushima nuclear disaster (2011), 169, 185, 331
Funada, Hajime, 311
Fu Ying, 143

G7: favorability ratings for, 114, 367, 369; foreigners residing in, 219, 223f; and relations with China, 138; and Trump, 57, 124
General Agreement on Tariffs and Trade (GATT), 79–80, 81–82, 112–113
General Headquarters of the Allied Occupation, 303, 305, 306
generational inequality, 14, 24, 216–219

Germany, 15; Basic Law amendments, 310; civic participation via internet in, 345; and historical justice, 272, 274, 275, 277f, 292; income disparity in, 213f; Japan compared with, 271, 272, 275; and nuclear nonproliferation regime, 176, 179, 185, 195, 271; public media spending per capita, 352; public opinion on immigration in, 220f, 221f, 222f; survey experiment responses about, 365–366
gino jisshu seido (technical internship program), 226, 229
globalization: as challenge to liberal international order, 10–12; and income disparity, 158; negative effects of, 125; populism as reaction to, 80, 205, 208. *See also* liberal trading order
gray zone operations, China's, 48, 50–52, 66–67, 70
Great East Japan Earthquake (2011), 331
Greece, 277f, 334f, 335f
green border adjustment taxes, 127
Guam Doctrine (1970), 188
Gulf War, 139, 308, 313

Hahn, Kyu S., 326
Haku, Shinkun, 227
hard news, 335
Harris, Harry, 56
Hashimoto, Toru, 239, 241, 245–248
Hatano, Yoshio, 121
hate speech, 247, 254, 258, 350–351
Hatoyama administration, 142, 287
healthcare coverage, 211, 212f, 213–214
Hendrix, Cullen, 88
Higashikokubaru, Hideo, 242
Hiranuma, Takeo, 258
Hiroshima, Obama's visit to, 290
historical justice, 28, 271–299: apologies by OECD countries, 276f–279f; apologies for Japan's invasions, 260, 284, 289; apology fatigue and growing tensions, 285–292; development of historical justice regime, 273–280, 292–294; evolution of history prob-

lem in Asia, 280–285; and Japan's leadership role, 271–273, 294–295; policy recommendations for, 294–299
historical revisionism, 259–260, 285
Horie, Takafumi, 339
House of Representatives, Japan, 312, 316, 317
How Democracy Ends (Runciman), 264–265
human rights, 2; abuses resulting from populism, 133; and COJ, 303, 304, 305–306, 309; and comfort women, 296; freedom of speech, 328–329, 330–331, 332, 340–341; and values diplomacy, 158
human rights diplomacy, 138–139
human security, 120, 140–141, 154f, 157, 158
Hungary: and historical justice, 277f; public opinion on immigration in, 220f, 221f, 222f
Hun Sen, 156

ichioku sochuryu (100 million, all middle class), 24, 210
identity politics, 239, 252–255, 326
Ikeda, Hayato, 214
Ikeda, Nobuo, 242
Ikenberry, John, 44, 174, 177, 196
immigration, 23; exclusion of foreign workers, 224–228; hate speech against, 247; LDP tough on, 258; loosening of restrictive policies, 228–231; populism as reaction to, 206–207; public opinion on, 219, 220f–222f, 259; restrictive policy on, 219, 223–224
Immigration Control and Refugee Act (1951), 224–225
imperial system, preservation of, 313
income disparity. *See* economic inequality
Income Doubling Plan, 214
independent governors, 242
India, 6; and nuclear nonproliferation regime, 174; public opinion on immigration in, 220f, 221f, 222f; and regional infrastructure cooperation, 97; security cooperation with, 63–64, 67, 145, 146; survey experiment responses about, 366, 370
Indonesia, 150, 227, 279f
inequality. *See* economic inequality
inequality, generational, 14, 24, 216–219
information treatment. *See* survey experiment
intellectual property, 83, 89, 93, 96
Intermediate-Range Nuclear Forces (INF) Treaty, 142, 167, 172, 189–190
International Atomic Energy Agency (IAEA), 169, 173, 174, 185, 190
International Campaign to Abolish Nuclear Weapons (ICAN), 170, 183
International Commercial Courts of China, 159
international law: constitutions on, 306, 307f; and PCA ruling on China's claims, 52–53, 56, 110. *See also* postwar Asia-Pacific security order
International Monetary Fund (IMF), 126; China's participation in, 86; criticisms of, 107, 111; favorability ratings for, 114, 367, 369
international organizations, 107–127; areas Japanese leadership could improve, 125–127; attacks on, 107; growth of, 109f; Japan as reformist status quo power in, 27, 108, 117–125; Japan's role in, 111–114; limits of power, 110; limits to Japanese leadership in, 117–118; problems/concerns with, 110–111; roles of in liberal international order, 108–111; survey experiment responses about, 367, 369
internet, as news source, 343, 344f, 353; and civic participation, 345; impact on Japanese triad, 327, 345, 349; internet TV, 349; newspapers' websites, 346. *See also* media, Japanese
internet sovereignty, 84
Ipsos MORI survey, 207, 219, 224

Iran, and nuclear nonproliferation regime, 168–169, 179–180, 195
Iraq, U.S. invasion of, 110, 142
Ishihara, Shintaro, 241, 247, 258, 287
Israel, and nuclear nonproliferation regime, 174, 179
Italy: and historical justice, 274, 275, 277f; public opinion on immigration in, 220f, 221f, 222f
Itō, Masami, 329
Iyotani, T., 225
Izumikawa, Yasuhiro, 134

Japan: as beneficiary of liberal international order, 1; civic culture in, 262–263; domestic politics in, 19–25; geopolitical position of, 4; influence of in Asia-Pacific region, 14–15; military expenditures of, 6; public media spending per capita, 352; UK and U.S. as role models, 325
Japan, public opinion on its leadership in liberal international order. *See* survey experiment
Japanese Broadcast Law, Article 4, 348
Japanese Communist Party (JCP), 209–210, 214, 311
Japanese males, in power roles, 332, 340, 350, 353
Japanese triad (political disinterest, public apathy, and indifference to media), 28–29, 327–354, 328f; and age demographics, 343–344f, 345; exceptions to, 345–346; and freedom of speech, 328–329, 330–331, 332, 340–341; internet's impact on, 327, 345, 349; media-politics exploration, 327, 337–342; media-public exploration, 327, 343–354; and polarization, 345–349; political disinterest, 333–336, 345; public-politics exploration, 327, 328–336, 345; soft news, Japanese preference for, 334–335, 336; and *sontaku* culture, 331–333; and voter turnout, 333–334, 336. *See also* media, Japanese; Western triad (polarization, populism, and distrust in media)
Japan Federation of Bar Associations (JFBA), 158
Japan First Party (Nippon Dai Itto), 258
Japan Innovation Party (Nippon Ishin no Kai) (JIP), 247, 248–249, 310–311, 312
Japan International Cooperation Agency (JICA), 146, 150
Japan Restoration Party. *See* Japan Innovation Party
Japan's Coast Guard (JCG), 51, 61, 66, 70
Japan Socialist Party (JSP), 137, 213–214, 281
Joint Comprehensive Plan of Action (JCPOA), 168–169, 179, 195
journalism in Japan. *See* Japanese triad; media, Japanese; newspapers

Kada, Yukiko, 242
Kagoike, Yasunori, 331
Kardon, Isaac, 53
Kassebaum-Solomon Amendment (1986), 122
Kawaguchi, Chinese residents in, 230
Kawamura, Takashi, 242
Kaye, David, 341
Kharas, Homi, 83
Kikuchi, Kiyoaki, 112, 114
Kim Dae Jung, 284
Kim Jong-un, 9, 180
kisha-kurabu (press club) system, 339–340
Kishi, Nobusuke, 213, 281–282
Kissinger, Henry, 4
Koguchi, Hidehiko, 246, 335–336
Koike, Yuriko, 239, 241, 250–252
Koizumi, Junichiro, 238, 241, 244–245; visits to Yasukuni, 245, 285–286, 287
kokumin futan ritsu (people's burden rate), 215
kōkyōsei (publicness), about media, 352–353
Komeito (political party), 68, 310, 312, 321

Kono, Taro, 23, 156
Kono statement (1993), 289, 295
Kuroda, Mizuo, 114
Kyoto Protocol, 126

labor shortages, 225, 226, 228–229
Latvia, 277f
LDP. *See* Liberal Democratic Party (LDP)
League of Nations, 108, 111–112
Lee Myung-Bak, 286–287
Lewis, Leo, 20–21
"liberal democratic malaise," 327, 328, 351
Liberal Democratic Party (LDP): adaptability of, 256–257; backlash to privatization, 245; and Cambodian elections, 156; coalition with Komeito, 68, 310; COJ amendment opinions, 260, 304, 309–313, 313–314, 316–317, 321, 330; and constitutional revision, 260; disputes within, 68, 311; dominance of, 237–238; and foreign workers, 226; and nationalism, 257, 258–259; opposition to, 251; public opinion on conservative turn in, 313–314; and Senkaku/Diaoyu islands, 288; and social welfare policies, 213–214; support for, 249, 335–336; and welfare system, 217–218. *See also* Abe administration
liberal international order: changes to, 2; debate over conceptualization of, 2–3; and domestic politics, 3; as ideological agenda, 2; support by advanced liberal democracies, 359; terminology referring to, 3; three pillars of, 2; U.S. ambivalence about continued support for, 359; what it is, 1–2. *See also* Constitution of Japan (COJ); economic order; security order
liberal international order, challenges to, 4–14; demographics, 12–14; and freedom of speech, 331; globalization and technological revolution, 10–12; shifting balance of power, 5–10

liberal international order, Japan's strategy for, 14–19; as exemplar, 118, 119–120; leading reforms, 118, 122–125; as mentor/supporting rising states' renegotiation, 118, 120–122
liberalism: and Abe administration, 23; and Japanese media, 338, 349–351, 352; populism in opposition to, 243. *See also* neoliberalism
liberal trading order, 26–27, 79–102; and domestic politics, 97–100; evolution of, 79–80; Japan's leadership in, 90–97, 101–102; stresses on, 81–89, 100–101; in survey experiment information treatment, 374, 375
Lithuania, 278f
Livedoor (internet company), 339
Luxembourg, 278f

Maas, Heiko, 58–59
Made in China 2025, 8, 84
Mahathir Mohamad, 7, 144
Mainichi (newspaper), 337, 342, 348f
the Maldives, 144, 147
Malstrom, Cecilia, 92
manufacturing, 84, 87–88
Maritime Self-Defense Force (MSDF), 51, 66–67, 70
Maruyama, Masao, 136, 330
Matsui, Ichiro, 249, 261
Matsuura, Koichiro, 123
Mattis, James, 53
Mazarr, Michael, 58, 196
media, Japanese, 28–29, 336, 337–354; and age demographics, 343–344f, 345; consumption habits by media type, 337–338, 343–344f, 349–350; corporate media as public utility, 337–339, 349; exceptions to norms in, 345–347; and Hashimoto, 245–246; international coverage in, 341–342; international monitoring of, 340–341, 353; internet, 327, 343, 344f, 345, 346, 349, 353; and *kisha-kurabu* (press club) system, 339–340; and *kōkyōsei* (publicness), 352–353; and

media, Japanese (*cont.*)
    liberalism, 349–351, 352; media-politics exploration, 327, 337–342; media-public exploration, 327, 343–354; and neoliberalism, 352; neutrality and objectivity principles in, 343, 345, 348; nonideological news sources, 337–338; and polarization, 345–349; political news in, 264; populism in, 240–241f, 251; and populist politics, 337; public broadcasting, 338, 352; stability in, 338–339; target market, as entire Japanese population, 349–350; television, 338–339, 343, 344f, 349. *See also* Japanese triad; newspapers
media distrust. *See* Western triad (polarization, populism, and distrust in media)
media indifference. *See* Japanese triad (political disinterest, public apathy, and indifference to media)
Meiji Constitution (1889-1946), 306, 307f, 310. *See also* Constitution of Japan (COJ)
Mexico, public opinion on immigration in, 220f, 221f, 222f
middle class, global increase in, 83
middle class, Japanese self-perception of (*ichioku sochuryu*), 24, 210
middle power diplomacy, 140–141
militarism: and COJ, 303, 305, 307–308, 314, 319; constitutions on, 306, 307–308. *See also* Article 9 (COJ); Self-Defense Forces (Japan)
Ministry of Health, Labor, and Welfare (MHLW), 211, 215
Ministry of Internal Affairs and Communication, 223
Ministry of Justice, 224, 230
Minobe, Ryokichi, 214
Mizuho Research Institute, 212
Modi, Narendra, 53, 64
Moon Jae-in, 180, 291
Morita, K., 225
Mudde, Cas, 3, 20, 242

Müller, Jan-Werner, 243
multilateralism: and China, 85; and regional security, 45–46; and values diplomacy, 153, 157; weakening of, 81–82, 90, 142. *See also* international organizations; liberal trading order; nuclear nonproliferation regime; postwar Asia-Pacific security order
Murayama statement (1995), 260, 274, 275, 295
Murdoch, Rupert, 338–339

Naka, Rei, 98–99
Nakakita, Koji, 245, 257
Nakano, Koichi, 347
Nakasone, Yasuhiro, 274, 283
nationalism, 21–22, 28, 257–260, 284, 288, 294. *See also* populism
national security. *See* security policy
national security council, Japan's (NSC), 61–62
National Security Strategy (2013), 26, 60–64; and ODA, 147–149; security cooperation in, 146–147; security cooperation with Asia-Pacific partners, 63–64, 70–71; strengthening and expanding Japan's capabilities and roles, 61–62; strengthening U.S.-Japan alliance, 62, 69–70; and values diplomacy, 146
National Security Strategy, US (2017), 48, 50
NATO, 177; favorability ratings for, 114, 364, 367, 369; in survey experiment information treatment, 374, 375
neoliberal institutionalism, 143
neoliberalism: and Hashimoto, 246–247; and Japanese media, 352; and Japanese populism, 239, 243; of Koike's administration, 250; of Koizumi's administration, 244
the Netherlands: and historical justice, 274, 275, 278f; populism in, 208; public interest in news coverage, 335f
neutrality, 157, 343
New Deal Democrats, 303, 330

new media. *See* internet
news: hard, 335; public interest in, 334f, 335f; soft, 335, 336. *See also* internet, as news source; media, Japanese
newspapers: age demographics of readership, 343–344f; *Asahi Shimbun,* 309, 311–312, 337, 339, 342, 346–347, 348f; *Mainichi,* 337, 342, 348f; market share battle, 337–338; *Nikkei,* 337, 342; *Sankei Shimbun,* 345–347, 348f; subscriptions to, 337–338, 343, 344, 349–350; *Yomiuri Shimbun,* 313–314, 337, 342, 347, 348f
New Zealand, 16, 43, 94, 220f, 221f, 222f
Next Generation Party (formerly Sunrise Party), 247, 258
NHK (public broadcaster), 338, 342
Nikai, Toshihiro, 156
Nikkei (newspaper), 337, 342
nikkeijin (people of Japanese descent), 226
Nippon-gata riberaru (Japanese-style liberals), 346
Nippon Hoso (radio station), 339
Nippon Ishin no Kai (Japan Innovation Party), 247, 248–249, 310–311, 312
Nippon Kaigi, 257
Nippon Shimbun Kyokai (Japan Newspaper Editors and Publishers Association), 339
Nitobe, Inazo, 112
Noda, Yoshihiko, 287
Normalization Treaty (1965), 291, 296
North American Free Trade Agreement (NAFTA), 87, 95
North Korea, 365; and nuclear nonproliferation regime, 168, 174, 180–182, 188; and shifting global balance of power, 9–10; survey experiment responses about, 366; and Trump administration, 57, 180–181
Norway, 278f, 352
NPT. *See* Treaty on the Non-Proliferation of Nuclear Weapons
NTTCom Online Market Solutions, 362

nuclear disarmament: divide over, 170, 183–184, 194; humanitarian approach to, 170, 183; Obama's call for, 290; and values diplomacy, 137
nuclear energy, 185–186, 187, 190–191, 193
nuclear nonproliferation regime, 9, 27, 167–197; atoms for alliance, 27, 171, 176–178, 190–191, 195; challenges in, 167–170, 178; disarmament gap, 170, 183–184, 194; fuel cycle policy, 190–193; and Iran, 178, 179–180; Japan's non-nuclear choice, 27, 187–190, 195–196; and liberal international order, 171–176, 193–194; nonproliferation commitment, 187–188, 190–193; and North Korea, 178, 180–182; policy recommendations for, 186–187; post-Cold War, 175–176; power shift in nuclear market, 184–187, 194; support for, 367
Nuclear Posture Review, US (2018), 48–49
nuclear power sector, civilian, 169–170
Nuclear Suppliers Group (NSG), 175, 186
nuclear weapons: acquisition of, 10; and North Korea threat, 57; and power distribution, 171–173
Nye, Joseph, 3, 44

Obama, Barack, 288, 290
Obama administration, 55, 290
Obuchi, Keizo, 284
OECD Development Assistance Committee (DAC), 144, 148
Official Development Assistance (ODA), 15; creation of charter for, 139; disbursements of, 149f; increase in contributions to international organizations, 115; for legal/judicial development, 150–151; and values diplomacy, 140, 145, 147–148
Ogata, Sadako, 120
Okada, Katsuya, 227–228, 230–231

Okinawa, regionalism in, 239, 243, 252–255
Okunoki, Nobuo, 230
Onaga, Takeshi, 239, 252–255
123 Agreements, 186
Onogi, Katsunobu, 25
Organisation for Economic Cooperation and Development (OECD), 113
Osaka, administration in, 246–247
Osaka Track, 17
Otake, Hideo, 242, 244
Oxford Dictionary, 331
Ozawa, Ichiro, 139

pacifism, 134, 135–136, 139–140; and COJ, 303, 309, 314, 319
Pakistan, 144, 174
Panmunjom Declaration for Peace, Prosperity, and Unification of the Korean Peninsula, 180
Paris Agreement, 107
Park Geun-Hye, 290
Partnership for Quality Infrastructure, 97
Party for Japanese Kokoro, 311
Party of Hope, 24, 250, 251
peace clause. *See* Article 9 (COJ)
Peacekeeping Operations (PKO) Cooperation Act (1992), 139
Pence, Mike, 49, 144
pensions, 211, 212f, 213–214, 217
People's Liberation Army (PLA) (China), 47, 48
People's New Party, 245
Permanent Court of Arbitration (PCA): China-Philippines ruling (2016), 52–53, 56, 57
Peru, public opinion on immigration in, 220f, 221f, 222f
the Philippines, 6; Economic Partnership Agreement with, 227; PCA ruling (2016), 52–53, 56, 57; survey experiment responses about, 366, 370
pluralism, 15, 20, 159, 250–251, 274
plurilateralism. *See* multilateralism

Poland: and historical justice, 278f; public opinion on immigration in, 219, 220f, 221f, 222f
polarization: "affective polarization," 326; on historical issue, 281; in Japanese media, 345–349
polarization, populism, and distrust in media triad. *See* Western triad (polarization, populism, and distrust in media)
policy recommendations, 29; for Asia-Pacific security order, 68–71; for constitutional revision, 321; for historical justice, 294–299; for Japanese media, 352–354; for Japan's role as reformist status quo power, 125–127; for liberal trading order, 96–97, 100, 102; for nuclear nonproliferation regime, 186–187; for values diplomacy, 156–158; for welfare systems, 231–232
political disengagement, 262–264. *See also* Japanese triad (political disinterest, public apathy, and indifference to media)
political inequality, 24
Politico, 206
politics, in Japan: and "affective polarization," 326; elected officials' opinions on amending Article 9, 311–313, 321; ideological surveys, 311–312; and party affiliations, 336; political news, 335; public's disinterest in, 333–336, 345; trust in candidates, 313–314, 316, 317; and voter turnouts, 333–334, 336. *See also* elections; Japanese triad (political disinterest, public apathy, and indifference to media); Liberal Democratic Party (LDP)
popular sovereignty, 309
populism, 19–21, 28; and Abe administration, 20–22; anti-liberalism of, 243; as backlash to undemocratic liberalism, 3; and civic attitudes, 208; defined, 20, 204, 242–243; education levels as predictor for, 207–208; effects on liberal trading order,

80–81; human rights abuses resulting from, 133; and Japanese culture, 360; and Japanese media, 337; Japan's insulation from, 203–204; and political institutions, 208; as reaction to economic insecurity, 205–206; as reaction to immigration, 206–207; reasons for/predictors for support of, 204–208; and structural factors in Japan's resistance to, 22–25; Western rise of, 204–208. *See also* populism, Japanese; Western triad (polarization, populism, and distrust in media)

populism, Japanese, 28, 237–266; features of, 242–244; and Hashimoto, 245–249; Japan's insulation from/resilience against, 237–238, 255–264; key issues of, 263; and Koike, 250–252; and Koizumi, 244–245; neoliberalism of, 239, 243; and Onaga, 252–255; perceptions of, 240–242; pragmatic responses to, 256–257; public interest in, 240–241f; and threat of economic inequality, 260–262; and threat of nationalism, 257–260; and threat of voter disengagement, 262–264

Portugal, and historical justice, 274, 275, 278f

Posen, Barry, 143

"post-truth" (2016 OED Word of the Year), 331, 332–333

postwar Asia-Pacific security order, 26, 39–72; and alliance system, 42–44; China's challenge to, 40, 47–54; constraints on Japan's leadership in, 64–68; Japan as champion of, 58–59; and Japan's national security strategy, 60–64; and Japan's postwar development, 39–40, 135–136; Japan's role as proactive stabilizer in, 41–42, 71–72; liberal characteristics of, 46–47; logic and evolution of, 42–47; North Korea's challenge to, 40, 181–182; policy recommendations for, 68–71; public opinion on importance of, 316–317; security cooperation and values diplomacy, 146–147; and shifting balance of power, 40; in survey experiment, 366, 375; and Trump administration, 40, 55–58; U.S. military commitment to, 305, 317, 318–320, 321

postwar democracy (*sengo minshushugi*), 330

power distribution, global: and nuclear weapons, 171–173; nuclear weapons determinants of, 171; shifting balance of, 5–10

preferentialism, 82, 101

privacy rights, COJ, 304, 316, 317, 321

privatization, 244, 245

Proliferation Security Initiative (PSI), 175

Public and Its Problems, The (Dewey), 329

public broadcasting, 338, 352

public-media relationship. *See* Japanese triad (political disinterest, public apathy, and indifference to media); media, Japanese; Western triad (polarization, populism, and distrust in media)

public opinion: on China, 259; on immigration, 207, 219, 220f–222f, 259; on international organizations, 367, 369; levels of nationalist sentiment, 259; on political engagement, 334–335; on TPP accession, 98; on Trump administration, 56; on trust in media, 337; on U.S. global leadership, 58; on welfare budget, 216. *See also* public opinion on amending COJ; survey experiment

public opinion on amending COJ, 304, 313–320; Article 9, 19, 305, 309, 313, 315, 317–320, 321; rationale, 315–320, 321; surveys, 309, 313–314f, 315–320, 368–369, 370; trust in elected officials affects, 313–314, 316, 317f; U.S. military commitment to Asia-Pacific region affects, 305, 317, 318–320, 321

public-politics relationship. *See* Japanese triad (political disinterest, public apathy, and indifference to media); politics, in Japan; Western triad (polarization, populism, and distrust in media)
Pyle, Kenneth, 3

the Quad (U.S., Australia, India, Japan security cooperation), 63–64, 67, 145, 146. *See also* Free and Open Indo-Pacific (FOIP) strategy

RAND Corporation, 7
RAND report (2018), 49
Ratner, Ely, 85
Reagan administration, 122, 192, 348
redistribution policies, 211, 212f, 216–217, 231, 247
Refugee Convention (1951), 223
refugee policy, 23, 223–224, 231, 368
Regional Comprehensive Economic Partnership (RCEP), 16, 93–94
regional security order. *See* postwar Asia-Pacific security order
reparations, 275, 276f–279f, 282, 292
Resolution Foundation, 207
Reuters Digital News Report, 325
Rice, Condoleezza, 146
Roh Moo-Hyun, 286
Rolland, Nadège, 85
Rose, Gideon, 2
Runciman, David, 264–265
rural areas: and income inequality, 216–217, 261; and populism, 24, 205; and welfare reforms, 214
Russia: and nuclear nonproliferation regime, 167, 172–173, 174, 179, 183, 185, 186; public opinion on immigration in, 220f, 221f, 222f; in survey experiment, 366, 368; as threat to liberal international order, 7, 56, 110

Sakaiya, Shiro, 313
sakoku (country closure) policies, 224
Sakurai, Makoto, 258

Sanders, Bernie, 55, 205–206
Sankei Shumbun (newspaper), 345–347, 348f
Sato, Eisaku, 137, 188
Saudi Arabia, 179, 220f, 221f, 222f
Scarborough Shoal, 52
SDF. *See* Self-Defense Forces (SDF)
Second Provisional Council for Administrative Reform (*Rincho*), 215
security legislation, Japan's (2015), 65–66
security order, 2, 42f. *See also* nuclear nonproliferation regime; postwar Asia-Pacific security order
security policy: and Abe administration, 18–19; COJ restricts, 304; state of emergency amendments to COJ, 311, 312, 316, 317; survey experiment questions on, 360, 362, 363–366, 368–371, 372–373, 375
Self-Defense Forces (SDF): Abe on, 311; and amending COJ, 19, 65, 308, 311, 316, 317–320, 321, 368–369; authorizations to use force, 65–66; budget, 66; and China's aggressions, 51; and constitutional revision, 19; deployment on peacekeeping missions, 139, 140, 320; and Gulf War, 308, 313; public calls for formal recognition in Article 9, 19, 316, 317–320, 321; strengthening of, 62
Sellek, Yoko, 225
Semba, Toshiro, 330–331
sengo minshushugi (postwar democracy), 330
Senkaku/Diaoyu Islands: China's provocations in, 50–51, 288; diplomatic crisis of 2010, 5, 142; and history issue, 288; and Japan-China relations, 142, 286; Japan's policy toward, 52; Noda's attempted purchase of, 287–288; policy recommendations for Japan, 295; and SDF/JCG, 61; survey experiment responses about, 368; and U.S.-Japan alliance, 5, 288–289, 290
September 11 terrorist attacks (2001), 175

Serbia, public opinion on immigration in, 220f, 221f, 222f
Shiba, Rei, 224
shigarami seiji (vested interest politics), 239, 243, 250
Shigemitsu, Mamoru, 113
Shimoji, Mikio, 255, 261
Singapore, 244, 370
Singh, Bhubhindar, 134, 139
Sinophobia, 259
Six-Party Talks, 45, 180
Slovak Republic, and historical justice, 278f
Slovenia, and historical justice, 278f
Small, Andrew, 85
Social Democrats, 311
social media, 246, 327, 343. See also internet, as news source; media, Japanese, structure and organization of
soft news, 334–335, 336
sontaku (to surmise the group sentiment to avoid conflicts and complications), 331–333
South Africa, public opinion on immigration in, 220f, 221f, 222f
South and East China Seas, China's sovereignty claims in/gray zone operations in, 46, 48, 50–52, 55, 110; and nuclear nonproliferation regime, 189; PCA ruling and China's claims, 52–53. See also Senkaku/Diaoyu Islands
Southeast Asian countries: China's influence in, 8; and values diplomacy, 151–152, 155–156. See also postwar Asia-Pacific security order
South Korea, 9–10; civic participation via internet in, 345; and historical justice, 272, 282, 283, 284, 288, 290, 291, 294; and Koizumi's visits to Yasukuni, 286; and North Korea, 180; public interest in news coverage, 334f; public opinion on immigration in, 220f, 221f, 222f; relations with Japan, 286–287, 295–298; security cooperation with, 64, 67, 146, 375; in survey experiment, 363, 364, 366, 374, 375; and trade policy, 101, 102
Spain: and historical justice, 274, 275; public opinion on immigration in, 220f, 221f, 222f
Sri Lanka, 144, 147
state-owned enterprises (SOEs), 84, 96
Strategic Arms Control Treaty (START), 167, 172, 183
Strategic Partnership Agreement (EU-Japan), 16, 153
Suga, Yoshihide, 217–218
Sunrise Party (later, Next Generation Party), 247, 258
supreme court (Japan), 308
survey experiment, 29, 68, 359–375; analysis, 321, 360, 361, 365–372; caveats in, 361, 371–372; COJ questions and opinions, 315–320, 321, 368–369, 370; economic treatment, 360, 362, 364, 365–371, 372, 375; future research implications, 361, 373; goals, 360, 361–362; information treatment in, 315–316, 317–318, 362–363, 369–371; posttreatment component, 315, 361, 363, 365, 367–369; pretreatment component, 315, 317, 361, 362, 364–367; results summary, 363, 364–365, 372–373; security treatment, 360, 362, 363–366, 368–371, 372–373, 375; static views assessed, 360; survey design, 315–318, 360, 361, 362–364; treatment groups, 315, 317–318, 361, 362–363. See also public opinion on amending COJ
Sweden, public opinion on immigration in, 220f, 221f, 222f
Switzerland, 141, 279f

Taira, Masaaki, 348
Takasu, Yukio, 123
Takeshima. See Dokdo/Takeshima islands
Takeuchi, Kumiko, 346
Tamaki, Denny, 255
Tanaka, Aiji, 336

Tanaka, Kakuei, 214, 293
Tanaka, Yasuo, 242
Taniguchi, Masaki, 311
Taniguchi, Mina, 98
tariffs, 88–89, 94–95, 100, 367, 375
technology: as challenge to liberal international order, 10–12; and China, 8, 11–12, 84, 133; digital trade, 16–17. *See also* internet, as news source
television, 338–339, 343, 344f, 349
territorial disputes. *See* Dokdo/Takeshima islands; Senkaku/Diaoyu Islands
textbooks, Miyazawa doctrine on, 283, 289, 295
third-country cooperation (economic projects between Japan and China), 152–153
Tiananmen Square incident (1989), 138–139
Tillerson, Rex, 48
Tokyo Electric Power Company, 331
Tokyo International Conference on African Development (TICAD), 140, 151
Tokyoites First, 250
Trade Expansion Act (1962) (United States), 88
trade liberalization, 16, 26, 342
trade policy. *See* liberal trading order
Trans-Pacific Partnership (TPP): and Abe administration, 204; as Asia strategy, 16; debate on accession to, 98; Japan's resurrection of (CPTPP), 16, 71, 92–93, 153, 204, 360; opposition to in U.S., 55; support for in Japan, 24, 367; U.S. withdrawal from, 88, 91, 142, 342, 360, 375
treaties, constitutions on, 306, 307f
Treaty of Mutual Cooperation and Security (1960), 2, 6; Article V, 51, 70
Treaty of San Francisco (1951), 282
Treaty on Conventional Forces in Europe (CFE), 172, 189–190
Treaty on the Non-Proliferation of Nuclear Weapons (NPT) (1968), 9, 173, 174, 183, 184, 185

Treaty on the Prohibition of Nuclear Weapons (TPNW) (2017), 170, 183
Trump, Donald J.: and decline of U.S. power, 5; election of, 325, 331; hostility toward international organizations, 88, 107, 117, 124; Japanese media criticizes decisions of, 342; and North Korea, 9–10, 180–181; opposition to immigration, 206–207; and polarized U.S. electorate, 325; relationship with Abe, 124; on relations with North Korea, 181; survey experiment responses about, 365; Trans-Pacific Partnership, withdrawal decision of, 88, 91, 142, 342, 360, 364, 375; and U.S.-Japan alliance, 5, 17; on withdrawal from JCPOA, 179. *See also* Trump administration
Trump administration: attack on liberal values, 142–143; on China challenge to security order, 48–49; global lack of confidence in, 56; and Indo-Pacific framing of security strategy, 64; and international organizations, 117, 124; and nuclear nonproliferation regime, 183, 195; and security order, 40, 55–58, 321; and shifting balance of power, 40; and trade policy, 80–81, 88–89, 95, 101. *See also* Trump, Donald J.
truth: "post-truth" (2016 OED Word of the Year), 331, 332–333
Tsurumi, Shunsuke, 330
Turkey: and historical justice, 274, 275, 279f; public opinion on immigration in, 220f, 221f, 222f
Turnbull, Malcom, 64
TV Asahi, 338–339, 349. *See also Asahi Shimbun* (newspaper)

Uemura, Takashi, 347
Ukraine, Russia's activities in, 48, 56, 168
unaffiliated voters, 238, 239, 242, 245, 249, 251, 263, 264, 336
unemployment, 87–88, 209, 218

United Kingdom: civic participation via internet in, 345; defense technology cooperation with, 64, 146; economic inequality in, 206, 213f; foreigners residing in, 223f; and historical justice, 274, 275, 279f; immigration in, 207, 220f, 221f, 222f; liberalism in, 350; and nuclear nonproliferation regime, 174, 179; plutonium stockpile in, 193; polarization in, 325–326; and populism, 80, 206; survey experiment responses about, 365. *See also* Western triad (polarization, populism, and distrust in media)

United Nations (UN): at center of foreign policy, 113, 114, 137; favorability ratings for, 114, 369; Japanese support for, 113–114, 122–123; Japan's status in, 112; public opinion on, 114; reform, 122–123

UN Charter, 113

UN Convention on the Law of the Sea (UNCLOS), 7, 8, 52, 55–56, 85

UN Democracy Fund (UNDEF), 145, 157

UN Educational, Scientific, and Cultural Organization (UNESCO), 107, 112, 116, 117, 122, 123

UN Framework Convention on Climate Change (UNFCCC), 107, 127

United Nations High Commissioner for Refugees (UNHCR), 223–224

UN Human Rights Council (UNHRC), 253–254

UN peacekeeping operations (PKOs), 139, 140

UN Security Council: Japan's membership in, 113, 121, 137, 141; and nuclear nonproliferation compliance, 174, 180; reform of, 111, 121

UN Security Council Resolution (UNSCR) 1540, 175

United States: aggressions undermining international organizations' norms, 110; ambivalence about continued support for liberal international order, 359, 360; civic participation via internet in, 345; democracy promotion activities, 150; economic inequality in, 205–206, 213f; education levels as predictor for populism in, 207–208; Fairness Doctrine in, 348; foreigners residing in, 223f; and historical justice, 274, 275, 279f, 288–289; incomplete support for security order, 55–56; and international organizations, 108, 117, 122; liberalism in, 350; and liberal trading order, 80–81, 87–89, 91–92, 100–101; and liberal values, 142–143; military commitment to Asia-Pacific region, 305, 317, 318–320, 321; and North Korea, 180–181; polarization in, 325–326; populism in, 80–81, 205–206; post-WWII grand strategy, 43; public media spending per capita, 352; public opinion on immigration in, 220f, 221f, 222f; security cooperation with, 63–64, 67, 146; and shifting global balance of power, 5–6; survey experiment responses about, 363, 364, 365, 367, 368, 370–373; trade negotiations with, 94–95; Trans-Pacific Partnership Agreement, Trump pulls from, 88, 91, 142, 342, 360, 375. *See also* Trump administration; United States, and nuclear nonproliferation regime; U.S.-Japan alliance; Western triad (polarization, populism, and distrust in media)

United States, and nuclear nonproliferation regime: "atoms for alliance" incentive program, 171, 176–178; and China's nuclear buildup, 167–168; Joint Comprehensive Plan of Action (JCPOA), 168–169, 179, 195; leadership of U.S., 174–175, 175–176, 194–195; and NPT, 174, 183–184; and nuclear market, 185; U.S.-Russia arms control regime, 172–173, 183, 189; withdrawal from JCPOA, 168–169, 179

United States Agency for International Development (USAID), 150
U.S.-centered alliance system, 42–44; China's opposition to, 54; sustainability of, 40–41
U.S.-Japan alliance: COJ's merits and limits in, 305, 315; and denuclearization of North Korea, 182; and history issue, 288–291, 295; insecurities in due to Trump administration, 57–58; and nuclear nonproliferation regime, 188, 189, 190–192, 195–196; and shifting global balance of power, 5–6; and Sino-Japanese territorial dispute, 288–291; strengthening as emphasis of national security strategy, 62, 69–70; in survey experiment information treatment, 374, 375; survey experiment responses about, 368, 370, 372; territorial dispute with China stresses, 290; and values in foreign policy, 136–137
U.S.-Japan Guidelines for Defense Cooperation (2015), 62
U.S.-Japan Nuclear Cooperation Agreement (1958), 192
U.S.-Japan Security Treaty (1951), 42–43, 281–282
U.S. military bases in Okinawa, opposition to, 68, 252–253, 254
U.S. New Deal Democrats, 303, 330
U.S.-North Korea summit meeting (Singapore, June 12, 2018), 9, 180–181
UTokyo-Asahi Survey, 311–312

values diplomacy, 27, 133–160; and Abe administration, 145–155; after Cold War, 138–141; analysis of discourse on, 153–155, 154f; during Cold War, 135–138; limitations in, 155–156; and ODA/foreign aid, 147–151; policy recommendations, 156–158; and security cooperation, 146–147; shifts in, 135; since 2000s, 141–145; studies of, 134; universality of, 145

vested interest groups, political attacks on, 239, 243, 250
Vietnam, 6, 46, 227, 366
voluntary export restraints (VERs), 82, 94
voters: disengagement of, 262–264; female, 251; unaffiliated, 238, 239, 242, 245, 249, 251, 263, 264, 336
voter turnout in Japan, 217, 333f–334, 336

Wakasa, Masaru, 250, 251, 252, 261
Wang Yi, 286
Wassenaar Arrangement (WA), 175
welfare state, 203–232; Abe's support for, 23; development of in Japan, 213–215; and egalitarian distribution policies, 209–215; and immigration policy, 219–231; and income disparity, 209–213; Japan's insulation from populism, 203–204, 209; relevance of Japanese model, 231–232; sustainability of, 215–219; and Western rise of populism, 204–209
Western triad (polarization, populism, and distrust in media), 325–328f, 331–333, 348; "affective polarization," 326; fake news, 325, 327; and Japanese culture, 326, 327, 337, 350; and "post-truth" culture, 331, 332–333; as result of "liberal democratic malaise," 327, 328, 351. *See also* Japanese triad (political disinterest, public apathy, and indifference to media)
West Germany, 138, 177, 225
Winkler, Christian G., 305, 309
Wohlstetter, Roberta, 187
women: economic inclusivity for, 13, 228; female voters, 251; ODA disbursements for women's equality organizations, 149f. *See also* "comfort women" of WWII
World Bank, 86, 107, 114
World Conference on Disaster Risk Reduction, 158

World Resources Institute, 158
World Trade Organization (WTO): Appellate Body of, 89, 124; China's entry into, 45, 83–84; creation of, 81–82; favorability ratings for, 114; negotiation in, 82; reform of, 27, 96, 124; rulemaking of, 83–84; survey experiment responses about, 367, 369; Trump administration hostility toward, 88–89, 124
World Values Survey (2010-14), 259, 262
World War II: and historical justice, 275, 276f–279f, 281; and international organizations, 108, 112; and pacifism, 135–136
Wright, Thomas, 49
Wu, Marc, 84

xenophobia, 247, 254, 257–258, 259
Xi Jinping, 54, 143, 288

Yamasaki, Shiro, 218
Yasukuni Shrine, official visits to, 295; and Abe, 289; Chinese responses to, 284; Koizumi's, 245, 285–286, 287; and Nakasone, 283, 284
Yomiuri Shimbun (newspaper), 240–241f, 313–314, 347, 348f; *Asahi* rivalry, 337, 342
Yoshida doctrine, 136

Zaitokukai (Association of Citizens against the Special Privileges of the Zainichi), 247, 258
Zeng Aiping, 159

Lightning Source UK Ltd.
Milton Keynes UK
UKHW010624051221
395058UK00001B/37